Forewor

The Bedford Series in History and Culture is designed so that readers can study the past as historians do.

The historian's first task is finding the evidence. Documents, letters, memoirs, interviews, pictures, movies, novels, or poems can provide facts and clues. Then the historian questions and compares the sources. There is more to do than in a courtroom, for hearsay evidence is welcome, and the historian is usually looking for answers beyond act and motive. Different views of an event may be as important as a single verdict. How a story is told may yield as much information as what it says.

Along the way the historian seeks help from other historians and perhaps from specialists in other disciplines. Finally, it is time to write, to decide on an interpretation and how to arrange the evidence for readers.

Each book in this series contains an important historical document or group of documents, each document a witness from the past and open to interpretation in different ways. The documents are combined with some element of historical narrative—an introduction or a biographical essay, for example—that provides students with an analysis of the primary source material and important background information about the world in which it was produced.

Each book in the series focuses on a specific topic within a specific historical period. Each provides a basis for lively thought and discussion about several aspects of the topic and the historian's role. Each is short enough (and inexpensive enough) to be a reasonable one-week assignment in a college course. Whether as classroom or personal reading, each book in the series provides firsthand experience of the challenge—and fun—of discovering, recreating, and interpreting the past.

Natalie Zemon Davis
Ernest R. May

iii

Preface

The Puritans of New England were avid diarists, and none more so than Samuel Sewall. His diary, covering more than a half century of his life in Massachusetts, has long been an invaluable source of information for students of colonial New England. As a prominent public figure whose career spanned the tumultuous years of the last quarter of the seventeenth and first quarter of the eighteenth centuries, Sewall was a witness to or participant in many of the most important imperial episodes of the period. Timing and circumstance had him well positioned to reflect on the collapse of the Puritan regime whose roots reached back to the Massachusetts Bay Company charter of 1629, the bewilderment that accompanied the rise of the Dominion government, the civil and ecclesiastical adjustments necessitated by the terms of the royal charter of 1691, and the evolution of the partisan factionalism that came to characterize provincial politics in the first decades of the eighteenth century.

But Sewall was more than simply a public figure. It is not merely fortuitous that the years of his diary keeping closely correspond to his years as a member of the South Church. Sewall's purpose in keeping a diary in the first place was directly related to his religious commitment. He understood, as did other Puritans, that the spiritual journey of the elect toward salvation was marked with signs: submission to God's commandments, awareness of one's sinfulness, fearfulness of the consequences of sin, doubt and despair, a spark of faith and a feeling of assurance in the knowledge of Christ, a disposition to live a meritorious life. The presence of these signs in a person's life was no guarantee that he or she was among the elect, but their absence was a guarantee that one was numbered among the damned. Puritan doctrine thus obligated the believer to engage in rigorous self-examination. Diaries, including Sewall's, were the products of such self-analyses; they were spiritual account books in which their keepers recorded their assets and liabilities in order to chart their standing with regard to saving grace.

That Sewall's diary goes well beyond self-examination of this sort has made it all the more valuable as a source of information on early New England. Since the 1960s, social historians have demonstrated again and again the value of studies that have as their focus the everyday lives of ordinary people. Sewall, to be sure, was no "ordinary" person, but even extraordinary people have everyday lives, and Sewall's diary is unsurpassed as an ongoing record of daily life in early Boston. This strength of the diary, however, its wealth of detail on public and private matters over a lengthy period, poses a major problem for any editor of an abridged edition of Sewall's journal. How does one convey a sense of the fullness of the diary with its thousands of daily entries and still address the issue of change and continuity over time?

My approach to this problem has been to select specific years from the Sewall diary and to reproduce them in their entirety. Readers are thereby able to follow Sewall closely for a full year and to gain an appreciation of the rhythms of his life: births, marriages, and deaths, fasts and thanksgivings, official news and rumors of remarkable providences, private devotions and public quarrels, accidents and illnesses, cold winter days and the arrival of spring. The selections are separated by ten-year intervals, thus allowing readers already familiar with a given year to consider the effects of the passage of time. The years I have selected for inclusion shed light on important themes in Sewall's life and in the life of the colony. However, they are also representative years for their respective decades in the sense that alternative years could have been presented without dramatically altering the final product. Indeed, having studied the selections contained in this volume, the reader should be able to place the other years of the Sewall diary in their proper context and to make sense out of them.

The danger of selecting whole years separated by ten years is obvious: Sewall's story might appear to be more disrupted than it actually was. To offset this possibility, Part 1 and the several introductions to the diary selections are intended to provide the reader with information necessary to bridge the gaps and to lend a certain coherence to the entire text. Taken together, these introductory essays should acquaint the reader with Sewall's world and place his life as well as his diary within the context of the times. Private losses and public crises did interrupt his routines and may have rendered his existence temporarily disjointed, but his life still revolved around certain perdurable themes in his family, church, and town.

ACKNOWLEDGMENTS

I am pleased to have this opportunity publicly to thank those who have
contributed to the completion of this book. Charles Christensen took an
early interest in the project, and his splendid staff at Bedford Books
greatly eased the transition from first draft to final product. I am especially grateful to Katherine E. Kurzman, Julie C. Sullivan, and Kate
Sheehan Roach for their patience and persistence in moving the manuscript forward. Peter Drummey, Librarian of the Massachusetts Historical Society, allowed me to view portions of the original Sewall diary,
and Chris Steele, Curator of Photographs, expedited the process of re-
producing illustrations in the Society's possession. Thanks are due also
to Georgia Barnhill of the American Antiquarian Society and Wayne
Furman of the New York Public Library for their assistance in securing
permission to reproduce material in the possession of their respective
institutions. Jack P. Greene (The Johns Hopkins University), David D.
Hall (Harvard Divinity School), Richard R. Johnson (University of Wash-
ington), Richard Godbeer (University of California, Riverside), and
Claudia L. Bushman (Columbia University) read and commented on an
earlier version of the manuscript. Although I was not able to follow all
of their suggestions, their carefully considered critiques assisted me in
my revisions and resulted ultimately in a better book. Donald Sullivan
and Warren Smith, my colleagues at the University of New Mexico,
helped me with English translations of the various Latin phrases and
passages in the diary. I am pleased also to take this opportunity to
thank Mary Carole and Jerry Wertheim and Georgia and Jim Snead
for their interest in and promotion of the study of history. I appreciate
the assistance I received under the auspices of the Snead-Wertheim
lectureship in History and Anthropology at the University of New Mexico. My wife, Jennifer, has been a constant source of support and
encouragement; she has been my "Hannah" for more than twenty
years. Finally, I wish to dedicate this book to my mother and to the
memory of my father.

Mel Yazawa

Contents

List of Illustrations

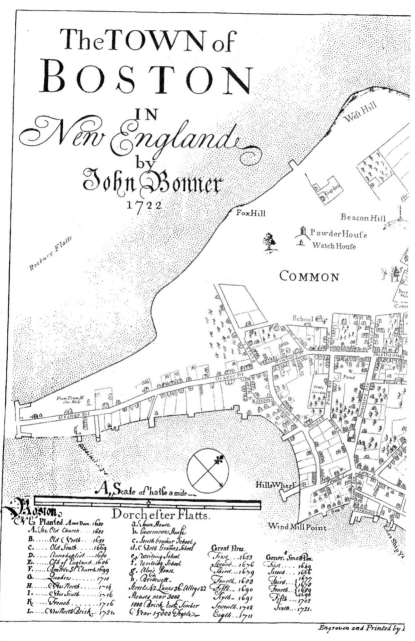

Figure 1.

Francis Dewing, after John Bonner, The Town of Boston in New England. Engraving, 1722. The Sewall home was on the south side of Marlborough Street, midway between Pond and Summer Streets (one block south of the Common).

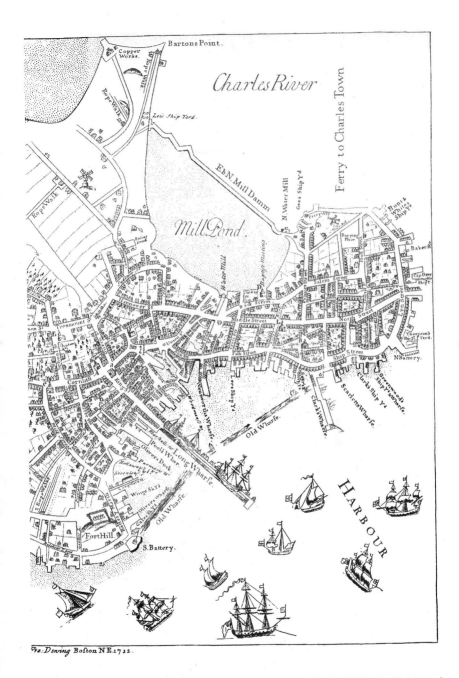

Courtesy, I. N. Phelps Stokes Collection, Miriam and Ira D., Wallach Division of Art, Prints and Photographs, New York Public Library, Astor, Lenox and Tilden Foundations.

PART ONE

Introduction:
The Life and Times
of Samuel Sewall

Samuel Sewall is perhaps best known for four episodes in his life. As a member of the special Court of Oyer and Terminer, Sewall was one of the judges who presided over the Salem witchcraft trials in 1692. His role in the conviction and execution of nineteen people later became a source of personal anguish and led to his public apology in 1697. Then, in 1700, Sewall wrote *The Selling of Joseph,* one of the earliest antislavery pamphlets in British America. "The numerousness of Slaves at this day in the Province, and the uneasiness of them under their Slavery," Sewall explained, had compelled him to question the rational and moral basis of the institution. Sewall's 1676 marriage to Hannah Hull has been immortalized in American literature by Nathaniel Hawthorne's short story "Grandfather's Chair," in which the fabled wealth of John Hull was reflected in a princely dowry for his new son-in-law. Finally, Sewall appears as an unsuccessful if not ridiculous suitor because, in 1718, nine months after Hannah's death had ended his marriage of forty-one years, Sewall began a series of courtships that have made him a figure of comical renown. The repeated rebuffs suffered by the sixty-eight-year-old suitor in his pursuit of Katharine Brattle Winthrop, the widow of Wait Still Winthrop, in particular, has been singled out as "the most celebrated passage in the Judge's *Diary.*"[1]

Unfortunately, an acquaintance with any of these popular images—remorseful witchcraft judge, pioneer antislavery writer, fortunate son-in-law, and overaged suitor—may frustrate a reader's full appreciation of Sewall's diary. About the first three episodes outlined above, Sewall had precious little to say. His 1697 apology for his role in the witchcraft trials five years earlier was prompted by the recent death of his two-year-old daughter Sarah and by his remembrance of the birth of a stillborn son the preceding May. Made "sensible" of his guilt by the "reiterated strokes of God upon himself and family," he appeared before the South Church congregation, accepted the "Blame and Shame" of his participation in the "late Commission of Oyer and Terminer at Salem," and asked for their prayers that "God . . . would pardon that Sin."[2]

With regard to *The Selling of Joseph,* Sewall recorded on June 19, 1700, that he had "been long and much dissatisfied with the Trade of fetching Negros from Guinea," but that his initially "strong inclination

---

[1] On the Salem witchcraft episode, compare Paul Boyer and Stephen Nissenbaum, *Salem Possessed: The Social Origins of Witchcraft* (Cambridge, Mass.: Harvard University Press, 1974), and Richard Godbeer, *The Devil's Dominion: Magic and Religion in Early New England* (Cambridge: Cambridge University Press, 1992). Samuel Sewall, *The Selling of Joseph* (Boston, 1700), reprinted in M. Halsey Thomas, ed., *The Diary of Samuel Sewall,* 2 vols. (New York: Farrar, Straus and Giroux, 1973), 2:1117–21, quotation on p. 1117; Nathaniel Hawthorne, "Grandfather's Chair," in *The Centenary Edition of the Works of Nathaniel Hawthorne,* ed. William Charvat, Roy Harvey Pearce, and Claude M. Simpson, vol. 6: *True Stories from History and Biography* (Columbus, Ohio: Ohio State University Press, 1972), 37–39; Richard S. Dunn, *Puritans and Yankees: The Winthrop Dynasty of New England, 1630–1717* (Princeton, NJ: Princeton University Press, 1962; New York: W. W. Norton, 1971), 285. Dunn's statement about the popularity of the diary passages relating Sewall's courtship of the widow Winthrop is supported by two earlier abridgments of the Sewall diary: Mark Van Doren, ed., *Samuel Sewall's Diary* (New York: Russell and Russell, 1963), 240–69; and Harvey Wish, ed., *The Diary of Samuel Sewall* (New York: Capricorn Books, 1967), 158–75, reprint entire portions of the diary relating to Sewall's courtship of Katharine Winthrop, Dorothy Denison, Abigail Tilley, and Mary Gibbs. Sewall's biographers—Ola Elizabeth Winslow, *Samuel Sewall of Boston* (New York: Macmillan, 1964), 165–86, and T. B. Strandness, *Samuel Sewall: A Puritan Portrait* (East Lansing, Mich.: Michigan State University Press, 1967), 169–81—also deal with Sewall's courtship of Katharine Winthrop and find much humor in it. "We read" about an "old man's stumbling attempt at courtship," Winslow writes, and "we smile at it, over his shoulder with apology." Strandness suggests that the courtships may be studied for "understanding" as well as "for amusement, for disparagement, or for quaint and curious lore," but he primarily reproduces wholesale with little analysis those passages dealing with Sewall and Winthrop.

[2] Thomas, ed., *Diary,* 1:366–67.

to write something about it . . . wore off." Only after reading a petition to the General Court on behalf of a black couple "unjustly held in bondage" and learning of a proposal to discourage the slave trade in Massachusetts by means of a forty-shilling-per-head tax on all slave imports did Sewall renew his commitment to "write this Apology for them." And even then, except for a rebuttal from fellow Bostonian John Saffin, Sewall's antislavery pamphlet was simply ignored by his contemporaries.[3]

Sewall recorded nothing in his diary about his courtship and marriage to Hannah Hull. In his autobiographical letter to his son Samuel, Jr., written in 1720, Sewall claimed that it was Hannah who, as a guest of Harvard President Leonard Hoar in August of 1674, "saw me when I took my [M.A.] Degree and set her affection on me, though I knew nothing of it till after our marriage." Perhaps the old man had exaggerated his appeal; nevertheless, there is no evidence to sustain Hawthorne's assertion that the young Sewall "had courted Miss Betsey [Hannah] out of pure love" or that John Hull had given him his daughter's weight in silver.

On the other hand, Sewall's descriptions of his courtship of the widows Dorothy Weld Denison and Katharine Brattle Winthrop do constitute a substantial portion of his diary entries for 1718 and 1720. However, to treat his advances as "an old man's stumbling attempt at courtship" or to "pity" Sewall for failing to see the humor of his situation is to distort seriously the context in which these failed courtships must be understood. The idea that Sewall court Katharine Winthrop was first broached by John Marion, deacon of the South Church, at the suggestion of Winthrop's nieces and nephews. Sewall himself, fully cognizant of his advanced age, was cool in his response, saying "twas hard to know whether best to marry again or no" and that "twas not five months since I buried my dear Wife." Yet he knew that Puritan doctrine cautioned against prolonged periods of mourning. The danger of crossing the line between a loving remembrance of the departed and the sin of "spiritual adultery," wherein one learns to "love the creature with that affection which is due only to Christ," must have figured into Sewall's decision finally to court Dorothy Denison (not Katharine Winthrop) in 1718 and to marry Abigail Woodmansey Tilley in 1719, two years after he had shed a "Flood of Tears" over the death of Hannah. Abigail's death seven months later led finally to Sewall's courtship

[3]Ibid., 1:432–33; Peter Kolchin, *American Slavery, 1619–1877* (New York: Hill and Wang, 1993), 64.

of Katharine Winthrop and his subsequent marriage to Mary Shrimpton Gibbs. Even a bare recitation of these events should make clear that the context for Sewall's courtships is more appropriately somber than comical. Hannah's death had devastated Sewall. "Lord help me to learn; and be a Sun and Shield to me, now [that] so much of my Comfort and Defense are taken away," Sewall prayed on the afternoon that Hannah died. Upon reading a note of condolence from Solomon Stoddard, Sewall "soked it in Tears." Abigail's sudden and unexpected death caused Sewall to bewail "this very Extraordinary, awfull Dispensation" and to anticipate his own death and entrance into a "house not made with Hands, eternal in the Heavens."[4]

The significance of Sewall's diary, then, is that it allows us to view these and numerous other lesser known events within the context of his everyday life. Sewall began his diary when he was twenty-two years old, and he continued to record what he saw and said and did on a daily basis for the next fifty-five years. As a result, we get to know Sewall with a degree of intimacy that is unsurpassed for any other individual of the time: riding to Dorchester with Hannah to eat cherries and raspberries, but "chiefly to ride and take the air"; listening to a complaint filed by the town's ministers against "mixt dances" being taught by dancing master Francis Stepney; scolding young Josiah Willard for wearing a wig; seeking meaning in a sudden and "very extraordinary storm of hail" that turned the ground white "as with the blossoms when fallen"; commiserating with Mary Obbinson whose husband had "kick'd her out of bed last night"; observing that a dog vomiting in the meetinghouse during Increase Mather's sermon had forced some to leave the building because it "stunk so horribly"; dreaming that he was a condemned criminal awaiting execution, which saddened him a "great

---

[4]Thomas, ed., *Diary*, 1:xxxii; 2:864, 872, 889, 890–93, 895–900, 904–8, 910–13, 927, 929, 931–33, 950, 951, 956–67, 988–93; Hawthorne, "Grandfather's Chair," 38. Hawthorne professed not to know the real name of John Hull's daughter (37) and thus settled on calling her "Betsey." The nineteenth-century editors of *The Diaries of John Hull*, estimating that Hannah's dowry of £500 was the equivalent of 125 pounds troy weight, have suggested that her dowry may have been equal to her body weight; see Thomas's recapitulation in *Diary*, 1:15. See Winslow, *Sewall of Boston*, 181, for statements on Sewall's "stumbling attempt" and the "pity" due him. The phrase *spiritual adultery* appears in *The Diary of Michael Wigglesworth, 1653–1657*, ed. Edmund S. Morgan (1951; reprint, Gloucester, Mass.: Peter Smith, 1970), 107. Edmund S. Morgan, *The Puritan Family: Religion and Domestic Relations in Seventeenth-Century New England* (1944; reprint, New York: Harper and Row, 1966), 48–64, discusses the Puritan concept of "rational love" between husbands and wives, which required them to control their affection for one another in order to ensure that it remained subordinate to their "highest love" for God. In this context, immoderate grief was proof that a widow or widower had not kept his or her love "within bounds."

while"; going fishing with John Bonner but catching only three cod because he grew seasick; using a chamber pot in bed and "not knowing the bottom was out" until he felt the "water"; finding his home "broken open in two places, and about twenty pounds worth of plate stolen away"; sitting in church on a day "so cold that the Sacramental Bread is frozen pretty hard, and rattles sadly as broken into the Plates"; and watching hopefully every April for the first signs of swallows returning to proclaim the arrival of spring.[5]

Given the wealth of detail contained in the diary, it is hardly surprising that we know a great deal more about Sewall as an adult than as a child or adolescent. From other sources, we know that the family's history in Massachusetts reaches back to 1634, when Sewall's father, Henry Sewall, Jr., first came to the Bay Colony at the age of twenty-two. The purpose of his migration was economic rather than religious: Henry, Jr., was charged with looking after his father's investment in a joint financial venture aimed at supplying the province with "Cattel and Provisions sutable for a new Plantation." Although the joint enterprise failed, Henry, Jr., remained in Newbury on the five hundred acres granted to him by the General Court as part of his father's share in the cattle-raising operation. Henry Sewall, Sr., then joined his son, and over the next twelve years the family prospered in Newbury. In 1646, however, shortly after his marriage to Jane Dummer, Henry, Jr., returned to England with his new wife and her parents. Samuel Sewall explained nearly three-quarters of a century later that the move was undertaken because the Dummers found the climate of New England "not agreeable." Hence it came to be that Sewall was born at Bishop Stoke, Hampshire, England, on March 28, 1652.[6]

During the family's residence in England, Henry, Jr., maintained some contact with his father in Massachusetts, and in 1659, two years after his father's death, he set sail for Newbury ostensibly to settle his inherited estate and to oversee the collection of rents, which had dwindled "to very little when remitted to England." Once in Massachusetts again, Henry, Jr., decided to stay. In 1661, he sent for the rest of his family "to come to him to New-England." Samuel Sewall later remembered in snapshot images his experiences as a nine-year-old embarking on the first grand adventure of his life: his mother hurriedly gathering

---

[5]Thomas, ed., *Diary,* 1:67, 83, 94, 330, 337, 358, 448–49, 518, 524, 543, 568; for characteristic entries on swallows in April, see 2:815, 893, 921, 946.

[6]Sewall traces the outlines of the family's history in his autobiographical letter to his son Samuel, Jr., April 21, 1720, in Thomas, ed., *Diary,* 1:xxix–xxxiii. See also Winslow, *Sewall of Boston,* 6–19; and Strandness, *Sewall,* 1–8.

the five young Sewall children to travel to London in preparation for the trip across the Atlantic aboard the *Prudent Mary;* members of the Dummer family taking their "leave with Tears"; a kindly uncle treating the children to "raisins and almonds"; the crew loading sheep on board at Dover; his growing fear during the eight-week journey because "we had nothing to see but Water and the Sky" and, later, his joy upon seeing "Land again"; a crewman carrying him ashore while "Mother kept aboard" in observance of the Sabbath; townspeople and newcomers joining together in "public Thanksgiving"; and finally, his father, who had hastened to Boston to greet them upon their arrival, accompanying them to Newbury.[7]

Sewall spent the next six years in Newbury and attended the school run by the "Reverend and Excellent Mr. Thomas Parker," whom he subsequently remembered as "my dear Master." In 1667, Sewall and his father traveled to Cambridge, where he entered Harvard College after successfully completing the oral examination in Latin and Greek administered by President Charles Chauncy. Characteristically, he developed a deep affection for the college and his classmates. Throughout the rest of his life, Sewall made a point of attending commencement exercises in Cambridge. Even in 1726, at age seventy-six and a "lame fainting Soldier," Sewall insisted on going to the Harvard commencement despite a driving rainstorm that made the trip something of an ordeal. He also kept in close touch with the ten men who graduated with him in 1671. In addition to following a routine schedule of visits, he met with John Norton to discuss personal matters of faith; prayed with John Bowles during the latter's bout with smallpox; grew ill himself while calling on Samuel Phipps and vomited in the Phipps's stove room; engaged in "refreshing converse" with Samuel Mather about seeing "one another in heaven"; and listened patiently during a long walk with Edward Taylor as Taylor told him of "his courting his first wife." In 1677, Sewall recorded the "lamentable newes" that Samuel Danforth had died of smallpox. Danforth was the first of the class of 1671 to die. Sewall, who outlived all of his classmates, was saddened with each passing. In late December of 1727, old and infirm, he attended the funeral of Peter Thacher and later summed up his situation: "I have now been at the Interment of 4 of my Class-mates. . . . Now I can go to no more Funerals of my Class-mates; nor none be at mine."[8]

---

[7]Thomas, ed., *Diary,* 1:xxx–xxxi; Winslow, *Sewall of Boston,* 12–13; Strandness, *Sewall,* 5–6.

[8]Thomas, ed., *Diary,* 1:xxxii, 40, 42, 276, 395–97; 2:845, 902, 1033, 1047–48, 1056–57.

Sewall left Harvard in 1674 with an M.A. degree, after having served both as a fellow of the college and keeper of the college library. He had been trained for the pulpit, but when a call came from the frontier town of Woodbridge, New Jersey, for his "coming thither to be their Minister," Sewall was singularly unresponsive. Perhaps he had already begun his courtship of Hannah Hull, who, as we have seen, he later claimed had "set her Affection on me" at the 1674 Harvard commencement. They were married on February 28, 1676. Regardless of whether John Hull showered his son-in-law with silver equal to Hannah's weight, he presented him with a clear alternative to entering the ministry. Within a year of his marriage, Sewall was intent on pursuing a mercantile career in the footsteps of his influential father-in-law. He later remembered that leading merchants who visited the Hull home, where he and Hannah had taken up residence, advised him to "Acquaint [himself] with Merchants, and Invited [him] (courteously) to their Caballs."[9]

Because diary entries for the period from 1677 to early 1685 are lost, we cannot trace in detail Sewall's rise as a merchant. What is clear, however, is that he worked for John Hull until Hull's death in 1683, and then inherited the Hull estate and mercantile practice. Because of his inheritance, by 1687 Sewall was clearly among the wealthiest residents of Boston. Out of a total of 1,036 persons on the 1687 tax roll, only two men, Samuel Shrimpton and Edward Shippen, rated above Sewall. He was one of only six taxpayers whose estates were valued at £130 or more. Thus a decade after his marriage to Hannah, Sewall's total taxable assets amounted to about £2,600. In 1684, Sewall gained election to the Court of Assistants, the upper house of the provincial legislature and also the colony's superior court of appeals, an honor that was in part a recognition of the economic position he had come to occupy by then.[10]

FAMILY

Although the Sewall diary is skimpy on the details of his economic enterprise, it constitutes an especially impressive commentary on the social milieu of the Sewalls and their neighbors. It is the best single source of information on the family life of Samuel Sewall. The Sewalls

[9]Ibid., 1:xxxii, 9, 32.
[10]The 1687 tax roll is reprinted in the appendix to the *Report of the Record Commissioners of the City of Boston,* First Report (Boston, 1881), 91–133. On Sewall's career as a merchant, see Winslow, *Sewall of Boston,* 47–78; and Strandness, *Sewall,* 45–56.

had fourteen children together, but only six reached adulthood. Sewall himself outlived eleven of his children. He witnessed their births, cared for them during their periods of illness, helped them through their adolescent crises, supervised their vocational training, involved himself in their courtships and marriages, saw four of them have children of their own, and buried all but three of them.[11] (See Table 1.)

Sewall's life as a Puritan father passed through at least three phases. The first, from the birth of John in 1677 to the birth of Sarah in 1694, had him concerned primarily with the establishment and growth of his family: the births of his children, their ongoing health problems, and the deaths of six of them during infancy. The second phase, from 1694 to 1700, were the years during which he dealt with the adolescent crises of his eldest children. Finding a calling for Sam, Jr., and comforting Betty as she struggled over questions of faith and salvation proved to be particularly taxing. The third phase began with the marriage of Betty in late 1700 and ended with Sewall's death in 1730. In this final stage of his paternal governance, he oversaw the courtships

Table 1. Sewall Children: Vital Statistics

NAME	DATE OF BIRTH	DATE OF MARRIAGE	AGE AT MARRIAGE (YEARS AND MONTHS)	DATE OF DEATH	AGE AT DEATH (YEARS AND MONTHS)
John	2 Apr 1677	—	—	11 Sep 1678	1.5
Samuel	11 Jun 1678	15 Sep 1702	24.3	27 Feb 1751	72.7
Hannah	3 Feb 1680	—	—	16 Aug 1724	44.6
Elizabeth	29 Dec 1681	17 Oct 1700	18.10	10 Jul 1716	34.6
Hull	8 Jul 1684	—	—	18 Jun 1686	1.11
Henry	7 Dec 1685	—	—	22 Dec 1685	0.½
Stephen	30 Jan 1687	—	—	26 Jul 1687	0.6
Joseph	15 Aug 1688	29 Oct 1713	25.2	27 Jun 1769	80.10
Judith	13 Aug 1690	—	—	21 Sep 1690	0.1
Mary	28 Oct 1691	24 Aug 1709	17.10	17 Nov 1710	19.1
Jane	7 Aug 1693	—	—	13 Sep 1693	0.1
Sarah	21 Nov 1694	—	—	23 Dec 1696	2.1
stillborn son	21 May 1696	—	—	21 May 1696	0.0
Judith	2 Jan 1702	12 May 1720	18.4	23 Dec 1740	39.0

[11] Winslow, *Sewall of Boston,* 204.

and marriages of his surviving children and began to involve himself in the lives of his grandchildren. These various stages of fatherhood naturally overlapped because nearly a quarter of a century separated the births of the first and last of the Sewall children. Thus Judith, the Sewalls' fourteenth child, was born in 1702, the same year that Sam, Jr., was married to Rebeckah Dudley, and more than a year after Betty's marriage to Grove Hirst. Judith would not marry until 1720, by which time Sewall had five grandchildren by Sam, Jr., eight by Betty, two by Joseph, and one by Mary. Nevertheless, there was a rhythm to Sewall's family life that corresponded to the life cycles of his children; thus we may examine his domestic history accordingly.

The events surrounding the birth of Sarah in 1694 tell us much about the routines of the Sewall household during parturition. Hannah, thirty-six years old and giving birth to her twelfth child, was having a difficult time on the morning of November 21. Sewall, who had been up since 3:00 or 4:00 A.M., sat praying in the kitchen with the Reverend Samuel Torrey of Weymouth. Eventually, the two were joined by Hannah's mother, Judith Hull, who left her daughter's bedside because the "more than ordinary extremity" of Hannah's situation was so taxing that "she was not able to endure the [birthing] chamber." Sometime before 9:00 A.M., Sewall left home to meet with the Reverend Samuel Willard of the South Church and inform him of Hannah's ordeal. After the meeting, as he entered the front gate of his home, Sewall was greeted by Elizabeth Peirce, one of Hannah's chamber attendants, who "wish'd me joy of my Daughter." Allowed, finally, to enter Hannah's room, Sewall noticed that the women who had tended to Hannah's needs throughout her travail were already dining on "rost Beef and minc'd Pyes, good Cheese and Tarts."[12]

Sewall's description of Sarah's birth highlights two important points. First, the birthing chamber was an exclusively female domain. Sewall was forced to pray in the kitchen while female friends and relatives comforted Hannah and midwife Elizabeth Weeden went about her work. The pattern was the same for the births of the other Sewall children. He and John Hull had to wait in the hallway during the birth of his first son, John, in 1677. News of the births of Henry in 1685 and Joseph in 1688 had to be conveyed to him by his mother-in-law in the first instance and by cousin Anne Quincy in the second. Only once did

---

[12]Thomas, ed., *Diary*, 1:324. My description of the birthing routines of the Sewall household follows the excellent discussion of parturition offered by Laurel Thatcher Ulrich in *Good Wives: Image and Reality in the Lives of Women in Northern New England, 1650–1750* (New York: Alfred A. Knopf, 1982), 126–45.

Sewall gain admission early into Hannah's chamber, and then it was at the invitation of the attending women. In 1702, during yet another difficult birth, Hannah's fourteenth and last, Sewall was confined to praying in another room until the "Women call me into the chamber, and I pray there."[13]

Sewall's description of the women dining on roast beef and tarts after Sarah's birth illustrates a second point. Evidently, the social occasion that parturition represented was not complete until the mother and her attendants had shared food together. After the birth of Judith in 1702, Hannah was bedridden for over a week. Once she recovered her strength, Hannah hosted a gathering of seventeen women in celebration. "My wife treats her Midwife and Women," Sewall recorded on January 16. While the women had a "good dinner [of] Boil'd Pork, Beef, Fowls; very good Rost-Beef, Turkey-Pye, [and] Tarts," Sewall was relegated to tending the "fire in the stove [that] warm'd the room." The Sewalls may have been especially conscientious about hosting private celebrations after a successful delivery because they were especially mindful of the dangers associated with childbirth. Hannah's "more than ordinary Extremity" with Sarah in 1694 was followed by the birth of a stillborn son eighteen months later. That more than five and a half years elapsed between the stillbirth of this "sweet desirable Son" and the birth of Judith in 1702, could only have added to the fears of the Sewalls.[14]

Given the possibility, indeed in the case of the Sewalls the probability, of infant death, a "comfortable Delivery" did not mark the end of parental prayers or worries. The Sewall children suffered their share of illnesses and misfortunes. Fevers and their resulting convulsions exacted a physical and emotional toll on parents and children alike. Two months after his birth in 1677, John, whose head had "received some harm" during delivery, suffered through his first bout of convulsions. Sewall described its onset: John was "asleep in the Cradle . . . [when he] suddenly started, trembled, his fingers contracted, his eyes starting and being distorted." By the time of John's death in 1678, the Sewalls' second child, Samuel, Jr., had been born. However, he too was wracked by convulsions. In desperation, the Sewalls sent their two-year-old son to Newbury to live with his grandparents "to see if change of air would help him against convulsions." The youngster remained in Newbury for a year. Hull, Henry, Mary, Jane, and Sarah also experienced infant "distempers" that were of a "convulsive nature." Convulsive fits were

[13]Thomas, ed., *Diary,* 1:41, 87, 175, 459.
[14]Ibid., 350, 460–61.

so commonplace during the illnesses of the Sewall children that their nonoccurrence was cause for commentary. When Stephen died in 1687 at the age of six months, Sewall noted that his "dear Son," who had been "very sick" for the preceding three days, had spent his last breath "in his Grandmother's Bed-Chamber" but suffered "no Convulsions."[15]

In addition to fevers and common colds, the Sewalls survived a major outbreak of the measles in 1688 and smallpox in 1690. Sam, Jr., first became ill on January 11, 1688, and within the next two weeks, both parents and the remaining Sewall children, Hannah and Betty, had "come out pretty full." At least two of the four deaths and three of the four cases of illness that Sewall recorded in his diary for January and early February were measles-related. Even more dangerous was the next epidemic. "Small Pocks appear," Sewall recorded simply on May 28, 1690. From late May to mid-June, Sewall was preoccupied with the progress of the disease. His diary entries are few, brief, and to the point: "Jane Toppan [Sewall's niece] is taken very ill"; "Betty and Joseph are taken"; "Betty very delirious"; "Joseph hath a very bad night"; "We put Sam to bed." Finally, on June 14, the crisis was over: "Have all my family together at Prayer, which has not been for many weeks before."[16]

The dangers posed by diseases were compounded by the perils of everyday life. Children at home and at play were frequently in harm's way. Sewall recorded almost routinely the accidents in which children were victims: a child dies after falling upon a knife which slits his cheek and throat; a young son accidentally shoots and kills his sister with the family gun; a boy is torn to pieces when he falls from his galloping horse and catches his foot on the stirrup; a four-year-old dies after he falls into a tub of scalding homemade beer; two youngsters drown when they fall through the ice while skating; a five-year-old is burned to death when his shirt catches fire; a young boy drowns while trying to save his friend, who also drowns. Winter and water, firearms and fire, took their toll of Boston children in the late seventeenth century.[17]

The Sewall children were involved in their share of accidents. Little Hannah fell against a chair and "grievously" cut her forehead "just above her left eye"; Joseph fell while playing and split his "forhead so as bleeds pretty much"; Mary fell into a neighbor's cellar and suffered a large gash on her head "more than two inches long"; Joseph hit Betty's

---

[15] Ibid., 43–44, 88, 145, 313, 337, 490.
[16] Ibid., 157–59, 259–60.
[17] Ibid., 61, 93, 119, 142, 151, 328, 360.

forehead with a brass knob and caused it to "bleed and swell"; and four-year-old Joseph swallowed a "bullet which for a while stuck in his throat" and put his parents in "great fear" until he safely voided the bullet two days later. The Sewalls were similarly in a "fright" when Hannah and Judith were run over by horses, and when Betty bled "pretty much" after she was accidentally struck on the side of her head with a goad swung by the driver of the children's sled.[18]

In 1694, at the age of forty-two, Sewall entered his second phase of fatherhood. Sam, Jr., his seventeen-year-old son, needed to be placed in an appropriate calling. Sewall had hoped that his namesake would become a minister, a calling that he himself had forsaken. But the youngster showed no talent for scholarship and little enthusiasm for schooling. Consequently, Sewall arranged to have the boy work as an apprentice with Boston bookseller Michael Perry. After only three months, however, Sam, Jr., was eager to quit the arrangement. His feet were "sore and swoln," Sewall told Perry, and "standing in the cold shop" only hindered their recovery. After Perry sent Sam, Jr., home, Sewall held a private fast and prayed that his son would "be disposed to such a master and calling, as wherein he may abide with God."[19]

For the next year and a half, Sewall sought out new opportunities for his eldest son. He placed him under the tutelage of merchant Samuel Checkley in 1695, but that arrangement had to be terminated after six months because Sam, Jr., could not adjust to the mercantile routine. The "numerousness of goods" in Checkley's shop made it "hard to distinguish them," Sewall heard his son complain, and the prices of the various items were not "marked; whereas books, the price of them was set down." The incongruity between Sam's last objection and his earlier complaints about his experience with bookseller Perry may have caught the attention of Sewall. In any case, in 1697 he settled his "valetudinarious son" in the shop of bookseller Richard Wilkins. Nearly nineteen years old by then, Sam, Jr., began finally to learn a trade and to apply himself in a calling.[20]

Whereas Sam's problems were primarily secular and social, Betty's major adolescent crisis was a crisis of faith that reached its peak the year before her brother found his calling. The Sewalls, like most Puritans, subscribed to the doctrine of predestination, the notion that God's grace alone, granted before birth, saved the believer. For fourteen-year-

[18]Ibid., 122, 180, 274, 300, 306, 336, 349, 484, 526.
[19]Ibid., 321–22, 327.
[20]Ibid., 336, 344, 347, 372, 500.

old Betty in 1696, the quest for reassurance that she was among the saved proved painful. The text of John Norton's sermon on the elusiveness of salvation, "Ye shall seek me and shall not find me," taken from the Gospel of St. John, "wounded" her and thus triggered her crisis. She "was afraid she should goe to hell, her sins were not pardoned," Sewall recorded. As Betty continued her struggle, at times in a state so confused that she was unable to give a distinct account of her distress, Sewall provided whatever comfort he could. In late February, a month after her initial bout of anxiety, and again in May, Betty was nearly inconsolable in her despair. Sewall prayed with his daughter, "with many tears on either part," and said what he could to help her "taste that sweetness in reading the Word which she once did." Perhaps hoping that a change of scenery might lift her spirits, Sewall sent Betty to Salem "to sojourn there awhile" with her uncle Stephen and his family. But the agony continued. During a private prayer session, Betty wept "so that [she] can hardly read" and confessed to Sewall her fear that she "was a reprobate."[21]

Precisely when Betty overcame her weeping bouts of despair cannot be known. When brother Stephen brought Betty back to Boston in late November of 1696, Sewall noted that his daughter returned from her three-month sojourn "well, blessed be God." Apparently, Betty had at last progressed beyond the stage of doubt and humiliation that preceded a renunciation of personal sinfulness in the Puritan morphology of conversion. It is important to note, however, that when Betty gained church membership in 1705, it was in Benjamin Colman's Brattle Street Church, where advocates of open communion had abandoned the older New England practice of requiring candidates for membership to relate their religious experiences before the assembled congregation. Betty may have considered her conversion experience too painful to be revisited in a public narration. In any case, Betty became the very model of the rectitude and moderation that stood at the center of the Puritan ideal of a church of visible saints. She dressed, for example, in accordance with the "decent customs of the town, but never in the extream." Indeed, "in her whole behavior," her husband Grove Hirst later testified, she "truly feared God and hated that which she knew to be sinful," and in no aspect of her life did she "affect the gaity and vanity of the world."[22]

---

[21]Ibid., 345–46, 348, 349, 355, 359.
[22]Ibid., 360. Charles Lloyd Cohen, *God's Caress: The Psychology of Puritan Religious Experience* (New York: Oxford University Press, 1986), 201–41, and Edmund S. Morgan, *Visible Saints: The History of a Puritan Idea* (New York: New York University Press, 1963;

Betty's marriage to Boston merchant Grove Hirst in 1700 marked the beginning of the third phase of Sewall's patriarchy. Not surprisingly, Sewall involved himself personally in the courtships and marriages of all of his children. What may be surprising is the degree to which marital decisions in the Sewall family were "participant-directed" rather than "parent-directed." We see this in operation from the outset of Betty's courtship. Sometime in late 1698, Sewall learned that Zechariah Tuthill, captain at Castle William and one of the founders of the Brattle Street Church, was interested in Betty. Upon making the appropriate preliminary inquiries and determining that there was no "blot" against Tuthill, Sewall allowed the courtship to commence. In January 1699, less than a week after Betty's seventeenth birthday, he arranged for Tuthill to meet the family and to speak with Betty. It was soon clear, however, that Betty did not share Tuthill's interest in marriage. When he came to call on her a second time, Betty "hid her self all alone in the coach for several hours till he was gon." On Tuthill's third visit, Sewall ensured that his elusive daughter talked to the good captain, but he had no intention of coercing Betty into a relationship she did not want. When Tuthill, a man not easily discouraged, made an encore appearance at the Sewall home the next night, Sewall sent him away.[23]

Betty's next suitor was Grove Hirst. Sewall clearly approved of Hirst, but Betty, initially receptive, seemed to grow cold to the idea of marrying him. After four weeks of diminishing expectations, Hirst's father, William, was ready to end the courtship. The elder Hirst approached the Sewalls in late October and informed them that he held little hope of a marriage resulting from the current situation between his son and their daughter. Although he was thankful for the courtesy shown his son by the Sewalls, he wanted it made plain by both families that the courtship was over, lest other interested parties think his son "was so involved that he was not fit to go any whether else." After the meeting, Sewall dashed off a letter to Betty, then visiting in Braintree, in which he warned her that her behavior thus far "will tend to discourage per-

---

Ithaca, N.Y.: Cornell University Press, 1965), 67–73, 148–50, discuss the various aspects of the Puritan conversion experience. Grove Hirst's description of Betty Sewall appears in Benjamin Colman's *A Funeral Sermon Preached upon the Death of . . . Grove Hirst* (Boston, 1717), 93–94.

[23]Thomas, ed., *Diary,* 1:405–6. Lawrence Stone, *The Family, Sex and Marriage in England 1500–1800* (New York: Harper and Row, 1977), 270–324, describes the change from "parent-directed" to "participant-directed" mating arrangements in seventeenth- and eighteenth-century England.

sons of worth from making their court to you." Having already heard Betty's complaints concerning Hirst, he explained that "when persons come to us, we are apt to look upon their undesirable circumstances mostly; and thereupon to shun them." But after such "persons retire from us for good," we are apt to appreciate "that which is desirable in them" and even to develop an exaggerated opinion of them "to our woful disquiet." Realizing this about human nature, Sewall advised, "you had need well to consider whether you [will] be able to bear his final leaving of you."[24]

Whether Sewall's advice influenced Betty's decision to marry Grove Hirst is unclear. She married him, but in October of 1700, fully a year after William Hirst's visit and Sewall's admonitory letter. Furthermore, it is likely that neither set of parents understood the true state of the courtship. While William was in Boston asking for a release for his son, Betty was receiving a visit from Grove in Braintree. It is also evident that Betty's emotional satisfaction was the paramount issue throughout her long courtship. To be sure, potential suitors approached Sewall before approaching Betty and, as William Hirst's appeal indicates, formal termination of a courtship was a familial responsibility. But Betty's preferences outweighed all other considerations. Sewall sent Tuthill away, but by then was anyone, with the possible exception of the hapless Tuthill, uncertain of Betty's disinterest? Similarly, Sewall's letter of admonition was really an appeal. As much as he liked Hirst, he was not ordering Betty to continue the courtship. On the contrary, he deferred to her judgment: "If you find in yourself an immovable, incurable aversion from him, and cannot love, and honour, and obey him, I shall say no more, nor give you any further trouble in this matter."[25]

The role Sewall played in the later courtships and marriages of the remaining Sewall children followed the pattern he established in Betty's case. Individual variations among the children were important, but the scope of Sewall's interaction with them and the flexibility he displayed in meeting their needs were constant. The length of Betty's courtship was exceptional, but that further supports the contention that Sewall recognized the necessity of accommodating personal differences. (See Table 2.)

That the third phase of Sewall's fatherhood only began with the marriages of his children is clearly seen in his ongoing involvement in the

[24]Thomas, ed., *Diary,* 1:415–16; Sewall to Elizabeth Sewall, October 26, 1699, in *Letter-Book of Samuel Sewall,* Massachusetts Historical Society *Collections,* sixth series, 2 vols. (Boston, 1886–1888), 1:213.

[25]Thomas, ed., *Diary,* 1:436; *Sewall Letter-Book,* 1:213.

life of Sam, Jr., and his wife, Rebeckah. After 1702, Sewall was a frequent visitor at the Dudley home, where Sam, Jr., and Rebeckah resided temporarily, and in Brookline, after the young couple moved into their own home. When Sam, Jr., and Rebeckah had their first child in 1703 and named him "Hull" in honor of John Hull and in remembrance of Sewall's own "little Hullie," Sewall was overjoyed. But Hull Sewall lived for only five months and, unfortunately, he was not the exception. Six of the seven children born to Sam, Jr., and Rebeckah died in infancy or early childhood. After Hull, Sam III died in 1708, Rebekah in 1710, and Mary in 1712—at ages one, five, and one, respectively. By 1713, the once promising marriage of Sam, Jr., and Rebeckah was in trouble. In February, Sam, Jr., told his mother that he was "very uncomfortable" in Brookline and that he wished to return home to Boston.[26]

The day after Sam, Jr.'s, confession to his mother, Sewall hurried to Brookline. His visit confirmed his worst fears. First, Sam, Jr., who had suffered through an episode of "Melancholy" a few years earlier, was still "abed" even though it was already eleven in the morning, and Sewall managed with difficulty to get him up and eating. Then, after admonishing Sam's servant "to be faithfull in his master's business," Sewall approached Rebeckah to ask "what might be the cause of my Son's indisposition, are you so kindly affected one towards another as you should be?" Rebeckah's curt response, "I do my Duty," stung Sewall and he left Brookline having "said no more." A week later, Rebeckah came to Boston to call on the Sewalls. Wishing to leave Hannah alone with Rebeckah, Sewall conveniently excused himself to deliver some letters. The result was a stormy session during which "very sharp"

Table 2.   Sewall Children: Courtship and Marriage

NAME	BIRTH ORDER	START OF COURTSHIP	DATE OF MARRIAGE	LENGTH OF COURTSHIP (IN MONTHS)
Elizabeth	4	2 Jan 1699	17 Oct 1700	21
Samuel, Jr.	2	20 Jul 1702	15 Sep 1702	2
Mary	10	31 Jan 1709	24 Aug 1709	7
Joseph	8	8 Apr 1713	29 Oct 1713	7
Judith	14	7 Dec 1719	12 May 1720	5

[26]Thomas, ed., *Diary,* 1:515, 576, 611; 2:641, 697, 705. The two other children who died early were Hannah in 1719, age ten, and John in 1724, age one.

A Neighbour's TEARS

Sprinkled on the Duſt of the Amiable Virgin,

Mrs. **Rebekah Sewall,**

Who was born **December** 30. 1 7 0 4. and dyed
.·. ſuddenly, **Auguſt** 3. 1 7 1 0. Ætatis 6.

Figure 2.
Headpiece from a broadside poem occasioned by the death of Rebekah Sewall (1704–1710). Rebekah was the second child born to Sam, Jr., and Rebeckah Dudley Sewall. Courtesy, Massachusetts Historical Society, Boston.

words were exchanged. Rebeckah "wholly justified her self" and accused Sam of such lascivious behavior that "if it were not for her, no Maid could be able to dwell at their house." In return, Hannah defended her son so vigorously that "at last Daughter Sewall burst out with Tears" and left in her carriage.[27]

Hoping that an intermediary might clear up the "dark wether at Brooklin," Sewall asked the Reverend Nehemiah Walter for assistance. Walter, who had married Sam, Jr., and Rebeckah in Roxbury more than a decade earlier, agreed to do what he could. But when Sewall broached the subject to Rebeckah, she dismissed it, saying "she knew not wherefore she should be called before a Minister!" Sewall explained that Walter was the "fittest moderator" because the "Govr [her father]

[27] Ibid., 1:557, 558; 2:706–7.

or I might be thought partial," but Rebeckah could not be persuaded. She became so animated in her own defense, insisting that the Sewalls had no idea how much "she had born" in the "performance of [her] Duty," that Betty's husband, Grove Hirst, thought it best to interrupt the discussion and lead Sewall away.[28]

By 1714, earnest prayers for Sam, Jr.'s, deliverance from his "melancholly circumstances" notwithstanding, the situation in Brookline had grown more complicated and, for Sam, Jr., in particular, more desperate. During one of his many sessions with his son, Sewall noted that Sam, Jr., was "full of pain" and that he predicted "with Tears that these sorrows (arising from discord between him and his wife) would bring him to his Grave." Sewall continued to search for a solution to his son's problems, but did so with less optimism than earlier. A December meeting with Rebeckah probably fueled his growing sense of the futility of further efforts at reconciliation. At that meeting, while he and his son Joseph, who was recently ordained as a minister of the South Church, waited to speak with Rebeckah in her chamber, they noticed that they were not alone. Rebeckah had invited a friend, Sarah Cummings, to sit "in the same room on the bed." Thus, although they spent "considerable time" together, "Daughter said nothing to us of her Grievances, nor we to her." The time for talking, it appeared, had passed.[29]

Barely two months after the disappointing December meeting in Brookline, Sam, Jr., moved back into the Sewall home in Boston. He lived with his parents for the remainder of 1715 and for all of 1716 and 1717. At least once, in late 1716, Sewall tried to arrange for his son's return to Brookline. He walked to Roxbury for a meeting with the Dudleys, but they seemed uninterested in effecting a reunion. Both Dudleys first "reckoned up the Offences of my son; and He the Vertues of his Daughter." Then, Sewall recorded in disbelief, the former governor proceeded to list the "hainous faults of my wife." Concluding that there was "no possibility of my Son's return" under the present circumstances, Sewall told the Dudleys that he remained open to their suggestions "and so left it."[30]

---

[28]Ibid., 2:712, 727, 728.

[29]Ibid., 2:732, 779. Joseph Sewall's description of his brother's "melancholly circumstances" appears in the "Diary of Joseph Sewall, 1711–1716," MS, Massachusetts Historical Society, May 22, 1713; for Joseph's prayers with his father for Sam, Jr., see his diary entries for December 25, 1712, February 17, 1713, and May 22, 1713. In April 1715, Sarah Cummings got married and moved to Newton. Sewall was delighted by the removal. "Sarah Cummins [sic] was married this day," he recorded on April 21. "This news will damp my daugter [sic] of Brooklin her Triumph." Thomas, ed., *Diary,* 2:791.

[30]Thomas, ed., *Diary,* 2:835–36.

The break in the deadlock between the Sewalls and the Dudleys and, consequently, the end of Sam's three years of exile from Brookline, came about unexpectedly. In December 1716, two months after the former governor and Mrs. Dudley had reckoned up the "Vertues" of their daughter, Rebeckah gave birth to an illegitimate son. The Dudleys were mortified. Lucy Wainwright Dudley, the wife of Rebeckah's brother Paul, took seven-year-old Hannah away from her mother, journeyed to Boston, and left the child with the Sewalls. When Joseph Dudley came to reclaim his granddaughter, he was clearly at a disadvantage. Sewall reminded him that "my son had all along insisted that Caution should be given" in dealing with the domestic crisis in Brookline. He now insisted on an acknowledgment from Dudley that Rebeckah's illegitimate son "should not be chargeable to his [Sam, Jr.'s] estate." For his part, after alluding to "Christ's pardoning Mary Magdalen" and admitting that "No body knew" who the father of the child was, Dudley merely "said 'twas best as 'twas."[31]

Sewall met with the Dudleys several times to discuss what he variously termed the "Affairs of Brooklin" or "Sam's business." He also consulted with the Reverend Nehemiah Walter, who advised Sam, Jr., to return "home to his wife." In February 1718, with Sewall and Dudley serving as witnesses, Sam, Jr., and Rebeckah met formally to "Sign and Seal the Writings" of both families. Immediately after the signing, Dudley presented Sewall with £100 and assured him that "he would perform all that he had promised to Mr. Walter." The occasion rekindled Sewall's hopes for his son and Rebeckah. He noted that the couple had formalized their reunion on the same day that he and Hannah had been married forty-two years earlier. "This was my Wedding Day. The Lord succeed and turn to good what we have been doing."[32]

Because he lived so long, until he was nearly seventy-eight years old, Sewall outlived Hannah, Betty, and Mary, three of his four daughters who survived beyond childhood and adolescence. During the third phase of his fatherhood, therefore, Sewall experienced the sadness of seeing some of his grown-up children precede him in death. Hannah's passing in 1724 is especially revealing because it came at the end of a ten-year ordeal. Hannah, Sewall's oldest daughter, never married; hence, she remained a presence in the Sewall home long after she had

[31]Ibid., 840, 850, 859–60.
[32]Ibid., 875, 886, 887.

Figure 3.
Joseph Dudley, governor of Massachusetts, 1702–1715. Artist unknown
(c. 1682–1686). Courtesy, Massachusetts Historical Society, Boston.

achieved adulthood. The nature of her presence, however, changed dramatically after the summer of 1714. "Hannah was coming hastily down
the new stairs, fell, and broke the pan of her right knee in two; one
part went upward, the other downward," Sewall recorded in August of

Figure 4.
Rebecca Tyng Dudley (Mrs. Joseph Dudley). Artist unknown (c. 1682–1686).
Courtesy, Massachusetts Historical Society, Boston.

that year. A year later, still hobbling from the first fall, Hannah fell down
the flight of stairs again. Sewall was "grievously surprised" to discover
that his luckless daughter had now broken her left kneecap and received a "great Gash" just below her previously broken right kneecap.

Thirty-five years old at the time, Hannah lived the rest of her life in pain.[33]

Although Hannah accompanied her mother to the meetinghouse in 1716, "after long restraint," and went to Salem to live temporarily with her uncle Stephen's family in late 1717, she was for the most part confined to her Boston home because the various plasters and ointments administered by her doctors failed to "abate her grievous pain." Then in early 1719, Hannah's right leg began to swell. The physician John Clark applied a compress to absorb the discharge from her ulcerated leg, but Hannah's prognosis remained gloomy. "Hannah's Right Legg swells much and water issues therefrom," Sewall observed in August, seven months after the initial swelling. In spite of some days when Hannah reportedly grew "better," her condition steadily deteriorated over the next few years. In a letter to the Reverend Timothy Woodbridge of Hartford, written in June of 1721, Sewall noted that Hannah was so "grievously fettered by Lameness" that she had "not gon out of doors since last December was two years." When he carried Hannah to Brookline to visit her brother Sam, Jr., in July, Sewall remarked that it was his daughter's first excursion "out of doors for two years and a half."[34]

Sewall anxiously monitored the health of his oldest daughter throughout the last years of her life. His reports to family and friends trace the deterioration of her condition. Hannah's "maimed knee" later became her "lameness" and still later her "Chronical Disease." By early 1724, Hannah's "disease" required almost constant attention. Sewall told Jonathan Dickinson that Mary Gibbs, whom he had married two years earlier, proved to be a "great Blessing to me and my family" because Hannah "could hardly Subsist without her." To the Reverend Solomon Stoddard of Northampton, Sewall wrote about the "necessary services of my wife, especially for me, and my daughter Hannah, whose Legg she dress'd once a day at least." And the task of changing the dressing on Hannah's leg, Sewall said, was now something that required "a great deal of diligence, skill, and Courage."[35]

In late July 1724, Hannah's condition worsened. She could not even rise from her bed on the 30th, Sewall noted, because she was not "able to get her foot on the ground." For the next week, various members of the Boston ministry called on the Sewalls. From the Brattle Street

---

[33] Ibid., 765, 792–93.

[34] Ibid., 797, 815, 816, 871, 915, 980; Sewall to Timothy Woodbridge, June 1, 1721, *Sewall Letter-Book,* 2:133.

[35] Sewall to Jonathan Dickinson, February 22, 1724, *Sewall Letter-Book,* 2:160; Sewall to Solomon Stoddard, March 14, 1724, ibid., 162.

Church, William Cooper, Judith Sewall's husband, came to pray on July 31 and again on August 4; from the Old North Church, Joshua Gee, Increase Mather, and Cotton Mather prayed with the Sewalls on August 3, 5, and 6, respectively; and from the New Brick Church, William Waldron came to pray and wait on the Sewalls on August 7. Joseph Sewall, now the senior pastor of the South Church, arranged to have John Webb of the New North Church preach in his place on August 2 so that he might remain at Hannah's bedside. "I think . . . all the Ministers of our Communion have been here," Sewall recorded on August 7. The family vigil continued until the 16th, when, shortly before 2:00 A.M., Sewall found Hannah "restless." He summoned the family to pray for Hannah, then positioned himself by her side while he quietly read the Twenty-seventh and Thirty-fourth Psalms to her. Later in the morning, he walked to the South Church to put up a public notice: "Prayers are desired for Hannah Sewall as drawing near her end." After attending a prayer meeting led by Thomas Prince, Joseph's South Church colleague, Sewall returned to find that Hannah had "expired half an hour past Ten."[36]

Sewall personally prepared Hannah's body for interment, wrapping it in "good Cere cloth" and applying a "convenient quantity of lime" in the coffin to ensure that the "noxious Humour flowing from her Legg may be suppressed and absorbed." On the evening of August 17, as he awaited the funeral scheduled for the next day, he ordered that Hannah be "removed into the best Room" in the house on the pretext that "Boston [Sewall's servant] will not have her put into the Cellar." Sewall's account of the events surrounding Hannah's death is itself evidence of his emotional attachment to his daughter. As nowhere else in his lengthy diary, he confessed that his recollection was a bit muddled, that his otherwise superb memory was at the moment failing him: "I do not remember the exact order of these things." Four years later, in 1728, as his eyesight faltered, Sewall honored his wife Mary by giving her a book of sermons "which had been my Daughter Hannah's, for whom she had laboured beyond measure."[37]

Until the very end, Sewall was a loving and watchful presence in the lives of his children. He died on January 1, 1730. His last diary entry dealt with the courtship of his granddaughter Jane Hirst. Jane had been living with the Sewalls since the age of eight, following the deaths of her parents, Sewall's daughter Betty in 1716 and Grove Hirst in 1717. On October 13, 1729, Addington Davenport, a former colleague on the

---

[36]Thomas, ed., *Diary,* 2:1018–19, 1020.
[37]Ibid., 1020–21, 1063.

Superior Court, called on Sewall on behalf of his son, Addington Davenport, Jr. After learning that Judge Davenport intended to build his son a house, give him the family pew in the South Church, and otherwise "deal by him as his eldest Son, and more than so," Sewall consented to the courtship. Jane and Addington, Jr., were married by Joseph Sewall two months later on December 23, 1729. It is only fitting that Sewall's diary ends with the commencement of a new chapter in the family's history, and that he was directly involved in arranging it.[38]

CHURCH

In late January of 1677, Sewall visited the Reverend Thomas Thacher to announce his "desire of communion with his Church." Two months later, he recorded in his diary: "I offered myself [for membership], and was not refused." Although the period between first mention and final admission was relatively brief for Sewall, it was nevertheless filled with doubts that could be allayed only through counseling and prayers. In the first place, he was "exceedingly tormented" by the fear that Thacher's South Church, formed a mere eight years earlier as a result of a schism within the First Church, might be violating "God's way in breaking off from the old." The "weakness or some such undesirableness in many of its members" compounded his discouragement. Seeking comfort in prayer, Sewall was "much relieved by the consideration" of the opening chapter of 1 Corinthians, in particular the verses "not many wise men after the flesh, not many mighty, not many noble, are called" and "God hath chosen the foolish things of the world to confound the wise; and God hath chosen the weak things of the world to confound the things which are mighty."[39]

Sewall was troubled also by his own shortcomings. To Thacher, he confessed his "continuance in sin, wandering in prayer." The very doubts he expressed about the membership of the South Church were rooted, he acknowledged, in his overweening "pride" and inability to trust wholly in "God's wisdom." On March 19, after discoursing with others regarding his "coming into the Church," Sewall met with Thacher once more, confessed his "temptations," and received some encouragement when Thacher allowed that his "stirring . . . was of God." Still, he was beset by a sense of his "own unfitness and want of Grace." Only the hope that his faith might be strengthened by partaking of communion and his desire to see his "then hoped for" child

---

[38]Ibid., 1066–67.
[39]Thomas, ed., *Diary,* 1:33, 39; 1 Cor. 1:26–27.

(John was born on April 2) properly baptized led Sewall finally to offer himself to the congregation. Shortly after he had successfully gained membership on March 30, however, after the "scruple of the Church vanished," he became even more distraught. "I began to be more afraid of myself," Sewall noted. And when Robert Walker, one of the founders of the South Church, failed to welcome him or to wish him well on the day after his admission, Sewall was "almost overwhelmed" and "could hardly sit down to the Lord's Table" the next day. He did, he explained, in part because he feared that a withdrawal would render him "less fit" to participate in any future "Sacrament day" and in part because he was determined to "do better" in seeking "God who many times before had touched my heart."[40]

That Sewall was at once despairing and hopeful, especially after he was "admitted into Mr. Thacher's Church," is instructive. Sewall and his Puritan neighbors knew that gaining church membership was an important milestone in the spiritual journey from sin to salvation, but it marked a beginning rather than the end of that pilgrimage. The "solemn covenant" Sewall made with the South Church included a promise to maintain a "watchfulness to Edification." And Sewall was watchful. He was quick to find larger meaning and occasion for religious instruction in everyday events. When four-year-old Joseph tried to hide behind a cradle to avoid being punished for playing during prayers and for throwing a brass knob against his sister Betty's forehead, causing it to "bleed and swell," Sewall took as a "sorrowful remembrance of Adam's carriage." When Richard Dummer, nine years old, died of smallpox in 1690, Sewall told eleven-year-old Sam that he too "had to prepare for death, and therefore to endeavour really to pray when he said over the Lord's Prayer." When a "bad fall" hurt his "right elbow and strained my self much," Sewall reflected on "how much hurt may one get when seemingly out of Danger! The Lord pity, and pardon, and raise me up." When another fall resulted in the lifting of the skin on his right leg and "a great deal of pain," Sewall pronounced his suffering to be "good" because through the "loss of some of my skin and blood I might be awakened to prepare for my own dissolution." When his front tooth came loose as he sat down for a funeral sermon, he understood it to be a "warning that I must shortly resign my head."[41]

For Sewall, these and numerous other events testified to the particular interest God had taken in the everyday lives of New Englanders. He did not believe that untimely deaths or unfortunate episodes were

[40] Ibid., 33, 38, 39–40.
[41] Ibid., 1:249, 300; 2:929, 976, 1056.

merely the products of chance. Unexpected occurrences were never accidents; they were "afflictions" visited upon the faithful as reminders of their ongoing need to seek perfection in the "love of Christ, which is altogether lovely." A bruised shin that kept Sewall hobbled and home-bound for nearly three weeks was an affliction to check his spirit, which was "apt to be too light." A "flux . . . so vehement" that it kept him from the Lord's Supper was an affliction to teach him to "profit by this con-finement." The sudden death of his five-year-old granddaughter Re-bekah was an "awful surprising" affliction through which the "Lord ef-fectually awaken[ed] us." The stillbirth of his thirteenth child was a "singular Affliction" to discourage his "Wandering and Neglect." The death of little Sarah, barely two years old, was an affliction to spur him toward being more "effectually carefull" in the defense of "those God has still left me." These repeated strokes, the Reverend Thomas Cheever explained to Sewall, were intended by God to perfect rather than to punish him. The "Afflictions of God's people" were like the blows of a goldsmith's hammer: "Knock, knock, knock; knock, knock, knock, to finish the plate." Sewall was so taken by Cheever's analogy that he "went and told Mr. Pemberton."[42]

Sewall's "watchfulness to Edification" was reinforced by his belief in apocalyptic prophecy, which predisposed him to link current events to events associated with the second coming of Christ. In particular, his ef-forts to interpret Saint John's visions in Revelation resulted in a blurring of all distinction between the natural world and the supernatural. Earth-quakes, hailstorms, clouds, lightning and thunder, falling stars, rain-bows, fires, and eclipses might be signs of the approaching millennium; in any case, they were providential in origin, and Sewall filled his diary with references to these natural phenomena. In the years covered by his diary, Sewall commented on at least twenty-eight rainbows, fifteen eclipses, six earthquakes, three comets, and dozens of lightning, thun-der, and hail storms. Often his comments were brief, probably because he was unsure of the precise meaning of that occurrence. But he was never discouraged. He understood that what John Danforth once called the "abstruse *Hieroglyphicks* of Heaven" was meant to be obscure. In-deed, as Benjamin Colman of the Brattle Street Church explained, God had purposely hidden the meanings of some of the prophecies in part "to teach us *Modesty* in our *Enquiries* after them."[43]

---

[42]Ibid., 2:961, 1056, 1061, 894, 641; 1:350, 364, 599.
[43]The best discussion of the eschatological ideas of colonial New Englanders is James West Davidson, *The Logic of Millennial Thought: Eighteenth-Century New England* (New Haven: Yale University Press, 1977), 37–121; the Danforth quotation appears on p. 43; the Colman quotation, on p. 40.

On more than a few occasions, however, Sewall alluded to the biblical or spiritual significance of a particular event. A "Noble *Rainbow*" appearing in an evening cloud after a day of "great Thundering, and Darkness, and Rain" was perhaps a "Token that Christ remembers his Covenant for his beloved *Jews* . . . and that He will make haste to prepare for them a city that has foundations." A "large Cometical Blaze, something fine and dim," glowing from the west after Increase Mather preached a sermon on "Rev. 22.16—bright and morning Star" and "mentioned sign in the Heaven," might be a sign of the second coming of Christ. A "great Flash of Lightening," sudden and solitary ("hardly any preceded or succeeded it"), striking Samuel Vetch's newly purchased house and no one else's, might be an indication that God was not pleased with Vetch, who had been implicated in a scheme involving trading with the enemy during Queen Anne's War. A "very extraordinary Storm of Hail" that broke through the kitchen windows of the Sewall home and "flew to the middle of the room, or farther" was perhaps a reminder from God: "He had broken the brittle part of our house . . . that we might be ready for the time when our Clay-Tabernacles should be broken."[44]

Seeking solace in prayer after the violence of the hailstorm was typical of the Sewalls' responses to other displays of "awful Providence." Living in a world full of mystery and meaning beyond mere human abilities to comprehend, the Sewalls turned first and foremost to prayer. At the most intimate level, prayers involved the devotions of the solitary believer in "secret." As Charles E. Hambrick-Stowe has pointed out, Matthew 6:6 provided the classic text for this practice: "When thou prayest, enter into thy closet, and when thou hast shut thy door, pray to thy Father which is in secret." In troubled times especially, Sewall seemed to resort to prayers in solitude. Two weeks after the death of his mother-in-law Judith Hull in June of 1695, in the middle of a crisis over finding a proper calling for Sam, Jr., Sewall kept a "day of prayer in secret." Six months later, with his son still adrift, he observed a "Day of Fasting with prayer for the conversion of my son and his settlement in a trade that might be good for soul and body." In February of 1704, fourteen months after Betty "was brought to bed of a dead child," he "fasted and prayed . . . for Daughter Hirst and [her five-day-old] little Mary." But secret prayers were not reserved for times of crisis alone. On the thirty-fifth anniversary of his marriage to Hannah, Sewall set aside some time for "meditation and prayer." He also routinely "spent some time in prayer" on his birthday. When court business kept him in Plymouth on March 28, he began his "birth-day in the [Plymouth]

---

[44]Thomas, ed., *Diary,* 1:462, 330–31; 2:1062, 762–63.

Meetinghouse." On one occasion, he visited the meetinghouse, "as I had done in former years," only to discover "it shut." Temporarily disappointed, he returned to his room in John Rickard's Plymouth tavern and there conducted a "solemn secret prayer." If public business or travel kept him from the meetinghouse on March 28, he went as soon as the opportunity presented itself. Once he went to the Plymouth meetinghouse on March 30; another time he "went into the Meetinghouse and spent some time in prayer" on April 1.[45]

Secret prayers constituted an essential part of the practice of piety, but they were still only a part of a larger pattern of devotion for most New Englanders. Sewall knew that solitary exercises were not enough. On the evening of March 28, 1721, he invited his son Joseph "to pray with us, that might redeem the time and turn over a new leaf." The occasion was his sixty-ninth birthday, and Sewall, his second wife having died ten months earlier, wished to surround himself with his children. As they gathered around their father, the children must have found and conveyed a sense of comfort in their accustomed setting. Hannah and Judith, age forty-one and nineteen, respectively, both of whom were unmarried and living at home, Joseph, age thirty-two, and Sam, Jr., age forty-two, had participated in family devotions all of their lives. For more than forty years, Sewall had been the very embodiment of Roger Clap's admonition: "Do not neglect Family Prayer, Morning and Evening. And be sure to Read some part of the Word of God every day in your Families." Sewall led the family in reading scriptures and singing psalms, but he expected the children to be contributors as well. Sam, Jr., was a full-fledged participant by the time he was eight years old. "My son reads to me Isa. 22 in his course this morning," Sewall recorded in May 1686; and, in August, "Sam read the 10th of Jeremiah." Furthermore, participation in family devotions was so important that few were excused. When wife Hannah was unable to leave her bedchamber because she was "very ill of the ague in her face," she did not join the family in prayer, but when eight-year-old Betty complained of "not being very well," she was encouraged to do her "share to read the 24 of Isaiah, which she doth with many tears."[46]

---

[45] Ibid., 1:336, 521, 477, 497; 2:655, 634–35, 616, 708. David D. Hall, *Worlds of Wonder, Days of Judgment: Popular Religious Belief in Early New England* (New York: Alfred A. Knopf, 1989), 71–116, 213–38; and Charles E. Hambrick-Stowe, *The Practice of Piety: Puritan Devotional Disciplines in Seventeenth-Century New England* (Chapel Hill: University of North Carolina Press, 1982), 9–15, 93–193 (quotation on p. 175), provide a larger context for many of the ideas discussed here and in subsequent paragraphs.

[46] Thomas, ed., *Diary*, 2:977; 1:114, 119, 249, 179; Roger Clap is quoted in Hambrick-Stowe, *Practice of Piety*, 143; on family prayers, see also Morgan, *Puritan Family*, 133–40.

Family prayers were, understandably, an integral part of the process of coping with grief. When the Sewalls' ninth child, whom they named Judith after her maternal grandmother and great-grandmother, appeared "ready to die" on September 20, 1690, Sewall asked Nehemiah Walter of the Roxbury church "to give her a lift towards heaven." Unable to sleep well that night, he arose at two the next morning to "read some Psalms and pray" with his month-old daughter, who continued to languish and moan. Between seven and eight, he summoned Samuel Willard of the South Church, "and he prays." In the afternoon, the Reverend John Bailey came to sit and pray with the Sewalls. Finally, between seven and eight that night, the "child died, and I hope sleeps in Jesus," Sewall recorded. The next night, Joshua Moodey and James Allen of the First Church and Cotton Mather of the North Church visited the Sewalls to offer their prayers. On the day of the funeral, "before we went, [the] children read the 18, 19, and 20th Chapters of John, being in course for family reading." Joshua Moodey then carried the coffin, on which "is the year 1690 made with little nails," to the Sewall family tomb.[47]

The devotional exercises the Sewalls engaged in during the period before and after the death of "little Judith" were repeated on other similarly sad occasions. Prayers in private, the notification of relatives and local clergymen, prayers by attending ministers, the family vigil, scripture reading, the funeral procession, and final condolences constituted a pattern of activities that was first revealed in Sewall's diary with the death of two-week-old Henry in 1685. The pattern was repeated in 1687 when Stephen died at the age of six months, in 1693 when Jane died after barely a month, and in 1696 when Sarah died at the age of two. It was essentially unchanged when older children died. When Mary died of complications in childbirth in 1710 at the age of nineteen, when Betty died of a "returning fever" in 1716 at the age of thirty-four, and when Hannah died of gangrenous infections in 1724 at the age of forty-four, the surviving members of the Sewall family followed the same sorrowful routine.[48]

That the Sewalls found relief in the prayers of their neighbors is clear; that they offered the same sort of relief to their neighbors is equally clear. On the day after Judith died, Sewall accompanied Joshua Moodey to John Hurd's home. Hurd, whose wife "Nurse Hurd" had

[47]Thomas, ed., *Diary,* 1:266–67. In 1690, Sam, Jr., was twelve years old; Hannah, ten; Betty, eight; and Joseph, two.
[48]Ibid., 89, 145, 313, 364–65.

kept watch over the Sewalls' first child in 1677 when the newborn's head "had received some harm" during delivery, was dying but unreceptive. Asked by his wife if he desired Sewall and Moodey to pray with him, he answered, "Hold your tongue" and "Let me alone, or, be quiet." Sewall, grieving over the death of his infant daughter, was startled by the old man's lack of charity. The Reverend Moodey proceeded to scold the dying tailor "pretty roundly," telling him he ought to have given a "penitent answer." Before leaving, Moodey thought to ask Hurd one last time whether he desired any prayers. "He answered, Ay for the Lord's sake." Hurd died early the next morning, on the day of Judith's funeral.[49]

Customary interaction among families in prayer was also in evidence during Betty's last illness. In April and June of 1716, Sewall not only held prayer meetings in his home, but he participated in similar meetings in the homes of others. On April 27, Sewall attended a prayer meeting at the home of Edward Bromfield, a fellow magistrate, whose son Henry had a "dangerous swelling on his neck." Also in attendance were the ministers of five of Boston's churches—Increase and Cotton Mather, John Webb, Benjamin Wadsworth, William Cooper, and Joseph Sewall—each of whom prayed in turn. Sewall then set the tune for the singing of the 116th Psalm, after which he "desired prayers for my daughter Hirst, which was done. *Laus Deo.*" A week later, at a "private meeting" in the Sewall home, the Sewalls prayed not for Betty alone, but again for Henry Bromfield and for Thomas Sewall, the ailing son of Sewall's younger brother John. Still later, on June 29, Eunice Willard, the widow of Samuel Willard who died in 1707, hosted a prayer meeting at which Boston's ministers Joseph Sewall, Webb, and Ebenezer Pemberton prayed for Henry Bromfield, Betty, and Thomas Sewall.[50]

The Sewalls frequently conjoined secret prayers and family devotions with days of fasting, which they and their like-minded neighbors observed in response to "awful surprising providences" or when they felt themselves to be too "solicitous about earthly things." One of the finest descriptions of a "private day of prayer with fasting" appears in Sewall's entry for February 10, 1708. Isolated in an upper chamber of his house, with the shutters fastened, Sewall commenced his praying by beseeching God's help in perfecting "what is lacking in my faith, and in the faith of my dear Yokefellow." He then moved on to "other important matters," progressing smoothly from his immediate family

---

[49]Ibid., 41, 267.
[50]Ibid., 2:816, 821, 823.

("convert my children, especially Samuel and Hannah"), to his servant ("make David [Sinclair] a man after thy own heart"), to the province ("steer the government in this difficult time, when the Governor and many others are at so much variance"), to other colonies ("save Connecticut . . . [and] N. York"), to the Western Hemisphere ("Reform all the European Plantations in America; Spanish, Portuguese, English, French, Dutch"), and finally to the world ("save Asia, Africa, Europe and America"). At the end, Sewall acknowledged the "bounteous grace of God" in helping him conclude a "very comfortable day."[51]

Other fasts—and Sewall participated in about a hundred of them—were not nearly as expansive. During little Hullie's ordeal of convulsions, Sewall invited all the provincial magistrates to a private fast at "our house." After the Dominion government under Edmund Andros appropriated the use of the South Meetinghouse, the Sewalls held a fast in response to the "difficult circumstances [of] our Church . . . regarding the Church of England's meeting in it." Following the death of their pastor Ebenezer Pemberton, the members of the South Church agreed to a fast "to humble ourselves for the breach made in the South church." As with Sewall's secret day, these fasts required a considerable commitment of time to prayers. Typically, a full morning of prayer and preaching was followed by a break and then an afternoon session of prayer and preaching. The fast occasioned by the Anglicans' appropriation of the South Church, for example, began with a morning prayer and sermon by Samuel Willard, which had as its text "For the Lord shall judge his people . . . when he seeth that their power is gone" (Deut. 32:36). The afternoon session included prayers by Cotton Mather and Joshua Moodey as well as a sermon by the latter on the text "Be still, and know that I am God: I will be exalted among the heathen" (Ps. 46:10). Willard then dismissed the assembly with a blessing. The private fast held for Hullie offers a more specific schedule. The fast began at 9:30 A.M. with a prayer by John Eliot, the longtime Roxbury minister known for his missionary work among the Indians, and a sermon by Willard on the text ("I am afraid of Thy judgments") given to him by Judith Hull, the convulsive boy's grandmother. After a prayer by James Allen of the First Church, the group took a half-hour break. The afternoon session included a prayer by Cotton Mather, a sermon by Increase Mather, and a closing prayer by Joshua Moodey that lasted "about an hour and a half." By the time Sewall "distributed some biskets, and beer, cider, [and] wine" to signify the end of the formal

---

[51] Ibid., 2:641, 961; 1:589.

proceedings, the group had spent perhaps four to five hours listening and praying together.[52]

Days of thanksgiving provided pious neighbors with similar opportunities for congregating in prayer. Evidence of God's special favor for New Englanders individually or collectively was the inspiration for thanksgiving: a son's "preservation" during a two-year trip abroad; a resident's safe return after service in England; the destruction of a pirate ship and crew; a proclamation of peace with France. For Bostonians, days of thanksgiving ordinarily entailed two sermons intermingled with prayers and psalm singing. During the smallpox epidemic of 1721, when the Reverend Thomas Prince of the South Church "offered it to consideration, that there might be but one sermon" for the upcoming day of thanksgiving, Sewall was much exercised by the proposal. "I spake against it," he said. "Twas the privilege we in Boston had, that might have two, which our Brethren in the country could not have, because of their remote living." Unable to secure a second for his own motion, Sewall claimed he "desisted." In fact, he had not given up the fight. Insisting that "so great an alteration should not have been made without the knowledge and agreement" of the magistrates who resided in Boston, he approached Penn Townsend in the Council chamber. Unfortunately, according to Sewall, although Townsend "was of opinion twas best to have two," he feared the "distress of the small pox" and would not "move a jot towards having two." On the day of thanksgiving itself, Sewall was reduced to noting: "Thanksgiving; but one sermon in most Congregations."[53]

The routines associated with days of thanksgiving were susceptible not only to the disruptions of epidemics but also to the tribulations of political manipulation. The situation in Massachusetts after the revocation of the old corporate charter in 1684 seemed to invite artful maneuvering. When Governor Andros issued an order for a day of thanksgiving in 1688 in honor of James II's second wife, the Catholic Mary of Modena, "being with child," the Puritan establishment demurred. Samuel Willard was responsible for announcing such events to his congregation, and on other occasions he did so with little hesitation. On this occasion, however, Willard "mentions not the Thanksgiving," Sewall observed, on the pretense that the governor's messenger had given

---

[52]Ibid., 1:63, 135, 136, 138, 139, 141–42. Hall, *Worlds of Wonder,* 233, says that Sewall participated in nearly a hundred fasts. John Eliot produced an Algonquian translation of the Bible in 1663.

[53]Thomas, ed., *Diary,* 1:300, 538; 2:983, 984.

him oral confirmation of the event but had "left no Order with him." Upon receiving the written order, Willard still refused to endorse it, saying merely that "such an occasion was by the Governour recommended to be given Thanks for." James Allen of the First Church, on the other hand, attempted to comply with Andros's order and sang portions of the Twenty-first and Seventy-second Psalms to his congregation, including the verses "The king shall joy in thy strength, O Lord . . . For thou hast made him most blessed for ever" and "Give the king thy judgments, O God, and thy righteousness unto the king's son." Allen's celebration, Sewall later learned, had given "offense to some of his Church." On a more personal level for Sewall, he noticed that neither Increase nor Cotton Mather was present at Elisha Cooke, Sr.'s, thanksgiving in 1692. Under ordinary circumstances, he expected to find the Mathers in the company of their Boston colleagues Willard, Allen, and John Bailey. But Increase Mather and Cooke had served together in London from 1690 to 1692 as agents of Massachusetts and had suffered a falling out over Mather's support of the 1691 royal charter. Cooke, who continued to hope in vain for a restoration of conditions under the old charter, suspected that Mather had acted from base motives. Both Mathers, father and son, were no longer welcomed at Cooke's home, and Sewall lamented their absence because of what it signified: "The good Lord unite us in his fear, and remove our animosities!"[54]

Days of fasting and thanksgiving were occasional observances and by their very nature supplementary to regularly scheduled days of worship. First and foremost among these was the Sabbath. Sunday services, morning and afternoon, were at the heart of all spiritual activity in Puritan New England, and these services consumed much of the day. Morning worship began around 9:00 A.M. and lasted until at least 11:00 A.M.; afternoon services began shortly before 2:00 P.M. and continued until about 4:00 P.M. Sewall expected to spend a minimum of four hours in church on Sundays. When circumstances prevented it, he found reason to comment or complain. Samuel Willard's morning sermon was over "before eleven by my clock" and his afternoon worship was concluded at a "quarter before four," Sewall said on one occasion. Given this rather rigid schedule, one of the difficulties posed by Andros's

---

[54] Ibid., 1:165, 166, 300. On Increase Mather and Elisha Cooke's experiences in England and their quarrel over the 1691 charter, see Richard R. Johnson, *Adjustment to Empire: The New England Colonies, 1675–1715* (New Brunswick, N.J.: Rutgers University Press, 1981), 136–241.

Figure 5.
Increase Mather, pastor of the North Church from 1664 to 1723. Detail from the portrait by Johan van der Spritt, 1688. Courtesy, Massachusetts Historical Society, Boston.

appropriation of the South Church for Anglican services was logistical. When would the Anglicans find the time to meet in the morning? Andros said that "they would begin at eight in the morning and have done by nine," but the members of the South Church were clearly skeptical:

"We said 'twould hardly be so in winter." James Graham, the attorney-general of the Dominion, thereupon offered a snappy rejoinder that earned him the enmity of the congregation: If he and his fellow Anglicans had to have "their service by candle-light what was that to any." Coordinating the afternoon sessions of worship posed similar problems. Once, when the South Church's morning service lasted until a little after noon, Andros was "angry that had done so late" and did not convene the Anglicans until "about a quarter past one." As a result, Sewall noted, the South Church's afternoon service had to be delayed until "a quarter past three . . . about 1 1/2 hour later than usual."[55]

Sabbath services ordinarily took four to six hours from beginning to end, but not all of that time was devoted to prayers, psalm singing, and sermons. On occasion, the admission of new members, a procedure that required of the candidates a narration of their spiritual preparation for salvation, took up a portion of the Sabbath: "Elizabeth Wisendunk and Abigail Winslow taken into Church"; "Francis Bromfield and Marshal's Negro woman" were admitted, "their Relations very acceptable"; "Mary Smith, widow, Mr. Wheelwright's grandchild, was taken into Church." Sewall, as we have seen, recorded his own admission into membership in the South Church in 1677: "Goodm[an] Cole first spake, then I, then the Relations of the women were read; as we spake so were we admitted." Also a vital part of the Sabbath services was the administering of the sacraments. Sewall recorded the baptisms of his children on various Sundays: Henry was "fine and quiet" during the service; Joseph carried his father's "hopes of the accomplishment of the Prophecy"; Mary was baptized on "a very pleasant day"; Sarah reflected her father's esteem for "Sarah's standing in the Scripture"; and Judith "cried not at all, though a pretty deal of water was poured on her." The administration of the Lord's Supper was a monthly or bimonthly ceremony. Again, we know from Sewall's own experience that the whole ritual could be nearly overwhelming for the newly admitted: "I . . . was afraid that because I came to the ordinance without belief . . . I should be stricken dead." Finally, the disciplining of the wayward constituted a part of the services on the Sabbath. "Elizabeth Monk . . . [was] restored" to good standing within the church after she "made a satisfactory confession" of her misdeeds before the congregation. Roger Judd, on the other hand, was "cast out of the Church for his con-

[55]Thomas, ed., *Diary,* 1:170, 171, 177; also, November 11, 1688: "Mr. Moodey preached with us in the forenoon . . . many got home just about a quarter after 11. Afternoon got home about half an hour by sun."

tumacy in refusing to hear the Church, and his contemptuous behaviour against the same and [against] Mr. Willard the Pastor."[56]

Being a part of the Sabbath observance was so important to Sewall that whenever official duties interfered with his "publick celebration of the Lord's day" at the South Church, he was uneasy. In New York in the spring of 1690 as a representative of Massachusetts commissioned to meet with Jacob Leisler in order to discuss matters of mutual defense against the French, Sewall confessed to a "great heaviness on my spirit." On Sunday morning, May 4, he attended the services of the Dutch Reformed Church of St. Nicholas and sang the Sixty-ninth Psalm with the assistance of an acquaintance who "lent me his Book [and] pointed to every syllable." But relief came to him only after he retired to his room and sang the Twenty-fifth Psalm, "which should have sung in course, if I had been at home this day." Clearly, Sewall was a creature of habit. The strangeness of his surroundings intensified his need to carry on as if he had been at home on that particular Sunday. The situation of his family at this time helps to explain further why he was not similarly distressed on other occasions in other places. A week before Sewall's departure for New York, Sam, Jr., had to have an "issue made in his left arm." Sewall hoped that the bleeding of his son would "prevent the swelling in his neck" from becoming cancerous. In addition, mindful of the fact that three of their last four children had died at or before the age of one, Sewall must have been apprehensive about Hannah's latest pregnancy. Hannah was five months pregnant at the time of the trip, and as it turned out, their daughter's birth was a month premature. Finally, there was a suggestion of smallpox in Boston. He had resolved, Sewall confessed later, "that if it pleased God to bring me to my family again, I would endeavour to serve Him better . . . labouring more constantly and thorowly to examine my self before sitting down to the Lord's Table." On his way home on May 8, Sewall prayed with the Reverend Samuel Lee in Roxbury and received an "account of the welfare of my family." The next day, in Boston, he found that Sam, Jr., was still bothered by the "sore in his neck, and Hannah droops as though would have the small pocks," but otherwise "all well."[57]

---

[56]Ibid., 40, 84, 87, 99, 175, 264, 283, 305, 407; Sewall noted that Judd, who had joined the Anglicans, "refused to be there [in the South Church]" at the time of his excommunication. Hambrick-Stowe, *Practice of Piety,* 99, offers the estimate that New Englanders spent six hours in church on Sundays.

[57]Thomas, ed., *Diary,* 2:699; 1:257, 258. Jacob Leisler took control of New York after Francis Nicholson, who had been in charge of the colony since its incorporation into the Dominion under Edmund Andros, fled to England in the summer of 1689. Leisler gov-

Shortly after his return, on May 21, Sewall learned that Roxbury minister John Eliot had died. "I visited him as I came from New York," he recalled. The following day, Sewall noted that the Reverend Nehemiah Walter, also of Roxbury, "preaches the Lecture, and so is the first who has such a publick opportunity to mention Mr. Eliot's death." The "lecture" to which Sewall referred was the regularly scheduled Thursday service in Boston. Sewall was nothing if not conscientious in his attendance at these weekday services. Indeed, he felt compelled to explain his absences: "By reason of the severity of the weather and great cold, I went not . . . to the Lecture." On days other than Thursdays, he frequented the lectures preached in surrounding communities. In a fairly typical period in January of 1688, he rode to the Cambridge lecture on Wednesday, accompanied his mother-in-law to the Roxbury lecture the following Tuesday, attended the Boston lecture on Thursday, and went to the Charlestown lecture on Friday a week later. He seemed to thrive on these days of public worship between Sabbaths. One of his most poignant complaints in later years was that his physical frailties kept him from maintaining his rigorous schedule. On Sunday, March 29, 1724, the day after his seventy-second birthday, Sewall traveled by coach to the South Church to partake of the Lord's Supper in the morning, but because of various ailments he dared "not venture out in the afternoon" and had to miss the second service. He grew despondent when persistent ailments forced him to miss the Thursday lecture. "I have now been deprived of four lectures by my fever and sore leg," he lamented.[58]

Lecture days were begun in Boston as days of instruction, the lectures being doctrinal elaborations of the sermons delivered on the Sabbath. By Sewall's time, however, weekday lectures had become indistinguishable from Sunday sermons, and lecture days had become a predictable part of the weekly cycle of worship. As he was wont to do for most of the sermons he heard on the Sabbath, Sewall identified the texts of the various Thursday lectures and sometimes repeated the preacher's application of the text: John Bailey preaching from "Eccles. 9.10. Whatsoever thy hand, &c."; Increase Mather from Jeremiah 2.21 "speaks sharply against health-drinking, card-playing,

---

erned New York for over a year. In March of 1691, he was forced to relinquish control of the colony to William III's duly appointed governor, Henry Sloughter. Leisler was then tried for treason and hanged in May, 1691. Four years later, Parliament overturned his conviction.

[58]Thomas, ed., *Diary,* 1:259, 385, 157, 158; 2:1014.

drunkenness, profane swearing, Sabbath-breaking, &c."; Samuel Lee from "Eccles. 7.13. From whence [Lee] exhorted to quietness under God's hand"; Samuel Willard from "1 John 2.1. My little children, these things write I unto you that you sin not. Doct[rine]. The proper tendency of the most evangelical doctrines of the Gospel is to keep men from sinning." On at least one occasion, Sewall thought the lecture was directed at him personally. When Cotton Mather railed against "hypocrites" who seemed to "strain at a Gnat and swallow a Camel," that is, men who were "zealous against an innocent fashion" while seemingly oblivious to "great immoralities," Sewall was mortified. He supposed that Mather's comments were meant for those, like him, who opposed the "wearing of perriwigs" as symbols of vanity or an unwillingness to accept God's ordinance. "I expected not to hear a vindication of perriwigs in Boston pulpit by Mr. Mather," Sewall fumed in his diary.[59]

As the occasion arose, Thursday lectures also involved criminals awaiting execution. It was customary in Boston for the condemned to be brought into the crowded meetinghouse and subjected to a final harangue before being led to the gallows. Ideally, the convicted person would repent and thereby reaffirm the established order of the community. In the case of Elizabeth Emerson, that seems to be precisely what happened. According to the indictment brought against her in the Court of Assistants in 1691, a court on which Sewall sat, Emerson had given birth to two "bastard children" on the night of May 7, killed

---

[59] Ibid., 1:92, 131, 383, 276; also, see Hambrick-Stowe, *Practice of Piety,* 99–100. Sewall was outspoken in his opposition to the wearing of wigs. Perhaps the most revealing episode in this regard occurred on June 10, 1701. Upon learning that Josiah Willard "had cut off his hair (a very full head of hair) and put on a wig," Sewall confronted the young man, who happened to be the son of Sewall's minister at the South Church, Samuel Willard. Was there some "extremity" that had "forced him to put off his own hair and put on a wig?" he asked rhetorically. Josiah's answer that fashion rather than necessity had dictated his choice, that he was unhappy with the appearance of his own hair because it "was straight and . . . parted behind," sent Sewall into a fury. "God seems to have ordained our hair as a test, to see whether we can bring our minds to be content to be at his finding; or whether we would be our own carvers, lords, and come no more at Him," he lectured the minister's son. After further admonitions of this sort, the young Willard "seemed to say [he] would leave off his wig when his hair was grown." But clearly Josiah was equivocating; he only "seemed" to say what he knew Sewall wanted to hear. Five and a half months later, surely sufficient time for his hair to have grown long enough to "cover his ears," Josiah still had not abandoned his wig wearing. Thus when the South Church invited Josiah to preach in his father's pulpit, Sewall refused to attend the scheduled service and opted instead to pray at the Brattle Square Church. "He that contemns the Law of Nature is not fit to be a publisher of the Law of Grace," Sewall wrote. Thomas, ed., *Diary,* 1:448–49, 458.

them both, hid their bodies in a "small bag or cloth sewed up," and then "did secretly bury" the bodies three days later in the yard of the Emerson home in Haverhill. The record of the trial proceedings is starkly formulaic: "The indictment examination & evidences were read, & the prisoner made her defense; the Jury return their verdict; the Jury say, That she [the] said Elizabeth Emerson is guilty according to indictment. The Court order, That sentence of death be pronounced against her." On lecture day, June 8, 1693, the day of Emerson's execution, Cotton Mather preached a "very good sermon to a very great auditory." Mather's sermon, which was subsequently published in his *Warnings from the Dead, or Solemn Admonitions unto All People,* included a purported confession by Emerson, the "dying expressions of her distressed soul." The statement that Mather read sounded a familiar theme about the wages of a wasted life and the hope of final redemption: "I am a miserable sinner"; "I was always of an haughty and stubborn spirit"; the "chief thing that hath brought me into my present condition is my Disobedience to my Parents"; I tried to "smother my wickedness by murdering of them"; I hope to "glorify God . . . by advising & entreating the Rising Generation here to take warning by my example"; I trust my distressed soul to the "Mercy of God in Jesus Christ." Take these "affectionate warnings" to heart, Mather told his lecture-day audience, and learn from the "dying speeches of the young woman whose execution you are to see this afternoon."[60]

In the days and weeks immediately following his admission into the South Church in 1677, Sewall prayed in private nearly every morning, received the prayers of Increase Mather when he grew "very sick," hosted a prayer meeting at his home, attended three prayer meetings at the homes of others, listened to at least one Thursday lecture, saw two women taken into membership in the South Church, partook of the Lord's Supper, and participated in the baptism of his first child on a Sabbath afternoon. He was already immersed in the round of devotional activities that would continue to occupy his attention over the course of the next half century. At times during those years, he may have thought that his family was more than usually afflicted, but he never despaired. He expected providential dispensations to be some-

---

[60] *Records of the Court of Assistants of the Colony of the Massachusetts Bay, 1630–1692,* 3 vols. (Boston, 1901–28), 1:357; Cotton Mather, *Warnings from the Dead, or Solemn Admonitions unto All People* (Boston, 1693), 35, 69–72; Thomas, ed., *Diary,* 1:310; Hall, *Worlds of Wonder,* 181–84.

Figure 6.
Cotton Mather, pastor of the North Church from 1684 to 1728. Mezzotint of Peter Pelham's portrait of 1727. Courtesy, Massachusetts Historical Society, Boston.

times painful, often mysterious, and always meaningful. Secret prayers, family devotions, fast days, days of thanksgiving, lecture days, and the Sabbath all conspired to help him cope with the presence of God in New England. When things went poorly, he prayed that he might profit from the experience; when things went well, he praised God, *"Laus Deo."*[61]

TOWN

When the nine-year-old Sewall arrived in Boston in 1661, he was unimpressed by the size of the town and the pace of provincial life. More than a half century later, the old man could fondly remember snacking on raisins and almonds in London as he and his brothers and sisters waited with their mother to board the *Prudent Mary* for their journey across the Atlantic to rejoin their father in Massachusetts. But he said nothing about his arrival save only that he was carried ashore in a canoe. If the young boy was unimpressed, however, it was probably because he was as yet unfamiliar with the colonial setting. A more knowledgeable visitor from London, John Josselyn, described Boston around the time of Sewall's arrival as the "Metropolis of this colony, or rather of the whole Countrey." With a population of about 4,000 persons in the 1660s and 14,000 by 1730, and a trading network that had dominated the region since the 1640s, Boston was by far the most urban of towns in British North America. Even in the 1720s, when New York's population approached 8,000 and Philadelphia's exceeded 6,000, and both towns had seriously eroded Boston's commercial dominance, the latter remained preeminent among provincial political and trading centers. Nevertheless, most modern readers might well conclude that Sewall's Boston was primarily an "overgrown village."[62]

The principal concerns of the inhabitants of this late-seventeenth- and early-eighteenth-century provincial city can be seen in the bylaws adopted by the 1701 Boston town meeting, when Sewall was nearly fifty years old and one of its leading residents. Altogether, Bostonians adopted forty-three separate regulations in their May 12 town meeting.

As Table 3 indicates, the largest single category of rules, accounting for about 23 percent of the total, comprised precautionary regulations addressing the threat of fire within the town's limits. These rules warned residents not to "carry fire" from one house to another except in a "safe vessell well covered," to keep in readiness a ladder, a hogshead of water, and a twelve-foot pole with a "large swabb fastened at the end," and to

---

[61] Thomas, ed., *Diary*, 1:41–43.

[62] Gary B. Nash, *The Urban Crucible: Social Change, Political Consciousness, and the Origins of the American Revolution* (Cambridge, Mass.: Harvard University Press, 1979), 3–21, quotation on p. 3. See also Carl Bridenbaugh, *Cities in the Wilderness: Urban Life in America, 1625–1742* (1938; reprint, New York: Capricorn Books, 1964), 143–300 passim; and G. B. Warden, *Boston, 1689–1776* (Boston: Little, Brown and Company, 1970), 15–33.

ensure that their chimneys were in good repair. Additional regulations required shipmasters to extinguish all shipboard fires between 10:00 P.M. and 5:00 A.M., prohibited the use of open fires within ten feet of any wooden structures, and ordered coopers, carpenters, and ropemakers to ensure that they themselves or "some carefull person stand by to watch" the fires they used in and around their shops.[63]

Like most of his neighbors, Sewall was aware of the dangers posed by fire. His diary entries make clear that the town was frequently "alarm'd" by the "Cry of Fire." An "ancient Woman rising early" discovered that the roof of a house near the harbor was on fire. Her early warning kept the fire from spreading; "praised be God," Sewall sighed. In 1688, the Sewall home was endangered and ultimately spared only because the "wind carried the flame into the Commonward." Others were not as fortunate, and the "sad Alarm" frequently interrupted everyday routines. Sermons, lectures, official meetings, and the stillness of night gave way to sudden alarms that sent residents "rushing out" of homes and meetinghouses. A 1676 fire, which Sewall promptly dubbed "Boston's greatest Fire," destroyed about fifty houses before a "considerable rain" mercifully checked "the (otherwise) masterless flames." Two years later, a midnight fire left "fourscore of thy dwellinghouses and seventy of thy warehouses in a ruinous heap," Cotton Mather observed. In 1690, fire destroyed at least a half dozen homes and nearly consumed the South Church, which "was preserv'd with very much difficulty, being in a flame in diverse places."[64]

Table 3.   Town Orders and Bylaws, 1701

CATEGORY	NUMBER OF REGULATIONS	% (TO NEAREST WHOLE)
Fire safety	10	23
Town officers	9	21
Public property	8	19
Public safety	5	12
Animal control	4	9
Sanitation	3	7
Sabbath restrictions	2	5
Food sales and purchases	2	5
Totals	43	101

[63] *Report of the Record Commissioners of the City of Boston* (hereafter BRC) (Boston, 1883), 8:9–17.

[64] Thomas, ed., *Diary*, 1:37, 52, 131, 132, 138, 162, 163, 226, 262, 266; Mather quoted in Bridenbaugh, *Cities in the Wilderness*, 59.

The provincial legislature in 1691, mindful of the fire hazards posed by extensive timber construction, passed an "Act for Building with Stone or Brick in the Town of Boston." Although intended to curtail the construction of new houses out of timber, the act was applied sparingly for about a decade. Under the law, Bostonians were allowed to petition the board of selectmen for exemptions to the ban against timber construction, and the selectmen readily granted such exemptions until after the turn of the century. In 1701 and 1702, for example, thirty-seven residents petitioned for exemptions. All were successful. In the ensuing years, however, the ban was more rigidly enforced. From 1703 to 1708, only six petitions were submitted to the selectmen for action, and none was successful. Among the unsuccessful petitioners was the French Protestant congregation in Boston, which sought to build a meetinghouse for services, and Samuel Green, who petitioned to build a house only "partly with timber."[65]

Regulations dealing with the duties and responsibilities of the town's officers constituted the second largest category of bylaws adopted in 1701. Of these, those that reaffirmed the role of the selectmen as the town's executive council were the most important. Selectmen were empowered specifically to appoint minor officers, lease town lands and buildings, compensate officers for services rendered, and authorize temporary encroachments on public property. In addition to these enumerated duties, most matters affecting the welfare of the town fell within the purview of the board of selectmen. When the widow Rebecca Philpot desired in 1701 to sell ale at her "victualing house," she petitioned the selectmen for a license to do so; when newcomers John Strong, his wife, and four children could not find a sponsor in Boston, they were warned by the selectmen to remove themselves from town; when Mary Davise experienced some financial difficulty because she needed to care for "her three Dumb Children," the selectmen abated her taxes by eleven shillings; when Hannah Jones enclosed a piece of the "Lower end of the Common," the selectmen issued a complaint against her; and when Daniel Turell failed to pay Goody Mulbery the £8 "due her for the maintenance of the Child born of the body of [her daughter] Abigail Mulbery," the selectmen ordered him to make the payment within a week.[66]

The relative importance of the selectmen is reflected in the town's choices of men to serve in that capacity. Each March, Bostonians elected a variety of town officers. Not only the town's selectmen, trea-

[65]BRC (Boston, 1884), 11:3–84 passim.
[66]All episodes are from 1701, ibid., 5, 8, 9, 12.

surer, constables, and recorder, but water bailiffs, scavengers, town cry-
ers, packers of flesh and fish, inspectors of brick, sealers of leather, surveyors, corders of wood, measurers of corn, and a number of other
minor officers served one-year terms. The historian G. B. Warden has
estimated that in the mid-1680s over 10 percent of Boston's adult males
were officeholders each year. Indeed, Warden argues, given the available pool of potential officers, "almost every adult male had a fair
chance to serve the town at least once in his life."[67] For our purposes,
however, it is important to note that, although officeholding was wide-
spread, residents tended to elect different sorts of men to different
sorts of offices. In the years 1685–89, for example, the town elected
nine men as selectmen each year. Yet a total of only fourteen men
served as selectmen, an average of three terms each. Furthermore, the
1687 tax roll (the only one extant for this period) reveals that those
who served as selectmen came from the richest quarter of the community. (See Table 4.)

In 1719, Sam, Jr., complained to his father that he had been snubbed
by the voters of Brookline. The March town meeting had elected Sam,
Jr., as a "Constable, though he has often served as Select-man." Sewall,
familiar with the hierarchical arrangement of town offices, understood
the reason for his son's complaint. Sam, Jr., it seems, had been reduced
to a lower office and relegated to the company of lesser neighbors. An
examination of the roster of Boston constables around the time of the
1687 tax roll illustrates this point. For each year from 1685 to 1689,
eight men served as constables, and none for more than one year. Of
the forty who served, thirty-three may be positively identified in the
tax roll. The taxable wealth of these thirty-three individuals covered a
wide spectrum: James Barnes, whose assessment of £50 ranks him in
the top 10 percent of all property owners, served with Thomas Barnard,
whose £3 assessment places him in the bottom 20 percent. However,
men like Barnes and Barnard were the exceptions. The average assessed wealth of the constables was £15.5, which, when compared with
the average assessment of nearly £38 for the selectmen, is indicative of
the respective positions of these men in Boston society. No one elected
to the board of selectmen one year was subsequently chosen to the office of constable. Indeed, because the constables' responsibilities were
numerous and burdensome—including the collection of provincial and
town taxes, supervision of the town watchmen, summoning of jurors,
serving of warrants, enforcement of fines, and suppression of disor-

[67]Warden, *Boston*, 32.

derly activities—men influential enough to gain election as selectmen, it seems, were also influential enough to avoid being saddled with the office of constable. Among those elected, many refused to serve. A few were excused after election by the town: Peter Wear pleaded that serving as constable would be "extreamly prejudiciall to him" under the "present circumstances of his family"; John Burneby escaped by going "on a voyage to sea"; Timothy Lindall alleged that "he is about to remove out of Town." Most, however, offered no excuses for their refusal, and beginning in 1673 the town regularly assessed a £10 fine on these unwilling freemen. Samuel Shrimpton paid the fine in 1673, which the town accepted "as full & ample satisfaction as if he had served the whole yeare." In 1674, all six constables had to be replaced because the men chosen during the March election meeting refused the office. Again, the town accepted "the payment of £10 [from] each man . . . as

Table 4. Boston Selectmen, 1685–89[a]

NAME	NUMBER OF TERMS (A)	ASSESSED WEALTH IN £ (B)	TOTAL TAXABLE WEALTH IN £ (C)	% AMONG ALL PROPERTY OWNERS (D)
Isaac Addington	1	30	600	Top 15
Henry Allen	3	20	400	Top 25
Elisha Cooke, Sr.	3	35	700	Top 12
John Fairweather	4	29	580	Top 15
Theophilus Frary	4	30	600	Top 15
James Hill	2	30	600	Top 15
Elisha Hutchinson	3	81	1620	Top 3
John Joyliffe	4	45	900	Top 8
Richard Medlecot	1	90	1800	Top 3
Timothy Prout	5	20	400	Top 25
Penn Townsend	2	60	1200	Top 5
Daniel Turell	5	24	480	Top 20
Edward Willis	5	40	800	Top 10
Adam Winthrop	2	55	1100	Top 5

[a]The town elected nine selectmen each year, except in 1688, when it elected only eight. Column (a) is from *Report of the Record Commissioners of the City of Boston* (hereafter BRC) (Boston, 1881), 7:173, 183, 191, 195, 196; column (b) is from the 1687 tax roll in BRC (Boston, 1881), 1:91–127; column (c) is computed on the basis of G. B. Warden's estimate in "Inequality and Instability in Eighteenth-Century Boston: A Reappraisal," *Journal of Interdisciplinary History* 6 (1976): 588, that real and personal property in 1687 was assessed at about 5 percent of true market value; column (d) is based on James Henretta's "Economic Development and Social Structure in Colonial Boston," *William and Mary Quarterly*, 3rd series, 22 (1965): 75–92.

full & ample satisfaction, as if they had served the whole yeare." By the end of the 1670s, the practice of paying a fine to gain release from service had become so ordinary that the town simply accepted the fines without appending the sort of exculpatory comment it had earlier offered.[68]

Thus, although "almost every adult male had a fair chance to serve the town," many did not welcome the opportunity, and not all offices were equally open to "every adult male." The hierarchical structure of Boston was reflected in its order of offices. Constables tended to come from the ranks of men below those of the selectmen; still lesser office-holders came from ranks generally below those of the constables. Beginning in 1672, for example, Bostonians annually elected certain "Officers about swine," along with their selectmen, constables, clerks, and surveyors. These officers, later called hog reeves, were empowered to enforce town ordinances concerning the capture and disposition of stray hogs in Boston's "streets, lanes, highways, [and] Commons." For comparative purposes, we may examine the list of men who served as hog reeves from 1685 to 1687. Of sixteen hog reeves elected during these years, twelve appear on the 1687 tax roll. The average property holding of these dozen men was £7.7, or about one-half the average assessment for constables and only slightly more than a fifth of the average assessment for selectmen.[69] Bostonians did not choose men to sit on the executive council one year and to chase stray hogs the next.

The "hazzard" posed by stray swine was only a part of the problem of animal control in Sewall's Boston. Town bylaws singled out for special attention not only hogs, but horses, cattle, sheep, and "tame fowl." Indeed, the everyday presence of such livestock, stray or otherwise, necessitated further complementary ordinances. Dog owners, in particular, were admonished to keep their animals in check. The town wished to be rid of any "curst or unruly dogg or bitch" that was "known to bite, seize upon, worry or do harm to man or beast." Four years earlier, in an effort to ensure responsible behavior, the town meeting had limited dog ownership to residents with at least "20 pounds ratable estate." Other local ordinances authorized inhabitants to "kill and destroy" all stray dogs they encountered. In 1676, only months after he had married Hannah Hull, Sewall recorded a near-tragic attempt to destroy an "ugly dogg." Upon seeing a strange dog in his father-in-law's kitchen

[68] For elections of constables, see BRC, 7:173, 183, 191, 195, 196; for refusals and payments of fines, ibid., 73, 85, 107, 116; for the 1680s, see 137–99 passim.

[69] Ibid., 65, 66, 173, 183, 191.

one evening, Sewall spoke to Hull's apprentice John Alcock. The apprentice set out in pursuit of the "shagged dogg." In the dark, however, Alcock mistook Seth Shove, the nine-year-old son of the Reverend George Shove, for the troublesome stray and "smote him so hard upon the bare head with a pipe staff" that only God's mercy saved young Seth from spilling "his Brains on the Ground." More than a half century later, stray dogs were still "worrying, chaseing & wounding" horses, cattle, sheep, and fowl. The problem of animals roaming at large in the streets of Boston seemed endless.[70]

Public safety issues went beyond those involving stray dogs and livestock. With a population of about 7,000 by 1700, Boston's busy streets could be unpleasant and even hazardous without proper regulations. Town laws warned residents not to shoot at birds or other targets in the "streets, lanes, or alleys," not to throw "dirt, dung, garbidge, carrion . . . or anything that may be an annoyance" out of their homes or shops, and not to construct any attachments to their houses that might impede the flow of traffic. In related matters, town orders strictly prohibited riders from proceeding at a "gallop or other extream pace within any of the streets, lanes, or alleys of this town." Carts were also prohibited from entering Boston without a "sufficient driver" capable of keeping his horse or horses "under command." Sewall almost certainly appreciated the wisdom of such prohibitions. In 1688, his eight-year-old daughter Hannah was "rid over by David Lopez" as she walked to school in the morning. Fortunately, although Hannah was "much frighted" and "her teeth bled" after the collision, she was "I hope little hurt," Sewall wrote.[71]

By the 1720s, street traffic was great enough to require further action by the town. Increased commercial activity and a population in excess of 10,000 were reflected in the presence of large carts and trucks of "extraordinary weight" and "unsutable length" in the narrow streets of Boston. Such vehicles posed a danger to passengers and passersby and caused "great damage . . . to the pavement." Consequently, the town ordered that henceforth all carts "whose sides exceed the length of sixteen feet" would be fined at the rate of twenty shillings per offense. Additionally, carters whose loads exceeded a ton or who used more than "two horses at a time" would have to pay a fine of five shillings for each infraction. Finally, the town ordered all wheels for carts and trucks to be a "full four inches in breadth and the nayles of

[70]BRC, 7:227; 8:15, 16, 92, 225; Thomas, ed., *Diary,* 1:29.
[71]BRC, 8:11, 12–13; Thomas, ed., *Diary,* 1:180.

the tire to be flat." In these ways Bostonians hoped to keep in check the "great charge" they had borne in constantly repairing their streets and alleys.[72]

One attempt to defray the mounting costs of street maintenance was a 1707 law requiring all resident free blacks and mulattoes to work on public projects in lieu of service as watchmen or militiamen on training days. Boston's selectmen began annually to assign the town's available free blacks to road repair duty. Between 1708 and 1718, an average of twenty-eight freemen per year worked on "repairing and cleansing" the streets of the town. Most were required to devote a total of six to eight days during the year; however, some spent only a day or two on road projects while others worked as many as twelve days. Because the minutes of the selectmen list by name the free blacks thus assigned, we are afforded a glimpse of yet another facet of life in Sewall's Boston. We know from the work of earlier historians that New Englanders tended to remain rooted in one place. Geographical mobility, especially in the relatively isolated rural communities of Massachusetts, was the exception rather than the rule for as long as arable land was available locally. Bostonians moved about much more frequently than their contemporaries in Andover or Dedham, but to present-day Americans they appear still to be remarkably immobile. Boston's free black population seemed rooted in place. Peter Quaco, Mingo Quinsie, Grandy Eliot, Sebasten Levensworth, Tom Rumny Marsh, and Joseph Jalla had resided continuously in Boston for at least a decade by 1718. Of the twenty-four freemen identified by the selectmen for street maintenance duty in 1718, fourteen had appeared on every list since 1708. An examination of the earlier 1712 list reveals that twenty-one of the twenty-nine men had been on all of the work crews for the preceding five years.[73]

Rootedness was related to and perhaps promoted by the practice of "warning out" undesirables. Sewall's Boston was an exclusive community. Since 1636, the town had forbidden any inhabitant from housing a stranger for more than two weeks without permission from the selectmen. In part, the town engaged in exclusionary practices in an attempt

[72]BRC, 8:211–12.

[73]BRC, Records of Selectmen, 11:73–74, 115–16, 137–38, 166–67, 210, 232–33; 13:8, 42. Kenneth A. Lockridge, *A New England Town, The First Hundred Years: Dedham, Massachusetts, 1636–1736* (New York: W. W. Norton, 1970); Philip J. Greven, Jr., *Four Generations: Population, Land, and Family in Colonial Andover, Massachusetts* (Ithaca, N.Y.: Cornell University Press, 1970); for a summary of work done in New England history over the past two decades, see Jack P. Greene, *Pursuits of Happiness: The Social Development of Early Modern British Colonies and the Formation of American Culture* (Chapel Hill: University of North Carolina Press, 1988), 55–80.

to ensure that "persons of ill behaviour belonging to other places" did not congregate in Boston. Of equal importance, however, was a practical concern: residents worried about the increasingly "great charges" they were forced to bear in supporting the "growing number of Poor among us." By 1677, when Sewall began regularly to attend town meetings in Boston, at least a portion of the day's agenda involved warnings to inhabitants and newcomers. On separate occasions in the early 1670s, the selectmen threatened Christopher Skinner with a fine of twenty shillings if he did not speedily arrange for the pregnant Elizabeth Walker to be "sent back to Coneticott"; ordered Stephen Sargeant to take Abraham Radford, whom he had brought to town, back to the "place from whence he brought him"; warned Joanna Porter to "remove out of this towne within one month" and notified John Lewis "who brought her in [to] take care that the order be observed"; and petitioned the county court for assistance in disposing of "Sebastian Bernardo, his wife, and two children," all of whom had arrived from Barbados with no securities given "to save the town from charge by them."[74]

As this last action indicates, Boston selectmen warned newcomers to depart "unless they find security to save the town harmless." Residents accepted the responsibility of caring for their own, but they refused to accommodate the "sick, aged & incapacitated" of other communities. Nicholas Warner, "above 80 years of age and infirm of body," was unwelcomed in Boston, as was Silvanus Warrow, a "molato man being lame," and Job Brown, "being troubled with fitts." Mary Phips, who claimed "her husband is lately gone to sea"; Elizabeth Pickworth, who came to Boston to "put her child to nurse"; Sarah Watts and her two young children, whose "circumstances" portended they would become town charges; and Christian Fortune, who was fleeing from her husband in Marblehead, received similar warnings to leave town. If Bostonians remained rooted in place, they wished others, especially the unfortunate and needy, to remain in their places.[75]

Beginning in 1701, the selectmen's minutes listed by name newcomers who had been admitted as inhabitants. These lists reveal at least two things about the population of early Boston. First, from 1702 to 1715, a total of sixty-six persons were officially recognized by the selectmen as having gained admission. Of these, not surprisingly, the vast majority

---

[74]BRC, Boston Records, 7:7, 54, 55, 58, 62–63; Bridenbaugh, *Cities in the Wilderness*, 79; Nash, *Urban Crucible*, 402 (appendix, table 10) offers estimates on average annual expenditure for poor relief in Boston from 1700 to 1775.

[75]BRC, 7:157; 11:25, 57, 59, 63, 66, 67, 70.

(82 percent) were men. It is important to note, however, that the selectmen's lists identified eleven of the twelve women individually; only once did they resort to using the generic appellation *and wife*. Furthermore, included among the women was Mary Harrison, whose admission was secured by Elizabeth Holmes, and "Bettey," a "Negro made free." Second, that the selectmen's lists are incomplete is perhaps indicative of their inability to exert closer control over the town's population. Clearly prescribed procedures notwithstanding, the town was too large for "warnings out" to be totally effective. The selectmen themselves admitted as much. Alexander Callman, a Quaker shoemaker who "came into the 3d Meetinge house in a bloody coate," and Peter Choke, a wine cooper "reported to be of vitious conversation," were relative easy targets, as was William Batt, "an idle person that refuseth to work." But others, equally undesirable, were either more elusive or more self-assertive. Nicholas Wardner, a tobacconist, demanded to be granted permission to "stay in the town . . . or [he will] complaine to England." Thomas Davis, a blacksmith "knowne to be a thief," avoided the constables by moving "from place to place" in town. The tactic employed by Davis was not unknown to the selectmen; as early as 1662, townspeople complained about the presence of "persons of ill behaviour belonging to other places" who had taken up residence in Boston and escaped apprehension by "shifting from house to house." At that time, the town meeting warned residents about receiving such miscreants into their homes and authorized the constables to collect a twenty-shilling-per-night fine from those who ignored the warning, but the problem proved to be persistent. Nearly forty years later, in 1701, Bostonians were still complaining that "poor and wild persons" from other towns were successfully evading the law by "shifting from place to place."[76]

As a justice of the peace and a member of the Council under the 1691 Charter, Sewall was acquainted with the problems posed by the transient poor. Whenever the constables' warnings failed to have their desired effect, the town turned to "Her Majesties Justices" for warrants to remove the undesirables in question. After Sarah Watts and her two children ignored warnings to depart "sundry times" and continued to "obtrude" themselves on the town, the selectmen applied for a warrant for their removal. Similarly, the selectmen requested a warrant against the wife of Edward Prat when she "againe returned" after once being removed. When Palmer Mullings, a "molatto man" from Dorchester,

[76]BRC, 7:7, 123, 241; 11:1–2; 139–40.

and his wife took up residence in Boston "without any orderly admission," the selectmen sought a warrant for "sending them out of this Town to Dorchester where they do belong." They asked for similar warrants to send Christian Fortune of Marblehead, Hannah Turner of Hingham, and John Orms of Newberry back to the communities from whence they came and to which they "doth properly belong." In the case of Sarah Boyce, "being in a helpless condition, big with child," the selectmen not only petitioned for her removal but asked that Charles Turner, who transported Boyce to Boston, be cited to appear before "some of Her Majesties Justices to answer for his so obtruding her upon this Town."[77]

In addition to hearing complaints against newcomers who resided in town "without allowance or consent," Sewall and the other justices met frequently with the town's selectmen in a joint effort "to prevent & redress disorders." By 1710, the selectmen, justices of the peace, and overseers of the poor routinely divided themselves into discrete groups and agreed upon specific dates for visiting "familyes in the several parts of this Town" and for otherwise suppressing the "growth of disorders." Ordinarily, the act of keeping the peace entailed little more than offering well-timed words of caution to men who were misspending their time or failing to provide for their families. On one occasion, however, the task proved far more difficult. On the night of February 6, 1714, Sewall learned of "disorders" at John Wallis's tavern, where a large company of men had consumed too much liquor and grown rowdy in violation of the law against drinking and keeping idle company on the evening before the Sabbath. Accompanied by fellow magistrate Edward Bromfield and constable Henry Howell, Sewall arrived at Wallis's tavern at approximately nine-thirty and found "much company" drinking to the "Queen's Health" and to "many other Healths" as well. Ordered to disperse, the merrymakers instead "drank to me," Sewall recorded. They were unmoved even when the justices "threaten'd to send some of them to prison." Exasperated and "in some heat," Bromfield suggested "raising a number of men to quell" the revelers, but Sewall proceeded simply "to take their names" and to tell Thomas Banister, the senior member of the group, that "he should set a good example in departing thence." Banister responded by announcing his intention to leave Wallis's and by inviting the company to join him at "his own house."[78]

On the Monday following the confrontation, Sewall and Bromfield

[77]BRC, 11:59, 67, 68, 70, 78, 84, 130, 134.
[78]BRC, 11:17, 134; Thomas, ed., *Diary,* 2:741–42.

presented Constable Howell with the names of the offenders and directed him to collect the appropriate fines from those willing to pay and to warn the others that they had to appear before the justices later that same day. Accordingly, at three o'clock that afternoon, John Netmaker, Francis Brinley, Andrew Simpson, and Alexander Gordon appeared before Sewall and Bromfield, heard that fines amounting to five shillings each would be levied against them, and promptly appealed their sentences. Netmaker, the rowdiest of the revelers, faced additional charges for contempt of government and "profane cursing." During the drunken encounter at Wallis's, he had apparently made disparaging remarks about the provincial government, saying that it had "not made one good law," and had cursed Constable Howell's assistant with a "God damn ye" when the latter would not drink healths with him. Although Netmaker willingly paid the five shillings fine for cursing, he would not post a £20 bond to appear before the next General Session of the Peace to defend himself against the contempt charge. Sewall and Bromfield nevertheless released Netmaker late that afternoon on his word that he would return at ten o'clock the next morning.[79]

At 11:00 A.M. on Tuesday, Sewall and Bromfield were still waiting for Netmaker. By the time Netmaker finally arrived, neither he nor the justices were in any mood to compromise. After all efforts "to bring him to some acknowledgment of his error" failed and Netmaker refused to post any sort of bond for himself, Sewall and Bromfield ordered that he be imprisoned. Netmaker would not go quietly. "Angry Words" passed between Netmaker and Howell, and Netmaker "threatened Constable Howell what he would do to him."

Netmaker's attitude and the actions of his supporters in the wake of his incarceration tell us much about the wider political implications of the duty to maintain order in Boston under the royal charter. In the end, not only was Netmaker released without penalty, but Sewall and Bromfield were the "parties complained of" in the Council. Netmaker, as it turns out, was General Francis Nicholson's secretary, and Nicholson, the former lieutenant governor of the Dominion of New England, was still a figure to be reckoned with in Massachusetts. At his urging, the Council met at the Boston Town House "late and duskish" on Tuesday. Crowded "round a little fire," Sewall "happened" to be seated next to Nicholson. The General "apply'd himself to me and Mr. Bromfield," asking "whether [we] did not know that Mr. Netmaker was his Secretary?" When Sewall answered that they knew, the general rose and

[79]Thomas, ed., *Diary*, 2:742–43.

shouted, "I demand JUSTICE against Mr. Sewall and Bromfield" and stormed out of the Council chamber. Pacing back and forth on the ground floor of the Town House, Nicholson continued "so furiously loud" that he could be "plainly heard" by Sewall and the others even with the Council door "being shut." With Nicholson's "roaring noise" in the background, Governor Dudley "vehemently urged the discharge of Netmaker" and admonished Sewall and Bromfield for failing to notify the general personally before having his secretary committed to prison. The majority of the Council, following Dudley's lead, then voted to release Netmaker, but not before Chief Justice Wait Still Winthrop objected to the Council's proceedings by saying "he understood not how it belonged to the Council to meddle" with Sewall and Bromfield's actions against the drunken antics of the general's secretary.[80]

Although Sewall was stung "pretty hard" by the Council's action, he had no time to dwell on the Netmaker episode. As a justice of the Superior Court of Judicature from 1692 to 1728, Sewall encountered problems far more disruptive of good order than the mischief caused by Sabbath violators. Because the Superior Court of Judicature was the highest court of the province, it was responsible for dealing with all cases in which defendants stood accused of serious crimes against persons or property. In 1714 alone, at the time of Sewall's involvement in the fracas at Wallis's tavern, the Superior Court ruled on at least a dozen cases of serious criminal wrongdoing, including two for murder, five for forgery or counterfeiting, three for adultery or bigamy, and one for buggery. During the preceding ten years, from 1704 to 1713, the Superior Court dealt with 110 cases of similar importance. Of these, 11 were for murder, 9 for assault, 4 for arson, 18 for burglary or robbery, 21 for counterfeiting, and 6 for adultery or fornication.[81]

Many of the stories heard by the Superior Court justices were truly tragic, and none more so than those involving charges of infanticide. John Chadwick, a tailor, beat his fourteen-month son Purchase until "blood came and run down his Childs face," and then "neglected to provide necessarys of meat & drink" for three or four weeks, "by which and other evill intreating," the infant "languished . . . & then dyed." Sarah Pilsbury appeared before the Court accused of having strangled her nine-month "bastard child" by tying a "handkerchief or some such

---

[80] Ibid., 744–45.

[81] Ibid., 745; Records of the Superior Court of Judicature, 1700–14, Massachusetts State Archives, Boston, Massachusetts (hereafter SCJ). For the most part, cases of serious criminal wrongdoing are listed under the heading of "Dominus Rex" or "Domina Regina."

like thing . . . about the neck of said child." Hannah Degoe, an unmarried mulatto woman from Bristol, was sentenced to be hanged for killing her "bastard child" with "malice forethought." Bettee, a black servant of Isaac Winslow of Marshfield, faced a similar sentence for having "willfully & feloniously concealed the death of a Bastard Child born of her Body & privately buried so that it could not come to light whether the said Child was born alive or not."[82]

Although cases of infanticide involved a disproportionate number of women, the bulk of the felony cases decided by the Superior Court dealt with criminal acts committed by men. Between 1700 and 1714, approximately 87 percent of all defendants were men. Furthermore, although the cases of Hannah Degoe and Bettee might seem to suggest otherwise, the vast majority, about 83 percent, of those indicted for serious crimes were white. Nevertheless, cases of arson and assault involving women, blacks, and Native Americans reveal a great deal about the undercurrents of life in Sewall's Boston. William Hack and Samuel Hall stood accused of assaulting Matthias Awhawton, "an Indian," by hanging him "by the heels & evilly intreating him." Samuel Hedges, an Eastham innkeeper, and his servant Mingo Negro were indicted for throwing Amos Sipson Indian "upon some stones which wounded his head & skull that in a few hours after he dyed of said wounds." Ebenezer Allen, a Bristol yeoman, and his sons Ebenezer, Jr., and Zebulon appeared before the Superior Court on charges of assaulting Ebenezer's "servant or slave" Andrew Negro. The Allens allegedly whipped Andrew "malitiously & unmercifully . . . on all parts of his body" and then "bound the said Negro with cords to a board & drew that board several feet from the ground with the said Negro bound to it." Left in that state for "several hours," Andrew Negro "languished & dyed of his wounds." In each of these cases, the defendants were found not guilty and released.[83]

Episodes involving actions taken by Native Americans or blacks

---

[82] SCJ, 1700–14, 69–70, 181–82, 253, 270. The best discussion of the crime of infanticide is Peter C. Hoffer and N. E. H. Hull's *Murdering Mothers: Infanticide in England and New England, 1558–1803* (New York: New York University Press, 1981).

[83] SCJ, 1700–14, passim. My tabulation reveals that between 1700 and 1714 a total of eight infanticide cases were tried before the Superior Court. Of these, only one, that of John Chadwick, involved a male as principal defendant. During this same period, a total of 163 defendants appeared before the Superior Court in "Dominus Rex" or "Domina Regina" cases. Of these, 142 involved men and 21 involved women. Furthermore, 135 defendants were white, 15 were black, 1 was a mulatto, and 12 were Native Americans. For individual cases cited in this paragraph, see SCJ, September 25, 1705, September 11, 1711, and March 13, 1714; pp. 165, 265, 296.

against whites are equally revealing. Joshua Chin, "Indian," after being convicted of beating Bristol husbandman Samuel Penfield "to the hazard of his life," was sentenced to be whipped ten stripes "severly layd on." Mingo, also known as "Cocho Negro," a Charlestown servant accused of raping Abigail Howse, was sentenced to be hanged. Coffee, William Shaw's slave, was convicted of stabbing Mrs. Shaw "to the very great danger of her life." The Court ordered Coffee to be whipped thirty-nine stripes and to stand at the gallows with a rope around his neck for one hour, after which he was to be "sold & transported into some [other] of Her Majestys Plantations." Sabina, "servant or slave" to Richard Saltonstal of Haverhill, was similarly sentenced to be whipped thirty-nine stripes and to be "sold & sent beyond [the] sea" after she was convicted of blowing up her master's house "to the danger of the life of him & his family." Given the dangers posed by fire in early Boston, it is perhaps not surprising to find the Court acting swiftly and severely against arsonists. Adino Bullfinch's slave, Rochester, convicted of setting ablaze the widow Elizabeth Savage's home and thereby "designing to consume the dwelling . . . and others adjoining," was asked by the Court to show cause why he should not be executed. After Rochester "made no Answer," Sewall read the Court's decision: he would "be hanged by his neck until he be dead."[84]

Crimes of this sort were probably rooted in deeply felt racial animosities. We are afforded additional glimpses of the problem in selected encounters. In 1712, William Hilton was forced to defend himself before the Superior Court against the charge that he had committed perjury when he swore before Governor Dudley and the Council that "three Indian scalps which he then & there produced were of the Indian enemy killed in fight, when they were not." What are we to make of the indictment? Was Hilton's solemn oath "false & wicked" because the scalps he displayed were not "enemy" scalps, not "Indian" scalps, or not scalps at all? Similarly, after "sundry of the inhabitants" complained in 1728 that "disorders and quarelling" were causing them great discomfort, the town meeting ordered that henceforth "no Indian, Negro, or Molatto" will be allowed to "carry any stick or cain . . . as may be fit for quarreling or fighting with." The fine for a first offense was five shillings; for a second, ten shillings. However, if any of the sticks or

---

[84] Ibid., September 25, 1705, November [9], 1705, May 18, 1709, January 12, 1712; pp. 165, 170, 238, 269. For an extended discussion of the subject of the Massachusetts judicial system and Native Americans, see Yasuhide Kawashima, *Puritan Justice and the Indian: White Man's Law in Massachusetts, 1630–1763* (Middletown, Conn.: Wesleyan University Press, 1986).

canes were tipped with an iron "spear or nayle," the fines would be doubled. The distressed inhabitants behind this ordinance were almost certainly white. But are we to assume that the quarrels they found so disquieting were principally between Native Americans and blacks or, alternatively, that white residents alone were to be trusted with instruments "fit for fighting with"? And were the targeted groups actually arming themselves with nail-tipped canes? If so, why? We know that Sewall was troubled by certain aspects of the treatment accorded to Native Americans and blacks. In 1716, he tried unsuccessfully to end the practice of "Indians and Negroes being rated [for taxes] with Horses and Hogs."[85]

In the summer of 1728, after more than thirty-five years of service on the Superior Court, the last ten as its chief justice, Sewall decided to retire from public life. Seventy-six years old by then, he knew that he was no longer able to do the work. His "sickness i.e. Lameness" kept him from traveling, even to religious meetings presided over by his son Joseph. On the one occasion when he ventured far from home to attend the funeral of his "dear friend" and Harvard classmate Peter Thacher of Milton, he fell and "raised off the skin" from his right leg, which caused him a "great deal of pain, especially when 'twas washed with Rum." An "extraordinary sickness of flux and vomiting" on the night of July 27, Sewall said, "quickened me to resign my places." Increasingly, he seemed to be contemplating his own death. After Thacher was buried, Sewall remarked that he had "now been at the Interment of 4 of my class-mates." The "skin and blood" he lost as a result of the fall awakened in him the need to "prepare for [his] own dissolution." On October 19, Sewall recalled "this to be the same day of the week and month that the wife of my youth expired eleven years agoe." Much "affected" by the sad anniversary, he wrote to Joseph and desired his son to "join [his] condolence."[86]

In what was perhaps his last letter, Sewall wrote to his kinsman William Dummer to congratulate him on his reappointment as lieutenant governor of Massachusetts. Above all, Sewall said, he was thankful that God had reserved men such as Dummer to assume the "weighty affairs of government" in anticipation of the "dark and difficult" times ahead. In writing thus to someone twenty-five years his junior, Sewall was informally marking the passage of provincial leadership from one generation to the next. He died three months later. The

---

[85]SCJ, December 20, 1712; BRC, 8:224; Thomas, ed., *Diary,* 2:822.
[86]Thomas, ed., *Diary,* 2:1051, 1052, 1056, 1057, 1061, 1063.

Boston of Sewall's final years was different from the one he encountered as a youngster: larger, politically fragmented, less homogeneous, and more susceptible to imperial interference. But there was a rhythm to life that must have seemed familiar to the old man. The town continued to meet in March to elect its moderator, selectmen, clerks, constables, viewers of fences, hog reeves, scavengers, and other officers. For selectmen, Bostonians still turned to a relatively small set of men. From 1724 to 1728, only fourteen men served as selectmen, for an average of 2.5 terms per person. John Fairweather, Theophilus Frary, John Joyliffe, and Elisha Cooke, Sr., the familiar names of the late 1680s, were gone, but in their places were men equally recognizable in the 1720s: Thomas Cushing, Nathaniel Green, Ezekiel Lewis, John Waldo, and Henry Dering. The election of constables, as before, proved to be a protracted affair. Of the fifteen men chosen on March 11, 1728, seven refused to serve and paid the necessary fines, five were excused, and only three agreed to be sworn into office. The town chose eleven replacements later that afternoon, but four refused to serve, two were excused, and one appealed his election. Seven more replacements chosen by the town to fill the remaining vacancies yielded only four who were willing to serve. The town then chose five additional replacements, but two refused to serve and one had to be excused. The election of two more replacements still later that same day resulted in one refusal. Finally, with the sixth election of the day, the town had its fifteen constables in place.[87]

In the last two years of his life, Sewall's lameness kept him from regular attendance at town meetings. The substantive issues confronted by Sewall's younger townsmen in his absence, however, were predictably familiar. David Colson, Benjamin Landon, Joshua Thornton, and Ebenezer Bridge petitioned for exemptions to the ban against the construction of timber buildings; Samuel Turell, Thomas Edwards, John Walker, and Joseph Belcher sought permission to encroach temporarily on public easements; Ann Norman, Elizabeth Ray, James Wright, and Samuel Boyce headed a list of ten women and eleven men who successfully petitioned to "sell strong drink as retailers"; Ambrose Tower, cordwainer, Richard Brown, cutler, Robert Gardner, wig maker, and James Pulman, tailor, gained official admission as inhabitants; the selectmen, justices of the peace, and overseers of the poor agreed to continue their practice of visiting the several wards of the town in order

[87]Sewall to William Dummer, September 11, 1729, *Sewall Letter-Book,* 2:275; BRC, 8:180, 185, 193, 201, 214–19.

"to prevent and supress disorders"; and finally, residents sought to control the dog population of Boston by limiting ownership to "house keepers that are qualified to vote in town meetings, and they no more than one at one time." In his final letter to Dummer, the aged Sewall ended on a hopeful note. "I take Leave," he wrote, praying that "your last days . . . be your best days." There was a timelessness to town life that allowed Sewall to take his leave anticipating difficult times but knowing that Boston would survive "this juncture of our distress."[88]

A NOTE ON THE SELECTIONS

My approach to the Sewall diary is markedly different from that adopted by earlier editors. There have been two previous abridgments of Sewall's diary, the first by Mark Van Doren in 1963 and the second by Harvey Wish in 1967.[89]

Both Van Doren and Wish selected passages from throughout the whole diary for inclusion in their abridged editions. The advantage of such an approach is that it offers the editor the opportunity to highlight certain episodes in Sewall's life. Thus Van Doren and Wish reproduce all of the passages relating to Sewall's courtships after the death of his wife Hannah. The disadvantage, as Table 5 illustrates, is that it insufficiently conveys a sense of Sewall's experiences for any given year and, consequently, does not allow readers adequately to trace the impact of time on the diarist and his world.

There is, of course, no way to compress the whole of Sewall's diary by deleting about 80 percent of its contents without making some sacrifices. Ultimately, my hope is to pique the interest and curiosity of the reader enough to have him or her turn to the larger editions of the diary. There are two superb full editions of Sewall's diary: the first appears as part of the Massachusetts Historical Society *Collections,* 5th series, vols. 5–7 (1878–82), and reprinted in three volumes (New York: Arno Press, 1972); the second is M. Halsey Thomas, ed., *The Diary of Samuel Sewall, 1674–1729,* 2 vols. (New York, 1973). I have used the Massachusetts Historical Society edition as the principal text for this edition. I have checked the accuracy of all passages against the Thomas version and consulted the original for all disputed or ambiguous entries. My working assumption in preparing the text for publication is

---

[88]BRC, 13:172–91; 8:223; Sewall to Dummer, September 11, 1729, *Sewall Letter-Book,* 2:275.

[89]Van Doren, *Sewall's Diary;* Wish, *Diary of Samuel Sewall.*

Table 5.   Editions of Sewall's Diary: Number of Entries for Given Years

YEAR	ORIGINAL DIARY	VAN DOREN (% OF ORIGINAL)	WISH (% OF ORIGINAL)
1685	162	36 (22)	36 (22)
1686	182	52 (29)	33 (18)
1696	75	26 (35)	15 (20)
1706	112	7 (6)	3 (3)
1717	118	15 (13)	13 (11)
Totals	649	136 (21)	100 (15)

one that was first voiced by L. H. Butterfield in his edition of the *Letters of Benjamin Rush:* "that literary works are primarily intended to be read, and that oddities, inconsistencies, and errors transferred from manuscript to printed page cause more distraction and more false effects of quaintness than they are worth as clues to the writer's meaning or feeling."[90]

I have thus taken the liberty of making corrections to the text whenever such emendations seemed warranted for the sake of clarity of expression or comprehension. More specifically, I have eliminated or standardized otherwise confusing contractions, punctuations, and capitalizations, expanded words with a tilde *(sup̃er, diñer, Cousin Duñer),* brought superior letters down to sentence level, and corrected a few obvious spelling errors. In the interest of readability if not aesthetics, I have used *"sic"* within square brackets only sparingly.

[90]L. H. Butterfield, ed., *Letters of Benjamin Rush,* 2 vols. (Princeton, N.J.: Princeton University Press, 1951), lxxvi.

PART TWO

The Diary

1

"Major Dudley Produced the Exemplification of the Charter's Condemnation"

John Winthrop, the first governor of the Massachusetts Bay Colony and the most influential member of the first generation of New England Puritans, died a mere twelve years before Samuel Sewall set foot in Boston, and his legacy was unmistakable. Not only were his children prominent inhabitants of Massachusetts and neighboring Connecticut, but the structure of government set up under his administration and the covenanted "City upon a Hill" ideal he had voiced in justifying the great migration across the Atlantic were substantially intact in 1661. Sewall thus grew to maturity in a Boston indelibly marked by the man who, as Cotton Mather wrote in his tribute to Winthrop in *Magnalia Christi Americana,* had been "chosen for the Moses" to carry God's people into the New England wilderness.[1]

Mather's advice that "posterity consider with admiration" Winthrop's life and the sacrifices he made for the success of the colony was certainly not lost on Sewall. When Deane Winthrop died in 1704 at the age of eighty-one, Sewall was honored to serve as one of the six coffin bearers at the funeral of the "last of Govr Winthrop's children." When he described the election of 1637 to a correspondent in London in 1704, he was at pains to establish a personal link with Winthrop: "my father . . . went on foot from Newbury to Cambridge [where the election was being held], forty miles," in order to "help strengthen Govr. Winthrop's party" and to ensure his victory over an upstart Henry Vane who was endeavoring to "confound and frustrate the whole business of the elec-

---

[1] Edmund S. Morgan, *The Puritan Dilemma: The Story of John Winthrop* (Boston: Little, Brown, 1958); Richard S. Dunn, *Puritans and Yankees: The Winthrop Dynasty of New England, 1630–1717* (Princeton: Princeton Univ. Press, 1962), 3–56; Mather quoted in Wesley Frank Craven, *The Legend of the Founding Fathers* (New York: New York Univ. Press, 1956; Ithaca, N.Y.: Cornell Univ. Press, 1965), 15.

tion, rather than that he himself should fail of being chosen." And when Joseph Sewall moved into the parsonage of the South Church in 1714, shortly after being ordained as one of its two pastors, Sewall wished his son the "blessing of Winthrop" as a reminder of the dwelling's first occupant.[2]

Throughout his long life, Sewall cherished the memory of "Govr Winthrop" because he subscribed to many of the ideas enunciated by the founder. Most importantly, Sewall followed Winthrop in the belief that the first migrants to Massachusetts were engaged in a covenanted relationship with God. "It is evident," he told William Dummer in 1723, "that our Almighty Saviour counseled the first planters to remove hither and settle here; and they dutifully followed his advice; and therefore He will never leave nor forsake them nor theirs." As Winthrop had foretold, a strict adherence to the terms of the covenant in establishing a holy commonwealth in the wilderness had resulted in God's "dwell[ing] among us as his own people." To be sure, Sewall's pronouncements lacked some of the militancy inherent in Winthrop's earlier vision. The notion that the principal reason for the existence of the Bay Colony was to serve as a base for reforming England from within had lost much of its appeal among the inhabitants of Massachusetts, including Winthrop, during the English civil war. But the commitment to the idea that New England was the chosen land continued unabated until long after the end of the 1640s. For Sewall, the assurance that the "families and churches which first ventured to follow Christ through the Atlantic Ocean into a strange land . . . were so religious; their end so holy; their self-denial in pursuing it so extraordinary" undergirded the hope that New England was the "New Jerusalem." In 1713, he managed to give a new twist, a hemispheric dimension, to the idea of a religious refuge. Christ's truth had been "trodden down" in Asia, "scorched and dried up" in Africa, and "choked with worldly hypocritical interest" in Europe; "why may we not . . . hope that the Americas shall be made the good ground that shall once at last prove especially and wonderfully fruitful?"[3]

[2]M. Halsey Thomas, ed., *The Diary of Samuel Sewall, 1674–1729,* 2 vols. (New York: Farrar, Straus and Giroux, 1973), 1:499; 2:740; Sewall to Edmund Calamy, January 24, 1704, in *Letter-Book of Samuel Sewall,* Massachusetts Historical Society *Collections,* 6th series, 1–2 (Boston, 1886–1888), 1:295; Sewall to James Noyes, March 9, 1714, ibid., 2:31.

[3]Thomas, ed., *Diary,* 2:1003; John Winthrop, "A Modell of Christian Charitie," in *Puritan Political Ideas, 1558–1794,* ed. Edmund S. Morgan (Indianapolis: Bobbs-Merrill, 1965), 92; Morgan, *Puritan Dilemma,* 176–81; Samuel Sewall, *Phaenomena Quaedam Apocalyptica* (Boston, 1697), 1–2; Sewall, *Proposals Touching the Accomplishment of Prophecies* (Boston, 1713), 1.

In the realm of politics, Sewall was a beneficiary of the governmental structure also established under Winthrop's direction. The charter that Charles I granted to the Massachusetts Bay Company in 1629 authorized the members of that joint-stock company, to whom the designation *freemen* was applied, to meet four times a year as a "General Court" to make "all manner of wholesome and reasonable orders, laws, statutes and ordinances, directions, and instructions, not contrarie to the laws" of the mother country. Company members were empowered also to elect annually a governor, deputy governor, and eighteen "assistants" to act as an executive council in the intervals between the meetings of the General Court. Theoretically, about a dozen company men were entitled legitimately to govern the entire colony. Realistically, however, Winthrop and his group knew that the large and rapidly growing population of the colony would not long tolerate such an oligarchical arrangement. Thus, from 1630 to 1634, they instituted three fundamental changes in the organization of the colony's government. First, they extended the circle of freemen to include all adult male church members. Second, they narrowed the definition of the General Court to include only the governor, deputy governor, and assistants. And third, they agreed to allow the newly expanded group of freemen to elect the members of the newly redefined General Court. These reforms achieved at least three desired ends: They extended political rights to a group far more numerous than the members of the joint-stock company, while ensuring that non-Puritans would never gain control of the government of the colony; they transformed what had been the executive council of the General Court into the General Court itself, thereby guaranteeing that legislative power would continue to be wielded by a select group of elites; and they affirmed the principle of the consent of the governed, especially with regard to the levying of taxes, without capitulating to the dictates of public opinion.[4]

The initial concessions made by Winthrop's administration, however, could not stem the tide of popular reform. In 1634, the freemen of the colony demanded a more direct role in matters of legislation. Winthrop was therefore forced to accommodate another innovation in the organization of the colony's government, one that allowed every town to "send their deputies" to the quarterly sessions of the General Court to "assist in making laws, disposing lands, etc." Each community

---

[4]Morgan, *Puritan Dilemma,* 84–95, 108–11; Charles M. Andrews, *The Colonial Period of American History,* 4 vols. (New Haven: Yale Univ. Press, 1934–1938), 1:430–41.

was henceforth entitled to elect representatives of its own to the provincial legislature. When the General Court became bicameral in 1644, the distinctiveness of the deputies' place in the government as elected officers closely linked to the freemen of particular localities was enhanced. Sitting in separate houses of the legislature, the assistants were more readily identified as "magistrates" and the deputies as "representatives." That the governor, deputy governor, and assistants alone constituted the Court of Assistants, which, increasingly after the 1640s, acted as the highest judicial authority in the colony, seemed to confirm the popular differentiation between magistrates and representatives.[5]

In 1661, the young Sewall arrived in a nearly autonomous colony whose political structure was well defined and whose founding religious ideals still resonated among its several congregations. Over the course of the next twenty-five years, he flourished in this Puritan commonwealth. He married Hannah Hull in 1676, became a member of the South Church the next year, and after the death of John Hull in 1683 inherited his father-in-law's business and promptly took his place among the richest men in Boston. Befitting his rising prominence, Sewall gained election to the General Court in 1684 as a nonresident deputy representing the western Massachusetts town of Westfield. The following year, with his election to the ranks of the assistants and a corresponding seat on the Court of Assistants, he assumed the judicial responsibilities that would be his life's calling. Even as Sewall rose to prominence in provincial society, however, changes were overtaking the colony to which he had grown so attached.

Beginning in 1675, the Lords of Trade, a standing committee of the Privy Council, assumed a central role in directing colonial affairs. As the Lords of Trade tightened royal control over the colonies and their trade, they grew increasingly concerned over reports of insubordination and rampant disregard of the Navigation Acts in Massachusetts. In 1676, they dispatched Edward Randolph to New England, ostensibly to check on proprietary business in New Hampshire, but really to determine whether Massachusets was complying with imperial trade reg-

---

[5] Andrews, *Colonial Period*, 1:442–43, 450–52; Morgan, *Puritan Dilemma*, 113; Dunn, *Puritans and Yankees*, 16; T. H. Breen, *The Character of the Good Ruler: A Study of Puritan Political Ideas in New England, 1630–1730* (New Haven: Yale Univ. Press, 1970), 75–80. Because it was the highest civil authority in the colony, the General Court was empowered to overturn the decisions of the Court of Assistants on appeal. Increasingly after the 1640s, however, as Yasuhide Kawashima points out in *Puritan Justice and the Indian: White Man's Law in Massachusetts, 1630–1763* (Middletown, Conn.: Wesleyan Univ. Press, 1986), 243, the General Court refrained from exercising its judicial powers.

ulations. Randolph's detailed reports were highly critical of the Puritan establishment, especially with regard to its persecution of Quakers, exclusion of the Church of England, and assumption of powers not granted in the 1629 charter. After returning to London, Randolph was influential in convincing Charles II to regulate the affairs of the Bay Colony more rigorously. In 1679, Randolph was back in Boston as a collector of customs for New England with authority to seize ships engaged in illegal trading. Resistance to Randolph and the actions of the Lords of Trade gave further credence to Randolph's earlier negative assessment of the Bay Colony and led royal authorities to commence the necessary judicial proceedings that resulted ultimately in the revocation of the colony's charter in 1684.[6]

For the next year and a half, the government of Massachusetts was in limbo. Although the revocation of the 1629 charter had destroyed its legal basis, the old government of the colony continued to operate because of delays in the implementation of royal rule. The death of Charles II in February of 1685 and the problems of succession encountered by the Catholic James II, in particular, left the old government pretty much intact but anticipating its own dissolution. Sewall's diary entries for 1685 were written in this atmosphere of uncertainty. Reports concerning the appointment of Colonel Piercy Kirke as the new governor of the colony only increased the apprehension of Sewall and his neighbors. The seemingly imminent arrival of "the Devil Kirk," whose earlier service as the governor of the English outpost of Tangier had earned him a reputation for severity, so alarmed Sewall that he attended a hastily scheduled meeting of the magistrates on July 8, despite an illness that had him alternately feverish and in a cold fit for the better part of the preceding week. As it turned out, Kirke never set sail for Massachusetts. In June of 1685, the Duke of Monmouth, Charles II's eldest and favorite illegitimate son, led a rebellion against James II, and the new king needed Kirke's help in suppressing the rebellion. Bostonians eagerly followed rumor after rumor regarding Monmouth's actions, as they had an earlier challenge to James II led by the Earl of Argyle in Scotland. Contrary to the hopes of the inhabitants of

[6]Wesley Frank Craven, *The Colonies in Transition, 1660–1713* (New York: Harper and Row, 1968), 165–74; David S. Lovejoy, *The Glorious Revolution in America* (New York: Harper and Row, 1972), 122–58; Michael G. Hall, *Edward Randolph and the American Colonies, 1676–1703* (Chapel Hill: Univ. of North Carolina Press, 1960), 24–47, 77–83; Bernard Bailyn, *The New England Merchants in the Seventeenth Century* (Cambridge, Mass.: Harvard Univ. Press, 1955; New York: Harper and Row, 1964), 154–59; Richard R. Johnson, *Adjustment to Empire: The New England Colonies, 1675–1715* (New Brunswick, N.J.: Rutgers Univ. Press, 1981), 36–51.

Massachusetts, the abortive rebellions of Monmouth and Argyle actually helped to secure James's claim to the throne.[7]

In 1686, the old government was finally replaced by a provisional government headed by Joseph Dudley. In a dramatic meeting of the General Court on May 17, Dudley "produced the Exemplification of the Charter's Condemnation," the proof that Sewall and others had insisted on seeing, and announced to the assembled magistrates and deputies that he "could treat them no longer as Governour and Company." Dudley's action signaled an end to more than a half century of relative freedom from imperial interference for Massachusetts authorities. After thanking God for "our hithertos of mercy 56 years," the General Court adjourned "with many tears shed." The changes, real and perceived, that accompanied the demise of the old order constitute an important part of Sewall's entries. On the last Sabbath in May, he noted that the Town House had been scheduled to host an Anglican service "by Countenance of Authority." Soon the manner of swearing oaths, burying the dead, and decorating the banner of the Ancient and Honorable Artillery Company became items of contention. Sewall was convinced that even everyday rowdiness had increased as a result of the collapse of the old regime. Following a drunken spree involving some of the supporters of the provisional government, he remarked that "such high-handed wickedness has hardly been heard of before in Boston."[8]

Diary
1685

Wednesday Febr 11, 1685. Joshua Moodey [minister of the First Church] and self set out for Ipswich. I lodge at Sparkes's [tavern].[1] Next day, Feb 12, goe to lecture which Mr. Moodey preaches, then I dine with Mr. [Thomas] Cobbet, and so ride to Newbury; visit Mr. Richardson sick of the dry belly ake.

[7] Craven, *Colonies in Transition,* 173–74; Lovejoy, *Glorious Revolution,* 173–78; Hall, *Edward Randolph,* 83–97; Thomas, ed., *Diary,* 1:69, 108.

[8] Thomas, ed., *Diary,* 1:113, 114–15, 116, 121; Craven, *Colonies in Transition,* 212–15; Lovejoy, *Glorious Revolution,* 180–82; Johnson, *Adjustment to Empire,* 71–74.

[1] Taverns and inns provided food, lodging, and drink to travelers in colonial Massachusetts. Sewall, as a member of the Court of Assistants and, later, the Superior Court, regularly spent a night or two in taverns as he rode the circuit to Plymouth, Springfield,

Monday Febr. 16. Get Mr. [Samuel] Phillips and [Edward] Payson to town and so keep a Fast-day, Mr. Moodey preaching forenoon, Mr. Phillips afternoon, Mr. [John] Woodbridge and Payson assisting in prayer, was a pretty full assembly, Mr. Moodey having given notice the Sabbath-day, on which he preached all day. At Wenham and Ipswich, as we went, we were told of the earthquake in those parts and at Salem (Feb. 8) the Sabbath before about the time of ending afternoon exercise; that which most was sensible of was a startling doleful sound; but many felt the shaking also, Peter and Jane Toppan. Mr. Phillips had not finished his sermon, and was much surprised at the sound, expecting when the house would have crackt. In several places exercise was over.

Tuesday Febr. 17. I and Brother, [and] sister Stephen Sewall ride to Sparkes's by the ferry, great part in the snow; dined with Ipswich Select-Men.

[February] 18th. I lodged there [Sparkes's]; the morn was serene; came to Salem, seeing Mrs. Hale by the way; staid Lecture, came [home] to Boston, found all well. *Laus Deo* [Praise God].

Tuesday March 10th, 1685. Deputies for Boston are Mr. Isaac Addington votes 90 and odd, Mr. John Saffin 70 and odd, Mr. Timothy Prout 50 and odd, Mr. Anthony Stoddard passed by, who hath been annually chosen about these twenty years: Mr. John Fayerwether left out. [Deputies] Are chosen for the year. Mr. [Isaac] Addington chosen a Commissioner also to seal up the votes and carry them. In the afternoon I carried my Wife to see Mrs. [Esther] Flint; wayes extream bad.

Thorsday, March 12, 1685. Mr. John Bayly preached from Amos 4.12 [prepare to meet thy God, O Israel], and Mr. [Samuel] Willard [of the South Church] from 2 Cor. 4. 16–18 [but though our outward man perish, yet the inward man is renewed day by day. . . . the things which are not seen are external]; both sermons and prayers excellent. In the even[ing] 2 first staves of the 46 Ps. sung. Watched [served as night

---

Salem, and Bristol. The historian David W. Conroy counted over 300 stops made by Sewall during his years as a Superior Court justice. Indeed, court sessions were frequently convened in taverns as a matter of convenience and cost effectiveness—to save on heating expenses in winter—as well as judicial preference. It seems quite certain, however, that Sewall was a model of restraint when it came to the consumption of alcohol. In 1716, in the midst of Sam, Jr.'s, marital turmoil, Sewall saw fit to "warn my eldest son against going to taverns." Sewall himself was an infrequent patron of Boston taverns, around thirty visits in fifty-five years. His use of taverns while on the road, therefore, as Conroy notes, constituted precisely the sort of "specialized patronage" that provincial officials had in mind when they issued licenses for such establishments. David W. Conroy, *In Public Houses: Drink and the Revolution of Authority in Colonial Massachusetts* (Chapel Hill: Univ. of North Carolina Press, 1995), 13–21; Thomas, ed., *Diary,* 2:815.

watch] with Isaac Goose and Sam Clark, had pleasant night, gave each watch 12*d.* to drink.

Satterday March 14th. went to Mr. Goddard of Watertown to buy hay, dined as I went with Thomas Danforth [Deputy Governor], Esq. and Lady; visited Mr. [Reverend John] Sherman as I came back.

Wednesday March 25th, 1685. went to Cambridge with Capt. Elisha Hutchinson, there meet with Lieut. Johnson; at Mr. [John] Cotton's Chamber the Deputy Governor tells how Major [William] Bordman dyed that morning; he had been College-Cook a long time. Dined with the Commissioners of Middlesex at the ordinary [tavern], then proceeded in our errand to Mr. Sherman from the Council to enquire when Easter Day was, and consequently our election, because by the rule in the Prayer Book it should be a week sooner. Mr. Sherman was pleasant and took it for granted 'twas as the Almanack had set it, *i.e.* an English Almanack, which I shewed him. Deputy Governour told the Commissioners this was the last time they were like to convene for such a purpose.

Thorsday March 26th, 1685. Went to the gathering of the Church at Sherborn and ordaining Mr. Daniel Gookin their Pastor. But six Brethren and three of the names Mors. Mr. [John] Wilson, Mr. [William] Adams and Mr. Nathaniel Gookin of Cambridge managed the work; Mr. Nathl Gookin the younger introduced the Elder, a happy type of the Calling the Jews. Mr. [Samuel] Torrey, [William] Brinsmead, [Moses] Fisk, [Joseph] Estabrooks, [Samuel] Man, [Joshua] Moodey, Hubbard (Neh.), [John] Sherman, [William] Woodrop, Rawson (Grindal), [John] Wilson junr there, and Fellows of the Colledge: Only Major General [Wait Still Winthrop] and self of magistrates. No relations were made, but I hope God was with them. I put up a note to pray for the Indians that light might be communicated to them by the candlestick, but my note was with the latest, and so not professedly prayed for at all.

Tuesday March the last, went to Weymouth, heard Mr. Brinsmead preach from Prov. 10. 29 [The way of the Lord is strength to the upright: but destruction shall be to the workers of iniquity]. After Lecture I took the acknowledgement of many deeds. In the even[ing] Angel Torrey brings word that little Hull was seized with convulsions; his first fit was when I was at Watertown, 25th March. Lodged with Mr. Brinsmead.

Wednesday morn April 1. Speaking to Mr. Brinsmead to pray for drying up the River Euphrates, he told me he had prayed that God would reveal to some or other as to Daniel of old, the understanding of the

Prophesies of this time, that so might know whereabouts we are.[2] Went home; Mr. [Samuel] Torrey accompanyed me to Monotocot Bridge; found things pretty calm at home and the child [Hull] sleeping.

Friday April 3rd, Mr. Joseph Eliot and I graft some walnut trees.

Apr. 14th, 1685. A ship arrives from New Castle and brings news of the death of Charles the 2nd, and proclamation of James the 2nd, King. Brought a couple of printed proclamations relating to that affair. News came to us as we were busy opening the nomination, just before dinner; it much startled the Governour and all of us. In the morn before I went the Governour said that a ship master had been with him from Nevis, who told him Govr. Stapleton should say, we should have a new Governour before he got to Boston. Master dined with magistrates and Commissioners at Capt. [John] Wing's. Carried my wife to [George] Bairsto's [in Roxbury] yesterday, April 13th.

Thorsday, April 16th, a vessel arrives from London. Mr. Lord, commander, brings orders to the several Colonies to proclaim the King. Mr. [William] Blathwayt writes to Simon Bradstreet, Esq. [Governor] superscribed For His Majestie's Service, advising that it would be best for us early to doe it; and our Charter being vacated in law and no government settled here, was the reason we were not writt to; copies and forms sent to us as to the other colonies, but no mention of Governour and Company. Also another letter was writt to Simon Bradstreet, Wm. Stoughton, Jos. Dudley, Peter Bulkeley, Sam'l Shrimpton, Richard Wharton, esquires, [Councillors] to proclaim the King. Suppose this was done lest the government should have neglected to do it. The Council agreed to proclaim the King before they knew of the letter. Major [John] Richards counted the votes for Mr. Dudley, totaled them twice over, and still found them 666, and so 'twas entered and sent to the towns.[3]

Monday April 20th. The King [James II] is Proclaimed; 8 companies,

---

[2] Sewall's reference to the "drying up" of the Euphrates was, as this passage indicates, related to his belief in, and his resulting quest to interpret, the signs contained in the book of Revelation. One of the series of visions recounted by St. John entailed the appearance of seven angels armed with orders to "Go your ways, and pour out the vials of the wrath of God upon the earth." The sixth angel "poured out his vial upon the great river Euphrates; and the water thereof was dried up." Rev. 16:12.

[3] Sewall and his cohorts' belief in biblical prophecy led them to look for telltale signs of the impending Apocalypse. Here, again, the reference is to the book of Revelation, wherein the number "six hundred threescore and six" is identified as the "number of the beast." In St. John's vision, the third angel proclaims that those bearing that mark "shall be tormented with fire and brimstone," and the vial poured by the first of seven angels visited "noisome and grievous sore upon the men which had the mark of the beast." Rev. 13:18; 14:10; 16:2.

the troop, and several gentlemen on horseback assisting; three volleys and then canon fired. This day a child falls upon a knife which runs through its cheek to the throat, of which inward wound it dies, and is buried on Wednesday. 'Tis one Gees child.

Thorsday, April 23, Mother [Jane Dummer] Sewall comes by water in Stephen Greenleaf to see us.

Sabbath, April 26th, I go to Meeting; staid at home last Sabbath and April 20th by reason of my sore throat, with which was taken the night before Mr. Lord came in.

April 27. Father Sweet buried.

Tuesday, April 28th Began to wean little Hull to see if that might be a means to free him of convulsions; he had one yesterday.

Wednesday, April 29th, The vessel of which Matthew Soley died master in London, arrives, and brings Gazettes to the 2d. of March. The King [Charles II] was buried 14th of Febr. in the even[ing] privately.

Friday, May the first, Mother Sewall goes to Salem; my wife and I go with her to visit Mrs. [Penelope] Bellingham [widow of former Governor Richard Bellingham], and so to the ferry boat in which met with a Hampshire man that had been well acquainted with Mr. [Reverend Henry] Cox and such Hampshire people, several of them, as mother knew: rode to Capt. Marshal's and there took leave. White Oaks pretty much put forth: 'tis a forward very green Spring. An Apsoon man arrives of about 5 weeks' passage, brings word that the King was to be Proclaimed the 23rd of April, and the Parliament to sit the 4th of May. Mr. Tho. Smith from Barbados brings the Honourable Francis Bond, one of His Majestie's Council for that island, and of a great estate, also one Mr. Middleton; former comes to recover his health. Father Town is buried at Cambridge this first of May. Sundry other vessels come from England, which I mention not. The like has hardly been known as to earliness.

Sabbath May 3rd, a letter read from the N[orth] Church wherein Mr. Willard and messengers desired to be sent in order to ordain Mr. Cotton Mather,[4] pastor of that Church; signed, Increase Mather, at the desire and order of the Church. The Governour and self with the Deacons, nominated to goe.

May 6th, General Court assembles; magistrates vote an Address to be sent by the ship now ready to sail, on which a negative put. A com-

---

[4]Cotton Mather, as his name indicates, was the embodiment of two of the most influential families in early Massachusetts, the Cottons and the Mathers. Together with his father, Increase, Cotton Mather served as minister of the North Church for four decades and was a revered figure among religious and secular authorities.

mittee chosen to revise the laws, at the earnest suit of the Deputies, which they would have had them made a report of next Tuesday, but agreed to be next Election Court. Took the word *"such"* out of the late law printed title *"Conveyancies";* made some freemen, it may be twenty; dissolved the Court on Friday May 8th, 1685.

Thorsday, May 7th. a youth was cut for the stone and a great one taken out as big as a hen's egg.

Friday morn, May 8th 1685, the lad dies at neighbour Mason's, and now his son will not be cut, seeing this stranger fare so ill. Mr. John Bayly preached the Lecture for Mr. [Increase] Mather, from Ps. 37.4. Delight thyself also in the Lord &c.

Friday May 8th—past 6, even[ing], walk with the honored Governour [Simon Bradstreet] up Hoar's Lane, so to the alms house; then down the length of the Common to Mr. Dean's pasture, then through Cowel's Lane to the New Garden, then to our house, then to our pasture by Engs's, then I waited on his Honour to his gate and so home. This day our old red cow is killed, and we have a new black one brought in the room, of about four years old and better, marked with a crop and slit in the left ear, and a crop off the right ear, with a little hollowing in. As came with his Honour through Cowell's Lane, Sam came running and called out a pretty way off and cried out the cow was dead and by the heels, meaning hanged up by the butcher. At which I was much startled, understanding him [to mean that] she had been dead upon a hill or cast with her heels upward, and so had lost her; for I was then looking for her and it was unexpected, mother having partly bargained and the butcher fetcht her away in the night unknown. Had served this family above ten years, above nine since my dwelling in it.

Satterday May 9th, Brother Stephen Sewall visits me.

Monday, May 11th, 1685, I accompanied Mr. [Joshua] Moodey to Mr. [John] Eliot's to persuade Mr. Benjamin [Eliot] to go to the ordination of Mr. Cotton Mather, in which I hope we have prevailed; the mentioning of it drew tears from the good father [John Eliot] so as to hinder his speech.[5] The father was abroad and preached yesterday. Vis-

[5]John Eliot, minister of the church at Roxbury, was known on both sides of the Atlantic for his efforts to convert the New England tribes to Christianity. Between 1650 and the mid-1670s, Eliot was responsible for the creation of fourteen "praying towns" for Massachusett and Nipmuc Indians who had supposedly accepted the "yoke of Christ." However, the total number of Eliot's converts remained small, and the outbreak of King Philip's War in 1675 destroyed most of the racial harmony he had cultivated in the course of his missionary work. Benjamin Eliot graduated from Harvard in 1665, but continued to live with his father until his death on October 15, 1687. Sewall, who seemed to take a special interest in the younger Eliot, described him as "much touch'd as to his Understand-

ited Mr. [Joseph] Dudley also. Deacon Parkes dyed last night, and Goodman Woodward of Dedham, father of the minister, is dead within a day or two. At Mr. Dudley's was Wm. Hahaton and David Indian, who acknowledged the papers I offered him in Feb. Court, at Capt. [Nicholas] Paige's, speaking English.

Tuesday, May 12th, I weary myself in walking from one end and side of the town to t'other to seek our lost cow.

Wednesday, May 13, 1685, Mr. Cotton Mather is ordained pastor [of the Second Church] by his father [Increase Mather], who said, My son Cotton Mather, and in his sermon spake of Aaron's garments being put on Eleazer, intimating he knew not but that God might now call him out of the world. Mr. Eliot gave the right hand of fellowship, calling him a lover of Jesus Christ. Mr. Benjamin Eliot was there who hath not been at town these many years.

Thorsday May 14th, Mr. [Samuel] Torrey and Unkle [Edmund] Quinsey dined here. Have agreed to have a Fast here at our house next Friday. 'Twas first to be on Tuesday, but altered it. I invited all the magistrates: to most writ the following words—"To Samuel Nowell, Esq., Sir—The ministers of this town are desired to pray and preach at my house next Friday, to begin about half an hour past nine; which I acquaint you with that so yourself and wife may have the opportunity of being present. Sam. Sewall. May 18, 1685."

Tuesday May 19th. 1685 went to Roxbury lecture, invited Mr. Eliot and his son to be with us on Friday next. When I come home I find Hullie extream ill having had two convulsion fits, one of them very long: the child is much changed.

Friday May 22d. 1685, had a private Fast: the magistrates of this town with their wives here. Mr. Eliot prayed, Mr. Willard preached. I am afraid of Thy judgments—text mother gave. Mr. [James] Allen [of the First Church] prayed; cessation half an hour. Mr. Cotton Mather prayed; Mr. [Increase] Mather preached Ps. 79.9 [Help us, O God . . . and purge away our sins]. Mr. Moodey prayed about an hour and half; sung the 79th Psalm from the 8th to the end; distributed some biskets, and beer, cider, wine. The Lord hear in Heaven his dwelling place.

Satterday May 23d, morn, thunder and lightning. Satterday 5 P.M.

---

ing." During a visit to the Eliots' home in August of 1687, Sewall noted that Benjamin kept "heaving up his shoulders," laughing at inappropriate times, and singing in notes that were "very extravagant." Benjamin "would have sung again before I came away" had not his father "prevail'd with him to the contrary, alledging the children would say he was distracted." Thomas, ed., *Diary,* 1:147–48.

Mr. [Richard] Wharton and [Judge John] Saffin offered me an Address, which I saw not cause to sign. Governour [Bradstreet] had signed, J. Winthrop, Capt. Fones and some others interested in the Narraganset lands. Mr. [Simon] Lynde, Mr. Smith (Nar.) [of Narragansett] and Mr. Brindley were by at the same time.

Sabbath May 24th, we read the ninety-seventh Psalm in course [in private devotions]; Mr. Francis Bond at our House.

Tuesday May 26th, 1685, Mary Kay comes hither to dwell in Hannah Hett's stead, who is upon marriage.

Wednesday, May 27, 1685, Election day, being very fair wether all day. Mr. William Adams [of Dedham] preaches from Isa. 66.2 [For all those things hath mine hand made, and all those things have been, saith the Lord]. Capt. [John] Blackwell and Mr. Bond dine with us: Mr. [Samuel] Philips craves a blessing and returns thanks, in which mentions the testimony of Jesus, that God would make us faithfull in it. Governour chosen without counting; Mr. Nowell (I think) came next. Mr. [Thomas] Danforth Deputy Governour clear. Assistants,

ESQRS.		ESQRS.	
D. Gookin	1312	P. Tilton	1234
J. Pynchon	1257	S. Appleton	1200
Wm. Stoughton	757	R. Pike	1168
J. Dudley	694	Elisha Cooke	1067
N. Saltonstall	1080	Wm. Johnson	932
H. Davie	1131	John Hathorn	1031
J. Richards	1267	Elisha Hutchinson	777
S. Nowell	1257	S. Sewall	1065
J. Russell	1263	Oliver Purchas	683

COMMISSIONERS UNITED COLONIES

Mr. Stoughton	307
Mr. Nowell	485

RESERVES

Mr. Danforth
Mr. Dudley.

PERSONS LEFT OUT THIS YEAR

Mr. [Peter] Bulkeley	667 ⎫	in last year—
Mr. [John] Woodbridge	559 ⎭	

In the room now Mr. Dudley, Oliver Purchas. Mr. [William] Brown had votes 398, Mr. [Bartholomew] Gidney 598, John Smith 608, Danl Pierce 471. Major General and Treasurer, no telling; Mr. [Isaac] Addington had a great many votes for Secretary. My dear child Hull had a convulsion fit in lecture time. Mr. Adams prayed after the election over. The Governour, Deputy Governour and about nine Assistants sworn, of which myself one; Court adjourned till Thursday 8 of the clock.

Thorsday about noon, one Jonathan Gardner of Roxbury commits bestiality with a mare; he is sent to prison, but one witness. Hull hath two convulsion fits which bring him extreme low; Mr. Philips prays with us.

Friday, May 29th. Mr. Nowell and I go to Mr. [William] Stoughton and [Joseph] Dudley to acquaint them with the freeman's choice of them, in the Court's name, and to desire them to come and take their oaths: I doubt Mr. Bulkeley's being left out will make them decline it. Mr. Eliot was ill and not at this election, which knew nothing of till Mr. Philips told me the last night.

Monday June 1, 1685. Artillery election [of officers] day; Eliakim [Mather] sets out to see his mother at N. Hampton, Connecticot. I train not. Mr. John Phillips is chosen Captain. Capt. Hill Lieutenant, Mr. Benj. Alford Ensign, Henry Dering eldest Sergeant, [Edward] Crick second, Seth Perry third, Sam Chickly fourth, Roby, Clark. The 46th Psalm sung at Mr. [John] Wing's, from the 6th verse to the end. About 3 of the clock in the afternoon this day, Cousin Anne Quinsey is brought to bed of a daughter [Ann].

June 2, 1685. In the afternoon Mr. Stoughton and Dudley come and confer with the Council thanking them for their respect in acquainting them with their choice, and to say they were not of another mind as to the substance than formerly, relating to the great concerns of the country, lest any might be deceived in desiring them to take their oaths. Also that if things went otherwise than well in that great trial [we] were like shortly to have, all the blame would be laid upon them. Said, supposed things would be so clear when the day came as that [there] would be a greater unanimity what to do than now was thought of. Deputy Governours Cloud and Pillar. Seemed, through the importunity of friends, ministers and others to incline to take the oath. Take leave. When gone Deputy Governour relates a saying of his wife.

June 3, very seasonable rain. Wednesday June 3d, '85, at night very considerable thunder and rain. I had dreamt[6] that I returned to New-

---

[6]Sewall recounted his dream in Latin as follows: *In somniis visum est mihi, me rediisse novoburgo vel alio aliquo oppido; et me absente, uxorem mortuam esse Roxburiae vel Dorcestriae; quam narrationem aegerrime tuli nomen saepius exclamans. Dum percontarer ubi esset socer, dixerunt eum in Angliam profecturum; filid scilicet mortud liberum esse ei ut iter*

bury or some other town, and that during my absence my wife had died at Roxbury or Dorchester. I took the tidings very hard, and repeatedly called her name out. While I was inquiring where my father-in-law might be, they said that he had started for England: since his daughter had died he was free to travel as he wished. Elizabeth [four-year-old Betty] whispered [something to me] that to that point had weighed heavily on me, namely that the death had occurred in part because of my neglect and want of love. When I shook off sleep, I embraced my wife for joy as if I had newly married her.

Thorsday, June 4th, Mr. [Increase] Mather preaches from Isa. 14. 32. Doct[rine] The Church of God shall stand and abide for ever. Probable that N.E. Church shall do so. The 87th. Psalm sung. Mr. Stoughton and Dudley dine with us. Mr. Stoughton inclines to take his oath; Mr. Mather, Capt. Scottow and Capt. Gidney dine with us likewise. This day the Chancery Bill is passed.

Monday, June 8th. 8 companies train: in the morn. between 7 and 8 o'clock. Asaph Eliot comes in and tells me a rumor in the town of the new Governour being come to New York, and the certain news, doleful news of Mr. [Reverend Thomas] Shepard of Charlestown, his being dead, of whose illness I heard nothing at all. Saw him very well this day sennight [a week ago]; was much smitten with the news. Was taken on Friday night, yet being [able] to preach and administer the Lord's Supper on Sabbath day, forbore physick, at least at first. This day Mr. Stoughton and Dudley come in, and in their places at Court in the afternoon, take their oaths. Charlestown was to have had a great bussle in training on Tuesday with horse and foot, Capt. [Lawrence] Hammond engaging some of Boston to be there; but now 'tis like to be turned into the funeral of their pastor; he dying full and corpulent. Mr. [John] Bayly, Sen'r dined with us at Mr. Pain's. The reverend Mr. Tho. Shepard was ordained May 5, 1680 by Mr. [John] Sherman, Mr. [Urian] Oakes [president of Harvard, 1675–81] giving the right hand of fellowship. Mr. Sh.'s Text Heb. 13. 20—That great Shepherd of the Sheep.

On the Sabbath June 7th '85, Cous. [Daniel] Quinsey had his daughter Anne baptized [see entry for June 1, above].

Tuesday, June 9th The Reverend Mr. Thos Shepard buried: Governour [Bradstreet], Deputy Governour [Danforth] and Magistrates there. Mr. [Peter] Bulkely dined with us and was there. Bearers, Mr.

---

faceret quo vellet. Hanc mortem partim ex incuria mea et amoris indigentia accidisse, Elizabetha susurravit quod adhuc me gravius pressit. Excusso somno prae gaudio uxorem quasi nuper nuptam amplexus sum. I have adopted a variation of M. Halsey Thomas's translation, *Diary,* 1:65.

[Increase] Mather, Mr. [Zechariah] Simmes, Mr. [Samuel] Willard, Mr. Hubbard [Nehemiah Hobart] of Cambridge, Mr. Nathaniel Gookin, Mr. Cotton Mather; the two last preached at Charlestown the last Sabbath day. It seems there were some verses; but none pinned on the herse. Scholars went before the herse. A pretty number of troopers there. Capt. [John] Blackwell and Counsellor [Francis] Bond there.

Tuesday, June 9th 1685. Govr Edw. Cranfield [of New Hampshire] sails away in his sloop from Portsmouth. It is like is gone to Barbados.

Thorsday Even[ing], June 11th Brother Steven Sewall lodges here: hath been extream ill.

Satterday, June 13th Capt. Benjn. Gillam buried. Govr Bradstreet's effigies [portrait] hung up in his best room this day.

Wednesday, June 17th a Quaker or two go to the Governour and ask leave to enclose the ground [on Boston Common] the hanged Quakers are buried in under or near the gallows, with pales [stakes]: Governour [Bradstreet] proposed it to the Council, who unanimously denied it as very inconvenient for persons so dead and buried in the place to have any monument.[7]

Thorsday, June 18. A Quaker comes to the Governour and speaks of a message he had which was to shew the great calamities of fire and sword that would suddenly come on New-England. Would fain have spoken in the Meetinghouse, but was prevented. Eliakim [Mather] comes home this day, brings word that Capt. [Daniel] Henchman is coming away from Worcester with his family. Noise this day of a French pirate on the coast, of 36 Guns.

Satterday, June 20th 1685. The Court not agreeing about the proviso in the end of the 2d section of the law, title Courts, adjourns till Tuesday July 7th except occasion be, and then the Governour is to call them sooner. Also the Dept. Governour goes to keep Court at York next week with Mr. Nowel, and several other magistrates will go out of town. The final difference between the magistrates and deputies is: The Governour and several with him would repeal the proviso, letting the rest of the law stand as it does; the deputies have voted the repeal of

[7]Contrary to the popular myth that a commitment to religious freedom was their inspiration for migrating to America, the Puritans were religious absolutists who regularly persecuted those who disagreed with them. By subjecting Quakers to the whipping post and the gallows, the Puritan majority in Massachusetts hoped to rid the colony of their presence. In 1708, when the Puritans were no longer able to dominate the colony as they had done earlier, Quakers in Boston petitioned the town's board of selectmen for permission to build a meetinghouse of their own. The selectmen ruled favorably on the petition, but when it was presented to the Council, Sewall was outraged: "I opposed it; said I would not have a hand in setting up their Devil Worship." See Thomas, ed., *Diary,* 1:600.

the proviso; and withall that the remainder of the law have this alteration, viz: in stead of greater part of the magistrates—greater number of the magistrates present—so to make the law new as [it] might be construed contrary to the charter: the Governour, Mr. Stoughton, Dudley and several others could not consent.

Voted the 16th of July to be observed as a Fast.

[General Court resolution:]

Publick Fast, [ordered] by the Governour and Company of the Massachusetts Bay in N.E. at a Genl. Court held at Boston May 27, 1685.

This Court having taken into their serious consideration, that in respect of afflictive sicknesses in many places, and some threatenings of scarcity as to our necessary food, and upon other accounts also, we are under solemn frowns of the Divine Providence; being likewise sensible, that the people of God in other parts of the world are in a low estate,

Do therefore appoint the sixteenth day of July next, to be set apart as a day of publick *Humiliation* by fasting and prayer throughout this colony, exhorting all who are the Lord's Remembrancers, to give Him no rest, till Isai. 62.7. He establish and make Jerusalem a praise in the earth: And do hereby prohibit the inhabitants of this jurisdiction all servile labour upon the said day.

By the Court, Edward Rawson Secretary.

Satterday, P.M. Carried my wife to Dorchester to eat cherries, rasberries, chiefly to ride and take the air: the time my wife and Mrs. [Esther] Flint spend in the orchard, I spent in Mr. [Josiah] Flint's study, reading Calvin on the Psalms &c. 45. 68. 24.

Sabbath, June 21, 1685. Mr. Solomon Stoddard preaches in the afternoon from Gal. 5.17. shewing that there is a principle of Godliness in every true Believer; and how it differs from moral vertue, &c. Some little disturbance by a Quaker about the time of baptism.

Wednesday, June 24, 1685. Carried my wife to Cambridge lecture; Mr. Willard preached from those words, He that knows and does not his Master's will, shall be beaten with many stripes. Dined with Mr. Nathaniel Gookin.

June 25. Mr. [John] Russel of Hadley preacheth the lecture from Zech. 7.5. Did ye at all fast unto me, even to me?

June 25th A ship comes in to Marble head, and brings news of the King's coronation.

June 26. Mr. John Cotton, and Mr. Solomon Stoddard dine here.

Satterday, June 27th It pleaseth God to send rain on the weary dusty earth.

Wednesday, July 1, 1685. Commencement day [at Harvard]; Peter

Butler comes in from London, brings news of the King's coronation, sermon and formalities, with a letter from Mr. [Robert] Humfryes [London attorney for Massachusetts], and a copy of the judgement entered up against us that [is] about 145 pages, cost £5 10s. having Pengry's rec[eip]t upon an outside leafe.

Cous. Nath[aniel] Dummer is brought by Cous. Jer[emiah Dummer] to our house this day, he came in [with] Mr. [Peter] Butler who came in late last night; so came not ashoar till this morn. Goes to the commencement with Eliakim [Mather]. Besides disputes, there are four orations, one Latin by Mr. [Thomas] Dudley; and two Greek, one Hebrew by Nath. Mather, and Mr. President [Increase Mather] after giving the degrees made an oration, in praise of academical studies and degrees, Hebrew tongue: Mr. [Edward] Collins, [Samuel] Shepard, &c. Dept. Governour and Mr. Nowell absent; not returned from keeping Court in the province of Maine. Governour there, whom I accompanied by Charlestown. After dinner the 3d part of the 103 Psalm was sung in the Hall.[8]

Thorsday, July 2d 1685. Mr. Cotton Mather preaches from 2 Cor. 5.5 [Now he that hath wrought us for the selfsame thing is God, who also hath given unto us the earnest of the Spirit]. In his father's turn, who keeps at Cambridge.

After the County Court is over, is a conference at his Honours; present the Governour, Mr. Stoughton, Dudley, [John] Richards, Sewall, Mr. [Samuel] Torrey, [William] Brinsmead, Willard, Adams. Were unanimous as to what discoursed, relating to our circumstances, the charter being condemned. Every one spake.

Satterday, July 4th 1685. Little Hull hath a convulsion fit: it took him sleeping in the cradle after dinner. I was taken ill myself very feverish so as feared the fever and ague, took some cardnus[9] drink at night, sweat pretty well, and so it went off, blessed be God.

Satterday, about 4 *mane* [in the morning] Isaac Woode dyes pretty

---

[8]Sewall regularly attended commencements at Harvard. By the mid-1680s, however, the occasion entailed more than the displays of scholarly achievement that seemed so pleasing to Sewall. President Mather here heaped "praise of academical studies" at the college, but elsewhere he expressed his concern about the "excesses and abuses" resulting from the consumption of prodigious quantities of wine by the young scholars and his hope that his presence on campus "might prevent disorder and profaneness." See Samuel Eliot Morison, *Harvard College in the Seventeenth Century,* 2 vols. (Cambridge, Mass.: Harvard Univ. Press, 1936), 2:465–67.

[9]Sewall may be referring to a medicinal drink made with the herb *Carduus Benedictus* or Blessed Thistle. Thomas Short's *Medicina Britannica* (Philadelphia, 1751), p. 49, prescribed the carduus drink for a variety of ailments, but noted that "its chief praise is for the plague, used inwardly to provoke sweat, either for prevention or cure."

suddenly, for was abroad the day before tho' had been not well a 14 night.

Monday, July 6th. I am taken with a feverish fit; yet go to court in the afternoon, the county court, where was read Major [John] Pynchon's letter to the Council; which is that 5 men came to one of the houses of Westfield (I think) about midnight 28th June, knockt at the door, the man bid him come in, so in they came all armed with drawn swords, and threatened to run the man and his wife through if they stirred: so plundered that house, and another in like manner: told they had 60 men in their company and that if they stirred out of door, they would kill them; so stayd in a great part of Monday, then when thought the coast was clear told the neighbours and some were sent to search after them; at last found them; one of the 5 snapt and missed fire, another shot, then one of ours shot so as to shoot one of theirs dead; another of the 5 fought one of ours with his sword, till another of ours knockt him down. One or two that were taken are brought to Boston, one at least is escaped. Major Pynchon writes 'twill cost near an hundred pounds.

An Indian was branded in court and had a piece of his ear cut off for burglary.

Tuesday, July 7th Brother [William] Moody [husband of Sewall's sister Mehitable] visits us. General Court sits in the afternoon. Time is spent in ordering a drum to beat up for volunteers about 30. Samson Waters, Capt., to go with Mr. Pateshal's brigenteen to fetch in two privateers that this morn are said to be in the Bay, a sloop and shalop; in the shalop, [the pirate] Graham.[10]

Wednesday [July 8] I take a vomit, after 12 sweat much, when cold fit past. Mr. Stoughton and Dudley visit me and Mr. Secretary. Thorsday morn take Cortex Peruvianus [made from the dried bark of trees and shrubs of the genus cinchona that yields quinine] in a glass of wine. Marshal Gen[era]ll [John Green] comes to speak with me, being sent to call me to Court because all the magistrates might be together to give their sence what to do when Col. Kirk comes, and how to receive him. Brother and Sister Gerrish [Moses and Jane Sewall Gerrish] lodged here last night. I had very little sleep.

Now about news comes to town that Panama is taken by one Banister an English man; and that by the help of the natives he intends to hold it.

---

[10]On July 8, 1685, the Massachusetts General Court decreed that "free plunder be offered to such as shall voluntarily lyst themselves" for action against pirates operating in local waters or, if such an incentive prove inadequate, "that a sufficient number of men be forthwith impressed to that service."

Friday, July 10th. I take another dose of the cortex: my fit stayes away. Brother and Sister Gerrish go home. Between 2 and 3 P.M. as Mr. [Moses] Fisk and Mr. [Edward] Wyllys were talking to me, it grew darkish, thundered, and a very sudden, violent storm of rain, wind and hail arose which beat so upon the glass and partly broke it, as startled us. The window of Mothers bed-chamber next the street hath many quarrels [panes] broken in it, all over, except the sidelong pane next [to] the shop. We were speaking about Col. Kirk's coming over.

Mr. Stoughton visits me and tells of the Court's adjournment till next Tuesday sennight [a week hence] and then the Elders to meet them and advise. Mr. Dudley and Mr. [Benjamin] Bullivant visit me at the same time. Mr. Stoughton also told me of George Car's Wife being with child by another man, tells the father, Major Pike sends her down to prison. Is the Governour's grandchild by his daughter [Dorothy Brad-street] Cotton.[11]

One Vicars drowned, the boat he was in being sunk in the harbour by the gust; our washer's son.

John Balston arrives; when was below, was some rumor that the [new] Governour [Piercy Kirke] was come. July 10th '85, brings news the Parliament had sat, and were adjourned for a day or two. Dr. Oates has been whipt and set in the pillory. Was set in the pillory before the Exchange, May 19, the day of the Parliament's sitting: 'Tis for perjury.[12]

Sabbath-day, July 5 [*sic*]. Mr. [John] Sherman the father is taken delirious in Sudbury pulpit; so fain to be born away; is now sick of the fever and ague. Orders go out to towns that have not sent, to send a deputy or deputies [to the General Court] at their peril against the 21 instant, and the Elder warned also to appear; I read the paper to Watertown. The deputies that were present on Friday, are to warn the respective Elders.

Wednesday, P.M., July 15. Very dark, and great thunder and lightening.

One Humphry Tiffiny and Frances Low, Daughter of Antony Low, are slain with the lightening and thunder about a mile or half a mile beyond Billinges farm, the horse also slain, that they rode on, and an-

---

[11]Ann Carr was the daughter of the Reverend Seaborn Cotton and Dorothy Brad-street Cotton—Governor Simon Bradstreet's daughter.

[12]In 1678, Titus Oates claimed to have uncovered evidence of a Catholic conspiracy to kill Charles II, install his brother James as king, and massacre large numbers of English Protestants. The alleged Popish Plot helped to inflame anti-Catholic fears in England. By 1684, Oates, never very reputable to begin with, had been further discredited and imprisoned. The "Exchange" was probably the Royal Exchange, where London merchants gathered for the transaction of business.

other horse in company slain, and his rider who held the garment on the maid to steady it at the time of the stroke, a coat or cloak, stounded, but not killed. Were coming to Boston. Antony Low being in town the sad bill was put up with [news] of that solemn judgment of God; Fast-day forenoon. July 15, 1685. 2 Persons, 2 Horses.

July 17. Mr. Allin makes me an issue in [bleeds] my left arm.

July 19th By accident the spear was not sent on Satterday, but this night; I not being very thoroughly recovered, Mr. [Isaac] Goose watches accompanied by Sam. Clark, and Cous. Nath. Dummer. This Sabbath-day Mrs. Sarah Noyes's house broken up in time of afternoon exercise; and money stolen; Ens[ign] Pecker's the Sabbath before.

A Bristow-Man [of War] comes in this day, and fires five guns at the Castle [fort on Castle Island in Boston Harbor], which a little startles us.

Tuesday July 21. Cous. Nath. Dummer goes to Salem in order to pass to Newbury next day, Brother Stephen [Sewall] coming for him.

This day about 31 ministers meet, Mr. [John] Higginson prayes excellently: Governour gives the question. Dine all together at Monk's [tavern]. After dinner about 3 or 4 aclock, they give their answer, i.e. Mr. [William] Hubbard [of Ipswich] speaks in behalf of the rest, that their opinion was the government ought not to give way to another till the Generall Court had seen and judged of the commission; so should be called if not sitting at the arrival of a commissioned Governour. But several expressed some dissent; and after, shewed themselves extreamly dissatisfied, saying that Mr. Hubbard had greatly abused them and that he was not ordered by the ministers that they knew to speak their minds, which six gave in under their hands. The meeting has been uncomfortable, and I doubt will breed great animosities.

Thorsday 23d July. Five ministers gave under their hands that Mr. Hubbard was appointed by the ministers to deliver their mind, and that [Hubbard] had delivered it right. First five were, Mr. John Higginson, Sam. Chiever, Joseph Estabrooks, Nicholas Noyes, Tho. Barnard.

The Governour goes from lecture sick of a cold, and dines not with us, nor comes to Court. Col. Pye dines with us, who comes hether by land from Mary-Land.

Friday, July 24. Governour not abroad, very sharp debates about submission &c. upon a Governour's arrival, occasioned by a vote from the deputies to the purpose that the Court be adjourned till 3d Wednesday in August except some demand of the government from His Majestie be made before, then that effectual order be taken for convening the Court by Governour, Dep. Governour or 3 magistrates of Boston, and no answer to be given till then. Magistrates past a negative and another vote for adjournment till 2d Wednesday in October. Address is past but several did not vote, of which self one. Mr. Stoughton and Dudley called as went home. Mr. Higginson gave in his opinion for submission this day in case a commissioned Governour come over.

Satterday, July 25. Governour is prevailed with to sign the Address. Court is adjourned by the Dept. Governour (for Governour at home) till the 2d Wednesday in August at one aclock: Several freemen first made.

July 29th Cous. Dummer returns, and brings word of Mr. [Edmund] Batters death this morn. He went from Court, as Mr. Addington the Speaker remembers, last Thorsday. Mr. Nath. Green arrives this day, comes from London June the 6. [Capt.] Jolls arrived in whom went the letter concerning the Kings proclamation.

Tho. Fayerwether a day or two before, by whom we hear of Argyle's rising in Scotland, landing there from Holland with the preparations against him. Act of Parliament for settling the King's revenue, as to the former King.[13]

Thorsday, July 30. Actions (33) being heard, Court is adjourned till Tuesday next, Jury not dismissed because of several criminals.

Friday, July ult. [William] Condey arrives, hath had the Small Pocks of which John Cutts, his own son, a youth, and one more are dead; but 'tis said have been well a 14 night. When came a little above the Castle, took in the colours and cast anchor, and a man coming from on board would not tell what the matter was, so began to noise it that the new Governour was come, flocking to the waterside. Not considering that Condey came out before Green [who, as Sewall noted above, had arrived on July 29].

Satterday, Augt 1. An order from the Council is signed to cause the [Condey] ship to remove lower to Lovel's island, and there the passengers, ship, and goods between decks to be aired; none to come to any town till further order. And none to entertain persons coming from the ship. Yet Mr. Vaughan and Wyar gone homeward. Mr. Saml Epps dyed in London last April. It seems upon the 30th of July Mr. Eliot riding home his horse stumbled and threw him, by which means his collarbone is broken near his shoulder which puts him in great pain.

Wednesday, Augt. 5. rode to Dorchester lecture with Cous. Nath. Dummer; was kindly entertained at Mr. Stoughton's after Lecture. Going thither I saw a few feet of ground enclosed with boards, which is

[13]In May of 1685, the Earl of Argyle landed in Scotland, where he hoped to provoke a rebellion among Scottish Presbyterians against the rule of James II. Argyle's supporters, numbering perhaps as many as 2,500 men, were quickly defeated, and Argyle himself was executed in Edinburgh.

done by the Quakers out of respect to some one or more hanged and buried by the gallows; though the Governour forbad them, when they asked leave.

Augt. 7th [Capt.] Eldridge sails for London, wherein goes the Address to King James the 2d. Hath been hindered from July 27 by running on a rock, essaying to go out at Broad Sound.

Satterday, 8 at night, August 8, 1685. The Reverend Mr. John Sherman dyes; seemed to be cheerly in the morn and on Friday; the wether extream hot; is buried on Monday August 10, 1685. Not many ministers there, I suppose knew not of it. Dept. Governour [Danforth], [and the following Councillors:] Major General [Daniel] Gookin, Mr. Stoughton, Dudley, [Humphrey] Davie, [John] Richards, [Samuel] Nowel, [James] Russel, [Elisha] Hutchinson, [Elisha] Cook, Sewall, there: Governour [Bradstreet] not present. I saw one or two coaches. He is much lamented as a godly, prudent, peaceable man. By Ed. Oaks I understand Mr. [Reverend William] Adams [Sewall's Harvard classmate] is seized again with his fever-ague, so that said Oaks preached there all day on the Sabbath. When return from the funeral, I find my little Hull extream ill.

Augt. 12. General Court meets.

Thorsday Augt. 13. Adjourns till 3d Wednesday in September, excepting emergency. This Court ordered Court of Assistant jurymen from Salem, and other towns, not of late usual. The Treasurer refused to send out warrants for valuation, without a special order of Court, lest thereby he should seem to accept of that office; so in his bill he drew up, mentioned their providing a Treasurer against October. So the Secretary is ordered to give forth warrants to the towns to send in votes for Treasurer to be presented to October Court. Is a rumor that a commission will be granted to some gentlemen here, before the Governour come.

Augt. 14. I go to the funeral of Robert Saunderson's young son and Mr. Danl Allen's young son. At night Mr. Willard, Jacob Eliot, Robt Walker, [Theophilus] Frary, Nath. Oliver, Benj. Davis meet here to discourse. Because the two last named desire to come into the Church without making any relation [narrative] at all; or having Mr. Willard report the substance of what they said to him.[14]

---

[14] New England Puritans ordinarily required candidates for church membership to appear before the congregation, make a narration of the manner in which they had experienced "saving grace," answer questions put to them by the assembled church members, and conclude with a profession of faith. Church members then voted on whether candidates deserved admission.

Tuesday, Augt. 18. The posthumous daughter of James Richards Esqr. is to be buried this day, died very suddenly.

Monday Morn. Augt. 17. The sad and unexpected newes of Mr. Adams's death came to town. Is to be buried on Wednesday. Relations of the young nymph above, are also relations to Mr. Adams.

Mr. Adams sat down to supper with us on Thorsday even[ing] Augt. 6, in company with Mr. [Samuel] Torrey. Mr. Torrey craving a blessing, thanked God for the interview. This day his election sermon came out, and Augt. the 7th Friday morn, he gave me the errata, which was chiefly carried *away* in stead of carried with ambition. Supped with a new sort of fish called Conners, my wife had bought, which occasioned discourse on the subject. Mr. Adams returned thanks.

Wednesday, Augt. 19th 1685. I ride to the funeral of the Reverend Mr. Wm Adams from Roxbury, in the company of Mr. Hutchinson, [Peter] Sergeant and their wives. Magistrates there, Dept. Governour, Mr. Stoughton, Dudley, Richards, Cook; four of our [Harvard] class [of 1671], viz: Mr. [Peter] Thacher, [John] Bowls, [John] Norton, Self. I took one spell at carrying him. Is laid in Mr. Lusher's tomb. Mr. [John] Wilson prayed with the company before they went to the grave. Dyed a strong death about sun-rise on Monday morn.

Augt. 20, 1685, Mr. [Joshua] Moodey preaches from Ps. 74.9. There is no more any Prophet, with respect to four Ministers taken away in less than twice so many moneths; shewed that 'twas a peculiar aggravation to all other afflictions and fears. Mr. Edw. Taylor [another member of the Harvard class of 1671] lodges here this night, he hastened to town [from Westfield] against lecture-day that so might see Mr. Adams among the ministers after lecture; but coming, found me gone to his funeral.

Augt. 26. Mr. Condey the shipmaster dyes about 9 last night. Hath been sick but a little while.

Augt. 27. Mr. Thomas Bayly preaches in Mr. [Increase] Mather's turn. After lecture Capt. Condey buried. Gloves given to the magistrates.[15] Eight companies warned to train next Monday. Capt. [Jacob] Eliot also warns the troop.

---

[15]By the latter part of the seventeenth century, New England funeral customs had become both elaborate and expensive. One of the rituals associated with funerals was the giving of gloves, scarves, and rings by the family of the deceased to close friends, ministers, and important lay officials. David E. Stannard in *The Puritan Way of Death: A Study in Religion, Culture, and Social Change* (New York: Oxford Univ. Press, 1977), 113, estimates that funeral costs often consumed as much as 20 percent of the deceased's estate.

Friday, Augt. 28, 1685. Mr. [Capt. John] Foy arrives from London, about 8 weeks passage, brings news of Argyle's being taken; and of Monmouth's being in arms in England, with rumors of a great engagement and 30 or 40,000 slain, which Solomon Raynsford told us at dinner. 'Tis said there are black boxes sent to Mr. Stoughton, Dudley, [Peter] Bulkly, and [Richard] Wharton. Many are clapt up in London, so that the halls full.

This day Augt. 28 is a church meeting at which 'tis consented that persons may be taken in, the church [members] only being present, and not the congregation; at the same time Mr. Benj. Davis, Mr. Nath. Oliver and Mr. Saml Checkly were propounded.

Monday, Augt. 31. Eight companies and the troop train. Dine with the South-Company, Capt. Blackwell, Mr. Brown of Barbados, Mr. Tho. Bayly, Capt. Gerrish, Capt. John Higginson, Cous. Dummer trained. This morn commissioners chosen, and by reason of the training, persons came and delivering their votes went away, and some came not at all, so that was but nine persons when they were proclaimed and but eleven at any time in telling. Most had 61 votes, generally 50 odd. Mr. Nowell and my self present for 2. After went to see my sick Ensign, and staid while Mr. Willard went to prayer with him, his life is feared. A ten-pound horse was stabbed and killed with a pike this day, John Bemis's; company made a gathering 16s. In the South-Company, Mr. [James] Allen [of the First Church] prayed, 5–9 verses 149 Ps. sung.

Thorsday, Septr 3d My ensign Mr. Asaph Eliot dyes about 3 post meridiem, of a fever. Is to be buried next Satterday about 2 of the Clock. Mr. John Bayly preached the lecture. Several desirable persons are lately dead at Watertown in a week or two.

Friday, Septr 4, '85. about 6 aclock Mr. Asaph Eliot, Ensign of the South-Company was buried; 'twas rainy wether, but had 7 files pikes and 6 musketeers. Mr. Eliot was about 34 years old.

Sabbath-day, Septr 6. in the time of afternoon-exercise, a considerable gust of thunder, lightening, rain. Suppose this to be the day that a barn was burnt by it at Roxbury.

Tuesday Sept. 8. A porpus was pursued and taken within the inward wharfs.

Wednesday, 7[th month, or September, under the Julian calendar]: 9th. Dined at Mr. Dudley's in company of Counsellor Bond, Mr. Stoughton, Blackwell, Davie, Torrey, Willard, [Samuel] Shrimpton, El[iaki]m Hutchinson, [Nicholas] Paige, King, Allen, Mrs. Willard, Mrs. Paige. Mr. Hutchinson shewed me his letter concerning his mill at Piscataqua, wherein is sollicited to build a fort, lest the Indians burn it. When came home heard of a body of Indians near Chelmsford, 3 or 400. The rumors and fears concerning them do much increase.

The Indians are near Albany; Wonolanset brings the news to Chelmsford; and mistrusts of their mischievous designs.

Thorsday 7[th month]: 10th Mr. John Cotton preaches the lecture. After lecture Counsellor Bond dines with the Court, thanks them all for their curtesy and kindness to him. Goes off in Mr. [Thomas] Smith['s ship].

Sabbath-day Septr 13, 1685. Mr. Benj. Davis, Nathl Oliver, Saml Checkly and his wife are received into the Church, which is a Sabbath or 2 sooner than I expected: The Lord's Supper not being to be administered till Octr 4th. Saml Checkly had most in his relation [narrative]; two wear perriwigs; viz: Davis, Checkly. Mr. Bond with us to day. Were first propounded Augt. 28.

Sept. 14, 1685. Go to Cambridge, and there hear Mr. [Michael] Wigglesworth preach excellently from those words, Fight the good Fight of Faith, Lay hold on eternal Life. Capt. [James] Hill chosen Capt., Mr. Lynde Lieut., Mr. Williams of New-Cambridge Ensign. Mr. Hill I think will not accept. Coming home, hear of Meadfield Mill being burnt, and their confusion at Malborough last Satterday night. A suspected Indian is put in prison. It seems were in arms last Sabbathday at Dedham, somway knowing of Meadfield Mill being burnt. People are much perplexed.

Tuesday, Septr 15. Take leave of Mr. Bond and give him Mr. Oakes's Artillery [election] sermon to read at sea, stitched in marble paper. Sails in Mr. Smith.

Tuesday, Septr 15, 1685. Mr. [James] Barns tells me the Governour of Carolina is come to town this day for his health: is so weak that stumbled at a pebble and fell down. Name, [Joseph] West. Mr. Willard speaks to the 7th Commandment, condemns naked brests; and seems to be against the marriage of First-Cousins.

Thorsday, Septr 17. News comes to town of the rising of the Negros at Jamaica. Proves nothing answerable to the rumor.[16]

Generall Court having voted that care be taken to see that all per-

---

[16]In July of 1685, about 150 Jamaican slaves began a rebellion among the northern coast settlements of the island. Although colonial authorities proclaimed martial law and sent out patrols to contain and kill the rebels, slaves continued to resist throughout the early months of 1686. Jamaican slaves rebelled more frequently than slaves in other British American colonies. A combination of factors probably accounts for their rebelliousness: the high ratio of blacks to whites, the preponderance of native-born Africans among the Jamaican slaves, and the comparatively easy access to mountain hideaways on the north coast of the island.

sons are furnisht with arms and ammunition according to law because of Indians, that Wonolanset have £10 given him to appease [him], because he alledges some of his [goods were] carried away contrary to [promise of] safe conduct, and for his late service; that the west end of the Town-House be secured with lead at the country's charge, Court is adjourned to the 2d Wednesday in October at one of the clock. Timo[thy] Prout made surveyor general in Mr. [Anthony] Stoddard's room, to look after stock of powder &c. Mr. Dudley, [Nathaniel] Saltonstall, Buckley [Peter Bulkeley], to say whether they will accept their commissions as Majors.

Sabbath-day night, Septr. 20, 1685. Watch with Isaac Goose, and Cous. Nath. Dummer. Sam. Clark keeps on board his brother's ship, intending a voyage to sea, having no work in the shop.

Sabbath-day, Septr 20. Mr. John Baily preached with us all day: Mr. Willard at Watertown. In the afternoon from those words of Job, Till my Change come. Doct[rine] Death a very great change.

Monday, 7r [September] 21. Shewed Mr. Tho. Chiever, schoolmaster, in the evening, what had received from Jamaica concerning [Stephen] Zadori [from Hungary].

Tuesday, 7r 22. 1685. John Gardener came in late last night; this morning the news he brings runs throw the town, viz. that James late D[uke] of Monmouth was beheaded on Tower-Hill on the 15th July last. Argyle drawn, hanged and quartered. Neighbor Fifield brought me the news, who had it from the Cryer of Fish. Mr. Nowel and Moodey called here, having been to see sick father [Abel] Porter, this morn 7r 22.

7r 22. This day Mr. Morgan, his Lady and family arrive from Barbados intending to dwell here for some time. By the same ship word is brought of the death of Mr. Henry Higginson of the small pocks.

7r 22. In the afternoon I visit Father Porter, and Mr. West late Governor of Carolina, who comes hether for cure of the dry gripes.

Wednesday 7r 23. Cous. Nath. Dummer and I ride to Milton lecture. Before lecture, I went to Anthony Gulliver and got him to go with me to Penny-Ferry and shew me the marsh [he] was to buy of Mr. Gardener. He owned that he hired the marsh 6 acres of my father [John Hull] at fifty shillings and would see me paid; seemed to say he hired it for his son. Dined at Mr. Thacher's.

Wednesday night, Septr 23. Mr. [William] Clutterbuck arrives from New-Castle and brings word that he saw Argile's head cut off June the last; and the certain news of the death of Monmouth about the middle of July. Dissenters in the North released, and Scotland in quiet. 'Tis remarkable that Clutterbuck should from ocular testimony contradict diametrically the rumors that were spread in town Friday was sennight [a week ago] and strongly propagated, said to come by Clutterbuck; which was a meer Lye.

Laurence Vandenbosk Fr[ench Huguenot] minister marries [Giles] Sylvester and Widow Gillam; though had promised the Court to do no more such things: this about the beginning 7r [September]; is since gone to New York.

7r 25. Brother and Sister Stev. Sewall visit us. His Honour [Governor Bradstreet] visits the Carolina Governour.

7r 26. John Turner arrives from Newfound-Land, brings above 20 passengers, though his vessel so very small. 14 n[igh]ts passage.

Monday, Septr 28, 1685. Meeting of Boston-Freemen to chuse a Treasurer for the country. Mrs. Stanbury buried last night. The last high tide carried away the bridge at Cambridge, part of it; so that Cous. Fissenden now keeps a ferry there. Seth [Shove, Sewall's attendant] tells me 'tis that part the Town was to maintain. Friday was sennight, by a raft of boards.

Septr 29. Cous. Nath. Dummer goes to Salem in Capt. More to try to sell what remains of his goods, for fish there. Cous. Fissenden calls in, all were well lately at Newbury, he having visited them.

Thorsday, Octr 1, 1685. Mr. Samson Stoddard arrives, who came from London the 25. July: brings the particulars of the taking and exe-cuting of the late Duke of Monmouth whose head he saw struck off. Persons confined are now released.

Friday, Octr 2. go to Andrew Gardener's at Muddy River [Brookline] to gather chestnuts in company Mr. Dudley, Shrimpton, [Charles] Lid-get, [Humphrey] Luscomb: 3 last I knew nothing of till came to Rox-bury. Made us eat there after came from nutting.

Monday Octr 5. Cloudy lowring [threatening] day, yet the Artillery company goes over to Charlestown: the 2 companies train: we divide into 2, and with Cambridge Artillery oppose them upon the hill in prospect of the Harbour. Mr. Cotton Mather prayed with us in the morn, and at breaking up. Capt. Wade with his troop there: the Major Generall [Winthrop] with a small guard. Major Richards, Mr. Trea-surer, Mr. Nowel, Cook, dine with us at Jackson's [tavern]. Mr. Cotton Mather craves a blessing and returns thanks. Got over about dark.

Wednesday, 8r [October] 7th Meeting at our house, Mr. Zech. Walker speaks from Gen. 6. 8, 9 [But Noah found grace in the eyes of the Lord . . . and Noah walked with God] to very good purpose, shewing how may walk to be in a way of finding favour in God's sight. Last direct[ive] was to carry it as inoffensively as might towards men, that our own rashness and indiscretion might not be the cause of our suffering.

Thorsday, Octr 8. [Capt. Andrew] Dolebery arrives being 7 weeks this day from London: brings little news that I hear of; only 'tis rumored, we are not like to have an alteration of the Government this year. A youth about nine years old, son to Emmanuel Wishart, drowned this day. County court dissolved.

Satterday, Octr 10, 1685. We read in course the defeat of Adonija; and the illustrious coronation of King Solomon.

Sabbath-day, Octr 11. A day of sore rain almost all day long: rained very hard going to and from Meeting forenoon and all Meeting time till 2 aclock, and great part afternoon, and now at dark rains hard. Hath been cloudy, rainy, dark wether above this week; but this day exceeds. Eliza. Foxcroft baptised this afternoon.

Monday, Octr 12. South-Company trains, rest discouraged by the wet because thought could not perform their intended exercise.

Tuesday, Octr 13. Is a rumor in town of [Capt.] Jolls's being cast away on the Cape and all the passengers lost but five persons; Mr. [Edward] Randolph drowned: but suppose all groundless.[17]

Friday, Octr 16. The Reverend Mr. Michael Wigglesworth is chosen by the magistrates to preach the next Election-Sermon.

Satterday, Octr 17. Yesterday Mr. Stoughton and Dudley were grossly abused on the road by James Begelo of Watertown, and others. Begelo lay in gaol [jail] all night, and to day bound over to the county court first Tuesday in November. Court adjourned till Tuesday morning next; partly because of the designed training. Before adjournment the Deputies sent down a smart bill, alledging that they were no blameable cause of the laws not being printed.

Monday, Octr 19th Training of six companies. Exercise was taking of the fort and advancing white colours with red cross, above the red colours; so it stood while went to dinner. Then retaken. Firings on the Common: vollies to the Governour. About nine aclock at night news comes to town of Capt. [Daniel] Henchman's death at Worcester last

---

[17]Sewall and the other rumormongers were probably engaging in wishful thinking when they spread the word that Edward Randolph had drowned. Most inhabitants of Massachusetts tended to blame Randolph for the loss of their charter in 1684. Randolph served on Joseph Dudley's provisional council in 1685 and later on Edmund Andros's Dominion council. Arrested and jailed during the Glorious Revolution in Massachusetts, Randolph returned to England in 1690.

Thorsday; buried on Friday. Very few at his funeral; his own servants, a white and black, carried him to, and put him in his grave. His wife and children following and no more, or but one or two more.

Tuesday, Octr 20th Mr. Torrey here, prays with me and my wife in the morning. Great rain and storm.

Octr 21, 1685. Capt. John Phillips finally refuses to be Treasurer; the Magistrates chuse Mr. Nowel: but the Deputies would have it done by the freemen, that their priviledges may not be clipt, as many of them have of late been. Mr. Walker speaks at Mrs. [Sarah] Oliver's from Isa. 59, 19. When the Enemy shall come in like a Flood, &c., being the place propounded by said Oliver. Very rainy day. Dined 5 times, as suppose [i.e., I believe].

Wednesday, Octr 21. '85. very high tide, went into our cellar over the wharf; but did not fill it; filled several other cellars.

Thorsday, Octr 22. Deputies reassume their vote as to the Treasurer and consent with the magistrates, provided it be not drawn into an example: so after lecture Mr. Nowel took his Oath as Treasurer, having first made a worthy speech. The bill is passed that persons must be arrested 14 days inclusive before the Court. Court adjourned to the 3d Tuesday in November at one aclock: except there be some great occasion to convene sooner. A half money-rate and whole rate in country-pay passed. Mr. Mather preached from Ps. 73. 28. first part: 'Tis good for all to draw near to God. No thanks-giving this session.

Octr 31, 1685. Mrs. Prout, the mother, is buried; rain part of the way, so but a few comparatively at the grave; rainbow seen. Little Hull had a sore convulsion fit this day about noon, so that I was sent for home from Court; had another near sunset.

Satterday, Octr 31. in the even[ing] I read in course in the family Mr. [John] Norton's sermon on John 8. 20. Libr. 22. 8th 3d 1659. Doct[rine] All engagements of spirit and advantages notwithstanding, the changes that befall men, they come neither before nor after, but in the appointed hour, or the precise time, foreappointed of God. Sometime this week a virulent libel was fixed on Mr. Dudley's fence, extreamly abusive, especially to him.

Novr 3d Capt. Brown dines with the court. Giles Goddard is brought in not guilty respecting Mr. Nowel's trunks, lost in time of the fire. 1679.

Novr 3d James Begelo fined 10£ and Stebbin 5£ for their abuses to Mr. Stoughton and Dudley. To find bond for good behaviour till next court, then appear; fees of court, standing committed till performed.

Wednesday, Novr 4th The county court was adjourned to Thorsday come sennight at 2 aclock.

Mr. Allin preached Novr 5. 1685—finished his Text 1 John 1.9 [If we confess our sins, he is faithful and just to forgive us our sins]; mentioned not a word in prayer or preaching that I took notice of with respect to Gun-powder treason.[18] Part of the 132d. Ps. sung; viz. from 11th v. The Lord to David sware—to the end. In the even[ing] I met at Serjt [John] Bull's with Capt. [Theophilus] Frary, Serjt. [Andrew] Gardener, [John] Pell, [Solomon] Raynsford, Corpll Odlin, Quinsey, Paddy, Clerk Mason, Wheeler; ten mentioned sat down to supper, Serjt. Bull and his wife waited: After by the fire spake as to an ensign, all said they were unanimous for Serjt Gardener upon Serjt Bull's refusal, who alledged, as formerly, the loss of his 4th finger of his right hand, and a pain in the same shoulder; and as to me, is not of any church, nor a freeman, nor of estate, besides the former objections. Although it rained hard, yet there was a bonfire made on the Common, about 50 attended it.

Friday night being fair about two hundred hallowed about a fire on the Common.

Friday, Novr 6. Mr. Willard calls in and tells me of a thanks-giving intended by the ministers through[out] the colony upon the 3d of the next moneth; go to the Governour to get his approbation, which he doth not presently grant; but will speak of it in Council on Thorsday next; whether convenient for the churches generally to attend such a day without an order from authority, as usual. The difficulty of printing an order is, lest by putting in, or leaving out, we offend England. Having occasion this day to go to Mr. [John] Hayward the publick notary's house, I speak to him about his cutting off his hair, and wearing a perriwig of contrary colour; mention the words of our Saviour, Can ye not make one hair white or black; and Mr. [Vincent] Alsop's sermon. He alleges, the doctors advised him to [wear] it.

Sabbathday Novr 8. By Mr. Willard's prayer in the morn, I understood some minister was dead; enquiring at noon was told by my wife,

[18]In 1604–05, Guy Fawkes and others, disappointed with James I's unwillingness to advance the cause of Catholicism in England, conspired to seize power from him. The "Gunpowder Plot" was to culminate on November 5, 1605, with the blowing up of Parliament buildings containing the king, Lords, and Commons. The discovery of the plot inflamed anti-Catholic fears in England and led to the commemoration of November 5 as Guy Fawkes Day, during which the populace affirmed its allegiance to the king by burning effigies of Fawkes. Sewall's entry indicates that New Englanders annually made some sort of reference to the Gunpowder Plot. In 1685, however, given the recent revocation of the Massachusetts charter and the reservations expressed by Sewall and others regarding the arrival of a new imperial governor, the Gunpowder Plot may have reminded Bostonians of the regicidal intentions of Fawkes and his cohorts.

from Mr. Willard, that it was Mr. Nathaniel Chauncy of Hatfield. Was a learned godly man.

In the afternoon Mr. Willard ordained our brother Theophilus Frary to the office of a Deacon. Declared his acceptance Jany 11th first, and now again. Propounded it to the congregation at noon; then in even[ing] propounded if any of the Church or other had to object they might speak: Then took the Church's vote, then [Willard] called him [Frary] up to the pulpit, laid his hand on his head, and said I ordain thee &c., gave him his charge, then prayed, and sung the 2d part of the 84th Ps. 4 children baptised before the ordination. Thomas Eyre; William, Eliza, Joseph. So God in some measure is building our house when pulling down others.

Going to Mr. Willard's I understand Mr. Thomas Cobbet died last Thorsday even[ing], to be buried tomorrow Novr 9th; was abroad at some of his neighbours the Monday before. Mr. Chauncey died on Tuesday last. So two ministers dead this last week.

Monday Novr 9. Mr. Cobbet buried about 4 in the afternoon. Flight of snow. This day about 6 or 7 at night a male infant pinned up in a sorry cloth is laid upon the bulk [counter] of Shaw, the tobacco-man; great search made tonight and next day to find the mother, so far as I can hear this is the first child that ever was in such a manner exposed in Boston.

Thorsday, Novr 12. Mr. Moodey preaches from Isa. 57. 1. [The right-eous perisheth . . . none considering that the righteous is taken away from the evil to come.] Mr. Cobbet's funeral sermon; said also of Mr. Chauncy that he was a man of singular worth. Said but 2 of the First Generation left.

After, the ministers of this town come to the Court and complain against a dancing master [Francis Stepney] who seeks to set up here and hath mixt dances, and his time of meeting is lecture-day; and 'tis reported he should say that by one play he could teach more divinity than Mr. Willard or the Old Testament. Mr. Moodey said 'twas not a time for N.E. to dance. Mr. Mather struck at the root, speaking against mixt dances.

An order is made to summon Mr. Shrimpton to answer Mr. Sergeant by virtue of the new law, about the fathers will, next Monday 14 night, which is the last of Novr. Mr. Shrimpton and Sergeant differ about will. Eclipse at night. County court adjourned till this day 14 night. Governour's hat blew off and fell flat on the ground just as went to go in at his gate. Hath a new border which began to wear catechising day or Sabbath last, as I take it. Dept. Governour not in town. New almanack comes out this day intituled New-England's Almanack, by Mr. Danforth.

The ship Capt. Berry went out master of to Jamaica, came in this day; he dyed in the voyage and was buried in the sea.

Friday, Novr 13. Barington arrives, brings word of the beheading my Lady Lisle, Mrs. Hez. Usher's mother, at Winchester. 4 executed at London, Mr. Jenkins's son, Alderm[an] Hayes son, and 2 more, and whipping the Taunton maids.[19] Capt. Jolls dead in London. Is a rumor that the [Massachusetts] government will be changed this fall or winter, by some person sent over, or a commission to some here.

It seems there was a thanksgiving kept at Deacon Allin's this day, which knew not of till Satterday. Madam Usher there. Have a Gazette to the 24th of August which mentions the raising the siege of Grann, taking Newheusel, defeating the Turkish Army by the Imperialists.

This Friday night began to read the Revelation in course, having begun Pareus [David Pareus, *A Commentary upon the Divine Revelation of the Apostle and Evangelist John* (Amsterdam, 1644)] just about the same time though not on purpose.

Sabbath-day, Novr 15, 1685. In the afternoon Mary Smith, widow, Mr. [John] Wheelwright's grandchild, was taken into Church; then Mr. Willard mentioned what the Elders had done as to a thanks-giving, and propounded to the Church that we might have one on the first Thorsday in December: because had fasted, and God had graciously answered our prayers; so should meet Him in the same place to give thanks for that, and any other providence that hath passed before us. Silence gave consent, no one speaking.

Monday, Novr 16. Brother Stephen here, and gives an account of what had done at Kittery, for which was glad, but sorely saddened by Hullie's being taken with convulsion fits that evening. Gave of Dr. Winthrop's physick and cordials.

Tuesday evening: Mr. Moodey here, prays with us; then I go with him to see Madam Usher, expecting to have seen some prints, but had only a letter from a sister which reached to the day of condemnation [of Lady Lisle]. Mr. Moodey prayed there; took leave.

Wednesday, Novr 18. Uncomfortable Court day by reason of the extream sharp words between the Deputy Governour [Danforth] and Mr.

---

[19]Lady Alice Lisle was executed in the wake of the Duke of Monmouth's unsuccessful rebellion. Her daughter Bridget was married to Boston merchant Hezekiah Usher. The harshness of the punishments meted out to suspected sympathizers of Monmouth by Lord Chief Justice George Jeffreys made him notorious and contributed to the downfall of James II in 1688–89.

Stoughton, Dudley and others. Some essay to have put a sanction upon the appointment for a thanksgiving; but it fell throw. I argued 'twas not fit upon meer generals, as (the mercies of the year) to command a thanksgiving and of particulars we could not agree. Governour would have had one article for the peace of England, according to his Majesty's proclamation.

Hollowells business heard, as to land: about that grew the fierceness in discourse. Mr. G[eorge] Boroughs dined with us. Major Generall not well. Mr. [George] Shove [Seth's father] comes to town today; but I see him not.

Thorsday, Novr 19. Mr. Mather preaches from Numb. 25. 11. Shewed that love was an ingredient to make one zealous: those that received good people, received Christ, Mat. 25. Said that if the government of N.E. were zealous might yet save this people. 2d part of 79th Ps. sung. Madam Usher, her daughter and husband in mourning. Mr. Stoughton and Dudley called here. 'Tis reported that a frigot is to come yet before spring with a commission for a governor here, upon the place; Mr. Dudley is talked of and 'tis said healths are drunk to the new governor already, and were so Novr 17, the day the ship came in. I presented a bill for Serjt. Andrew Gardener to be ensign of the South-Company, which passed the magistrates, the whole Court.

Mr. Tho. Weld is approved by about 11 magistrates Novr 19th in his intended work of gathering a church the 16th of December next, Wednesday.

Friday Novr 20th a very rainy and dark day, and in the afternoon turns to a storm of snow: Court is adjourned to Tuesday, February 16th at one of the clock, except some frigot or ships arrival from England with his majesty's commands that may call for one sooner; then the Secretary, or if he sick or dead, the Treasurer, to send forthwith to the members of the Court, and to such others as freemen may chuse to convene two days after the date of such signification, to which time the Court is adjourned in such case. No freemen made, nor prayer. Ground covered with snow by that time Court done, which is even quite dark. Mr. Stoughton and Dudley not here today. 'Twas essayed again to have had a sanction put on the thanksgiving; but 'twas again pleaded, to do it without mentioning particular causes would be to impose too much on those commanded: so fell.

Monday night Novr 23, 1685. I go the rounds [night watch] with Cous. Quinsey and Isaac Goose, a very severe night for cold, yet 'twas fair and comfortable; came home at 5 *mane* [in the morning].

Novr 25, Wednesday. Just before I went to the meeting at Brother

Hayward's, where I was to speak from Ps. *79. 8* [O remember not against us former iniquities . . . for we are brought very low], John Turner, master of the brigenteen, came in and told me that James Mudge, one of his seamen, having carried a pass to the Castle, coming on board again, fell between the boat and brigenteen into water and was drowned. He several years since gave his daughter to Capt. Chips daughter at Charlestown. Thawing wether.

Novr. 26, Thorsday. Nurse [Susanna] Goose dyes about 2 or 3 aclock in the night; having lien sick about a week; was here it seems Wednesday was sennight. Was helpful to her self all along till this last sickness; washt her own cloaths. She saw her great grandchildren; was a good woman.

Mary an Indian, James's Squaw, was frozen to death upon the [Boston] Neck near Roxbury gate on Thorsday night Novr 27th 85, being fudled [drunk].

Novr. 30. Nurse Goose buried. Was not well yesterday, feverish and tossing most of the night; so not at the Court nor meeting of magistrates, nor at the funeral. Mr. Willard here, I returned [Reverend Vincent] Alsop['s sermon] of Scandal. Mr. Secretary here.

At night viewed the eclipse, which in the total obscuration was ruddy; but when began to receive some light, the darkish ruddiness ceased. Horizon somewhat hazy. Read in course the Eleventh of the Revelation.

30 Novr Cous. Nath. Dummer visits us.

Wednesday, Decr 2. Elias Parkman comes in, and hath a man drowned near the Castle, as E[liaki]m [Mather] tells me. See last Wednesday.

Friday, Decr 4th Being at Mr. [Isaac] Addington's upon business, he tells me Mr. Shrimpton's answer in writing last Monday was, that the Court proceeded upon a law made since the vacating [of] the charter, and therefore he should not attend; so that this Monday we [the government under the old charter] begin palpably to dye.[20]

Sabbath-day, December 6. Hull hath a convulsion fit as he sits in his

---

[20]See Sewall's entry for November 12 above. Samuel Shrimpton inherited an estate worth nearly £12,000 when his father, Henry, died in 1666. By this time in 1685, he was probably the richest man in Boston, with vast property holdings and a trading operation that included the exportation of fish and logwood and the importation of manufactures. The particulars of the dispute between Peter Sergeant and Shrimpton are unknown; however, the latter's insistence that the revocation of the corporate charter had disqualified the Court of Assistants from sitting in judgment on him was clear evidence of the unsettledness of the Massachusetts government at this time. As we shall see, Shrimpton would be summoned by the Court in early 1686 to answer to charges of sedition.

grandmother's lap at table, dining, with which we are much surprised. *Monday, Decembr 7th 1685.* About one in the night my wife is brought to bed of a son, of which Mother Hull brings me the first news; Mrs. [Elizabeth] Weeden midwife.

Wednesday Decr 9th 1685. Our neighbor Gemaliel Wait eating his breakfast well, went to do something in his orchard, where Serjt. Pell dwells, there found him self not well and went into Pell's his tenant's house, and there dyed extream suddenly about noon, and then was carried home in a chair, and means used to fetch him [back to life] again, but in vain. To the children startled about him he said, here is a sudden change, or there will be a great change, to that purpose. Was about 87 years old, and yet strong and hearty; had lately several new teeth. People in the street much startled at this good man's sudden death. Govr [Thomas] Hinkley [of Plymouth Colony] sent for me to Mr. [Edward] Rawson's just as they were sending a great chair to carry him home.

Satterday, Decr 12, '85. Father Wait buried; magistrates and ministers had gloves. There heard of the death of Capt. Hutchinson's child by convulsions, and so pass to the funeral of little Samuel Hutchinson about six weeks old, where also had a pair of funeral gloves.

Peter Butler comes in this day, several have had the small pocks; buried a Negro. Several very green, hardly recovered; among whom Nathl Parkman is one. Snowy day.

Esther Kein at her time [in childbirth], falls into convulsion fits, and dyes last Thorsday; no likelihood of the child's being born.

Sabbath-day, Decembr 13th 1685. Mr. Willard [of the South Church] baptizeth my son lately born, whom I named Henry; David Stoddard, the son of Mr. Simeon Stoddard, was baptized next, and then several other grown children. Nurse Hill came in before the Psalm was sung, and yet the child was fine and quiet; Mr. Willard preached from John 15th, 8. Herein is my Father glorified, that you bear much fruit, so shall ye be my disciples; which is the first sermon my little son hath been present at.

Monday, Dec. 14. County-court meets about Mr. Sergeant's business chiefly; Mr. Shrimpton's letter [contending that laws made after the revocation of the old charter were without legal foundation] is read; but 'tis not agreed on to proceed, and some heat, the vote being in a manner equal. Mr. Stoughton and Majr. Richards not there. Mr. Shrimpton pleads that he has fullfilled his father's will dated July 17th one thousand six hundred and six, and cannot submit to this arbitrary way, especially the law being made since the dissolution of the charter of this place. Govr. seems somewhat resolute; the Court adjourned till Thorsday; something of Bushnell, the barber's, relating to his estate was now also done. He dyed in '67 just about the same time Mr. [John] Wilson [former minister of the First Church] did, as I remember.

This Monday a jury is summond who sit on the body of Joseph Johnson, and the verdict they find, a wound an inch or 2 above his navel which they judge to be the cause of his death, and that they were informed James Morgan did it with a spit. So were sworn in Court Decr 14, 1685, and James Morgan ordered to have irons put on him. He committed the fact last Thorsday night.

Wednesday, Dec. 16. A very pleasant day for gathering the church at Dunstable, and ordaining Mr. Thomas Weld.

Thorsday, Decr 17th Mr. Mather preacheth from Mat. 16, former part of the 25th verse. For whosoever will save his Life shall Lose it. At county-court nothing done in Mr. Sergeant's business; so he makes a speech when the court open, that if the court did nothing they would give him a record of it, that he might go elsewhere for he would not be kept out of his money; speaking warmly.

Mr. Francis Stepney, the dancing master, desired a Jury, so he and Mr. Shrimpton bound in 50£ to January Court. Said Stepney is ordered not to keep a dancing school; if he does will be taken in contempt and be proceeded with accordingly. Mr. Shrimpton muttered, saying he took it as a great favour that the court would take his bond for £50.

Sabbath, Decr 13, 1685. John Maryon, the father, faints in the Old Meetinghouse [First Church], in time of worship, which obstructs Mr. [Reverend James] Allen, and makes considerable disturbance.

Decr 17. One Trescot, an ancient woman of Dorchester, riding over the Neck, tide being high, her horse drowned and she hardly saved; questioned whether she may live or no. This night Little Hull hath a convulsion fit, as he lay with me in bed. Henry very restless.

Friday, Decembr 18, 1685. Father John Odlin, one of the very first inhabitants of Boston, dies; know not of above one more [of the first generation still alive] besides the Governour [Bradstreet].

Satterday, Decr 19th Father John Odlin buried in the first burying place as father Wait the Satterday before.

Friday Dec. 18. Begun in course to read the New-Testament, having ended the Revelation the night before.

Satterday Dec. 19. Mr. Willard prayes with my little Henry, being very ill.

Sabbath-day, Dec. 20. Send notes to Mr. Willard and Mr. Moodey to pray for my child Henry.

Monday, about four in the morn the faint and moaning noise of my child forces me up to pray for it.

21. Monday even[ing] Mr. Moodey calls. I get him to go up and pray with my extream sick son.

Tuesday Morn, Dec. 22. Child makes no noise save by a kind of snoaring as it breathed, and as it were slept.

Read the 16th of the first Chron. in the family. Having read to my wife and nurse out of John, the fourteenth chapter fell now in course, which I read and went to prayer. By that time had done, could hear little breathing, and so about sun-rise, or little after, he fell asleep, I hope in Jesus, and that a Mansion was ready for him in the Father's House. Died in Nurse Hill's lap. Nurse Hill washes and layes him out; because our private meeting hath a day of prayer tomorrow, Thursday Mr. Willard's lecture, and the child dying after sunrise (wether cloudy), have determined to bury on Thursday after lecture. The Lord sanctify his dispensation, and prepare me and mine for the coming of our Lord, in whatsoever way it be. Mr. Tho. Oakes our physician for this child. Read the 16th chap. of the First Chronicles in the family.

Tuesday night read the 15th John in the chamber, out of which Mr. Willard took his text the day Henry was baptized; in the family, the 3d of Matthew, both requiring fruit.

Wednesday, Dec. 23. Go to the private fast at Brother [Nathaniel] Williams's. Capt. [Joshua] Scottow begins and is enlarged and fervent in praying for the church and Christ's witnesses: Made me conclude. Sung part 137. Ps. But if I Jerusalem, &c. Just before I went, Brother [William] Longfellow [husband of Sewall's sister Anne] came in, which was some exercise to me, he being so ill conditioned and so outwardly shabby. The Lord humble me. As I remember, he came so before; either upon the funeral of my father [John Hull] or Johnny [the Sewall's first child].

Thorsday, Decr 24th 1685. We follow Little Henry to his grave: governour and magistrates of the county here, 8 in all, beside my self, eight ministers, and several persons of note. Mr. [Samuel] Phillips of Rowley here. I led Sam., then Cous. [Ephraim] Savage led Mother [Jane Dummer Sewall], and Cousin [Jeremiah] Dummer led Cous. [Daniel] Quinsey's wife [Ann], he not well. Midwife Weeden and Nurse Hill carried the corpse by turns, and so by men in its chestnut coffin 'twas set into a grave (the tomb full of water) between 4 and 5. At lecture the 21 Psalm was sung from 8th to the end. The Lord humble me kindly in respect of all my enmity against Him, and let his breaking my image in my son be a means of it. Considerable snow this night. At night little Hull had a sore convulsion fit.

Friday-morn Dec. 25. [Hull] had another [fit]; wave upon wave. Mr. Phillips prayes with Hullie. Receive news this 25th Dec. that Brother Stephen Sewall hath a son.

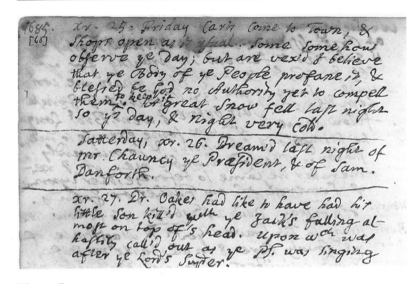

Figure 7.
Sewall diary entries for December 25, 26, 27, 1685. Courtesy, Massachusetts Historical Society, Boston.

Dec. 25. Friday. Carts come to town and shops open as is usual. Some somehow observe the day; but are vexed I believe that the body of the people profane it, and blessed be God no Authority yet to compell them to keep it.[21] A great snow fell last night so this day and night very cold.

Satterday, Dec. 26. Dreamed last night of Mr. [Charles] Chauncy, the President [of Harvard], and of Sam. Danforth.

Dec. 27. Dr. Oakes had like to have had his little son killed with the jack's falling almost on top of his head. Upon which was hastily called out as the Psalm was singing after the Lord's Supper.

Dec. 28. Cous. Fissenden here, saith he came for skins last Friday, and [noticed there] was less Christmas-keeping than last year, fewer shops shut up.

Dec. 30th An Indian man is found dead on the Neck with a bottle of

[21] Puritan New Englanders shunned the celebration of the holy days of the Anglican church. "Bacchanallian Christmasses" especially, John Cotton said, had degenerated into days of "revelling, dicing, carding, masking, mumming, consumed in compotations, in interludes, in excess of wine, in mad mirth." Alice Morse Earle, *Customs and Fashions in Old New England* (1893; reprint, Williamstown, Mass.: Corner House Publishers, 1969), 214. Sewall was especially concerned about Christmas celebrations in 1685 because the General Court, in response to the revocation of the colony's charter, had recently annulled several laws, including a 1659 statute "against keeping Christmas."

rum between his legs. Fast at Charlestown this day. Mr. Cotton Mather preaches forenoon, mentions the notion Mede [Reverend Matthew Mead] has about America's peopling. Mr. Moodey preaches afternoon excellently. Hull (as suppose) hath a sore fit in the night; but I asleep, and find it by the effects.

Dec. 31. Mr. Allen preaches from 2 Tim. 2. 19. [Let every one that nameth the name of Christ depart from iniquity.] Saith should pray for the Natives that they may name Christ. Spoke against observing the 25. Instant, called it Antichristian heresie: Spoke against the name [Christmas]. Canker began in the tongue.

Diary

1686

Satterday, Jany 2d Last night had a very unusual dream; viz. That our Saviour in the dayes of his flesh when upon earth, came to Boston and abode here sometime, and moreover that He lodged in that time at Father Hull's; upon which in my dream had two reflections. One was how much more Boston had to say than Rome boasting of Peter's being there. The other a sense of great respect that I ought to have shewed Father Hull since Christ chose when in town, to take up His quarters at his house. Admired the goodness and wisdom of Christ in coming hither and spending some part of His short life here. The chronological absurdity never came into my mind, as I remember.

Jany 1. 1686 finished reading the godly learned ingenious [David] Pareus on the Revelation.

Satterday, Jany 2. discoursed with Ralf Carter about [the tree] *Lignum Vitae* [wood of life]. He saith thinks 'tis found no where but in America, there a common wood at Antego [Antigua] and other places. Is physical [medicinal].[1]

---

[1] Sewall's dream and his comments about *Lignum Vitae* reflect his belief that America was God's chosen land. In 1688, Sewall explained further his interest in a tree with curative powers: "If the tree of life mentioned in the two and twentieth of the Revelation should be found growing and flourishing in Antego, which doth so plentifully produce Lignum Vitae, how proper and proportionable would Gods providences appear to be." Sewall to Nathaniel Barns, October 26, 1688, in *Letter-Book of Samuel Sewall,* Massachusetts Historical Society *Collections,* 6th series, 1–2 (Boston, 1886–1888), 1:90.

January 5th The infant exposed the beginning of the winter, is buried this day. Mr. [Joshua] Moodey [of the First Church] and his wife visit us after the catechising. He full of great pain.

Thorsday, Janr 7th Mr. Moodey preached excellently from those words, Ye are my friends if ye do what I command you: Exhorted not to disown Christ when in adversity, i.e. his members in a low condition. A very blustering, snowy day that hindered many from going to Meeting, which took special notice of in prayer; and God's letting us stand another year in His vinyard. At his lecture this day twelvemonth we had the newes of our charter's being condemned, just as going to meeting. Some coming over the Neck to day, had much ado to find the way.

Satterday, Janr 9th A very great storm of snow and wind. Mr. Tho. Oakes here, who tells me there is news come to town of the French king's death.[2]

Sabbath-day afternoon. My wife goes to meeting, which is the first time since her lying-in [7 December 1685].

Tuesday, January 12. I dine at the Governour's [Simon Bradstreet], where Mr. [Joseph] West, Governour of Carolina, Capt. [John] Blackwell, his wife and daughter, Mr. Morgan, his wife and daughter, Mis. Brown, Mr. Eliakim Hutchinson, and wife, Mr. Peter Sergeant, and wife, Mr. Secretary [Edward Rawson], and S. S. Mrs. Mercy sat not down, but came in after dinner well dressed and saluted the two daughters. Madam Bradstreet and Blackwell sat at the upper end together, Governor at the lower end. I sat next Mis. Frances, Capt. Blackwell's daughter. After dinner Madam Blackwell swooned, or very ill, so was lead into the chamber.

Wednesday, Janr 13th very cold day. Meeting at Brother Allen's; I speak from Eph. 4.3 [Endeavouring to keep the unity of the Spirit in the bond of peace].

Thorsday exceeding cold; Mr. John Bayly preaches the lecture for Mr. [Increase] Mather from Eccles. 9. 10. Whatever thy hand, &c. After lecture the court sat, and adjourned till Tuesday 1 aclock, to hear Mr. Shrimpton's case, i.e. Mr. Sergeant's complaint against him. Mr. Shrimpton resolves to appeal to the Court of Assistants upon the pleas he hath made. Mr. [William] Stoughton, [Joseph] Dudley, and Mr. Thomas called here; their horses all broke away, and fain to run beyond Capt. [Theophilus] Frary's before any had stopt, it being night and excessive cold.

Satterday, January 16. Notwithstanding the three very severe nights last past and snow in abundance lately fallen, yet, by reason of the

[2]An inaccurate report of the death of Louis XIV.

spring tides, and wind 2 of the nights, the harbour remains fairly open, and the channel between the Castle [fort on Castle Island] and Dorchester Neck; though much loose ice floating up and down. Isaiah Tay told me yesterday, that the 17th January last year he went on the ice to the Castle, and nine hundred were told by their company going and coming on the ice, and at the Island.

Sabbathday, Janr 17th 1686. Rain and thaw all day. This day Mr. [Samuel] Willard [of the South Church] begins to preach upon the 11th of the Hebrews. Faith is the substance, &c.

Wednesday Janr 20th Went to Dorchester lecture. Mr. [John] Danforth preached from Rev. 22. 17. Said that chapter treated of Heaven, that Christ dyed for mankind.

[*January 21*] On Tuesday last the Court [of Assistants] sat, and as it fell out, I was not there. Agitation was about Mr. Shrimpton's business. 2 *pro.* 2 *con.* of those that pretended to vote; Mr. [Isaac] Addington knew not what to enter. Governour [Bradstreet], Mr. Stoughton and Dudley went away thinking the Court ended; 'tis said Mr. [Humphrey] Davie gone also but called back, and he, Mr. [Elisha] Cook and C[apt. Elisha] Hutchinson adjourned the Court to the Governour's that evening, and from thence 'twas adjourned to the Town-House on Thursday after Lecture, Janr 21. Was very hot discourse about the irregular pretended adjournment of the Court. Mr. Stoughton and Dudley fell especially on Mr. Cook. After much hot dispute nothing at last done as I know. Mr. Stoughton argued the new law was not determinal and so worth nothing, and that the ordinary [Court of Assistants] could not act after an award and mutual agreement as was produced in this case; must be relieved by some superiour court, as Chancery. Thus the symptoms of death are on us [i.e., on the institutions established under the old charter].[3] This morn about 5, Hull had a fit. Mr. Willard preached excellently from *Buy the Truth.* Must have a care of being

---

[3]In March, the Court of Assistants would issue a summons to Samuel Shrimpton to answer the charge that he had "in a proud & contemptuous manner declared himself that there was no Governor & Company . . . & therefore he would make no answer" to the court in a matter pertaining to his civil case. When Shrimpton appeared before the court in April, he reiterated his earlier statement to the effect that "there is no Governor and Company of this place in being," that the "Governor had a signification of the dissolution of the charter of this colony," and that, therefore, he "was not willing to submit to laws" enacted since the revocation. Shrimpton's words, which a grand jury said he "repeated over & over again with diverse other seditious words & expressions," resulted in his being indicted for causing "such a tumult in the Court as evidently tended to the high breach of his Majesties government here & . . . to the peace of our Sovereign Lord the king." *Records of the Court of Assistants of the Colony of the Massachusetts Bay, 1630–1692,*

cheated, our natures encline to falshood. Must not take great men, rulers, for our rule, but the written word of God. Must have no man's person in admiration. Mr. Stoughton and Dudley called here. It seems Mr. [Jeremiah] Hubbard's son of Long Island, presented a gun at his sister and it went off and killed her. Cous. Fissenden tells me there is a maid at Woburn who 'tis feared is possessed by an evil spirit. Mr. [Jacob] Eliot not at lecture Janr 21, which I think is the 3d day of his absence.

Friday, Janr 22. Hull hath another fit about 5 or 6 *mane* [in the morning], and is extream ill after it. Mr. Willard prays with him in the evening, Capt. [Joshua] Scottow present. Joseph Redknap of Lin buried, being about 110 years old; was a wine-cooper in London, was about 30 years old at the great frost. Ralph King *teste* [witness].

Sabbath, Janr 24. Friday night and Satterday were extream cold, so that the harbour frozen up, and to the Castle. This day so cold that the sacramental bread is frozen pretty hard, and rattles sadly as broken into the plates.

Monday, Janr 25. I call in Andrew Gardiner and deliver him his commission for ensign, he disabling himself, I tell him he must endeavour to get David's heart; and that with his stature will make a very good ensign. Capt. Scottow present, to whom have lent my gr. testament, and Governor Pen. Mrs. Harris and Baker present their mutual offences against each other as to their seating, before Mr. Willard and the overseers.[4]

Tuesday, Janr 26. Walked [kept watch] with Isaac Goose and Cous. [Daniel] Quinsey: though the snow extream deep by reason of this

---

3 vols. (Boston, 1901–1928), 1:297–99. The court apparently was dissolved before it could rule on Shrimpton's case. It is interesting to note that although Shrimpton welcomed the collapse of the Puritan establishment and the rule of the provisional government in 1686, even to the point of hosting the first marriage performed by an Anglican clergyman in New England (see the entry below for May 18), by 1689 he had come to oppose Edmund Andros and the Dominion of New England. Because Andros filled the council with his favorites, many of whom were New Yorkers unknown to the inhabitants of Massachusetts, Shrimpton and other prominent Boston merchants joined the revolution against the Dominion. See Bernard Bailyn, *The New England Merchants in the Seventeenth Century* (Cambridge, Mass.: Harvard Univ. Press, 1955; New York: Harper and Row, 1964), 176, 192–93.

[4]Seats in New England meetinghouses were assigned to members, sometimes by specially chosen seating committees, on the basis of social standing in the community. Consequently, as Ola Elizabeth Winslow points out in *Meetinghouse Hill, 1630–1783* (New York: Macmillan, 1952; New York: W. W. Norton, 1972), 142, "lotting out" the seats was the seventeenth-century equivalent of the current-day social register. Where one sat in the meetinghouse was thus a sensitive issue capable of dividing a congregation.

day's snow and what was before, yet had a very comfortable night. Nehemiah Perce's wife is brought to bed of a daughter.

Wednesday, Janr 27. Peter Butler is non-suited in suing for his 500£ legacy, at which I doubt Mr. [Samuel] Nowell [Butler's stepfather and a member of the Court of Assistants] and his wife [Butler's mother Mary Butler Usher Nowell] grieved. Is talk of a ship below and some think it may be [Capt. Thomas] Jenner from London.

Thorsday, January 28. Mr. Jenner having lodged at Capt. [Roger] Clap's last night, with Mr. [Andrew] Belcher and others, come near twenty together to Serjt. [John] Bull's over the ice and bring the news of the Rose frigot ready to come and bring Mr. [Edward] Randolph, who is to be Deputy Governour, and Mr. [Joseph] Dudley Governour. Sheriff Cornish executed [in London], and a woman burnt about the [Popish] Plot and such like treason.[5] The town much filled with this discourse. Jenner came from Isle Wight the 13 of November. When Mr. Jenner came in the magistrates went all off the bench to hear his news in the lobby. Mr. Addington also came in. Isa. 33.17 was preached from, by Mr. Cotton Mather. Thine eyes shall see the King, &c. whose sermon was somewhat disgusted for some expressions; as, sweet-sented hands of Christ, Lord High Treasurer of Ethiopia, Ribband of Humility—which was sorry for, because of the excellency and seasonableness of the subject, and otherwise well handled. Doct[rine] 'Tis a matchless priviledg to behold Christ in his beauty. Mr. Eliot not at lecture. Mr. Jenner rumors that the Oxford frigot is to come in the spring, and bring a Governour from England, and that one Vincent, brother to the minister, most talked of; which Mr. Dudley laughs at.

Friday, Janr 29th Isaac Goose proves his mother's will. Mr. Belcher dines with the Court. It seems there's a discourse that the K[ing] should motion to have all the Negroes at Jamaica baptized. Mr. Francis Stepney [dancing teacher] has his jury to try his speaking blasphemous words; and reviling the government. 'Tis referred till next Tuesday.

Sabbath, Janr. 31, 1686. 125th Psalm sung by us in course in the family, They that trust in the Lord, &c. In publick *mane* the 56th from 8th verse, *ad finem* [to the end], of all my wanderings, &c. Mr. Willard speaking of faith, instanced in things past before we had a being, and things to be, as destruction of the man of sin, seemed very much concerned for God's people. Madam Br[idget] Usher taken into the First

---

[5]On Titus Oates's revelations about the existence of a plot to replace Charles II with his Catholic brother James II; see footnote 12 on p. 82.

Church, and Mr. [Daniel] Royse taken in and baptized in the North Church. Gallant warm thawing weather.

Feb. 1. Nath. Man brings me a letter wherein am told of my Brother St[ephe]n child's death last Friday about noon. Had from the Satterday before till then more than 200 fits.

Feb. 1 In the afternoon a great cake of ice comes from Cambridge-ward and jostles away the body of ice that lay between the outward wharfs and Noodle's Island: so now our harbour open again.

Feb. 2. Several ships sail. This day Return Wait is by sentence of Court turned out of his Marshal's place, many complaints coming against him. The persons injured left to their remedy in law against him.

Wednesday, Feb. 3. Mr. Henry Phillips is buried with arms, he having been an ensign at Dedham, and in Boston several years of Capt. Oliver's company. Capt. Hutchinson led the souldiers, his and Capt. [Penn] Townsend's company springing of said Oliver's. Capt. Townsend and Capt. [James] Hill each of them trailed a pike: were about 24 files, 4 deep. Snow very deep; so in the New-burial place [Copp's Hill], 3 paths, 2 for the 2 files of souldiers, middlemost for the relations. Edw. Cowel and Mr. [John] Winchcomb go before the Governour. Return Wait is refused though I see he was there. About eight of the South-Company there attending. Bearers, Deacon [Jacob] Eliot, [Robert] Saunderson, [Deacon Henry] Allen, [Joseph] Bridgham, [Deacon Theophilus] Frary, and Mr. [Ezekiel] Chiever.

Thorsday Feb. 4. Francis Stepney fined 100£. 10£ down, the rest respited till the last of March, that so might go away if he would. He appeals; Mr. Shrimpton and [Humphrey] Luscombe his sureties. Mr. Moodey preaches from Luke 12. 4. Especially this day from those words, My friends [Be not afraid of them that kill the body, and after that have no more that they can do].

Friday, Feb. 5. Fast at Cous. [Jeremiah] Dummer's: I and Mother [Hull] there.

Sabbath, Febr. 7th 1686. Went to the first Meeting House [First Church] both parts of the day, sat down there at the Lord's Table. Mr. Moodey preached from Isa. 12. 1. beginning upon that Scripture this day—In that day thou shalt say, &c. shewing that 'twas chiefly a directory of thanksgiving for the conversion of the Jews; and that should get our praises ready before hand. Very warm day, and so till Wednesday Feb 10, when Mr. Willard preaches at Maccartas from Rom. 8.1 [There is therefore now no condemnation to them which are in Christ]. Seems very sensible of the countries danger as to changes.

Febr. 12th Ice breaks up from Gill's Wharf.

Febr. 13th Satterday, pretty well clear our dock of ice by a passage cut open. Shut up about 7 weeks. [Capt. John] Balston sails. An Indian squaw died on the Neck last night. Mr. [John] Eyre's little son dyed, went well to bed; dyed by them in the bed. It seems there is no symptom of overlaying [being accidentally smothered].

Sabbath-day, Febr. 14. Little Hull speaks *Apple* plainly in the hearing of his grandmother [Judith Hull] and Eliza Lane; this the first word. At the burial of Mr. Eyr's child, Mr. Moodey discoursed of the grievous spreading of the small pocks in, and round about Portsmouth, at Exeter, &c.

Tuesday, Feb. 16, 1686. Generall Court meets. Dine 3 times. Is a discourse this day of a strange beast killed at Middletown, or 4 miles off that place, last Dec., 10 foot his tail, as tall as a two year and vantage horse; had a dead horse and two dear lay at its den, and Indians waiting for him, at last saw him coming with another in its mouth, as a cat carries a mouse almost. Indian shot him down.[6] Great disorder in the town by cock-skailing;[7] I grant 2 warrants. Tho. Barnard has one, and James Barns the other, whereby several companies broke up; but for want of a law and agreement shall find much ado to suppress it.

Mr. Eliot at meeting on lecture day.

The Arrow against dancing comes out.[8]

Friday the Court adjourns to the 11th of May on the conditions of former adjournment. The law about wills is made in a new edition. Some freemen made, and I think Sam. Chekly an ensign. Order for a fast to be on March 25, 1686. Great heat about the libel, and Mr. Clark's fine the occasion of the discourse at this time.

Satterday, Febr. 20. I send for Edw. Cowel and blame him for his ill carriage at Richd. White's wedding, Dec. 10. He denys the fact, and saith he came not nigh her (i.e. the bride) and stooped down only to take up his hat taken off in the crowd.

Wednesday, Feb. 24. Privat meeting at our house: Mr. Willard preached excellently from Act. 1.7 [It is not for you to know the times or the seasons]. I had prayed before, privatly, and he prayed at the Meeting in the very same words, that God would make our houses bethels [houses of God]. Question was, How shall we attend known duty with cheerfullness and constancy, though God impart not so much

---

[6]Sewall later noted in the margin of his entry: "all untrue."

[7]Cock-skailing or cock-throwing was a game played on Shrove Tuesday in which the participants threw sticks at a cock tied to a post, the object being to knock it down and kill it.

[8]Increase Mather, *An Arrow against Profane and Promiscuous Dancing* (Boston, 1684). Mather's pamphlet, written for the "Ministers of Christ at Boston in New-England," was directed against the activities of dancing master Francis Stepney.

of his counsel to us as we could desire? Which Mr. Willard propounded and opened excellently, shewing the reference to the foregoing and following verse, as was desired. Many people present.

Thorsday, Feb. 25. The law about wills and administrations is published [announced]; and almost as soon as the drum had done beating, Mr. [Peter] Serj[ean]t comes with his petition; and an order is made for a hearing next Monday, 3 weeks, the 22d of March; some would have had it sooner, and Mr. [Samuel] Nowel and self thought it very indecent that it was so soon, especially considering, the order made upon a law scarce yet out of the marshal's mouth.

Mr. John Winchcombe is made Marshal of Suffolke, his oath is given him; and the Marshal Generall [John Green] declares it. Very rainy fore-noon, and dark most part of the day.

Sabbath-day, Feb. 28. A jury is summoned to sit upon the body of Sarah, daughter of Henry and Mary Flood, about 13 weeks old, for that said Mary was suspected of murder. So now 3 in prison for suspected murder.

Tuesday, March 2. Brother St[ephen Sewall] and wife visit us. Mr. Chickly [Anthony Checkley] is cast in his attaint. Morgan, Indian and Flood put upon tryal.[9]

Wednesday, March 3d James Morgan is brought in guilty by the jury, Saml Phips Fore-Man. Mr. [Edward] Wyllys cast by Anna Haugh, as to Haugh's farm. Mr. Stoughton calls at night and shews me the names of the persons in the commission, telling me that a copy of the commission is come to town. Comes by [Capt.] Eldridge, who bore away to Montserrat. The address sent to his present Majesty, is sent back to

---

[9]Anthony Checkley was seeking to have a jury verdict against him reversed; he "attainted the jury of 17 Sept [16]85 for errors & mistakes." Sewall and the other members of the Court of Assistants, meeting in March of 1686, considered the "evidences in the case" and upheld the earlier verdict of the jury. The March session of the court also ruled on the cases of James Morgan, Joseph Indian, and Mary Flood. Morgan was brought to trial for the murder of Boston butcher Joseph Johnson. (See the entry above for December 14, 1685.) He pleaded not guilty to the charge of "running a spit into his [Johnson's] belly a little above the navel of which wound about three days after the said Johnson died." The jury, after considering the evidence against Morgan, found him guilty, and the court sentenced him to be "hanged by the neck till you be dead." Mary Flood, the wife of Boston cordwainer Henry Flood, was indicted for murdering her "youngest daughter about thirteen weeks old by giving it several strokes of her fist." The jury found her not guilty. Joseph Indian was on trial for murdering "his squaw or wife" by inflicting "several mortal wounds on her head." Although the jury found him not guilty on the charge of murder, they convicted him of "unnaturalness and barbarous cruelty towards his wife." The court sentenced Joseph "to be severely whipt with thirty stripes and also pay forty shillings . . . within a week or be sold by the treasurer out of this country to any of his majesties plantations discharging your prison fees." *Records of the Court of Assistants,* 1:282, 287, 294–96.

Mr. Dudley by Mr. [Robert] Humphrys [London attorney for Massachusetts]. Sabbath-day, or Monday, we hear of the death of Abel Porter and above 60 more, going from Scotland to Pensilvania. Tuesday, March 2, hear of the death of Jeremiah Green at Salt Tatoodas [Tortugas]; was a hopefull young shipmaster, Mr. Nathaniel's son.

Thorsday, March 4. Mr. Moodey preaches. After lecture, James Morgan is condemned to dye: He said was murdered; but spake not of appealing, which I expected he might.

Friday 5. Joseph Indian is acquitted. James Morgan is sent to, and acquainted that he must dye next Thorsday, and ordered that Mr. [Increase] Mather be acquainted with it who is to preach the [execution-day] lecture.[10] Mr. Stoughton and Dudley voted not in the judgment, and went off the bench when sentence was to be passed. Major [John] Richards slid off too. Judgment was voted at George Monk's [tavern] before rose from table, on Thorsday.

Friday, March 5. Capt. Clap's son, a very desirable man and gunner of the Castle, though Mr. [Nicholas] Baxter hath the name, at the Castle Island hath one of his eyes shot out, and a piece of his scull taken away by the accidental firing of a gun as he was going a fowling.

Satterday, March 6. James Morgan sends a petition by one Vaughan, signed with said Morgan's own hand, wherein he acknowledges his own sinfull life, the justness of the Court's sentence; and desires longer time to live, but 'tis not granted.

Sabbath-day, March 7th. P.M. Capt. Clap hath a bill put up, wherein he desires prayers that the untimely death of his son may be sanctifyed to him; dyed this day.

Monday, March 8th 1686. Anniversary town-meeting: Select-Men as last year; Mr. [Elisha] Cooke, [Elisha] Hutchinson, [John] Joyliff, [Timothy] Prout, [Theophilus] Frary, [Henry] Allin, [John] Fayerwether, [Edward] Wyllys, [Daniel] Turell. Mr. Hutchinson had 86 votes, which were the most: Capt. Frary 82. Constables: Wm Sumner 90 votes, the highest; Jabez Negus, Wm Rawson, Isaiah Tay, Tho. Adkins, Henry Emes, Joshua Windsor 51. Saml Marshall 37, being chosen after the refusal [to serve as constables] of Joseph Parson, Edw. Bromfield, Benj. Alford, Humphry Luscombe, which 4 last fined. Mr. Wyllys chosen Treasurer by the town, and Mr. Joyliff Recorder. Meeting very comfortably held, being not so full as sometimes, and not such contention about priviledges. Mr. Nowell begun with prayer, and I, by mere accident being left, was fain to conclude. 7 sworn by Major Richards same day, viz: all

---

[10]Increase Mather, *A Sermon Occasioned by the Execution of a Man Found Guilty of Murder* (Boston, 1687).

save Isaiah Tay. The Governour seems to mention it with some concernment that the 18 said to be of the commission are publickly to be seen at the notaries; so there is a nomination before we put in votes.

Tuesday, March 9th 1686. Supply Clap, gunner of the Castle, is buried at Dorchester by the Castle-Company about noon; after the vollies there, several great guns were fired at the Castle; both heard by the town.

Mr. Tho. Kay our maid's father, dyes about 8 or 9 aclock. An order is given for the execution of Morgan next Thorsday; which the Marshal Generall [Green] acquaints him with.

Court sits, so the votes for nomination are put in, in the other room. Dine 5 times.

Wednesday morn about 5 aclock, little Hull hath a convulsion fit in bed. *March 10th* about 8 aclock this evening Father Abel Porter dyeth. Mr. Kay buried this day. Robert Orchard comes to town.

Thorsday, March 11. Persons crowd much into the Old Meetinghouse [First Church] by reason of James Morgan; and before I got thether a crazed woman cryed the gallery or meetinghouse broke, which made the people rush out with great consternation, a great part of them, but were seated again. However, Mr. Eliot, the father, speaks to me that I would go with him back to the Governour, and speak that the meeting might be held in our Meeting-house [South Church] for fear of the worst. Deputy Governour [Thomas Danforth] forwarded it, so Governour [Bradstreet] proceeded, met Mr. Mather, paused a little and then went to our house, the stream of people presently following and deserting the Old: first part of the 51 Ps. sung. Mr. Mather's text was from Num. 35. 16. And if he smite him with an instrument of iron, &c. Saw not Mr. Dudley at meeting, nor Court; suppose he might not be in town. Mr. Stoughton here. Morgan was turned off about 1/2 an hour past five. The day very comfortable, but now 9 aclock rains and has done a good while.

Know not whether the mad woman said the [meeting] house fell, or whether her beating women made them scream, and so those afar off, not knowing the cause, took it to be that; but the effect was as before; and I was told by several as I went along, that one gallery in the old Meetinghouse was broken down. [The mad woman was] the daughter of Goodm[an] Bishop, master of Morgan. She went in at the southwest door, beat the women, they fled from her; they above supposed they fled from under the falling gallery. Mr. Cotton Mather accompanied James Morgan to the place of execution, and prayed with him there.

Friday, March 12. Father Porter laid in the Old Cemetery; is acknowledged by all to have been a great man in prayer. A very winterly day by which means many hindered from coming to the funeral. I perceive there is a considerable disgust taken at the use of our [meeting] house yesterday [for the ceremonies preceding Morgan's execution].

Sabbathday. Mr. John Bolt and John Nichols are received into our church. Mr. Bolt mentioned profane courses he had been entangled in after conviction. Relations [confessions of faith] of both well accepted, being such as gave good hope.

Monday, March 15th. Mr. [Michael] Wigglesworth here, speaks about a council respecting Mr. Thomas Chiever.

Tuesday, March 16. 1686. Went to Muddy-River [Brookline] and met with the Deputy Governour [Danforth] to adjust the matter of fencing; measured from a stake by the crick 16 rods marsh, then upland 40, 40, 52 which reached a little above the dam, then guessed that might be 16 rods to the beginning of the ditch. Then measured from the dam to about a rod below an elm growing to Boston-side of the fence, which accounted the middle; Deputy Governour to fence thence upward above the dam 16 rod to the ditch; Simon Gates to fence downwards to the stake by the crick where by consent we began. Had a good dinner at Simon's; Capt. Scottow accompanied me. Deputy Governour expressed willingness for Simon and his wife to go on foot to Cambridge Church directly throw his ground.

When came home, found all well; but they told me the small pox was in town, one that came in Peter Butler being sick of it at one Wolf's, whose house stands on some part of Capt. [Peter] Oliver's land, in the Town-House-street.

Wednesday, March 17. 1686. Little Hull had a sore convulsion between 5 and 6, a little after his mother and I gone to our private meeting. A cry of fire this night but not one house burnt quite down; 'twas Bachelour White's that fell on fire thereabouts where Mr. Sanford dwelled.

[Resolution:] General Court on adjournment Febr. 16, 1685. Publick fast. This Court considering how apparent the threatening hand of God is, by reason of the spreading of that infectious disease of the small pox in some towns in the countrey; (Portsmouth, Exeter.); together with other evils impending our selves and the churches of Christ abroad, as also the more than ordinary severity of the winter, and the loss of many of our cattel occasioned thereby; have appointed the 25th day of March next to be kept as a Day of Solemn Humiliation and Prayer throughout this colony; That we may obtain favour from God for the diverting these tokens of his anger, and his smiles towards us in the spring and seed-time approaching: And to this end do recommend it to the elders and ministers of the respective churches, to promote this work on the said day; forbidding servile labour to all people within this jurisdiction, thereon.

Edw. Rawson, Secrt.

Monday, March 22. 1686. Went to Braintrey, viewed Albies Farm, and treated with Jonathan Paddleford about letting of it to him; Lodged in the lower room of Unkle [Edmund] Quinsey's new house.

Tuesday, March 23. Went and run the line between us and Tho. Faxon: and between us and John French, the father; came home in company Ephr[aim Hunt] and John Hunt; found all well; but hear of the sad consequences of yesterday's county-court, Mr. Shrimpton's saying there was no Governour and Company. Heat between the members of the court. I can't yet understand that Mr. Nowell, Cook, or Hutchinson were there. Some are much offended that Mr. Shrimpton was not sent to prison.

Fast-day, March 25, 1686. Mr. Willard exerciseth all day, Mr. [John] Bayly being constrained to keep house by reason of the gout. Tho. Hollinsworth, sick of the small pocks, prayed for.

Friday, March 26, 1686. Court of Assistants. Go to the Governour's and accompany him to Court; was slow to go out till knew the Court pretty full: Deputy Governour and about 1/2 duzen went down, among whom Mr. Stoughton; Mr. Dudley went not. At the Town-House debated what was best to do respecting Mr. Shrimpton: Mr. Stoughton related matter of fact. Governour had adjourned the Court from Thorsday to Monday, beside the appointment to hear Mr. Sergeant, which was done Feb. 25. The Court not being full as the Governour alledged, several malefactors were called and sentenced, before which ended, Mr. Stoughton and Dudley came in; a while after the Governour said to Mr. Sergeant, Will you have your case called now, Here is but a thin Court—which was somewhat grievous to Mr. Stoughton; at length Mr. Sergeant and Shrimpton called, Mr. Shrimpton in a great fury, said he was no thief, &c. though called among them; and he perceived he was to answer Mr. Sergeant and not the Court, because of the Governour's speech above; told the Governour he had wronged him much, which some apply to his arbitraitorship, some otherwise; said there was no Governour and Company, and the Governour had notice of it from Mr. Humphryes, and would not answer; substance was what subscribed before in his paper given in more silently; but now spoken, in a great croud with contemptuous pride and rage. Govr, Stoughton, Dudley, Davie, Richards. Court cleared the room, debated among themselves. None but the Governour spoke to send Mr. Shrimpton to prison, one reason was because he had given the essence of it in writing long before, and nothing had been done to him; but would have spoken to him and the people, desiring the Governour to begin; Governour said he despised it, or the like, speaking to Mr. Davie who propounded it inconveniently: So went away angry, and rest followed him; so is extream displeasure among the people, against Stoughton and Dudley chiefly. This 26th Shrimpton sent for, not coming, (was not at home) Court and Council is adjourned to the next Thorsday after lecture, and marshal ordered to summon him.

Satterday, March 27th Capt. Eliot, Mr. Wyllys, Allin, Frary go to the Governour's to comfort him and strengthen his hands, seeming to be extreamly concerned. I vindicated Mr. Stoughton, being the senior magistrate, all that ever I could; but I question whether it takes much place or no. Mr. Addington entered nothing, and professed before the Council that was so surprized and 'twas such a sudden gust, that scarce knew what he said: and all say 'twas extream sudden and tumultuous: I perceive sundry oaths are taking, what avail they'll be of as to things done in Court, I know not.

Ship comes in from Dartmouth to Salem this week, about 8 weeks passage, brings news of horrid progress of the persecution in France;[11] of several [news items] relating to England, Parliament prorogued to May; Rose-Frigat set out for Portsmouth, &c.

Natalis [Sewall's birthday]. March 28. 133 Ps. sung in the morn in course: The Lord give me a holy godly life without end. Letter read from Maldon directed to the three churches in Boston, desiring council respecting their Pastor Mr. Tho. Chiever, who is charged with scandalous immoralities, for which hath not given satisfaction. Mr. Eliot and my self to accompany Mr. Willard thither next Wednesday come sennight [a week], 7th April.

March 29. I visit Mr. [Increase] Mather, and Mr. Nowell confined by his lameness. About 6 aclock P.M. Hull hath a very sore convulsion fit.

March the last, walked [night watch] with Isaac Goose and Cous. Quinsey, had a very pleasant moon-shiny night.

Thorsday, April 1, 1686. Mr. Shrimpton comes before the Council, gives in a paper shewing that March 22 he did say there was no Governour and Company in being in this place, which he still did averr, and was ready to prove if called to it. Council adjourned to April 15th and the Essex magistrates writt to, to be here. Mr. Shrimpton said he never did disown a government here, but honoured them. Mr. Secretary [Edward Rawson] in writing the letter writt *Henry,* in stead of

---

[11]Louis XIV revoked the Edict of Nantes on October 17, 1685, which resulted in the persecution of French Protestants.

Samuel. Am afraid little can or will be done, we shall only *sentire nos mori* [see ourselves die]; for Governour seemed to own before the people that the charter was vacated in England, and insisted upon a proclamation sent him; and the Deputy Governour said the government must not be tumbled down till his majesty called for it, or to that purpose: Such discourses and arguings before the people do make us grow weaker and weaker. Said 'twas voided as much as London's; and they durst not since hold a Common-Council.

April 2, 1686. Mr. Thomas Thacher dyes about 9 or 10 aclock. Hath had a pretty long indisposition. Buried on the Sabbath afternoon.

Monday, Apr. 5. Mr. Nehemiah Hobart chosen to preach the next Election-Sermon Artillery, hardly any other had votes, though Mr. Cotton Mather is even almost son in law to the Capt and a worthy man.

Apr. 7. 1686. Get up about 4 *mane* to go and accompany Mr. Willard to Maldon, went most by water, some by land. Those that went by water were landed at Switzer's Point, then went about 2 miles on foot.

Apr. 8. Came home about 4 or 5 P.M. Visited Mr. Nowell. Mr. Tho. Bayly preached the lecture. *Vide Locos Communes, quoad Concilii factum* [appeared at the usual public places until the Council convened].

Thorsday, Ap. 8 the bell was rung; went in publick. Mr. moderator prayed, read the Council's report. Mr. Wigglesworth spake, thanked him and the Council; said had cause to condemn themselves, as for other sins, so their sudden laying hands on Mr. Chiever; and now God was whipping them with a rod of their own making. Mr. Chiever the father, stood up and pathetically desired his son might speak, but Mr. moderator and others judged it not convenient, he not having by what he said given the Council encouragement. Mr. Allin prayed; went to dinner; Council adjourned to that day 6 weeks. Came home well.[12]

[12] On April 7, a council of the churches of Boston convened in Malden to rule on the case of Thomas Cheever, the pastor of the Malden church. Cheever stood accused of repeatedly violating the Third Commandment, most recently at a tavern in Salem where he was overheard uttering "obscene expressions (not fit to be named)." Although Cheever "absolutely deny'd some things" attributed to him, especially the "filthy words" allegedly spoken at Salem, the church council was inclined to believe his accusers. In the end, the fifteen members of the council, which included Sewall, were not disposed to be charitable toward Cheever because they failed to see "that humble and penitential frame in him" when he appeared before them to answer charges "so fully prov'd against him." Fearing that the pastor was "too much accustomed to an evil course of levity and profaneness," the council advised the Malden church to "suspend Mr. Cheever from the exercise of his ministerial function" for at least six weeks; if in that time he should manifest a proper "repentance," the congregation might "improve him again in the Lord's work among them." The Malden church ultimately dismissed Cheever, and he retired to Rumney Marsh (Chelsea). In 1715, the members of the newly established Chelsea church chose him to be their first minister. Thomas, ed., *Diary,* 1:104–6, reprints Sewall's record of the church trial in Malden.

Monday, Apr. 12. Mr. Lewis['s ship] (in whom Mr. [Nathaniel] Wear goes for England to answer for Hampshire) going out, runs on shore upon a rock a little below the Castle, at high-water: so judged the voyage may be much obstructed. High wind, and flurries of hail.

Tuesday, Apr. 13, 1686. Have news by Madera that Col. Kirk was set sail in order to come hether.[13]

NOMINATION.

S. Bradstreet Esq.	1144	Rob. Pike	1113
T. Danforth	1052	E. Cooke	1121
D. Gookin	1002	W. Johnson	872
J. Pynchon	1097	J. Hathorn	983
W. Stoughton	656	E. Hutchinson	978
J. Dudley	619	S. Sewall	868
P. Bulkly	475	J. Smith	619
N. Saltonstall	852	I. Addington	510
H. Davie	1127	O. Purchis	507
J. Richards	896	D. Pierce	474
S. Nowell	1203	Jn Blackwell	331
Jam. Russell	1095	Left Out,	
P. Tilton	1125	Wm Brown	99
Bar. Gedny	387	Jn Woodbridge	325
S. Appleton	1129		

Persons that came next are—Capt. [John] Phillips of Charlestown, 307—Lt. Thurston of Meadfild, 207—Saml. Partrigge of Hadley, 176—Capt. Daniel Epps 146. Mr. [John] Saffin had very few votes. Mr. Stoughton not present. Mr. Dudley dined (as I think) at Mr. Shrimpton's, which will go near to give great offence. Commissioners dined at Wezendunk's [tavern], Governour gave us his company there, and Mr. Dudley came and abode with us some time; said remembered not 'twas the day for opening the nomination.

Thorsday, Apr. 15. After lecture the Court meets, Mr. Shrimpton sent for, evidences sworn. Considered how to hear him, as county court, I voted for the county court, and three more, or [Court of] Assistants. When some were for Satterday, others for next Thorsday; first carried it because of Major [Samuel] Appleton and [Robert] Pike; so juries to be summoned then to appear. Mr. Shrimpton would not take any blame to himself as to substance of what had said, and pleaded that might be

---

[13]Sewall and others were still apprehensive about the appointment of Piercy Kirke as governor.

heard by the county court, else refused to give bond to appear. The Deputy Governour said his case was capital, which Mr. Stoughton earnestly spake against. In the hurry Deputy Governour adjourned the Court, bid the Marshal Generall [Green] look to Mr. Shrimpton; Marshal Generall required a warrant which Secretary [Rawson] would not grant because the Court adjourned: So Mr. Shrimpton under no obligation to appear. Boston to chuse jury-men for the county court, Friday 3 aclock all under one [ballot] and read the nomination-bill. This Thorsday 15 April, Capt. Ephraim Savage's maid is known to have the small pocks, to the great saddening of the town, besides all our other deaths.

Warrants run for the jury to appear 17th inst. at 8 aclock *mane* to try a case that concerns limb, life, or banishment; and for a grand jury. Doubt the terms of the warrant extream inconvenient.

Thorsday, 15 April, po[st]merid[iem]. The companies warned to train. News is brought by Mary-Land that Mr. Randolph alone was come for N[ew] England. Am told a letter from Mr. [John] Ive of Dec. 10 saith was then in the Downs waiting for a wind. So that the report that the Devil Kirk was coming (as was said the mariners called him) now abates.

Satterday, April 17, 1686. After much discourse an indictment [against Shrimpton] is drawn up, the grand jury find the bill *per* Pen Townsend, foreman. Mr. Shrimpton appears not: so an attachment ordered to goe out for him against next Thorsday, upon which the marshal is to take bond of him with sureties of 1000. which if refuse to give, to carry him to prison. The towns sent to as far as Weymouth sent their jury men very soon Satterday morn; which was to me a very rare sight, seeing the warrants to arrive a Thorsday night. Mr. Stoughton and Dudley called here. Mr. Stoughton said would not come again till after the election, [even if such action] should make me lose all my votes.

Sabbath, Apr. 18. Capt. Ephr. Savage puts up a bill to have God's hand sanctified in sending the small pocks into his family.

Apr. 19. Mr. Seaborn Cotton dyes.

Thorsday, Apr. 22. Court [of] Assistants. Mr. Shrimpton gives no bond, but is sent to prison, marshal did not light on him before. In the afternoon pleads against the illegality of the indictment it having no date; which suppose will be granted; is dismissed tonight on his parole to appear tomorrow. Acknowledged was ashamed of the manner of his behaviour in the county court, but stood to the substance, that [there was] no Governour and Company [because of the revocation of the old charter].

Mr. Tho. Smith comes to Nantasket; was much feared to be lost. Cous. Nath. Dummer here. Mr. Cotton's sermon printed off [John Cotton, *God's Promise to His Plantation* (Boston, 1686)]. Apr. 22, 1686. *Satterday, Apr. 24.* Court makes a decree in the admiralty case. Mr. Shrimpton's paper satisfies not; Court overrules his plea as to the indictments not having a date; because alledge the giving in to Court makes it have a date sufficient and determines 22d March last past, and order the Secretary to underwrite it when received in open Court: near half the magistrates could not vote for either. Court is adjourned to the 14th May, 8 aclock, Mr. Shrimpton promises then to appear, and jury ordered to attend. Is a rumor that the frigot hath been long at sea. Gave the magistrates one of Mr. Cotton's sermons [*God's Promise*] on 2 Sam. 7.10 [neither shall the children of wickedness afflict them anymore], each of them one, being now just come out. Ap.24, 1686.

Monday, Apr. 26, 1686. I and my wife set out for Newbury with little Hull; brother St[ephen] Sewall meets us at the gate next the little bridge near where Boston and Cambridge road join; yet Eliakim [Mather][14] went on to Salem, whether we got well in good time. Was kindly entertained by Capt. [Bartholomew] Gedney, Mr. [John] Hathorn, [Daniel] Epps; visited by Mr. [Nicholas] Noyes.

Tuesday, Ap. 27. Being in a strait for a horse, brother [Stephen] accidentally meets with Stephen Jaques, who had a horse exceeding fit for our purpose, and was a Newbury man; so got to Newbury very well in good time.

Wednesday, May 5, came home-ward, took Rowley-lecture in the way. Text—Denying the power, shewed that true goodness was a powerfull principle. Came to Salem, Gilbert Cole to our great benefit overtaking and accompanying us, and bringing my wife from Salem, else must have troubled brother.

Thorsday, May 6, 1686. Got home about four aclock, found all well, blessed be God. 'Twas lecture-day at Lin too and is so once a moneth, but we have missed both; and indeed my wife's painfull flux such, that had we known of Lin lecture before past the place, could not have took it. Mr. [Richard] Wharton buried a child since our going; and Mr. Cotton Mather married Mrs. Margaret Phillips before Major Richards (Mr. Russell and Capt. Hutchinson also present) Tuesday May 4th 1686. 'Tis said was a great wedding, but Eliakim [Cotton Mather's cousin] not bidden [invited].

---

[14]Eliakim Mather, the eighteen-year-old son of the Reverend Eleazar Mather, was probably serving as Sewall's attendant at this time.

Going to Newbury, at Ipswich Farms met with Richard Waldron, who told me what an eastward master reported about the coming out of the Rose-frigot, shewing me a letter written to the Capt. of the Rose at Boston in N.E. which causes great thoughts and expectation. Left Hull well at our coming away. God did graciously help us out and home this journey, and answer prayer. Capt. Frary met us and bid us wellcom home.

May 10th. Went to Charlestown and wished Mr. Cotton Mather joy, was married last Tuesday.

Monday, 10th May, night and Tuesday morn, plenty of warm refreshing rain which was extreamly wanted.

Tuesday Morn. Mr. Mather's maid, a member of [blank] Church is brought to bed of a child. Nothing suspected before that I hear of. 'Tis said he has turned her out of his house.

May 12, 1686. Pleasant day. Governour ill of his gout, goes not to meeting. Mr. Wigglesworth preaches from Rev. 2.4 [Nevertheless I have somewhat against thee, because thou hast left thy first love] and part of 5th v. and do thy first works [or else I will come unto thee quickly], end of the text. Shewed the want of love, or abating in it, was ground enough of controversy, whatsoever outward performances a people might have. In his prayer said, That may know the things of our peace in this our day, and it may be the last of our days. Acknowledged God as to the election, and bringing forth him as 'twere a dead man—had been reckoned among the dead—to preach. Governour being at home [we] adjourned to his house, and there the Deputy Governour and Assistants took their oaths, being much obstructed and confused by the drums and vollies from which the souldiers would not be refrained.

Gookin	1107	Gedny	509
Pynchon	1295	Appleton	1272
Stoughton	664	Pike	1229
Dudley	500	Cook	1143
Bulkly	436	Johnson	987
Saltonstall	1036	Hathorn	1176
Davie	1260	Hutchinson	1066
Richards	1160	Sewall	957
Nowell	1269	Addington	903
Russell	1273	Smith	842
Tilton	1178		

Thorsday, May 13. Major Richards and I were sent by the magistrates to wait on Mr. Stoughton to invite him to take his oath; called at Major Dudley's for extract of his letter.

Friday, May 14. The Rose-frigot arrives at Nantasket, Mr. Randolph up at town about 8 *mane;* takes coach for Roxbury; Major [John] Pynchon and Mr. Stoughton are sent to the magistrates to acquaint them with the king's commands being come, and that Mr. Deputy, with whom he pleased to take with him, might go to Capt. [Nicholas] Paige's and see the commission, exemplification of the judgment [against the Massachusetts charter] and seals. Mr. Shrimpton in the morn was sent for and told, by reason of the Governour's absence, and other business, should not now proceed with his tryal, and that the Court would be adjourned and he should be acquainted with the time. Had a small admiralty case. Jury dismissed after dinner. Major Pynchon has not took his oath, I saw him not till came in with Mr. Stoughton.

Elder [James] Humphryes of Dorchester buried this day. Major Richards and self saw his grave digging when went to Mr. Stoughton's.

Satterday, May 15. Govr Hinkley [of Plymouth Colony], Major Richards, Mr. [James] Russell and self sent to by Major Dudley to come to Capt. Paige's, where we saw the exemplification of the judgment against the charter, with the broad seal affixed; discoursed about their acceptance; had some thoughts of shewing their seals to the magistrates and deputies, though not to them as a Court; but before we returned, the magistrates were gone to the Governour's and from thence they adjourned till Monday one aclock. Major Generall [Wait Still Winthrop] came home and dined with me. Went to George Monk's [tavern] and paid him in full, drank half a pint of wine together.

Friday morn Capt. Townsend is chosen deputy for Boston in his brother Addington's room. Mr. John Saffin is chosen Speaker the day before. Mr. Nicholas Noyes, the minister, told me the first news of the frigot.

Sabbath, May 16. The Lord's Supper administered with us; in the morn the 2d Ps. sung from the 6th v. to the end. In the family, sung the 139th in course. Mr. Randolph at meeting, sat in Mr. Luscombe's pue. Mr. Willard prayed not for the Governour or Government, as formerly, but spake so as implied it to be changed or changing. It seems Mr. [Samuel] Phillips at the Old Church, prayed for Governour and Deputy Governour. Govr Hinkly, Major Pynchon, Rawson and self with Mr. Willy [Edward Wyllys] in the fore-seat at the sacrament.

Monday, May 17th 1686. Generall Court sits at one aclock, I goe thither, about 3. The Old Government draws to the north-side, Mr. Addington, Capt. Smith and I sit at the table, there not being room; Major [Joseph] Dudley the President [of the interim government], Major Pynchon, Capt. Gedney, Mr. [Robert] Mason, Randolph, Capt.

[Adam] Winthrop, Mr. Wharton come in on the left. Mr. Stoughton I left out; came also Capt. [of] king's frigot, Govr Hinkley [of Plymouth], Govr West [of Carolina] and sat on the bench, and the room pretty well filled with spectators in an instant. Major Dudley made a speech, that was sorry could treat them no longer as Governour and Company; produced the Exemplification of the Charter's Condemnation, the commission under the broad-seal of England—both: letter of the Lords, commission of Admiralty, openly exhibiting them to the people; when had done, Deputy Governour [Danforth] said supposed they expected not the Court's answer now; which the President took up and said they could not acknowledge them as such, and could no way capitulate with them, to which I think no reply [was made]. When gone, Major Generall [Winthrop], Major Richards, Mr. Russell and self spake our minds. I chose to say after the Major Generall, adding that the foundations being destroyed what can the righteous do; speaking against a protest, which some spake for. Spake to call some elders to pray tomorrow which some think inconvenient, because of what past, and the commissioners having several times declared themselves to be the king's council when in the Town-House.

Tuesday, May 18. Mr. Willard not seeing cause to go to the Town-House to pray, I who was to speak to him refrain also. Major Bulkley and Mr. Jonathan Tyng came to town last night. Mr. Phillips had very close discourse with the President [Dudley], to persuade him not to accept [his new appointment]: 'twas in Mr. Willard's study Monday after noon just at night. Mr. Stoughton and [Increase] Mather there too. Now are reading the beginning of the Psalms and the Acts.

Tuesday, May 18. A great wedding from Milton, and are married by Mr. Randolph's chaplain, at Mr. Shrimpton's, according to the [Anglican] Service-Book, a little after noon, when prayer was had at the Town-House: Was another married at the same time. The former was [Thomas] Vosse's son. Borrowed a ring. 'Tis said they having asked Mr. Cook and Addington, and they declining it [to perform the marriage], went after to the President [Dudley] and he sent them to the parson [Anglican clergyman Robert Ratcliffe]. In the evening, Mr. [Joshua] Moodey, [James] Allen, [Samuel] Willard, Addington, Frary visit me. It seems neither of the Mathers [Increase and Cotton], nor Baylys [John and Thomas], nor Major Richards were at the fast.

Wednesday, May 19. Capt. [Jacob] Eliot tells me that he hears Salem troop is to be here on Friday, Capt. [John] Higginson is Mr. Wharton's brother in law, and Capt. Gedney is of Salem, commands one of the companyes. Mr. Higginson and Mr. Noyes steady for submission; the former is the Captain's father. My son [Sam, Jr.] reads to me Isa. 22 in his course this morning. In the afternoon Major Richards and self sent for to Capt. Winthrop's, and desired to have our companyes in arms next Tuesday, Boston troop to bring the President from Roxbury; what was thought of the former notion is now laid aside.

Friday, May 21, 1686. The magistrates and deputies goe to the Governour's. I was going to them about 11 aclock, supposing them to be at the Town-House, and seeing a head through the Governour's room, and, [Joseph] Brisco in the Street, I asked if magistrates there; so went in and they were discoursing about delivering the keys of a fort which had been asked, seemed to advise him not to do it till the gentlemen sworn. Mr. Nowell prayed that God would pardon each magistrate and deputies sin. Thanked God for our hithertos of mercy 56 years, in which time sad calamities elsewhere, as massacre Piedmont; thanked God for what we might expect from sundry of those now set over us. I moved to sing, so sang the 17 and 18 verses of Habbakkuk.

The adjournment which had been agreed before, second Wednesday in October next at 8 aclock in the morning, was declared by the weeping Marshal-General. Many tears shed in prayer and at parting.

This day the President [Dudley] goes on board the frigot a little below the Castle, so the flag is hung out at the main top. About 4 or 5 P.M. she comes up with a fair wind, Castle fires about 25 guns; a very considerable time after the frigot fires, then the sconce and ships, Noodles Island, Charlestown battery, frigot again, ships with their ancients out, and forts their flags. Not very many spectators on Fort Hill and there about, I was for one, coming from warehouse. I waited on the President in the morn to speak with him, and so accompanied him to town. Wednesday, Major Richards and I were sent for to Capt. Winthrop's to speak with us about attending with our companyes on Tuesday; this was near night. Were advised to consult our officers; Major Richards objected the discontent of the souldiers and may be it might prove inconvenient. On Thorsday, before lecture, at Capt. Paige's, I told the President thought I could do nothing to the purpose. On Friday waited on him on purpose and propounded Lieut. Hayward; when came home, after dinner went to speak with Lieut. Hayward, found him at George's [Monk's tavern]. There he was speaking with his Capt., the President having spoken to him; he was to return an answer to the President. I hear no more of it, so I suppose 'tis left with him. On Wednesday Major spake of warning by corporals not drum.

May 25, mane we read the seventeenth Psalm in course, a precious seasonable prayer for this day.

Wednesday, May 26. Mr. Ratliff the minister [Anglican Robert Ratcliffe], waits on the Council; Mr. Mason and Randolph propose that he may have one of the 3 [meeting] houses to preach in. That is denyed, and he is granted the east-end of the Town-House, where the deputies used to meet; untill those who desire his ministry shall provide a fitter place. No body that I observed went to meet the President at his first coming to town that I know of.

Thorsday, May 27. Lieut. [Samuel] Checkly and I wait on the President and Mr. Stoughton [now the deputy president] to Mr. Allin's [First Church]. Mr. [John] Whiting of Hartford preaches. Mr. Danforth [no longer deputy governor] sits in the gallery, Major Gookin with me. Ministers generally dine with the President and co[mpany].

Friday, May 28. I pay my respects to Mr. Stoughton as Deputy-President, break fast with him, and ride part of the way to town. Then I goe with Capt. Eliot and adjust the line between him and me at Muddy-River [Brookline]. Visit Mr. Benj. Eliot as we come back. Yesterday a very refreshing rain.

Sabbath, May 30th 1686. My son [Sam, Jr.] reads to me in the course the 26th of Isaiah—In that day shall this Song, &c. And we sing the 141 Psalm, both exceedingly suited to this day. Wherein there is to be worship according to the Church of England as 'tis called, in the Town-House, by countenance of authority. 'Tis deferred 'till the 6th of June at what time the pulpit is provided; the pulpit is movable, carried up and down stairs, as occasion serves; it seems many crouded thether, and the ministers preached forenoon and afternoon. Charles Lidget there.

Satterday, June 5th. I rode to Newbury, to see my little Hull, and to keep out of the way of the Artillery election, on which day eat strawberries and cream with sister [Anne Sewall] Longfellow at the falls, visited Capt. Richard Dummer, rode to Salem, where lodged 2 nights for the sake of Mr. Noyes's lecture, who preached excellently of humility, from the woman's washing Christ's feet. Was invited by Mr. [Reverend John] Higginson to dinner, but could not stay, came alone to Capt. Marshal's, from thence with Mr. Davie, who gave me an account of B[enjamin] Davis Capt., Tho. Savage Lieut. and Sam Ravenscroft Ensign, [results] of the Artillery [election]; John Wait was chosen but served not. Mr. Hubbard preached from Eccles., There is no discharge in that war.

Friday, June 11. Waited on the Council, took the Oath of Allegiance, and received my new commission for Capt. Was before at a private fast at Deacon Allen's; so Capt. Hutchinson and I went about 5 aclock, and all the rest were sworn, Capt. Hutchinson at present refuses. I read the oath myself holding the book in my left hand, and holding up my right hand to heaven.

Friday, June 18. My dear son, Hull Sewall, dyes at Newbury about one aclock. Brother [Jacob] Toppan [husband of Sewall's sister Hannah] gets hither to acquaint us on Satterday morn between 5 and 6. [Hull had been living with Hannah and Jacob Toppan since April 26.] We set out about 8. I got to Newbury a little after sun-set, where found many persons waiting for the funeral; so very quickly went; Mr. [John] Woodbridge and [John] Richardson there; bearers Mr. Saml. Tompson, John Moodey, John Toppan, Johnny Richardson. Had gloves. Gave no body else any because 'twas so late.

Sabbath-day Morn. Goodman Pilsbury was buried just after the ringing of the second bell. Grave dug over night. Mr. Richardson preached from 1 Cor.3.21,22 [Therefore let no man glory in men. For all things are your's; Whether . . . the world, or life, or death, or things present, or things to come], going something out of his order by reason of the occasion, and singling out those words *Or Death.*

On *Monday [June 21]* I distributed some gloves, and in the afternoon about 6 aclock came with Deacon [Nathaniel] Coffin to Salem about 10 at night. From thence early in the morn by reason of the flaming heat, and got to Winnisimmet [Chelsea] before the ferry-men up. Got home about 3/4 after seven, found all well. Hullie was taken ill on Friday morn. Mr. [Jonas] Clark of Cambridge had a son of 9 years old drownd the Tuesday before. Two women dyed suddenly in Boston. James Mirick that lived just by my father at Newbury, had his house suddenly burnt down to the ground on Sabbath-day even[ing] before this Friday.

The Lord sanctify this third bereavement.[15]

Tuesday, June 22, 1686. Betty Lane's father dyes suddenly.

Wednesday, Junii ulto [June 30] Went to a fast at Dorchester, Mr. Danforth and Williams exercised, and no other. In the evening supped with Major Gidney, [and ministers of the First Church] Mr. [Joshua] Moodey [and James] Allin, at Mr. Stoghton's.

Friday, July 2. Mis. [Thomasine] Chancy, widow, dyes having been sick a day or two, of a flux. Her body is carried in the night to Roxbury there to be buried.

July 9. Mr. Richard Collicot buried.

---

[15]The two other deaths Sewall is referring to here were his sons John, who died in 1678 at age one and a half, and Henry, who died in 1685 two weeks after his birth.

Monday, July 12. Mr. Thomas Kellond dyes, is to be buried on Thorsday between 4 and 5. Is the only son of Madame Kellond, and Mrs [Susanna Kellond] Luscombe is now her only child. Conversed with Mr. Thomas when at Newbury in the beginning of June. He was so fat and corpulent that most thought he could not live.

Wednesday, July 21. Went to Cambridge-lecture and heard Mr. [Charles] Morton. Considerable rain this day. Dined at [Jonathan] Remington's.

Mr. John Bayly preaches his farewell sermon from 2 Cor. 13.11 [Finally, brethren, farewell. Be perfect, be of good comfort, be of one mind, live in peace]. Goes to Watertown this week. July 25, 1686.

July 26, 1686. More rain this day. Major Richards and most of the Captains gave in some military orders for the Council's approbation and passing; and before the Council agreed that this day fortnight be a training-day.

July 27, 1686. Mr. Stoughton prayes excellently, and makes a notable speech at the opening of the Court. The foreman of the grandjury, Capt. Hollbrook, swore laying his hand on the Bible, and one or two more. So Mr. [Jarvis] Ballard, foreman of the petit jury, and one or two more. Others swore lifting up their hands, as formerly. Attorneys are sworn and none must plead as attorneys but they.

July 28. A considerable troop from Watertown come and fetch Mr. Bayly, some of ours also accompany them. Francis Stepney the dancing master runs away for debt. Several attachments out after him.

Thorsday night, July 29, 1686. I goe the grand rounds with Isaac Goose and Matthias Smith; comes eight dayes sooner than it ought because Capt. [Charles] Lidget's lieut. refuses, and so the rest of the company.

Friday, July 30. Church meeting, at which Richard Draper, Mrs. [Mary Atwater] Clark, Sarah Chapin, and Eliza Lane admitted. About the same time Wm Johnson Esqr. is sharply reproved by the Council for his carriage on the fast-day, staying at home himself and having a dozen men at his house. Told him must take the Oath of Allegiance; he desired an hour's consideration, then said he could not take it; but when his *Mittimus* [warrant of commitment to prison] writing, or written, he considered again, and took it rather than goe to prison. Objected against that clause of acknowledging it [new government] to be lawfull authority who administered; would see the seals.

Augt 4. Mr. Moodey [conducts devotional] exercises at our house, being our meeting-day. Mr. [George] Shove [minister of Taunton, Mass.] in town.

Augt 5. Wm Harrison, the bodice-maker, is buried, which is the first that I know of buried with the [Anglican] Common-Prayer Book in Boston. He was formerly Mr. Randolph's landlord. This day Capt. Paige hath a judgment for Capt. Keyn's [Robert Keayne] farm: Mr. Cook appeals. Mr. Morton preaches the lecture. One John Gold, chief commander of the military company at Topsfield, is sent to prison for treasonable words spoken about the change of government, is to be tryed this day fortnight. Council said he was not bailable.

Sabbath-day, Augt 8. 'Tis said the sacrament of the Lord's Supper is administered at the Town-House. Cleverly there.

Augt 9. Pretty sharp thunder and lightening.

Augt 10. Ride to Braintrey in company of Mr. Pain, and Mr. Joseph Parson, and home agen. 'Tis said a Groton man is killed by his cart, bowells crushed out; and a boy killed by a horse at Rowley; foot hung in the stirrup and so was torn to pieces; both about a week ago.

Augt. 10 at night. Two brothers die in one bed, the mate and purser of the ship which brought the Frenchmen. Died of a malignant fever.

Augt 11. Buried together. Mr. [Samuel] Parris spake at Mrs. [Sarah] Noyes's.[16]

Augt. 18, 1686. Went and came on foot to Cambridge-lecture. Dined at Mr. [Nathaniel] Gookin's in company of Mr. Hubbard [of] N[ew] Cambr[idge] and others.

Augt. 21. mane Mr. Randolph and [Benjamin] Bullivant were here, Mr. Randolph mentioned a contribution toward building them [Anglicans] a Church, and seemed to goe away displeased because I spake not up to it.

Friday, Augt. 20. Read the 143, 144 Psalms *mane,* and Sam read the 10th of Jeremiah. I was and am in great exercise about the cross to be put into the colours, and afraid if I should have a hand in it whether it may not hinder my entrance into the Holy Land.[17]

Sabbath-day, Augt. 22. In the evening seriously discoursed with Capt. [Jacob] Eliot and Frary, signifying my inability to hold [continue as Captain of the South Company militia], and reading Mr. Cotton's arguments to them about the cross, and sayd that to introduce it in Boston at this time was much, seeing it had been kept out more than my lifetime, and now the cross much set by in England and here; and it could scarce be put in but I must have a hand in it. I fetcht home the silk

---

[16] In 1689, Samuel Parris became the minister of the church in Salem Village and an influential participant in the 1692 witchcraft episode.

[17] Sewall, like most of his Puritan neighbors, believed that the use of the cross on flags or pennants bordered on idolatry and popery.

Elizur Holyoke had of me, to make the cross, last Friday morn; and went and discoursed Mr. [Increase] Mather. He judged it sin to have it put in, but the Captain not in fault; but I could hardly understand how the command of others could wholly excuse them, at least me who had spoken so much against it in April 1681, and that summer and forward, upon occasion of Capt. [John] Walley's putting the cross in his colours.

Augt. 22. [Capt. John] Balston arrives.

Monday, Augt. 23. At evening, I wait on the President and shew him that I cannot hold because of the cross now to be introduced, and offered him my commission, which he refused, said would not take it but in Council. Received me very candidly, and told me we might expect Sir Edmund Andros, our Governour, here within six weeks; for ought I know that might make him the more placid. Came over the Neck with Mr. Sherman. *Laus Deo* [Praise God].

Balston arrives Augt 22: came from Graves-End June 24, 1686. Had news there by several vessels that the Rose-frigot was arrived here. Mr. [Samuel] Lee and another minister came over with many passengers.

Augt. 29. Lord's day. Mr. Lee, the minister, now come over, came to our meeting in the forenoon, and sat in my pue.

Augt. 30. Eight companyes train, but I appear not save to take leave in the morning, getting Mr. Willard to goe to prayer. Lieut. [Elizur] Holyoke led the [South] Company which had Lt. Cols. colours; in the morn Lt. [Richard] Way came to me and told me the likelihood of Mr. [Samuel] Lee's being my tenant; so invited said Way to dinner. Gave each souldier a sermon: [John Cotton's] God's Promise to his Plantations and 20s.

Augt. 31. Mr. Nowell, Moodey and [Edward] Rawson visit me and comfort me. Mr Lee views the house at Cotton-Hill in order to taking it.

Septr 1. Went to Natick lecture, Simon Gates shewing me the way; called as went at Noah Wiswall's; came home accompanied by Major Gookin and his son Sam till the way parted. Mr. Danl. Gookin preached; were about 40 or 50 men at the most, and a pretty many women and children [at the Indian Meetinghouse]. Called at the President's as came home, who was very pleasant; excused my giving himself and the Deputy President [William Stoughton] occasion to say what they did on Thorsday night. Met with there, Capt. [John] Blackwell and Mr. [John] Hubbard and his wife, with whom I came over the Neck.

Septr 3. The report about Sir Edmund Andros coming, is refreshed by Martin in his way to New York.

Friday, Septr 3. Mr. Shrimpton, Capt. Lidget and others come in a coach from Roxbury about 9 aclock or past, singing as they come, being inflamed with drink: At Justice Morgan's they stop and drink healths, curse, swear, talk profanely and baudily to the great disturbance of the town and grief of good people. Such high-handed wickedness has hardly been heard of before in Boston.

Monday, Septr 6. Artillery training. Not one old Captain there. Dartmouth frigot arrives from Barmudas last night. Lieut. Holyoke's little daughter buried today; died on Satterday.

Tuesday, Septr 7th The Dartmouth frigot comes up. I goe with my wife, Cous. Ruth [Quincy], Savages [Ephraim and Mary Quincy] and Mrs. Baker and their children to Hog-Island. We put off just as the frigot and ships and town salute each other mutually. Got home by 9 aclock.

I little thought of its being the day signed by the almanack for the Court of Assistants, till coming home I accidently spyed. It has been a great day of feasting on board Capt. Head. Mr. Lidget and Shrimpton there. I suppose they are little concerned for being bound over in the morn for their Friday night revel.

Monday, Septr 13, 1686. Mr. Cotton Mather preaches the election sermon for the Artillery, at Charlestown, from Ps. 144. 1 [Blessed be the Lord my strength, which teacheth my hands to war, and my fingers to fight]. Made a very good discourse. President and Deputy President there. As I went in the morn I had Sam [eight years old] to the latin school, which is the first time. Mr. Chiever [Ezekiel Cheever] received him gladly. The Artillery Company had like to have broken up; the animosity so high between Charlestown and Cambridge men about the place of training. Were fain at last to vote the old officers to stand for next year, in general. Major Gookin, Richards and self, by as spectators. Major Gookin to order.

Wednesday, Septr 15. Mr. David Geffries marries Mrs. Betty Usher before [Anglican minister] Mr. Ratcliff.

Monday, Septr 20. The President, Deputy President, Capt. [John] Blackwell, Councillour [John] Usher, Mr. Moodey, Lee, Morton, Allen, Willard, Cotton Mather, and self, goe and visit Mr. Baylye [John Bailey] at Watertown, and there dine.

Septr 23. Lecture day. Govr Bradstreet is gone with his Lady to Salem. President and Deputy President called here.

Septr 24. Friday. Capt. [Roger] Clapp leaves the Castle; about nine guns fired at his going off. It seems Capt. Clap is not actually come away, but Capt. Winthrop, and Lieut. Thomas Savage did this day there receive their commissions.

Satterday, Septr 25. The Queen's birthday is celebrated by the captains of the frigots and sundry others at Noddles Island. King and Council's proclamation of Novr 6 last, was published by beat of drum throw the town to hinder their making bonfires in the town however. Went with their boats to the ships and vessels and caused them to put out their ancients. Many guns fired. A kind of tent set up at the Island and a flagg on the top on it. Made a great fire in the evening, many hussas.

Sabbath, Septr 26. Mr. Willard expresses great grief in his prayer for the profanation of the Sabbath last night. Mr. Lee preaches with us in the afternoon from Isa. 52.7 [How beautiful upon the mountains are the feet of him that bringeth good tidings . . . that saith unto Zion, Thy God reigneth!]. Said that all America should be converted, Mexico overcome, England sent over to convert the Natives, look you do it. Read in course this day Cant. 6. vid. [Thomas] Brightm[an's *Commentary on the Canticles* (London, 1644)] fol. 121.

Septr 27. Hannah [six years old] clambring to the cupboard's head upon a chair breaks her forehead grievously just above her left eye: 'twas in the morn.

Septr 28. Mr. Edward Grove who kept the Salutation [tavern], dyed this day of the bloody flux. Yesterday's training was hindred by the rain. No drums beat.

Wednesday, Septr 29. Set forth toward Narraganset, went to Woodcock's [tavern near Rehoboth].

Octr 2d. Mr. Joseph Eliot and I went from Joseph Stanton's to Stonnington [Conn.] and kept the Sabbath with Mr. [James] Noyes.

Octr 6. Went with Mr. [Nathaniel] Byfield to Rode-Island about the middle on it, go to Bristow [Bristol], there lodged.

Octr 7. Went to Newport and back again to Mr. Byfield's.

Octr 8. Rode to Plat's Farm.

Octr 9. Satterday. Mr. [Jacob] Eliot and I got home about one aclock, and found all well. *Soli Deo gloria* [Glory to God alone].

Sabbath-day, Octr 10. By reason of the fires the Meeting-houses are much filled with smoke; so 'twas a lecture-day, one might feel it in ones eyes. Mr. Willard preached in the afternoon from Ps. 43. *ult.*

Wednesday, Octr 6. Mr. Bayly is ordained at Watertown, but not as Congregational men are.[18]

Thorsday, Octr 7. Deacon [Henry] Bright carrying home chairs, &c. used at Mr. Baylys [ordination], is hurt by his cart none seeing, so that he dyes Octr 9. Satterday. It seems he was the only officer left in that church. Several of his ribs broken.

---

[18]John Bailey refused to follow the ritual of the laying on of hands, which had been part of the ordination ceremony in Massachusetts since the 1630s. When Charles Morton became the ordained minister of Charlestown, he, too, refused to follow the "Congregational" way.

Octr 12. Mr. [George] Shove [minister of Taunton] dines with us.

Wednesday, Octr 13th Carry Mistress Bridget Hoar behind me to Cambridge-lecture, where Mr. Lee preached. After lecture was invited to dinner by the late [i.e., former] Deputy Governour [Danforth]; at his table sat down Deputy Governour and his lady, Mr. Lee, Morton, Bayly, [Nehemiah] Hubbard of the village, [James] Russell, Sewall, Wyllie, [Jarvis] Ballard, [John] Leverett, [William] Brattle, [John] Williams [of] Derefield. Mr. Lee craved a blessing and returned thanks. Came home in company Mr. Hez. Usher and Lady, and from widow Clark's, with Capt. [Jacob] Eliot and his sons Elizur Holyoke [husband of Mary Eliot] and Mr. Joseph [Eliot]; got home about 8 aclock at night. Went in company of the same save Mr. Hez. Usher and lady who were not ready.

Wednesday, Septr 29. Capt. Clap went to Dorchester-lecture, so to Boston, where he dwells, having actually left the Castle this day 29th September. Gunner [Nicholas] Baxter also is here, having laid down his place, and both aged.

Thorsday, Octr 14. Many guns fired, and at night a bonfire on Noddles Island, in remembrance of the king's birth-day; 'tis the more remarkable because Wednesday Octr 13th was the day the Generall Court was adjourned to at 8 aclock. Upon Thorsday before lecture the guns fired; some marched throw the streets with viols and drums, playing and beating by turns.

Satterday, Octr 16. Accompanied Judge Stoughton as far as Dorchester burying place, at his return from the eastward.

Monday, Octr 18. Pretty deal of rain. *Sabbath, Octr 17.* Mr. Edw. Taylor preaches in the forenoon.[19]

Tuesday, Octr 19. Wait on Major Richards to Braintrey, where he joins in marriage his cousin John Hunt and cousin Ruth Quinsey; present, Capt. [Edmund] Quinsey the father, Mr. [Moses] Fisk [minister of Braintree] who prayed before and after, his wife, Cap. Daniel Quinsey and Exper. Quinsey, wife, Capt. Savage and wife [Mary Quincy], Lieut. Tho. Hunt and wife, [Ephraim] Hunt of Weymouth and wife, Mr. Sam Shepard. Came home after dinner. Wedding was about one of the clock. This day Mr. Smith and Butler come in from London. I receive Gazettes next morn to the 26th of August. 'Tis reported that the King-Fisher rides no longer admiral [as flagship] in the Downs as being ready to sail and bring Sir Edmund Andros our Governour.

---

[19]Edward Taylor, Sewall's classmate at Harvard and minister of Westfield, was an accomplished Puritan poet.

Satterday night, Octr 23, about 7 aclock the frigot fires many guns, drums and trumpets going. I heard the guns.

Sabbath-day, Octr 24. A man swoons in our Meeting-house [South Church], and falls down, which makes much disturbance, yet Mr. Willard breaks not off preaching.

Tuesday, Octr 26. I set sweet-briar seeds at the pasture by Mr. [Robert] Saunderson's, next the lane at the upper end. Little red heifer is this day brought from Braintrey to be killed.

Octr 29. Mr. Saml Danforth preaches at the meeting at Cousin Quinsey's, Luke 3.8 [Bring forth therefore fruits worthy of repentance].

Friday, Novr 5. Mr. Morton is ordained the pastor of the church at Charlestown; propounded to the church and to all if any had [reason] to object; then the churches vote was had; Mr. [Increase] Mather gave him his charge, Mr. Allen, Moodey, Willard prayed. Mr. Morton's text was out of Rom. 1.16 [For I am not ashamed of the gospel of Christ]. Took occasion to speak of the 5th of November [the Gunpowder Plot] very pithily, and said the just contrary to that epistle was taught and practised at Rome. Mr. Mather spoke in praise of the Congregational way [of ordination], and said were [he] as Mr. Morton, he would have hands laid on him. Mr. Moodey in his prayer said, though that which would have been gratefull to many was omitted, or to that purpose. I dined about 3 or 4 aclock at Mr. Russel's.

Friday, Novr 5. One Mr. [Josias] Clark [Anglican minister] preaches at the Town-House. Speaks much against the Presbyterians in England and here.

Satterday, Novr 6. One Robison Esqr., that came from Antego, is buried; first was had to the Town-House and set before the pulpit where Mr. Buckley preached. The President and many others there. [Anglican Book of] Common-Prayer used.

Monday, Novr 8. [Capt.] Lewis arrives. I have a Gazette to the 6th of September, by which are informed of the taking of Buda [by the Imperialists], which heard of before by a vessel from Bilbao.

Novr 9. Mr. Shove at our house, went on to Roxbury, after had sat with me awhile. I am ill of a cold I took on Friday, lies much in my head.

Novr 10, 1686. Second year of His Majesties reign.

Thorsday, Novr 11. I delivered my commission to the Council, desiring them to appoint a Captain for the South-Company; left it with them to put them in mind on it. As was coming home Capt. [James] Hill invited me to his house where unexpectly I found a good supper. Capt. [Elisha] Hutchinson, [Penn] Townsend, Savage, [John] Wing and sundry others to the number of 14 or 15 were there. After supper sung the 46th Ps.

Friday, Novr 12. I go to the meeting at the schoolhouse.

John Griffin is this week buried with the [Anglican] Common-Prayer: which is the third funeral of this sort, as far as I can learn.

In the preamble to the order for thanksgiving, are these words—As also for that His Majesties kingdoms, and other His Majesties plantations, flourish in all happy peace and tranquillity. It is therefore ordered &c.

Tuesday, Novr 16. I goe to Roxbury lecture, and hear Mr. [John] Eliot, the father, pray and preach. Came home with Mr. Moodey. This day [John] Gardener arrives and brings Gazettes to the 16th of September, in one of which is that on the 13th of September His Majestie accepted of Rode-Island surrender by their address. At night brother [William] Longfellow [husband of Sewall's sister Anne] lodges here.

Wednesday, Novr 17. At parting I give him [Longfellow] 2 French crowns and 15s English money, and writt to Stephen [Sewall] to furnish him with cloths to the value of £5., and charged him to be frugal.

Novr 18. John Neponet [Indian], alias Nemasit, executed. Mr. Eliot hopes well of him.

This day sent for my coat home from Capt. [William] Gerrishes, where I suppose I left it the 25th May, and now the cold wether made me look after it.

Friday, Novr 19. Went to Capt. Gerrish and paid him 18d., which laid out for crying [carrying?] my coat, from thence Eliakim [Mather] calls me to Mr. Moodey, so we together viewed the eclipse. As to the time and digits the Cambridge Almanack rightest; had he not unhappily said 'twould not be visible. Clouds hindered between whiles that could not so well see how much the moon eclipsed, but when near half darkened, and when emerging, had a good view.

This night Eliza Damon, servant to Nash the currier, dyes about midnight of the small pocks, to our great startling, lest it should spread as in 1678. Had hoped the town was clear of it. But one that I know of dyed on it before, and that a great while since.

Satterday, Novr 20. Capt. [Benjamin] Davis buries his sarjeant, Henry Messenger, in arms.

Tuesday night, Novr 23. Mr. James Whetcomb dyes.

Wednesday, 24. Robert Combs taken up drowned.

Thorsday, 25. Public thanksgiving.

Friday, Novr 26. [Capt.] Marshal arrives from England.

Monday, Novr 29. Mr. Whetcomb buried. Coffin was lined with cloth on the outside, and below the name and year a St. Andrew's Cross made, with what intent I can't tell. Bearers, Mr. [Richard] Wharton, [John] Joyliff, Hutchinson, James Paige, [Peter] Sergeant, [John] Nelson. Gave scarvs to the President, Mr. Bradstreet and the ministers, and Mr. [Thomas] Oakes. Should have been buried on Friday, but the storm of rain hindred.

This day Wm Clendon the barber and perriwig-maker dies miserably, being almost eat up with lice and stupified with drink and cold. Sat in the watch-house and was there gazed on a good part of the day, having been taken up the night before.

Decr 8, 1686. Going to Cambridge-lecture, a little beyond Daniel Champney's I saw a rainbow to the North, being just about noon; only Herl. Simons [Harlakenden Symonds] with me just then; but Capt. [Jacob] Eliot and Mr. Tho. Oliver saw it, with whom rid over the causeys [causeway]. Mr. Oliver said he had not before noted a rainbow in the north. Cloud rose suddenly very black and hailed afterward. Ministers pray together at Boston this day.

Sabbath, Decr 12. [Capt. William] Clutterbuck arrives, brings news of Capt. [Thomas] Jenner's death, Widow Winsley's son; and that the Capt. of the Kings-fisher expected to sail in a day or two; this was Octr 13, and then in the Downs. Mr. Cotton Mather preaches with us.

Decr 13. [Boston ministers:] Mr. [Increase] Mather, [Samuel] Willard, Mr. Cotton Mather, Mr. [Joshua] Moodey, [James] Allin visit me. Very pleasant wether.

Tuesday, Decr 14. Capt. [Samuel] Legg arrives, who brings 60 beds for soldiers, and a considerable quantity of goods for the Governour. 120 soldiers to come. This day Mrs. Crines, Mr. [Henry] Dering's daughter, dies of the small pocks.

Sabbath, Decr 19, 1686. Day of the Fort-fight. As I was reading the exposition of Habakkuk 3d, which this morn sung and read in the family, I heard a great gun or two, as I supposed, which made me think Sir Edmund [Andros] might be come; but none of the family speaking of it, I held my peace. Going to Mr. Bradstreet's, Tho. Baker told me Sir Edmund was below, which [John] Winchcomb and [Joseph] Brisco confirmed; said they saw the frigot with the flag in the main top, and sundry gone down. President and Deputy [Joseph Dudley and William Stoughton] come to town; President comes and hears Mr. Willard, whose text was Heb. 11.12. Therefore sprang there of one &c. 113 Psalm sung. Mr. Willard said he was fully persuaded and confident God would not forget the faith of those who came first to New England, but would remember their posterity with kindness. One doctrine: Faith usu-

ally reaps the greatest crops off the barrenest ground. Between sermons, the President and several of the Council goe down. Mr. Lee
preaches with us in the afternoon from Zech. 3.9 [I will remove the iniquity of that land in one day], 10 [In that day . . . shall ye call every
man his neighbour under the vine].

Mercy Lincorn and [blank] Dinsdale baptized. John Eastman taken
into Church, Mis. Harris as to her owning the Covenant dismissed. A
youth, one Bradish, of about 10 years old, that was drowned, buried.
Fine, serene, moderate wether.

Mr. Secretary indisposed, so I wait on Madam Bradstreet morn. and
even. Capt. Wing absent.

Monday, Decr 20. 1686. Governour Andros comes up in the pinnace,
touches at the Castle, lands at Govr. Leveret's wharf about 2 P.M. where
the President, &c. meet him and so march up through the guards of
the 8 companyes to the Town House, where part of the commission
read: He hath power to suspend Councillors and to appoint others if
the number be reduced to less than seven. He and Council to make
laws. Then took the Oath of Allegiance and as Governour, then about
eight of the Council sworn. Court cleared. Governour stood with his
hat on when oaths given to Councillours. It seems speaks to the ministers in the library about accommodations as to a meeting-house, that
might so contrive the time as one house might serve two assemblies
[Anglican and Puritan].

Last Satterday, Mr. [Elisha] Cook not prosecuting his appeal, possession was given by Major [Peter] Bulkly and Marshal [John] Green,
of the farm to Capt. [Nicholas] Paige and his wife. The constables were
ordered this day to come and take new staves, little thinking the government should have been before altered, or at this time. Mr. Nath.
Oliver was the person first spyed the frigot under sail about 7 *mane*
Sabbath-day, knowing her by the flag; he went to Capt. Davis, Capt.
Davis to the President. Governour was in a scarlet coat laced; several
others were in scarlet. Mr. Bradstreet and Mr. Danforth there, to meet
the Governour at the wharf. At dinner Mr. [Increase] Mather craved a
blessing. The day was serene, but somewhat cold. Major Richards
made the South-Company change their colours for the 8th colours. Andrew Gardner led them.

Tuesday, Decr 21. There is a meeting at Mr. Allen's, of the ministers
and four of each congregation, to consider what answer to give the Governour; and 'twas agreed that could not with a good conscience consent that our Meeting-houses should be made use of for the [Anglican]
Common-Prayer worship.

Decr 22. Kings-fisher comes up but neither salutes the Castle nor the town. In the evening Mr. Mather and Willard thorowly discoursed his Excellency [Andros] about the Meeting-houses in great plainness, shewing they could not consent. This was at his lodging at Madam [Rebecca Stoughton] Taylor's. He seems to say will not impose.

Friday, Decr 24. About 60 Red-Coats are brought to town, landed at Mr. Pool's wharf, where drew up and so marched to Mr. [Robert] Gibb's house at Fort-hill.

Satterday, Decr 25. Governour goes to the Town-House to [Anglican] service forenoon and afternoon, a Red-Coat going on his right hand and Capt. George on the left. Was not at lecture on Thorsday. Shops open today generally and persons about their occasions. Some, but few, carts at town with wood, though the day exceeding fair and pleasant. Read in the morn the 46 and 47 of Isa., and at night Mr. [John] Norton from John 9.3. Neither this Man nor his Parents.

Thorsday, Decr 30. The Council meets. Gentlemen from Plimouth and Rhode-Island here and take their oaths without any ceremony, perhaps for sake of the Quakers, who have promised to deliver up their charter. Mr. Lee preaches the lecture from Isa. 4.5, 6 [And the Lord will create . . . a cloud and smoke by day, and the shining of a flaming fire by night . . . And there shall be a tabernacle for a shadow in the daytime from the heat, and for a place of refuge]. But the Governour and most of the Councillours absent. Mr. Stoughton, Govr Hinkley, Mr. Usher and some other at lecture.

2

"Love to Thee and Our Dear Quaternion: S.H.E.J."

The arrival of Edmund Andros in December 1686 marked the end of the rule of the provisional government under Joseph Dudley and the beginning of more than two years of centralized control under the auspices of the Dominion of New England. At its height in 1688, the Dominion encompassed not only all of New England, but New York and New Jersey as well. As its governor, Andros ruled over a territory larger than England and possessed the power to make laws, levy taxes, and administer justice, limited only by the consent of his Council. For the colonists in general, the powers granted to Andros raised serious questions of a constitutional nature. Could a royal governor demand more of the colonists in America than the king could demand of Englishmen at home? Were the colonists entitled to all of the rights of Englishmen? For Sewall, two of the actions taken by the new governor seemed to be particularly vexing. First, shortly after his arrival in Boston, Andros insisted on using the South Meetinghouse, Sewall's church, for Anglican services. Even after a delegation that included Sewall presented the governor with proof that the "Land and House is ours" and declared to him that "we can't consent to part with it to such use," Andros commanded a reluctant sexton to "ring the bell and open the door" for the Anglicans. As late as the summer of 1688, Andros was still asking questions about "who the House belonged to." Told once again that the "title to the House was on record," he responded with a curt "we will have that looked into."[1]

Andros's thinly veiled threat against the rights of property was the

---

[1] M. Halsey Thomas, ed., *The Diary of Samuel Sewall, 1674–1729,* 2 vols. (New York: Farrar, Straus and Giroux, 1973), 1:135, 171.

basis of Sewall's second complaint. The governor's instructions directed him to require provincial landowners to petition the crown for royal patents to all land they claimed under the old charter. In July 1688 Sewall learned that the nearly five hundred acres he owned on Hogg Island in Boston Harbor were in jeopardy, that "there is a Writt out against me for Hog-Island, and against several other persons for land as being violent intruders into the King's possession." He promptly forwarded a petition to Andros in which he beseeched the governor's "favour that he may obtain His Majesties Grant and Confirmation of the said Hogg-Island."[2] Additionally, Sewall set sail for England in November hoping to confirm his rights to all of his properties in New England. By the time Sewall arrived in London, however, James II had already fled England and William and Mary merely awaited a joint coronation in order to complete the Glorious Revolution.

In Massachusetts, the Dominion government collapsed in the wake of the Glorious Revolution. Andros, Edward Randolph, and Joseph Dudley, among others who supported the Dominion, were arrested and imprisoned. A revolutionary coalition, headed by some of the most prominent men in Boston, many of them Sewall's friends, decided that the officers last elected under the old charter were to resume their positions until the new king's will was known. Ideally, agents of the colony dispatched to England in 1690 hoped for a new charter that would restore the sort of autonomy that Massachusetts had enjoyed for more than fifty years under the 1629 Bay Company charter. What they got instead was a charter in 1691 that reimposed royal control over the colony.

The new charter was an improvement over the Dominion government, but Sewall and his cohorts were little cheered by its provisions. Under the 1691 charter, the governor of the colony, now a royal appointee who served at the pleasure of the crown, was empowered to call, prorogue, or dissolve the meetings of the General Court, exercise a veto over all legislation, and appoint judges, sheriffs, and local administrative officers. The freemen of the colony retained the right to elect their representatives to the Assembly, the lower house of the General Court, but freemanship was henceforth divorced from church membership. After 1691, the franchise was extended to all males possessed of a freehold worth forty shillings a year or personal property worth £40 sterling. The political base of the Puritan establishment was

[2]Ibid., 172, 173.

thus undermined. Furthermore, although the Assembly elected the members of the Council, the governor was authorized to negate at will the election of any councillor.[3]

For the rest of Sewall's life, Massachusetts politics was characterized by a struggle between those who supported the new charter or sought an amicable accommodation of it under successive governors and those who repudiated the document or were determined at least to contain the powers of the governor under the new system. This division first manifested itself in the tension that existed between Elisha Cooke, Sr., and Increase Mather. After the fall of the Dominion, the revolutionary government appointed both men to a commission of four whose purpose was to secure a restoration of the old charter. By the end of 1691, however, Cooke and Mather had taken up diametrically opposed positions. Whereas the latter defended the new charter as a "MAGNA CHARTA" that secured the liberties and properties of the king's subjects in Massachusetts, the former so despised the 1691 charter that he refused to return home in the same ship that carried Mather, the document itself, and Sir William Phips, the newly appointed royal governor of the colony, across the Atlantic. When Phips vetoed Cooke's election to the Council in 1693, partisan tensions came to a head. "Mr. Danforth labours to bring Mr. Mather and Cooke together," Sewall noted, "but I think in vain." The governor's disallowance of Cooke's election had provoked "great wrath," and most "supposed Mr. Mather is the cause" of the governor's veto.[4]

Sewall and Thomas Danforth were more than usually interested, and perhaps more than usually uncomfortable, in the evolving contest between the Assembly and Governor Phips. Both men had been supporters of the old charter and had served in privileged positions under it, Sewall on the Court of Assistants and Danforth as deputy governor, but both had accepted appointment as justices of the Superior Court and election to the Council under the 1691 charter. Their situation became even more discomfiting in 1693 when Phips sought to lessen the influence of his Boston critics by limiting their numbers in the Assem-

---

[3]G. B. Warden, *Boston, 1689–1776* (Boston: Little, Brown, 1970), 34–36; Wesley Frank Craven, *The Colonies in Transition, 1660–1713* (New York: Harper and Row, 1968), 245–46.

[4]Richard L. Bushman, *King and People in Provincial Massachusetts* (Chapel Hill: Univ. of North Carolina Press, 1985), 99–108; T. H. Breen, *The Character of the Good Ruler: Puritan Political Ideas in New England, 1630–1730* (New Haven: Yale Univ. Press, 1970), 182–95; Warden, *Boston*, 36–47; Richard R. Johnson, *Adjustment to Empire: The New England Colonies, 1675–1715* (New Brunswick, N.J.: Rutgers Univ. Press, 1981), 274–85, Mather quoted on p. 311; Thomas, ed., *Diary*, 2:310.

bly. The governor, knowing that some Bostonians in the lower house were elected to seats from towns and villages in which they did not reside, advocated a law requiring that "none be chosen representatives [to the Assembly] but persons resident in the towns for which they are chosen." The bill provoked a heated dissent in the Council and prevailed by the narrowest of margins, nine votes to eight, with Sewall and Danforth voting for Phips's proposal and in opposition to some of their closest associates.[5]

The dispute over residency and representation was the climax of the confrontation between the governor and the Assembly. By early 1694, tensions within the colony had begun to ease, in large part because Phips was increasingly preoccupied with defending himself in London against charges of misconduct. Eager to expand the basis of support for his administration in Massachusetts, the governor became decidedly more tractable. He withheld his veto when the Assembly elected Cooke to the Council in 1694 and even expressed a willingness to work for a return to the conditions that prevailed under the old charter. Nevertheless, when William III ordered Phips to return to England to answer the charges leveled against him, few seemed to mourn his departure. In 1692, the governor arrived on a Saturday evening with little fanfare, Sewall recorded in November 1694, "and so tis at his going off, both in darkness, and uncomfortable because of the Sabbath." Phips died a month after his arrival in London; when news of his death reached Boston in May of 1695, Sewall reported only that "people are generally sad."[6]

Dissension within Massachusetts remained muted during the adminstration of Phips's successor, Lieutenant Governor William Stoughton. Political experience and personal temperament combined in Stoughton to produce an executive determined to refrain from engaging in confrontations with the Assembly. During his predecessor's tenure, Stoughton had openly disagreed with Phips. Unlike Sewall, he had voted against the residency bill, and when the crown ordered that evidence pertaining to the purported misdeeds of Phips be sent to London, Stoughton joined in collecting documents unfavorable to the gov-

---

[5] Johnson, *Adjustment to Empire,* 314–15; Breen, *Character of the Good Ruler,* 192–93; Warden, *Boston,* 45–47; Thomas, ed., *Diary,* 1:314–15.

[6] Johnson, *Adjustment to Empire,* 281–84; Warden, *Boston,* 47; Breen, *Character of the Good Ruler,* 193–94; Thomas, ed., *Diary,* 1:323, 331–32. Phips had gotten the General Court to pass a resolution supporting his administration in November of 1693, but with a bare majority and considerable opposition in the lower house. In colonial New England, Sabbath observances began with meditations on Saturday evening.

ernor's case. His first public act as governor was to invite an array of local worthies to a "splendid treat" at the home of Boston merchant Thomas Cooper. Among the "councillors, ministers, [and] justices" in attendance were Elisha Cooke and Increase Mather. That old adversaries joined in celebrating the "occasion of the government's being fallen" on Stoughton was hardly happenstance; it was the result of calculated effort. In preparing for the "treat," the new governor had consulted with Sewall, and presumably others, about "whom he had best to invite." Stoughton's conciliatory administration rendered provincial politics relatively quiet for the next several years.[7]

On a more personal level, the demise of the Andros regime meant that much of Sewall's initial purpose in traveling to England in 1688 was rendered moot. Still, the usual round of family visits and the outbreak of King William's War prevented his speedy return to Boston. By the summer of 1689, he was homesick. He had visited Canterbury Cathedral, measured the galleries of the Bodleian Library, ridden between the massive slabs at Stonehenge, viewed the stars through Royal Astronomer John Flamsteed's telescopes, enjoyed the gardens at Emmanuel College, and marveled at the petrified cheese at St. John's, but he missed his family. To Hannah, he wrote: "Love to Brothers, Sisters, and to thee and our dear Quaternion. S.H.E.J."[8]

Sewall's beloved quaternion comprised Sam, Jr., Hannah, Elizabeth (Betty), and Joseph, the four Sewall children then living. By the time Sewall ventured to England in 1688, he and his wife Hannah had lost four of their eight children in infancy. Henry and Hull, as we have seen in the preceding selections, died in 1685 and 1686. Stephen, born on January 30, 1687, died six months later. The birth of Joseph on August 15, 1688, may have provided the Sewalls some solace; he "put up a bill for thanksgiving" the morning after the safe delivery of his son, whom he named, Sewall explained, "not out of respect to any relation, or other person, except the first Joseph." But tragedy continued to stalk the Sewall family. In the half dozen years between Sewall's return to Boston in 1689 and Joseph's beginning his studies with schoolmistress Ann Kay in 1695, Hannah gave birth to four daughters: Judith, Mary, Jane, and Sarah. Judith, whose birth on August 13, 1690, "wholly surprised" the family because it was one month premature, died after barely a month of life. Jane, born on August 7, 1693, also lived a short life. On September 9, a month after her birth, Jane was "not well." On September

[7]Johnson, *Adjustment to Empire,* 284; Thomas, ed., *Diary,* 1:315, 324–25.
[8]Thomas, ed., *Diary,* 1:233.

12, Sewall, whose misfortune it was to be practiced in looking for signs of early death, remembered his son Henry's desperate last hours some eight years earlier and recorded forebodingly that the infant Jane "looks like Henry in his sickness." The next night, his saddest expectations were realized as "little Jane expires, much as Henry did."[9]

Diary

1696

Second day [Monday], Jan. 6th 1696. Kept a day of fasting with prayer for the conversion of my son [Sam, Jr.], and his settlement in a trade that might be good for soul and body. *Uxor praegnans est* [wife is pregnant]. Governour's [Earl of Bellomont] expected arrival, which will bring great changes.[1] Supply for the South-Church. Three courts sit tomorrow. Lord's Supper the next Sabbath-day. Mr. [Joshua] Moodey's entanglements, Watertown. Church of England. New England. My hair. Read Epistles to Timothy, Titus, Philemon, Hebrews. Sung the 143, 51, and 130 Psalms. I had hope that seeing God pardoned all Israel's iniquities, He would pardon mine, as being part of Israel.

Seventh-day [Saturday], Jan. 4th. The Revd. Mr. Edward Bulkly, of Concord, dies at Chelmsford in a good old age; is buried at Concord.

Jan. 7th. Deacon Henry Allen dies. Col. [Bartholomew] Gedney's wife [Hannah] is dead within this week.

Jan. 8th. Unkle [Edmund] Quinsey lodged here last night, having

---

[9]Ibid., 89, 313.

[1]Sir William Phips returned to England in January of 1695 to answer charges leveled against him by his opponents in Massachusetts and London that he was abusing his vice-admiralty powers in his selective enforcement of the Acts of Trade. Phips died a month after his arrival in England, before his case could be settled. After Phips's death, the king's Lords Justices recommended that Richard Coote, Earl of Bellomont, be named governor not only of Massachusetts but of New York as well. The advantage of the dual appointment was clear: the new governor might draw his salary from New York and thus avoid the problems that Phips had encountered when the Massachusetts assembly refused to vote him a regular salary. Bellomont's commission made him governor of a confederation of the colonies of Massachusetts, New York, and New Hampshire. Although Bellomont's powers in no way matched those given to Sir Edmund Andros under the Dominion, Sewall and his friends were apprehensive; hence, Sewall's comment that Bellomont's anticipated arrival "will bring great changes." Bellomont finally arrived in New York in 1698, resided in Boston for only fourteen months in 1699–1700, and died in New York in March of 1701.

received a letter from Mr. [Daniel] Gookin [who had been married to Quincy's daughter Elizabeth, now deceased] to desire him, agrees to bind Daniel Gookin [Jr., fourteen years old] to Cous. [Jeremiah] Dummer [silversmith] for 8 years from the 10th of March next. Not being able to stay, desires me to see it effected. Bulkley and Edmund Quinsey dine with us.

Jan. 11. 1696. I write a letter to Mr. Zech. Walker acquainting him with his mother's death and funeral; that some recompence ought to be made to Mehetabel and Mary for their faithfull and laborious attendance on their grandmother. Although I reckon my self abundantly satisfied for any little service I did or could doe for our dear friend, by her desireable company and hearty thanks; yet I earnestly desire your prayers, that my aged father and mother may live and die with such like faith and frame of spirit as this our Sarah did.[2] I delivered this letter to be given to the post on second day morning, Jan. 13, 1696.

About 10 aclock *Jan. 13, 1696.* Cous. Dummer came to invite me to goe along with him to Cambridge to visit Mr. [Thomas] Danforth. About noon we set out, and at Mr. Danforth's gate, meet with Mr. N[ehemiah] Hobart and [James] Trowbridge; Mr. Danforth made us dine there; then after awhile, Mr. Hobart was called in to pray, which he did excellently, Mr. [Charles] Morton being by, who came with us from the college. When were there at first, Mr. Danforth bad me look on the cupboard's head for a book; I told him I saw there a law-book, Wingate on the Common Law. He said he would lend it me, I should speak to [Jacob] Amsden to call for it; and if he died, he would give it me. Again when took leave after prayer, he said he lent me that book not to wrap up but to read, and if misliked it, should tell him of it. By that time Cous. [Dummer] and I could get to the ferry twas quite dark. Capt. [Samuel] Hunting told us the river was full of ice and no getting over. But I went to [William] Sheaf and he hallowed over John Russell again. Boat came to Ballard's Wharf below the lodged ice, from whence had a very comfortable passage over with Madam [Elizabeth] Foxcroft.

When I came in, past 7 at night, my wife met me in the entry and told me Betty [fourteen years old] had surprised them. I was surprised

---

[2]Sarah Walker died on December 21, 1695. Walker had tutored Sewall's daughters Hannah and Betty in the 1680s and remained a close friend of the family. After her funeral on December 23, Sam, Jr., was "overwhelmed with Sorrow" and "shed many tears." Sewall hoped that the "removal of one of his [Sam, Jr.'s] best friends may put him upon seeking unto God betimes and making Him his Hiding Place." M. Halsey Thomas, ed., *The Diary of Samuel Sewall, 1674–1729,* 2 vols. (New York: Farrar, Straus and Giroux, 1973), 1:343.

with the abruptness of the relation. It seems Betty Sewall had given some signs of dejection and sorrow; but a little after dinner she burst out into an amazing cry, which caused all the family to cry too; her mother asked the reason; she gave none; at last said she was afraid she should goe to hell, her sins were not pardoned. She was first wounded by my reading a sermon of Mr. [John] Norton's, about the 5th of Jan. Text John 7. 34. Ye shall seek me and shall not find me. And those words in the sermon, John 8.21. Ye shall seek me and shall die in your sins, ran in her mind, and terrified her greatly. And staying at home Jan. 12, she read out of Mr. Cotton Mather—Why hath Satan filled thy heart, which increased her fear. Her mother asked her whether she prayed. She answered, Yes; but feared her prayers were not heard because her sins not pardoned. Mr. [Samuel] Willard though sent for timelyer, yet not being told of the message, till [two words illegible in MS] was given him; he came not till after I came home. He discoursed with Betty who could not give a distinct account, but was confused as his phrase was, and as had experienced in himself. Mr. Willard prayed excellently. The Lord bring sight and comfort out of this dark and dreadful cloud, and grant that Christ's being formed in my dear child, may be the issue [end] of these painfull pangs.

Feb. 1. 1696. Sam Haugh came to speak about Frank's burial; I sent Atherton [Sam's brother] away before and spake to Sam as to his mistress' maid being with child, and that she laid it to him, and told him if she were with child by him, it concerned him seriously to consider what were best to be done; and that a father was obliged to look after mother and child. Christ would one day call him to an account and demand of him what was become of the child: and if [he] married not the woman, he would always keep at a distance from those whose temporal and spiritual good he was bound to promote to the uttermost of his power. Could not discern that any impression was made on him. I remarked to him the unsuitableness of his frame under a business of so great and solemn concern.[3]

Third-Day. Feb. 4. Mr. Willard, Major [John] Walley, Capt. [Theophilus] Frary and Seth Perry *pater* [father] met here about the difference between said Frary and Perry. Capt. Frary seems now again to justify his oath, and what he did before was out of surprize. Major Walley desired Mr. Elliot and [Elizur] Holyoke to meet on lecture day,

---

[3] Samuel Haugh, aged twenty and indentured to Thomas Savage, had once been Sewall's ward; hence, Sewall continued to maintain an active interest in the young man's wellbeing.

Feb. 6, which they did, and sent for Mr. Perry. This day sennight [one week] is assigned him to bring his account.

Sixth-day, Feb. 7th. Mrs. [Elizabeth] Alden [wife of shipmaster John Alden] is buried. Bearers were Mr. [Ezekiel] Chiever, Capt. [James] Hill, Capt. [Nathaniel] Williams, Mr. [Major John] Walley, Mr. [Capt. John] Ballentine. Capt. Frary was passed by, though there, which several took notice of.

Last night Sam [Jr., seventeen years old] could not sleep because of my brother's [Stephen Sewall] speaking to him of removing to some other place, mentioning Mr. [Hezekiah] Usher's. I put him to get up a little wood, and he even fainted, at which brother was much startled, and advised to remove him forthwith and place him somewhere else, or send him to Salem and he would doe the best he could for him. Since, I have expressed doubtfullness to Sam as to his staying there.[4]

He [Sam, Jr.] mentioned to me Mr. [Benjamin] Wadsworth's sermon against idleness, which was an affliction to him. He said his was an idle calling, and that he did more at home than there, take one day with another. And he mentioned Mr. [Solomon] Stoddard's words to me, that should place him with a good master, and where had fullness of imployment. It seems Sam overheard him, and now alleged these words against his being where he was because of his idleness. Mentioned also the difficulty of the imployment by reason of the numerousness of goods and hard to distinguish them, many not being marked; whereas books, the price of them was set down, and so could sell them readily. I spake to Capt. [Samuel] Checkly again and again, and he gave me no encouragement that his being there would be to Sam's profit; and Mrs. Checkly always discouraging. Mr. Willard's sermon from those words, What doest thou here Elijah? was an occasion to hasten the removal.

Feb. 10. Secund-day. I went to Mr. Willard to ask whether had best keep him [Sam, Jr.] at home today. He said, No; but tell Capt. Checkly first; but when I came back, Sam was weeping and much discomposed, and loath to goe because it was a little later than usual, so I thought twas hardly fit for him to go in that case, and went to Capt. Checkly and told him how it was, and thanked him for his kindness to Sam. Capt. Checkly desired Sam might come to their house and not be strange there, for which I thanked him very kindly. He presented his service to my wife, and I to his who was in her chamber. Capt. Checkly gave me Sam's copy-book that lay in a drawer.

[4]Sam, Jr., had been an apprentice to the merchant Samuel Checkley for less than a year. Earlier, in 1694, he had served a brief apprenticeship with bookseller Michael Perry.

Just before I got thether, I met Mr. [Thomas] Grafford who told me that Mumford said I was a knave. The good Lord give me truth in the inward parts, and finally give rest unto my dear son, and put him into some calling wherein he will accept of him to serve Him.

Feb. 12. 1696. I rode to Brooklin with one Ems, a carpenter, to view the widow Bairsto's house, in order to repairing or adding to it. From thence to G[eorge] Bairsto's again, to [John] Devotions, to treat with him about a piece of ground to sell it [to] me and issue [end] the controversy about a way. From thence to Cambridge, to Mr. Wadsworth's chamber, where found [Lt.] Govr. [of New Hampshire John] Usher, Mr. Secretary [Isaac Addington], &c. with them came home, got to Mr. [James] Allen's [minister of the First Church] by 4 P.M. Supped. Sung two staves of the 132d Ps. begin at the 13th verse. Went to the meeting at Mrs. [Sarah] Noyes's.[5]

Sabbath, Feb. 16. 1696. Mr. [John] Emmerson preaches twice in the new Meetinghouse at Watertown, which is the first time. Capt. Checkly's son Samuel is baptized with us. I was very sorrowfull by reason of the unsettledness of my Samuel.

Feb. 22. 1696. Betty comes into me almost as soon as I was up and tells me the disquiet she had when waked; told me [she] was afraid [she] should go to hell, was like Spira, not elected.[6] Asked her what I should pray for, she said, that God would pardon her sin and give her a new heart. I answered her fears as well as I could, and prayed with many tears on either part; hope God heard us. I gave her solemnly to God.

Feb. 26. 1696. I prayed with Sam alone, that God would direct our way as to a calling for him.

It seems John Cornish essayed yesterday to goe to carry cloth to the fulling-mill [mill for cleaning and processing cloth], and perished in the storm; this day [his body] was brought frozen to town, a very sad spectacle.

By reason of the vehemency of the storm yesterday, but ten deputies

---

[5] Sarah Noyes was the widow of John Noyes, who died in 1678 of smallpox and whom Sewall described in his autobiographical letter as one of "my special Friends." Thomas, ed., *Diary,* 2:xxxiii.

[6] Francis Spira was a sixteenth-century Venetian Catholic who first professed a belief in the Lutheran doctrine of grace and then publicly recanted. Upon recanting, however, Spira was convinced that he was "utterly undone," that he was now destined to "eternall damnation." Inconsolable, he lived out the rest of his life in agony. In the seventeenth century, as David D. Hall points out, Spira's story was such an integral part of the everyday religion of New Englanders that the mere mention of his name conjured up images of God's justice and the terrors to be visited upon sinners. See David D. Hall, *Worlds of Wonder, Days of Judgment: Popular Religious Belief in Early New England* (New York: Knopf, 1989), 132–33.

assemble, so that the Lieut. Governour [William Stoughton] questions whether the [General] Court be not fallen, because 40 constitute a house.

Fifth-day, 27th. 32 deputies appear.

Sixth-day. [*Feb. 28*] Have fourty [deputies] or upward. Chuse Major [Penn] Townsend Speaker. Lieut-Governour was much disturbed as fearing the Court could not legally be held, because was not that appearance the first and second day as the law prescribes.

Sabbath, Apr. 12, 1696. About 8 m[ane; i.e., in the morning]. it begins to snow; by noon the houses and ground were covered, and at 5 P.M. I saw an isicle seven inches long. This new snow was plentifully to be seen on the ground for about three days space.

Fifth-day, Apr. 23, 1696. News is brought of several of our men killed at Tartooda [Tortuga], and six vessels taken.

Mr. Daniel Oliver marries Mrs. Elisabeth Belchar.

Apr. 24. Lydia Moodey visits me, and tells me that Mr. [Samuel] Phillips of Rowley dyed the last Wednesday, the same morn we read— The prophets do they live for ever? in Zech. 1. The Lord help me to redeem the time.

Sabbath, May 3, 1696. Betty can hardly read her chapter for weeping; tells me she is afraid she is gone back, does not taste that sweetness in reading the Word which once she did; fears that what was once upon her is worn off. I said what I could to her, and in the evening prayed with her alone.

Fifth-day, May 7, 1696. Col. [Samuel] Shrimpton marries his son to his wife's sister's daughter, Elisabeth Richardson. All of the Council in town were invited to the wedding, and many others. Only I was not spoken to. As I was glad not to be there because the lawfullness of the intermarrying of Cousin-Germans is doubted;[7] so it grieves me to be

---

[7]That Sewall was opposed to such marriages is clear. In 1704, when his nephew John Sewall told him that he had been advised to marry the widow of his "Cousin German," Sewall responded in no uncertain terms. "Tis [a] pity that any have been so unadvised themselves as to prompt you to do a needless thing," he wrote. "It is not easy to conceive how a man's marrying his Sister should be a capital crime, and yet the marriage of Cousin Germans should be blameless and commendable." When John suggested that "Cousins-German" were not "so near as Second-Cousins by blood," Sewall told him that he was "plainly mistaken." Scripture "reckons Cousins Germans among Brothers and Sisters, and so uncapable of intermarriage." If John entertained even the smallest doubts about such marriages, Sewall advised, then he should "do that which is safe, which is most safe, in a matter of the greatest importance. Be sure you have the license of Heaven to produce." Sewall to John Sewall, February 23, 1704, *Letter-Book of Samuel Sewall,* Massachusetts Historical Society *Collections,* 6th series, 1–2 (Boston, 1886–88), 1:290–93.

taken up in the lips of talkers, and to be in such a condition that Col. Shrimpton shall be under a temptation in defence of himself, to wound me; if any should happen to say, Why was not such a one here? The Lord help me not to do, or neglect any thing that should prevent the dwelling of brethren together in unity. And, Oh most bountifull and gracious God, who givest liberally and upbraidest not, admit me humbly to bespeak an invitation to the marriage of the lamb, and let thy grace with me and in me be sufficient for me in making my self ready. And out of thy infinite and unaccountable compassions, place me among those who shall not be left; but shall be accepted by Thee here, and taken into glory hereafter. Though I am beyond conception vile! Who may say unto Thee, What doest thou? Thou canst justify thy self in thy proceedings. And O, Lord God forgive all my unsuitable deportment at thy Table the last Sabbath-Day, that wedding day; and if ever I be again invited (invite me once again!) help me entirely to give my self to thy son as to my most endeared lord and husband. And let my dear wife and all my children, partake in this priviledge, and that not as umbras [shadows], but on their own account.

May 11th 1696. Joseph [eight years old] falls down and breaks his forhead so as bleeds pretty much.

May 11th 1696. Town-meeting to chuse Assembly-men, 134 there; Mr. [John] Eyre had 88. Major Townsend 85. Capt. [Nathaniel] Byfield 82. Mr. [Nathaniel] Oliver 74. Mr. Tho. Brattle had 67. Left out Mr. [Edward] Bromfield, [Timothy] Thornton, Frary.

May 12, 1696. Cous. [Jeremiah] Dummer, Mr. Eyre, Bromfield, went with me to Mr. Increase Mather and acknowledged that his preaching the lecture once or twice was very pleasing to us, and that we were thankfull for it, and desired more; that he would please to preach in course, as being as diffusive a way of doing good, as any in our little Israel. He treated us with respect and some encouragement, I hope.

Fourth-day, May 13, 1696. Mr. Willard, Capt. [Edward] Wyllys, Capt. Frary, and Mr. Sheaf met at my house about the difference between said Frary and Mr. Perry; Wyllys, Sheaf and I told him plainly that it had been well the matter had been issued [ended] by their mutual confession to each other at their privat meeting, as was once intended. He persisted and said he knew certainly that what he had sworn was true; I told him the less was said of that nature, the better twould be, it was so long agoe; and if Mr. Eliot was possessed, Mrs. Eliot his mother must be his tenant; whereas the father's will made him her servant, and nature too, he being under age; and the Scripture saith the heir under age differs little from a servant.

May 18. By reason of the Major Generall's [Wait Still Winthrop] illness, I am forced to go to Ipswich court; and being to go, my wife desired me to go on to Newbury [where Sewall's parents lived]; I went with brother [Stephen] on Wednesday night. Visited father, mother, friends, returned to Salem, got thether about nine. Supped well with the fish bought out of Wenham pond. Between eleven and noon, Tho. Messenger comes in, and brings me the amazing news of my wife's hard time and my son's being still-born. We get up our horses from the ship, and set out by starlight about 12, yet the bells rung for five before we got over the ferry. Found my wife as well as usually; but I was grievously stung to find a sweet desirable son dead, who had none of my help to succour him and save his life. The Lord pardon all my sin, and wandering and neglect, and sanctify to me this singular affliction. These tears I weep over my abortive son.

A reason for life and for death has been revealed to me at the same time;
 I alone am not allowed to have as many as thirteen [children],
Yet let this hope sustain grieving parents,
 Jesus is able to come into me.[8]

Fourth day, May 27, 1696. Election. Rainy day, which wet the troops that waited on the Lieut. Governour [Stoughton] to the town. Mr. Cotton Mather preaches. Pouring out water at Mispeh, the text.

Votes.—Stoughton 60—[Thomas] Danforth 65—[John] Pynchon 61—[James] Russel 55—[Bartholomew] Gedney 69—Winthrop 58—[John] Hathorn 62—Hutchinson[,] Elisha 79—Sewall 70—[Isaac] Addington 71—[Elisha] Cook 72—[William] Brown 55—[John] Phillips 58—[Jonathan] Corwin 46—Shrimpton 57—[John] Foster 62—[Daniel] Perce 53—[Peter] Sergeant 45. Major [Robert] Pike had 32, so Col. Shrimpton comes in his room.

Plimouth—[William] Bradford 65—[Barnabas] Lothrop 67—[Nathaniel] Thomas 66—[John] Thacher 41.

Main[e]—E[liaki]m Hutchinson, [Charles] Frost, [Samuel] Wheelwright, votes so unanimous that they were not parted.

Sagadahoc—Joseph Lynde 41. Mr. Tho. Brattle had 21.

At large. Vagum [at large]. [John] Walley 39. [John] Saffin 39. Capt. John Appleton had 26. I have fallen 7 [votes] since last year; the Lord advance me in real worth, and his esteem.

---

[8]Sewall rendered his tribute to his abortive son in Latin as follows:

Causa parata mihi est, et vitae, et mortis, ibidem;
 In tredecim, Solus denegor, ire foras,
Spes tamen haec maneat, stimulante dolore, parentes,
 Ad memet Jesus introijsse potest.

May 28. Our two old nurses got my wife on the pallat-bed [temporary straw bed], which much discomposed her, put her in great pain, and all in great fear. Grows better by morn. May 29.

Sabbath, May 31, 1696. Mr. Willard is so faint with his flux, that is not able to come abroad, and so there is a disappointment of the Lord's Supper, which should otherwise have been celebrated this day. Mr. Cotton Mather preaches, exhorts us to examine our selves, whether we were prepared for that ordinance. And said that humiliation for the disappointmt, and mourning after Christ, God might make as profitable to us as the ordinance.

May 30. Post brings from New-York a confirmation of the news about the plot, and a printed proclamation for the thanksgiving in England; It seems the Governour has a packet.

Second-day, June 1, 1696. Mr. [Michael] Wigglesworth preaches the Artillery sermon, from Ephes. 6, 11. Put on the whole Armour of God, that ye may be able to stand against the wiles of the Devil. In the applications, said 'twas necessary we should doe so by reason of the evil of the times or else of Popery, or something as bad as Popery should come to be set up. What should we doe? Mentioned Rev. 16.15 [Blessed is he that watcheth, and keepeth his garments], said the garments there and armour in the text were the same. About dinner time the guns were fired at the Castle and battery for joy that the plot was discovered.

June 11, 1696. I strove with my might that in stead of Tuesday, Thursday, and Satterday in every week, it might be said, third, fifth and seventh day in every week; but could not prevail, hardly one in the Council would secund me, and many spake against it very earnestly; although I asked not to have it changed in the fairs. Some said twas the speech of the English nation; mend it in the fasts; mend it every where or no where, others said persons would scarce know what days were intended; and in England would call us Quakers. I urged that the week only, of all parcells of time, was of Divine institution, erected by God as a monumental pillar for a memorial of the creation perfected in so many distinct days.[9]

June 19. News is brought to town of Capt. Berries [Thomas Berry, son-in-law of former Harvard president John Rogers, who had died in 1684] being slain.

June 20th. Wm Veisy is bound over for plowing on the day of thanksgiving &c. News comes that the embargo is kept strictly in England.

[9]Because he deemed the days of the week to be a memorial to God's work as recorded in the book of Genesis, Sewall opposed the use of pagan names as corruptions.

Legendum [Sermon].

At Edinburg Octr 27, 1695, in the Colledge, it being the Sabbath, and their Sacrament day, one Mr. John Moncrife, preaching on that text, Jer. 3, 22, Return you backsliding children, and I will heal your back-slidings: Behold we come unto Thee for thou art the Lord our God—Between the hours of 10 and 11, there came such a downpouring of the spirit of God on the whole congregation (supposed to be 3 or 4000), that they all cryed out, not being able to contain themselves; so that the minister could not be heard; but was forced to give over preaching to the people; and sung a psalm to compose them. A person present adds, that he and 100 more never saw heaven on earth before, being like Peter on the Mount, or Jacob in Bethel, or Paul in a rapture. For the Lord came down with the shout of a king among them, so that they could have been content to have built tabernacles there; which has dashed the Jacobite party more than all the kings forces could doe.

From London by the ships that arrived July 12, 1696.

July 12, 1696. By reason of fire on Mrs. [Hannah] Phillips stone house over against the Town house, the morning exercise was tumultuously interrupted, both at the old meetinghouse [First Church] and ours [South Church]. The North [Church members] who had no impression from this, were much disturbed by the alarm from the Castle, which a man rashly told them of as were celebrating the Lds Supper. About one [o'clock] the drums beat throw the town, all goe into arms. Nantasket beacon began. Had order it seems on the sight of 2 great ships to fire it, because of the 2 who lately took Capt. [Wentworth] Paxton. In the afternoon some went to meeting; abt 30 men in all at ours. North [Church] met not till abt 5 P.M. when our exercise was over; went to the Townhouse and after a while by Mr. Whittingham received the packet which makes void many of our laws; viz. courts, colledge, habeas corpus, forms of writts &c. and confirms many others.[10]

July, 23. In the evening were much startled by a letter from Govr Usher, of many ships seen off and their province in arms upon it. Lt. Govr [Stoughton] came in his charet to my house, and sent for the Council. Majr Genl [Winthrop], Mr. [Elisha] Cook, Mr. Secretary [Addington], Mr. [John] Foster, [Peter] Serjeant, Majr [John] Walley came, Majr [Penn] Townsend also sent for and came: After a while, the captain of the Castle comes in, and informs us that twas the mast-fleet

[10]The 1691 Massachusetts charter required all of the colony's laws to be transmitted to England for approval by the Privy Council.

from England, so were comfortably dismissed between 9 and 10 of the clock.

July 26. We hear that Mr. [Benjamin] Bullivant and Mr. [Samuel] Myles [both prominent Anglicans and former associates of Sir Edmund Andros] are come.

27th At the Council the Lt. Govr reads the letters that give notice from the Lords [Board of Trade and Plantations] of a French squadron intending for America; they will afford us what assistance they can under the present circumstance of affairs. Reads also Mr. [William] Blathwayts letter recommending the subscribing the Association by all in publick place and trust, with one drawn for that purpose.[11] This day also received an express from Col. [John] Pynchon, of Count Frontenac's coming agt the 5 Nations, or Albany, or N.E., or all, with 2000 French and 1000 Indians: Casteen with 4 or 500 to hold us in play the mean while. The wind coming North last night ships arrive at Nantasket this morn. Mr. Myles and Bullivant come to town.

July 26. Mr. Veisy [William Vesey, Jr.] preached at the Church of England; had many auditors. He was spoken to to preach for Mr. Willard [at the South Church]; but am told [Vesey is unwilling to do so because] this will procure him a discharge [from the Anglican church].

Third day Augt 4. Pemmaquid fort [Fort William Henry] is summond by the French; the two ships which took the Newport galley, and said galley; besides many hundreds by land.

Fourth day Augt 5th summond them again, and for fear of their guns, bombs and numbers, Capt [Pascoe] Chub surrendred, and then they blew up the fort.[12] This news came to town Augt 10. Capt. Paxton brought it; just after publishing the act referring to navigation [Navigation Act of 1696].

Fourth-day Augt 12, 1696. Mr. [Jacob] Melyen, upon a slight occasion, spoke to me very smartly about the Salem witchcraft; in discourse he said, if a man should take Beacon hill on his back, carry it away; and then bring it and set it in its place again, he should not make any thing of that.

---

[11]Members of the House of Commons, fearing attempts on the life of William III, entered into an association for the defense of the king by signing a declaration of fidelity to William on February 25, 1696. Massachusetts legislators signed the association's oath on September 18, 1696.

[12]Captain Pascoe Chubb, the commander of Fort William Henry on the Maine frontier, surrendered the garrison to the French on July 15, 1696. The French and their Indian allies killed a few of the ninety-five Massachusetts men they had captured and plundered the fort. Massachusetts authorities subsequently arrested Chubb and dismissed him from further military service.

Seventh-day, Augt 15th Brother Stephen Sewall comes to town; gets an order to Col. [John] Hathorne for erecting a beacon on Pigeon hill on Cape-Anne, and for pressing 20 men at Marble-head. This day vessels arrive from Barbados, bring news of 10 great ships at Petit Quavers, of between 60 and 90 guns. Mr. Williams, the physician, and his wife are both dead. Mrs. Hatch and her children in tears for the death of her husband, which was brought to her about an hour by sun. We are in pain for Saco [Maine] fort. Guns were heard thrice on fifth day all day long. One Peters and Hoyt scalped at Andover this week; were not shot, but knocked on the head.

Augt 24. Betty rides to Salem, to sojourn there awhile [at Stephen Sewall's home]; Sam carries Joanna Gerrish [daughter of Sewall's sister Jane Gerrish] to Newbury [where Sewall's parents resided].

7r [September] 5th Little Mehetabel Fifield dies, being about 8 weeks old.

Septr 7th Jane [Gerrish] sets sail for Newbury with little Sarah [Sewall's youngest daughter, aged a year and ten months]; suppose got thether the next day.

Septr 8 Mr. Benja[min] Wadsworth is ordained pastor of the First Church. Mr. [James] Allin [also of the First Church] gave the charge, Mr. I. Mather gave the right hand of fellowship; spake notably of some young men who had apostatized from New England principles, contrary to the light of their education; was glad that he [Wadsworth] was of another spirit.[13] Mr. Willard was one who joined in laying on of hands.

Septr 9. Purchase Capen had been gunning, or shot a fowl by the by as was at work; charged his gun which others knew not of, laid it down as was about to go home at night; a lad took it up in sport and held it out, it went off and killed the owner.

Septr 10. Mr. [Nehemiah] Walter preaches the lecture, made a very good sermon. The fear of the Lord is to hate evil.

Letter. Mrs. Martha Oakes. Not finding opportunity to speak with you at your house, nor at my own, I write, to persuade you to be sensible that your striking your daughter-in-law before me, in my house, is not justifiable; though twas but a small blow, twas not a small fault; especially considering your promise to refrain from [indiscreet] speech itself; or at least any that might give disturbance. As for New England, it is a cleaner country than ever you were in before, and, therefore, with

---

[13]Mather is probably referring to the rejection by some ministers of the ordination ritual of the laying on of hands. In 1686, John Bailey and Charles Morton refused, as Sewall observed, to be ordained "as Congregational men are." Mather, who delivered the charge at Morton's ordination, bemoaned the latter's refusal to follow the "Congregational way." See footnote 18 on p. 129.

disdain to term it *filthy,* is a sort of blasphemie, which, by proceeding out of your mouth, hath defiled you. I write not this to upbraid, but to admonish you, with whom I sympathize under your extraordinary provocations and pressures; and pray God command you freedom from them. S.S.[14]

7r [September] 14. 1696. Went with Mr. [Joshua] Moodey, and visited Mrs. [Martha] Collins, John Soley, and Mr. [Michael] Wigglesworth and his wife [Sybil], dined with them; I furnished New England salt.

7r 16. Keep a day of prayer in the east end of the Town-House, [Lt.] Govr, Council and Assembly. Mr. Morton begun with prayer, Mr. Allin prayed, Mr. Willard preached—If God be with us who can be against us?—Spake smartly at last about the Salem witchcrafts, and that no order had been suffered to come forth by authority to ask God's pardon.

Mr. [Samuel] Torrey prayed, Mr. Moodey; both excellently; all prayed hard for the persons gone forth in the expedition.[15]

7r 17th Mr. Moodey preacheth the lecture from Act. 13.36. For David after he had served his own generation &c.; made a very good sermon; dined with Mr. Danforth, Winthrop, Gedney, Russel, [Stephen] Sewall—about 10, at [James] Meers's [tavern].

7r 18, P.M. The Council and Representatives subscribe the Association [pledging allegiance to William III]. In the morn had warm discourse whether the [General] Court could sit or no, because the writ by which twas called was made void; at last spake round and were then quiet. [Lt.] Govr said he was resolved to hold the Court if so many would abide with him as were capable.

7r 25th 1696. Mr. John Glover is buried. Col. Pynchon, Mr. Cook, Mr. P. Sergeant and Mr. [Thomas] Oakes were there. Drew up a letter to the Duke of Shrewsbury.

Octr 3. David Edwards is buried. The revival of courts is published; and the Court adjourned to the 18 Novr 1 P.M. Some moved for a dissolution, saying feared we were not on a good bottom, which angered the Lt Govr. Septr 29. 1696. Mr. Wigglesworth and his wife lodge here.

Octr 3. 1696. Mr. Joseph Baxter lodges here, being to preach for

[14]Martha Oakes was a member of a prominent New England family. Her husband, Thomas Oakes, a Boston physician, had served in England as an agent for Massachusetts. Thomas's brother, Urian Oakes, was the former president of Harvard (1675–81).

[15]Massachusetts mounted an expedition against the French in retaliation for the destruction of Fort William Henry. Three British ships transported five hundred men under the command of Benjamin Church to Penobscot, but the French forces were no longer in the area.

Mr. Willard on the Sabbath: Deacon [Theophilus] Frary came to me on Friday; told me Mr. Willard put him upon getting help on the fifth day at evening, because disappointed of Mr. [John] Sparhawk [minister of Bristol]. He [Frary] sent that evening to Braintrey; but for fear of failing rode thether himself on Sixth-day morn and secured him [Baxter]: After the meeting at brother [Joseph] Wheelers, [Frary] came and told me of it, and earnestly proposed to me that he [Baxter] might lodge at my house; which I thought I could not avoid except I would shut my doors against one of Christ's servants; which I also inclined to, only was afraid lest some should take offence. And my library was convenient for him.

Octr 10. Bro[the]r [James] Pemberton dies.

Octr 12. Lt Governour goes to Cambridge, Mr. Secretary, Major Wally and I goe to Dorchester and wait on his Honour from thence; Mr. Cook, Mr. Hutchinson, Foster, Russel, Lynde there: Mr. [Nathaniel] Williams made an oration (Mr. [Ebenezer] Pemberton should have done it but was prevented by his fathers death). Lt. Govr complemented the president [Harvard president Increase Mather] &c. for all the respect to him, acknowldged his obligation and promised his interposition for them as become such an alumnus to such an alma mater; directed and desired the president and fellows to go on; directed and enjoined the students to obedience.[16] Had a good dinner; came home; Mr. Danforth not there. Mr. Cotton Mather took off [former presidents of Harvard] Mr. [Charles] Chauncy and [Urian] Oakes's epitaphs as I read them to him.

Oct. 13 [Lt.] Govr goes to view the Castle, I went not because of a flux. Mr. Simms [Zechariah Symmes] dined with me to day, spake of the assaults he had made upon periwiggs; and of his repulses. Seemed to be in good sober sadness.

4th d[ay]. Octr 21. 1696. A church is gathered at Cambridge North-farms [Lexington]; no relations [statements of conversion] made, but a covenant signed and voted by 10 brethren dismissed from the churches of Cambridge, Watertown, Wooburn, Concord for this work. Being declared to be a church, they chose Mr. Benj. Estabrooks their pastor, who had made a good sermon from Jer. 3.15 [And I will give you pastors according to mine heart, which shall feed you with knowledge and understanding]. Mr. [Joseph] Estabrooks, the father, man-

---

[16]On June 27, 1692, the new Massachusetts legislature passed an act (re)incorporating Harvard College, a move made necessary by the abrogation of the Massachusetts Bay charter in 1684. However, the Privy Council disallowed the act of incorporation and thus left Harvard in a state of uneasiness.

aged this [Benjamin's ordination], having prayed excellently; Mr. Willard gave the charge; Mr. [Jabez] Fox the right hand of fellowship. Sung part of the 4 Ps. From the 9th v. to the end, O God, our Thoughts. Mr. Stone and [Moses] Fisk thanked me for my assistance there. Cambridge was sent to though had no teaching officer; they sent Elder [Jonas] Clark. [Walter] Hasting, [Jonathan] Remmington.

Sabbath, Octr 25. Towards the latter end of Mr. [Increase] Mathers prayer, a dog vomited in the ally [aisle] near the corner of Mr. Willards pew, which stunk so horribly that some were forced out of the house; I and others could hardly stay; Mr. Mather himself almost sick. Just about duskish we know there is an house on fire, it proves [to be] Peter Butlers, just by my Lady's [widow of former governor Sir William Phips], where Mr. [Samuel] Nowell once dwelt. Mr. [Bartholomew] Green, who married Mr. Mathers daughter [Maria], is one of the tenants; he and his family were at Charlestown, keeping Sabbath there.

Fifth day Octr 22. Capt. [Nathaniel] Byfield marries his daughter Debora to James Lyde, before Mr. Willard. Mr. Sparhawk would have had her [was an unsuccessful suitor].

Octr 29th Clouds hinder our sight of the eclipsed moon; though tis apparently dark by means of it.

Octr 30. Mr Wigglesworth tells me that one John Bucknam of Malden, above 50 years old, has been perfectly dumb near 18 years, and now within about 3 weeks has his understanding and speech restored. He is much affected with the goodness of God to him herein.

2d day, Novr 2. Mary [five years old] goes to Mrs. [Deborah] Thair's to learn to read and knit.

3d d[ay]. Novr 10. Ride to Salem with Mr. Cooke, get to Lewis's [tavern] 1/4 of an hour before Mr. Danforth; were met there by Mr. Sheriff, Mr. Harris and Brown; Mr. Howard went with us; in the even[ing] visit Govr Bradstreet, who confirms what had formerly told me about Mr. Gage his being in the expedition against Hispaniola and dying in it.

Novr 11. Grand jury present Tho. Maule for publishing his scandalous book. Jury of Tryals, of whom Capt. [John] Turner and Capt. King were two, bring him in not guilty, at which he triumphs. Mr. Bullivant spake for him, but modestly and with respect.[17] In the evening,

[17]Thomas Maule, Boston merchant and Quaker critic of the Puritan establishment, wrote *Truth Held Forth and Maintained According to the Testimony of the Holy Prophets . . . with Some Account of the Judgments of the Lord Lately Inflicted upon New England by Witchcraft* (New York, 1695). On December 19, 1695, Sewall recorded that Massachusetts authorities ordered Maule's book to be "burnt, being stuff'd with notorious Lyes and Scandals," and Maule himself to appear before the court.

visited Major [William] Brown, there sung first part of 72 ps. and last part 24th. But first visited Mr. [John] Higginson, though had dined with us. He tells me that the protector, Oliver Cromwell, when Genl, wrote to Mr. [William] Hook of Newhaven, and therein sent comendations to Mr. [John] Cotton; upon which Mr. Cotton was writt to by Mr. Hook and desired to write to the Genl, which he did, and advised him that to take from the Spaniards in America would be to dry up Euphrates [as in the book of Revelation]; which was one thing put him upon his expedition to Hispaniola, and Mr. Higginson and 3 more were to have gone to Hispaniola if the place had been taken. O. Cromwell would have had Capt. [John] Leverett to have gone thether [as] Govr, told him twas drying up Euphrates, and he intended not to desist till he came to the gates of Rome. This Mr. Cook said he had heard his father Leverett tell many a time. Govr Leverett said, My lord let us make an end of one voyage first, and declined it; at which Oliver was blank. One told Mr. Leverett, Jamaica was the Protector's darling, and he had disadvantaged himself in not consenting to goe.

Novr 12. Dine with fish and fowls at Major Brown's. Col. Gedney went out of town, so that we saw him not all the Court. Major Brown, Mr. Benj. Brown, brother [Stephen Sewall], Mr. [John] Emmerson, Col. Hathorn brought us going as far as the Butts. Mr. Cook asked me which way would goe, I said we will goe [with] Mr. Danforth as far as the [blank], so came home by Charlestown very comfortably. I set Betty to read Ezek. 37, and she weeps so that can hardly read; I talk with her and she tells me of the various temptations she had; as that [she] was a reprobate, loved not God's people as she should. Intends to come home [to Boston from Stephen Sewall's place in Salem] when she has done her cusheon. Find all well at home.

Novr 13. Mr. Addington comes to me, and tells me I was summoned to Dorchester by the Lt Govr to dine. I told him of Mr. Simon Wainwright, and asked his advise about putting his name out of the commission, he made me no answer; at which I was a little disappointed and looked on him; he stood up and said he was very ill. I reached the elbow chair to him and with my arms crowded him into it; where he presently became like a dying man: I sent for Mr. Oakes [physician Thomas Oakes], who was not at home. But he [Addington] quickly revived and said he was in a sweat, would sit a little and then goe; said twas well I got him into the chair, else should have fallen. He gave me an almanack in Mr. [John] Ushers name, desired me to present his duty to the Lt Govr and went home. I fear twas a fit of the apoplexy. Went with Majr Wally and Capt [Cyprian] Southack to the Lt Govr's, where dined; [diners included:] Capt Kiggin, Jesson, [John] Eyre, [John] Fayerwether, Tho. Brattle, [Andrew] Belchar, [Joseph] Dudley, Southack, Davenport, Edw. Turfry, [Thaddeus] Maccarty, Mr. Leverett, Danforth, Major Townsend, Major Walley, Sewall; Govr Usher, Lt. Governour and Mr. Usher sat at the end of the table, Capt Kiggin next on the Lt Govrs side, then Capt Jesson, Mr. Eyre. Sewall sat next on Mr. Usher's side, then Major Wally, Major Townsend. 'Twas about sunset by the time we got home.

Novr 20 6th day, Madam Saml [i.e., Elizabeth] Bellingham, Capt [Nathaniel] Thomas, Mr. Willard and their wives, Mr. Woodbridge and his kinsman Brockherst dined here.

Novr 25. 1696. Brother [Stephen Sewall] brings home Elizabeth, who is well, blessed be God. Went thither Augt 24.

Novr 25. Mr. Wm Brattle was ordained at Cambridge. He and Mr. [Increase] Mather, the president [of Harvard], preached. Twas first ordered that Mr. Brattle should not preach, but many being troubled at it, twas afterward altered. Mr. Brattle also procured the church to order that Elder Clark should not lay his hand on his [Brattle's] head when he was ordained; and he [Clark] refrained accordingly. So that Deacon [Obadiah] Gill coming home, said he liked all very well except the bill of exclusion. I was feverish by reason of cold taken the day before, and so abode at home.

Wednesday, Novr 25. 1696. As I sat alone at home in the old room, I had the notion first; Tis when martyrs *seen,* not *slain* [as a fulfilment of prophecy in the book of Revelation].

Second-day, Novr 30. Many scholars go in the afternoon to scate on fresh-pond; William Maxwell, and John Eyre fall in and are drowned. Just about candle-lighting the news of it is brought to town, which affects persons exceedingly. Mr. Eyre the father cryes out bitterly.[18]

Decr 1. The body of John Eyre is brought to town. Decr 3. is buried. Ministers of Boston had gloves and rings, Counsellors gloves, of Boston. Bearers, Hutchinson, Dudley, Sim. Bradstreet, Dummer Jer[emiah], John Winthrop, Belchar. Maxwell was buried at Cambridge. Paul Miller, his 2 sons, and about 4 more drowned last week; vessel and corn lost coming from Barstable.

Decr 2. 1696. Now about Capt. Byfield brings in a long bill from the deputys for a fast and reformation, written by Mr. Cotton Mather, to

---

[18]Increase Mather preached a sermon on the occasion, *A Discourse Concerning the Uncertainty of the Times of Men, and the Necessity of Being Prepared for Sudden Changes & Death* (Boston, 1697).

which a streamer [supplement] was added expressing that partiality in courts of justice was obvious; with a vote on it that 500 [copies] should be printed, should be read; and sent up for concurrence; 'twas denied [by the Council]; and our bill for a fast was sent down; deputies denied that. Govr told them the way was unusual, they had taken, sending out a committee, calling the ministers, voting all, and never letting the Council know; that it pertained principally to the Govr and Council to set forth such orders with a motion from them. A while after Capt. Byfield came in, and said 'twas no new thing, and they had taken no wrong step. Little was said to him. It seems this message is entered in their book. The Council were exceedingly grieved to be thus roughly treated.

About Decr 18, Mr. [Increase] Mather, Allen, Willard, C[otton] Mather give in a paper subscribed by them, shewing their dislike of our draught for the [Harvard] college charter, and desiring that their names might not be entered therein. One chief reason was their apointing the Govr and Council for visitor.[19]

Decr 19. Mr. Allin prays, and the Court is prorogued to the 17th Febr. at 1 P.M. Lt Governour said that hoped by praying together, our love to God and one another should be increased. This is the first prorogation that I know of.

Nota, Deputies voted our bill for the fast at length. Mr. Byfield brought it in, said, they would have *doubtless* instead of *probably.* And would have those words—*and so revive that joyful Proverb in the world, One flock, one Shepherd*—left out. Their reason was because God's conversion of the American heathen did not make it good. Therefore would have the word *Obey* added after our *hear,* and let that be the close.[20]

Nota. I had by accident met with and transcribed Mr. [William] Strong's notes on Rev. 12th about the slaying of the witnesses, the evening before this fell out; the last words were, prepare for it. I doe not know that ever I saw the Council run upon with such a height of rage

---

[19]The Council drew up a bill for a new charter for Harvard in September of 1696. Increase Mather, Harvard's president at that time, objected principally to two of its provisions: that the president must "dwell and reside at the college," and that the governor and Council be named as Visitors, a position that might include the power to intervene in the administration of the college. Although the bill was signed by Lieutenant Governor William Stoughton on December 17, it never took effect because Mather and other officers named in the 1696 charter refused to serve under it. As Sewall's entry makes clear, Increase and Cotton Mather, James Allen, and Samuel Willard demanded that their names not be listed among the college's officers.

[20]See the entry for December 2 above. Mather's original draft of a bill for a day of fasting and prayer was rejected by the Council on December 11. The Council's bill, which was a version of Mather's, but with his criticism of the judiciary left out, was eventually accepted by the deputies, with the modifications suggested in this entry.

before. The Lord prepare for the issue. I dont remembr to have seen Capt. Byfield or [Daniel] Oliver at prayers. And the ministers will go to England for a [college] charter, except we exclude the Council from the visitation. Allege this reason: because the K[ing] will not pass it, and so shall be longer unsettled.

Note[:] *Decr 12. 1696.* Capt. [Benjamin] Davis's eldest daughter dyes very suddenly. Was a great funeral next week.

Decr 21. A very great snow is on the ground. I go in the morn to Mr. Willard, to entreat him to chuse his own time to come and pray with little Sarah [two years old]: He comes a little before night, and prays very fully and well. Mr. [Increase] Mather, the president [of Harvard], had prayed with her in the time of the Courts sitting.

Decr 22. being catechising day, I give Mr. Willard a note to pray for my daughter publickly, which he did.

Note[:] This morn Madam Elisa[beth] Bellingham came to our house and upbraided me with setting my hand to pass Mr. [Richard] Wharton's account to the Court, where he obtained a judgmt for Eustace's farm. I was wheadled and hectored into that business, and have all along been uneasy in the remembrance of it; and now there is one come who will not spare to lay load [to blame, reproach]. The Lord take away my filthy garments, and give me change of rayment. This day I remove poor little Sarah into my bed-chamber, where about break of day Decr 23, she gives up the ghost in Nurse [Hannah] Cowell's arms. Born, Nov. 21. 1694. Neither I nor my wife were by; Nurse not expecting so sudden a change, and having promised to call us. I thought of Christ's words, could you not watch with me one hour! and would fain have sat up with her, but fear of my wife's illness, who is very valetudinarious, made me to lodge with her in the new hall, where was called by Jane's [Sewall's sister Jane Gerrish] cry, to take notice of my dead daughter. Nurse did long and pathetically ask our pardon that she had not called us, and said she was surprized. Thus this very fair day is rendered foul to us by reason of the general sorrow and tears in the family. Master [Ezekiel] Chiever was here the evening before, I desired him to pray for my daughter. The chapter read in course on Decr 23 mane was Deut. 22. which made me sadly reflect that I had not been so thorowly tender of my daughter; nor so effectually carefull of her defence and preservation as I should have been. The good Lord pity and pardon and help for the future as to those God has still left me.

Decr 24. Sam recites to me in Latin, Mat. 12. from the 6th to the end of the 12th v. The 7th verse [But if ye had known what this meaneth, I will have mercy, and not sacrifice, ye would not have condemned the guiltless] did awfully bring to mind the Salem tragedie.

6th day, Decr 25, 1696. We bury our little daughter. In the chamber, Joseph [eight years old] in course reads Ecclesiastes 3d a time to be born and a time to die. Elizabeth [Betty, four days shy of her fifteenth birthday], Rev. 22. Hannah [sixteen years old], the 38th Psalm. I speak to each, as God helped, to our mutual comfort I hope. I ordered Sam [eighteen years old] to read the 102 Psalm. Elisha Cooke, Edw. Hutchinson, John Baily, and Josiah Willard bear my little daughter to the tomb.

Note[:] Twas wholly dry, and I went at noon to see in what order things were set [in the Sewall tomb]; and there I was entertained with a view of, and converse with, the coffins of my dear Father Hull, Mother Hull, Cousin Quinsey, and my six children, for the little posthumous [Sarah] was now took up and set in upon that that stands on John's [father Hull's coffin]; so are three [coffins], one upon another twice, on the bench at the end. My Mother lyes on a lower bench, at the end, with head to her husband's head; and I ordered little Sarah to be set on her grandmother's feet. 'Twas an awful yet pleasing treat; having said, The Lord knows who shall be brought hether next, I came away.

Mr. Willard prayed with us the night before; I gave him a ring worth about 20s. Sent the president [Mather of Harvard] one, who is sick of the gout. He prayd with my little daughter. Mr. Oakes, the physician, Major Townsend, speaker, of whose wife I was a [coffin] bearer, and was joined with me in going to Albany and has been civil and treated me several times. Left a ring at Madam [Mehitable] Cooper's for the Governour. Gave not one pair of gloves save to the bearers. Many went to the church this day, I met them coming home, as went to the tomb.

7th day Decr 26. Roger Judd tells me of a ship arrived at Rhode Island from England, and after, that Mr. [John] Ive has written that most judged the King of France [Louis XIV] was dead, or dying.[21] Ship comes from New Castle, several weeks after the Falkland.

---

[21] As with other rumors, this one proved to be false.

3

"My Dear Wife May Now Leave Off Bearing"

At daybreak on January 1, 1701, Sewall was awakened by four trumpeters on the Common blaring their horns to signal the beginning of the new century. As he listened further, he heard the town's bellman read the verses he had given him for the occasion:

> Once more! our God vouchsafe to shine:
> Correct the Coldness of our Clime.
> Make haste with thy Impartial Light,
> And terminate this long dark night.

Although nothing could be done to temper the cold New England winters, Sewall tried to ensure that "false Religions shall decay, And Darkness fly before bright Day." In 1697, he published his first book, *Phaenomena Quaedam Apocalyptica ad Aspectum Novi Orbis Configurata,* a piece of prophetical speculation intended to inspire his neighbors to do good by demonstrating that New England might be the "seat of the *New Jerusalem*" when Christ returned to earth. Sewall, like most New England Puritans, believed that America was God's chosen land. "Of all the parts of the world" advancing claims to "entitle themselves to the Government of Christ," he asserted, *"America*'s plea . . . is the strongest." His 1686 dream about Christ's spending some time in Boston at John Hull's home and his comments about the wood of life, *lignum vitae,* as we have seen, reaffirmed his long-standing interest in the subject. Above all, he was convinced that the New Jerusalem would be noted for its "Humility, Purity, Self-Denial, Love, Peace, and Joy in Believing." Compared to such traits rooted in the souls of New Englanders, "what signify the most sumptuous and magnificent buildings of Europe?"[1]

---

[1]M. Halsey Thomas, ed., *The Diary of Samuel Sewall, 1674–1729,* 2 vols. (New York: Farrar, Straus and Giroux, 1973), 1:440; Ola Elizabeth Winslow, *Samuel Sewall of Boston*

Sewall's work with the Company for the Propagation of the Gospel in New England, or the New England Company, to which he had been appointed as an American commissioner in 1699, was a part of his continuing commitment to do good.[2] His New Year's Day poem of 1701 spoke narrowly of his hope "That they [Indians] Religion may possess, Denying all Ungodliness." The New England Company's principal purpose was to encourage missionary activity among the Indians, and Sewall, as its treasurer until 1721, deflected other causes, however worthy, when they threatened to distract the company. In one instance, he advised Governor Gurdon Saltonstall not to support a proposal for a "New Edition of the Indian Bible" because such an undertaking would consume the precious time of "all men the most essential to the Indian Service" and prove so costly that other projects, including "the Evangelical work among the Indians," might "fall to the ground." Far better for the Indians themselves, Sewall said, would be to "Anglicise" them, especially in the use of the English language, so that the "great things of our Holy Religion" may be "brought unto them in it."[3]

The first decade of the eighteenth century was a busy period for Sewall. In addition to his work as treasurer of the New England Company, he continued to ride the circuit as a justice of the Superior Court of Judicature and, beginning in 1702, served regularly as town moderator. The first order of business of the several Boston town meetings of the period was the election of a moderator to preside over that particular meeting and to "demand and keep silence and attention in the assembly." Town rules authorized the moderator to impose a fine of five shillings per head on those who failed to abide by his instructions. Before 1700, Sewall was elected town moderator once, in 1698; however, from 1702 to 1711, he was second only to Penn Townsend in the frequency of his service as presiding officer. Of the forty-two separate

---

(New York: Macmillan, 1964), 153; Sewall to Benjamin Wadsworth, March 8, 1726, in *Letter-Book of Samuel Sewall,* Massachusetts Historical Society *Collections,* 6th series, 1–2 (Boston, 1886–88), 2:201; Samuel Sewall, *Phaenomena Quaedam Apocalyptica* (Boston, 1697), 2–3; also, Sewall, *Proposals Touching the Accomplishment of Prophesies* (Boston, 1713), 4–5.

[2]The Company for the Propagation of the Gospel in New England and the Parts Adjacent in America was originally chartered by the Long Parliament in 1649 for the purpose of converting the Indians of the region to Christianity. This New England Company must not be confused with the Society for the Propagation of the Gospel in Foreign Parts, chartered in 1701, which served as the missionary arm of the Anglican church. Sewall served as the secretary and treasurer of the New England Company from 1701 to 1724.

[3]Thomas, ed., *Diary,* 1:440; Sewall to Governor Saltonstall, October 1710, *Sewall Letter-Book,* 1:401–2.

town meetings held during these years, Townsend acted as moderator twelve times and Sewall eight. Only two others, Henry Dering and John Bridgham, served as many as five terms. Together, these four men presided over 70 percent of the town meetings. Sewall was by far the wealthiest among them, but all of them fell within the top 10 percent of the taxpayers of Boston.[4]

In provincial politics, the appointment of Joseph Dudley as royal governor in 1702 signaled an end to the relative quiet that had prevailed in Massachusetts since the departure of Sir William Phips in 1694. Thirteen years earlier, after the collapse of the Dominion, the revolutionary government of the colony had imprisoned Dudley, charged him with 119 illegal acts, and sent him to London for trial. Across the Atlantic, however, Dudley was quickly exonerated, managed to gain influential patrons in court circles, and, after a prolonged period of maneuvering in lesser offices, succeeded in getting the governor's commission. At the time of Dudley's appointment, nine of the members of the provincial Council had been among his jailers in 1689, and they probably knew the man well enough to know that he was not one to forget past "injustices" committed against him. Nevertheless, the Council sent a delegation of four to greet the new governor upon his arrival in Boston on June 11. Sewall, speaking for the delegation, congratulated Dudley on the occasion of his return "in the quality of our Governor." Dudley's appointment, Sewall said, was a "very fair first fruit" of Queen Anne's intention to treat her subjects in Massachusetts with special "favour."[5]

The etiquette of politics notwithstanding, Sewall noted that he was "startled at 2 or 3 things" during his meeting with the governor. In the first place, with Dudley was his lieutenant governor, Thomas Povey, a cousin of one of Dudley's most important patrons in England, William Blathwayt. That Blathwayt was the clerk of the Privy Council and a charter member of the Board of Trade meant much to Dudley but mattered little to Sewall and his friends. As far as they were concerned,

[4] *Report of the Record Commissioners of the City of Boston* (hereafter BRC), (Boston, 1883), 7:22–87 *passim.* Sewall presided over the meetings held on June 3, 1702; February 16, 1703; June 1, 1703; March 11, 1706; May 14, 1706; April 29, 1709; March 13, 1710; and August 3, 1711. Wealth estimates are based on the 1687 tax list in BRC (Boston, 1881), 1:91–127.

[5] Richard L. Bushman, *King and People in Provincial Massachusetts* (Chapel Hill: Univ. of North Carolina Press, 1985), 64–67; T. H. Breen, *The Character of the Good Ruler: A Study of Puritan Political Ideas in New England, 1630–1730* (New Haven: Yale Univ. Press, 1970), 226–29; Richard R. Johnson, *Adjustment to Empire: The New England Colonies, 1675–1715* (New Brunswick, N.J.: Rutgers Univ. Press, 1981), 333–38; G. B. Warden, *Boston, 1689–1776* (Boston: Little, Brown, 1970), 58–59; Thomas, ed., *Diary,* 1:468–69.

Povey was "a stranger . . . whom we knew [not] nor heard anything of before." The situation was perhaps all the more startling because Dudley's success in gaining the governorship was in part facilitated by his professed advantage of being a native-born New Englander. Accompanying the new governor also was an "ancient minister" who, in answer to Sewall's inquiry, was identified as George Keith, once a Quaker schoolmaster and preacher in Philadelphia and now an Anglican missionary with the Society for the Propagation of the Gospel—in either case, an unwelcome presence in Sewall's Boston. "I looked on him as Helena aboard," Sewall remarked, anticipating that Keith's coming portended future discord. Dudley himself was adorned with a "very large wig," and when he took his oath of office before the General Court and "as many else as could crowd in" the Town House, he kissed the Bible. Sewall, we know, opposed the wearing of wigs and preferred that oaths be taken in the New England way, as he took them: "holding the book [Bible] in my left hand and holding up my right hand to heaven."[6]

Despite these less than encouraging first signs, Dudley was charming when he chose to be, and Sewall was impressed when the governor called on him the next day to thank him "for my kindness to his family." He was even more pleased when Sam, Jr., called on the Dudleys' twenty-one-year-old daughter Rebeckah, and the two of them seemed to get along so well. What ensued was a whirlwind of family visits that resulted in the marriage of Sam, Jr., and Rebeckah exactly two months after their initial meeting. Later, as we have seen, problems developed in the marriage of Sam, Jr., and Rebeckah, and those problems would engulf the Sewalls and Dudleys in a sometimes bitter contest that continued for more than three years. But all of that was at least a decade removed from the ceremony conducted by the Reverend Nehemiah Walter in the governor's home in Roxbury. For the moment, Sewall seemed to welcome the union as a guarantee of further access to the sources of provincial power.[7]

Dudley's talent for seeking out and gaining favor with a few influential Bostonians, as evidenced by his ability to overcome Sewall's initial apprehension, was enhanced by his power to reward friends with patronage appointments and to punish foes by withholding the same. Within two months of his arrival, Dudley's shake-up of the government had led some to complain that "Govr Dudley put men in place that were

[6]Bushman, *King and People,* 65; Johnson, *Adjustment to Empire,* 330, 397; Thomas, ed., *Diary,* 1:117, 469–70.
[7]Thomas, ed., *Diary,* 1:470–71, 473, 475.

not good." His most inflammatory actions in this regard were the appointment of his son Paul as the province's attorney general and his vetoing of the Assembly's election of Elisha Cooke Sr. to the Council. In the case of the former, even Sewall thought the action so unwise that he saw fit to complain. In a bit of classic understatement, Sewall made it known that it would be "very inconvenient" for the governor's son to bring action before the General Court over which his father presided and wherein "nothing can be done without the governor's consent in writing." Dudley's action against the election of Cooke was a reversal of the policies of immediate predecessors, William Stoughton and Richard Coote, Earl of Bellomont, both of whom had refrained from negating the election of any councillor. Dudley not only vetoed the election of Cooke and other councillors he found disagreeable, but he was soon writing to the Board of Trade to advise them that "nothing will proceed well here" until the system of constituting the Council through the "people's election" was changed. Specifically, he recommended that the Council be made up of royal appointees. Receiving no reply from imperial authorities, Dudley continued to try to shape the Council through the use of his veto. The Assembly elected Cooke to the Council every year, and every year Dudley vetoed his election.[8]

Sewall's family life during these years was in a state of transition. He was forty-eight years old in 1700, and Hannah was forty-two. Their family together was very nearly complete; Hannah had their last child on January 2, 1702. Two days later, after the Reverend Samuel Willard had baptized the child "Judith, in remembrance of her honoured and beloved Grandmother Mrs. Judith Hull," Sewall reflected on Hannah's "many illnesses," including a fall that kept her bedridden for the last five weeks of her pregnancy, and thanked God for being "wonderfully merciful to us in her comfortable delivery." Nevertheless, their earlier fears over "what the issue would be," coupled with the fact that Hannah's last pregnancy five and a half years before had resulted in the delivery of a stillborn son, led Sewall to conclude correctly that "it may be my dear wife may now leave off bearing."[9]

While Sewall anticipated the completion of his immediate family, he and Hannah had already begun their lives as grandparents. Unfortunately, it was a beginning marked by sorrow. Betty, who had married Grove Hirst in October of 1700, "was brought to bed of a dead child" on

[8]Ibid., 472; Sewall to Nathaniel Higginson, October 21, 1706, *Sewall Letter-Book,* 1:339; Breen, *Character of the Good Ruler,* 231; Warden, *Boston,* 60–61.
[9]Thomas, ed., *Diary,* 1:459–60.

November 28, 1702. The Sewalls' second grandchild, Hull, the first child of Sam, Jr., and Rebeckah Dudley, was born on July 19, 1703, but he too died prematurely. On December 14, less than five months after welcoming Hull's birth, Sewall recorded that the dead child was brought to Boston for burial. The next day, the "little corpse," borne by family friends Nathaniel Oliver and David Stoddard, led a mournful procession to the Sewall tomb, where it was laid to rest atop a box containing "his great grandfather's bones." Their next three grandchildren, Sam, Jr., and Rebeckah's daughter Rebekah, and Betty and Grove Hirst's children, Mary and Samuel, provided the Sewalls with more lasting joy. Sewall was especially gratified by the birth of his namesake on October 23, 1705. "Little Samuel Hirst is baptized by Mr. Colman," he recorded on October 28; "tis a very rainy day."[10]

Diary

1706

Jany 9. Guns are fired at Boston upon the supposal of Mr. [Jonathan] Belchar's being married at Portsmouth yesterday; very cold wether.

Jany 10. I corrected David [Sinclair, Sewall's servant] for his extravagant staying out, and for his playing when his mistress sent him of errands.

Jany 11th I visited languishing Mr. Bayley,[1] carried him two pounds of currants, which he accepted very kindly. Is in a very pious humble frame in submitting to the afflicting hand of God.

This day I met Mr. [John] Leverett in the street at Boston, who told me, he had by the Governour's [Joseph Dudley] direction, written to Col. [John] Hathorne to come to town. I asked him, whether as a Councillor, or Judge; he said both; the Governor had drawn up a declaration relating to Winchester and Trowbridge. I enquired whether it might not be as well be let alone till the trial; it seems Mr. Leverett's letter went by the post.

I called at the Governour's, only his Lady at home. Slander. It seems

---

[10] Ibid., 477, 489, 493, 496, 515, 530–31.

[1] James Bayley had been a contemporary of Sewall's at Harvard in the late 1660s. Sewall first learned of Bayley's illness at the funeral of another Harvard schoolmate, Thomas Weld, on July 22, 1704.

some have reported that I should say I saw quarts of blood that run out of Trowbridges-horses. I answered, I have never seen, nor thought, nor reported any such thing.[2]

Seventh-day, Jany 12 1706. A Council is called to meet at eleven aclock. Govr called [John] Maxwell, bid him go to Major [John] Walley, and tell him the Govr and Council were sitting, and would have him there also. Maxwell answered that Major Walley was sick. Twas said also that Mr. [Edward] Bromfield was sick. Mr. Leverett was called in, and bid to sit down. The Governour's declaration was read as to the fray xr [December] 7th with Winchester and Trowbridge, carters. The Govr said he did not know whether he should live to the time of the Court; bid Mr. Secretary [Isaac Addington] keep it for the Court. Govr mentioned the story of the blood, I said before the Council, as had said before. Govr said some minister, mentioning Mr. [James] Allen, had reported that he [Dudley] swore; whereas he said he was as free from cursing and swearing vainly, as any there. Made a ridicule of Winchester's complaint about Mr. Dudley's striking him last Monday. I mentioned Mr. Taylor's striking, which was inconvenient for a justice of peace. The Govr answered, he did well. Brought that as an argument for himself, his drawing his sword; a justice of peace might punish sev-

[2] On December 7, 1705, Governor Dudley and his son William were involved in a confrontation with two farmers, Thomas Trowbridge of Newton and John Winchester, Jr., of Brookline. Despite variations in the opposing depositions, the outlines of the episode are clear. As the Dudleys approached Meetinghouse Hill, a slight elevation about a mile from the governor's estate, they encountered "two carts in the road loaden with wood" and driven by Trowbridge and Winchester. William Dudley ordered the farmers to make way for the governor's coach. When they refused, a fracas ensued, during which the governor drew his sword and Winchester "layd hold on the Govr. and broke the sword in his hand." In his deposition, Dudley maintained that he and his son remained calm throughout the confrontation and that he drew his sword only to "secure himself" against the surly carters. He had no intention of hurting them, or even "once pointing or passing at them." Trowbridge and Winchester painted a different picture of the governor and his son. In the first place, there were "two plaine cart paths" up Meetinghouse Hill, and the governor appeared to have deliberately chosen the path the farmers were already using. When Trowbridge suggested that it might be easier for the governor to take the other path than for them to vacate the one they were on, William "gave out threatening words," drew his sword, and made "several passes at me." Winchester substantiated Trowbridge's account. He said that he approached the governor only after William persisted in his "rash" behavior. "I then told his Excellency if he would but have patience a minute or two, I would clear that way for him." But Dudley, allegedly shouting "run the dogs through," struck Winchester on the head and stabbed him in the back "with his naked sword." In his own defense, he "catcht hold" of the governor's sword, "and it broke." On November 5, 1706, eleven months after the incident, the Superior Court, with Sewall present, ruled in favor of the farmers and "discharged them by solemn proclamation." M. Halsey Thomas, ed., *The Diary of Samuel Sewall, 1674–1729,* 2 vols. (New York: Farrar, Straus and Giroux, 1973), 1:533–35, reprints the conflicting depositions.

eral offences against the laws upon view. After dinner I went and told Mr. [Samuel] Willard what was reported of himself and me. He said he knew nothing of it. Col. [Elisha] Hutchinson was not at Council. I laid down this as a position, that of all men, twas most inconvenient for a justice of peace to be a striker.

Jany 12. Capt. [Andrew] Belchar appears at Council in his new wigg; said he needed more than his own hair for his journey to Portsmouth [to attend his son's wedding on January 8]; and other provision was not suitable for a wedding.

Jany 13th [Belcher] appears at meeting in his wigg. He had a good head of hair, though twas grown a little thin.

Jany 18. Sister Stephen Sewall [Margaret Mitchel Sewall], son [Grove] Hirst and his wife [Sewall's daughter Betty], dine with us; Major Walley droops with his cold and cough; he was not abroad on the Lord's day, nor lecture-day; wears plaisters or poultices to his right side to ease the intolerable pain his coughing causes him.

Lord's Day, Jany 20th My Dame Mary Phipps, (Lady Sergeant, *alias* Phypps [i.e., formerly the widow of Sir William Phips]) dies about sunrise; Majr Genl [Wait Still Winthrop] tells me she was dying from Satterday noon. Has bled excessively at the nose. Mr. [Peter] Sergeant [Mary Phips's husband] was at meeting in the afternoon. Mr. [Robert] Butchers son Alwin taken into [South] Church and a woman; Mr. Ezek. Lewis dismissed [transferred] from Westfield, and entered into covenant with them [at the South Church]. Major Walley not at meeting.

Jany 20. Mrs. Jane Pembrook dies in the afternoon, was taken on Wednesday. Her husband is at Connecticut.

Tuesday, Jany 22. Mrs. Jane Pembrook buried in the New Burying place. Saw no minister there but Mr. [Benjamin] Colman [minister of the Brattle Street church] and Mr. [Pierre] Dallie [minister of the French Huguenot church]. I and Mr. E[liaki]m Hutchinson went together; Capt. [Samuel] Legg was there.

Wednesday, Jany 23. Storm of snow, for which reason the funeral of my Lady [Phips] is put off to Friday.

Jany 23. Mr. Jonathan Belcher and his bride dine at Lt Govr [John] Usher's, come to town about 6 aclock: About 20 horsmen, three coaches and many slays. Joseph [seventeen years old] came from college [Harvard] to visit us, and gave us notice of their coming before hand.

Jany 24th. Comfortable day: Mr. Willard not abroad in the forenoon by reason of pain; but preaches excellently in the afternoon. Mr.

[Jonathan] Broadhurst of Albany, Mr. Hirst and family, cousin Saml and Jonathan Sewall, dine with us &c.

Jany 25th Friday, My Lady Phipps is laid in Mr. Sergeant's tomb in the New Burying place. Bearers, Mr. [Wait Still] Winthrop, [Elisha] Cook; Elisha Hutchinson, Addington; [John] Foster, [Andrew] Belcher. Govr [Dudley] and Lt Govr [Thomas Povey] there. Mr. [James] Russel and I go together. I had a ring. Mr. [Jonathan] Corwin and B[enjamin] Brown there from Salem. Mr. [John] Holman married cousin Ann Quinsey a week ago.

Jany 26. I visit Mr. Sergeant, who takes my visit very kindly, tells me, my Lady [Phips] would have been 59 years old next March, and that he was two months older. It seems Mr. [Ezekiel] Chiever buried his daughter Abigail, about an hour before my Lady was entombed.

Jany 29th 1706. Col. Hathorn, Leverett, and S[ewall] hold the court at Charlestown; storm began by noon; yet I got home at night with difficulty.

Jany 30. Extraordinary storm; yet at noon I rode to John Russel's with very great difficulty by reason of the snow and hail beating on my forehead and eyes hindering my sight, and the extravagant banks of snow the streets were filled with. Waited 3 hours or more, and at last the Charlestown boat coming over, I went in that very comfortably; got thither a little before four. Lodged at Capt. [Samuel] Hayman's with Mr. Leverett.

Jany 31. Got not home till six at night, by reason of much ice in the river; fain to land at the Salutation [tavern], having got below the ice on Charlestown side.

Feb. 11. Mr. John Marion, the father, buried; bearers, Mr. Cook, Col. [Penn] Townsend; Elder [Joseph] Bridgham, [David] Copp; Deacon [Isaiah] Tay, [Thomas] Hubbard. Great funeral. I think Mr. Chiever was not there.

Feb. 27. My neighbour [David] Deming came to me, and asked of me the agreement between himself and Joanna Tiler; I told him I was to keep it for them both and could not deliver it; he said he was going to Cambridge to ask Mr. Leverett's advice, he would bring it safe again. When he still urged and insisted, I told him I would not have him lose his time, I would not deliver it; I would give him a copy if he pleased. He said he was in haste and could not stay the writing of it. I said, you would not take it well that I should deliver it to Tiler; no more could I deliver it to him. He said some what sourly, I am sorry you have not more charity for him. And going away, murmuring said, passing out of the stove-room into the kitchen, I have desired a copy, offered money and am denyed. I was then more moved than before, and said with some earnestness, will you speak false to my face? He went away, and came not again, but his son came, and I gave him a copy of the agreement, written with my own hand. I thank God, I heartily desired and endeavoured a good agreement between him and his neighbour as to the bounds of their land: although he be thus out of tune, upon my denying to grant his unjust petition.

Satterday, March 2. I visit my son and daughter [Sam and his wife Rebeckah Dudley] at Brooklin and little Rebecka [Sewall's granddaughter, a year and two months old]: Visited Mr. Bayley as I came home. Most of the way over the Neck is good summer travelling.

March 4th Cousin [Jeremiah] Dummer and I take bond of Mr. Rust 30£, to prosecute his son's master, John Staniford, for misusing and evil entreating his servant; left Robert Rust with his father in the mean time. The invincible fear of the mother [Mrs. Rust], who came from Ipswich on purpose, and the high hand wherewith Staniford carried it, did in a manner force it. Mr. John Colman said, if his servant should answer so, he would trample him under his feet; afterward mentioned that scripture, Obey in all things. Staniford said scoffingly before us: The boy would do well with good correction; words were directed to the mother.

Wednesday, March 6. Council of Churches held at Mr. Willard's. They advise that after a month, Mr. Joseph Morse cease to preach at Watertown farms. Adjourned to the first of May. Sharp thunder the night following. Mr. [Daniel] Gookin, Capt. Morse and Deacon Larned dine with us. Cousin [Cutting] Noyes lodges here, and tells of many sheep being drowned by the overflowing of Merrimack River. At the breaking up of the river, which was furious by the flood in Febr. The ice jamed and made a great dam, and so caused the river to rise so much and suddenly.

March 6. 1706. At night, a great ship, of 370 tuns, building at Salem, runs off her blocking in the night and pitches ahead 16 foot. Her deck nut bolted off, falls in; and opens at the bows; so that twill cost a great deal to bring her right agen; and Capt. [Jonathan] Dows thinks she will be hundreds of pounds the worse.

March 13th Mr. [Samuel] Torrey comes to town; on Thorsday evening, Mr. [Benjamin] Wadsworth came to visit him. Mr. Torrey told him of his Elder Rogers's carriage towards him; and craved his pardon for chusing him; acknowledged his fault and plainly seemed to renounce that office.

March 16. A storm of snow.

Friday, March 22. Michael Gill arrives from Lisbon, came out 11th Febr. By him have news from London of the 1st of Jany. This day Mr. Jer[emiah] Cushing dyes at Scituat. John Turner dies there suddenly P.M. the same day; he has the character of a drunkard, and striker of his wife.

March 23. Set out for Weymouth with Sam Robbison, stopped at Gibbs's to shelter our selves from a gust of wind and rain. Twas dusk before got to Mr. Torrey's. I asked Mr. Torrey about laying the hand on the Bible in swearing; he said he was against it, and would suffer anything but death rather than do it.

March 24. Mr. Torrey preached out of Amos, 8.11 [I will send a famine in the land, not a famine of bread . . . but of hearing the words of the Lord]. Four children baptized in the afternoon.

March 25, 1706. Dined at Barkers [tavern]; surprised the Sheriff and his men at the flat-house; got to Plymouth about 1 1/2 by Sun.

March 26. Major Walley and Leverett come from Barker's.

March 27th I walk in the Meetinghouse. Set out homeward, lodged at Cushing's [tavern at Scituate]. I prayed not with my servant [David Sinclair], being weary. Seeing no chamber-pot called for one; a little before day I used it in the bed, and the bottom came out, and all the water run upon me. I was amazed, not knowing the bottom was out till I felt it in the bed. The trouble and disgrace of it did afflict me. As soon as it was light, I called up my man [Sinclair] and he made a fire and warmed me a clean shirt and I put it on, and was comfortable. How unexpectedly a man may be exposed! There's no security but in God, who is to be sought by prayer.

March 28, mihi natalis [my birthday], got home about 1/2 hour after 12, dine with my wife and children.

Apr. 1. 1706. Col. Townsend, Mr. [Edward] Bromfield, Burroughs and I went in the hackney coach [rented coach] and visited Mr. [Peter] Thacher, dined with him and Mrs. Thacher. Mrs. Niles is there to ly in; but saw her not. Got home well. *Laus Deo* [Praise God].

Apr. 4, 1706. Last night I dreamed I saw a vast number of French coming towards us, for multitude and huddle like a great flock of sheep. It put me into a great consternation, and made me think of hiding in some thicket. The impression remained upon me after my waking. GOD defend!

Friday, Ap. 5. I went and visited Mr. Baily whose paroxisms are returned to once every hour. Carried him two pounds of currants which he accepted with wonderful kindness. When left him, went forward for Brooklin, and going up the Meetinghouse Hill fell in with the Governour's coach with two horses; in it were his Excellency and Lady, Madam Paul Dudley, and Madam Thomas Dudley. I followed the coach mostly, especially at Mittimus [Meetinghouse] Hill, and observed, that the coachman of his own accord took the road next Boston, which was refused Decembr 7, and nothing to incline to it but the goodness of the way. Took it also returning. Mrs. Kate Dudley, little Allen, and Capt. [Benjamin] Gillam's little maiden daughter rode in a calash. Capt. Thomas Dudley rode on horseback.

Tuesday, Apr. 9. Mr. Danl Oliver and I ride to Milton, and there meet with Mr. Leverett, and as spectators and auditors were present at Deacon Swifts when Mr. Leverett discoursed the Punkapog intruders. Dined at the said Swift's with Mr. [Peter] Thacher. Seth Dwight waited on us.

Ap. 8. Monday, poor little Sam Hirst [Betty's five-month-old son] went through the valley of the shadow of death through the oppression of flegm.

Ap. 9. Wife takes physick, has a comfortable night after it. *Laus Deo* [Praise God]. Brother [Stephen Sewall] visits us.

Ap. 14. Capt. [Andrew] Belchar is kept at home by the gout.

Ap. 15. Abraham Hill arrives; makes us believe the Virginia fleet is arrived.

Ap. 16. I first hear and see the swallows: they are now frequent. Mr. [Thomas] Banister says they were seen by him 2 or 3 days ago. Mrs. Gates lodged here last night. At night the air being clear, the eclipse of the moon was very much gazed upon.

Tuesday, Apr. 23. Govr. comes to town guarded by the troops with their swords drawn; dines at the Dragon, from thence proceeds to the Townhouse, illuminations at night. Capt. Pelham tells me several wore crosses in their hats; which makes me resolve to stay at home; (though [John] Maxwell was at my house and spake to me to be at the Councilchamber at 4 P.M.) Because to drinking healths, now the keeping of a day to fictitious St. George, is plainly set on foot. It seems Capt. [Thomas] Dudley's men wore crosses. Somebody has fastened a cross to a dog's head; Capt. Dudley's boatswain seeing him, struck the dog, and then went into the shop, next [to] where the dog was, and struck down a carpenter, one Davis, as he was at work not thinking anything: Boatswain and the other with him were fined 10s each for breach of the peace, by Jer. Dummer Esqr; pretty much blood was shed by means of this bloody cross, and the poor dog a sufferer.

Thomas Hazard came in from Narragansett about the time [I] should have gone to the Townhouse, said he came on purpose to speak with me; so 'twas inconvenient [for me] to leave him.

Midweek; Apr. 24. Private meeting at our house; read out of Mr. [Joseph] Caryl[3] on those words, the Lord gives, and the Lord takes, Blessed—preface my reading with saying, I will read now what [was] read in course to my family because of the great and multiplied losses. Cousin [Ephraim] Savage and Capt. [James] Hill prayed, had a pretty full and comfortable meeting notwithstanding the much rain and dirt. Sung 1 part and last v. of 48th Ps. 119.

7th day, Apr. 27th Joseph [eighteen-year-old junior at Harvard] visits us, it seems he had a tooth pulled out by Madam Oliver's maid, on midweek night.

Lords-Day, April 28. Brief is read. Bowditch arrives.

Monday, Apr. 29. Cousin Gookin, his wife and son Richard lodge here.

Tuesday, Apr. 30. I carry Capt. Belchar my letter to Mr. [John] Bellamy [in London], and he sends me the Comons votes. Lords Resolution is dated Decr 6. Comons conferred with them about it the 7th. Agree to it Satterday xr [December] 8. Address upon it agreed to by the Comons xr. 14th[4]

May 1. 1706. Eclipse of the sun, not seen by reason of the cloudy wether.

May 2d Mr. Penn Townsend junr dies about 10 m[ane]. May 3 is buried; bearers Mr. Nathanl Williams, Major Adam Winthrop, Capt. Oliver Noyes, Capt. John Ballentine junr, Mr. Habijah Savage, Mr. Elisha Cooke; all scholars [contemporaries of Townsend at Harvard in the 1690s].

May 2d, 1706. Capt. Stukely arrives from Barbados in the Deptford, 3 weeks passage; was not suffered to bring the fleet with him, neither can they go for salt; but are embargoed at Barbados. Tis much feared that Nevis is taken [by the French].

May 4th Mr. [Thomas] Brattle [Harvard treasurer] and I send the school and college deeds by Mr. N[athaniel] Niles to be recorded. Niles tells me that Monotocott [Braintree] Meetinghouse is raised; he came that way, and saw it.

---

[3]Joseph Caryl (1602–1673), Oliver Cromwell's chaplain in Scotland, wrote extensively on the book of Job. Sewall so admired Caryl that in 1716, upon learning that the new governor of Massachusetts, Samuel Shute, was the grandson of Caryl, he hoped that it was one of the "omens for good, that will not fail." Later, in a letter to Governor Shute, Sewall mentioned his hope that the "blessings of your excellently Pious and Learned Grandfather, the Revd. Mr. Joseph Caryl, may be plentifully showered upon you." Sewall to Jonathan Belcher, July 28, 1716; Sewall to Samuel Shute, February 19, 1717, *Letter-Book of Samuel Sewall*, Massachusetts Historical Society *Collections*, 6th series, 1–2 (Boston, 1886–88), 2:55, 67.

[4]Sewall is referring to the Bill for the Better Security of Her Majesty's Person and Government, and of the Succession to the Crown of England in the Protestant Line.

Mid-week, May 15th 1706. Went to Brooklin, visited my daughter [Sam's wife, Rebeckah] and little grand-daughter [Rebekah]. Visited Mr. Bayley.

May 16. Capt. Benja Gillam buried about 7 P.M.

May 20. Set out for Ipswich with Major Walley by Winisimet [Chelsea]; ride in the rain from Lewis' [tavern at Lynn] to Salem; staid there, and assisted at the funeral of Mrs. [Elizabeth] Lindal, Capt. [George] Corwin's only daughter, a vertuous Gentlewoman. Was buried in the tomb in a pasture; brother [Stephen] was one of the bearers.

May 21. Set out early for Ipswich; got thither seasonably. Twas late ere Mr. Leverett came. Sarah Pilsbury, tryed for murdering her young child, was acquitted.

May 23. Mr. [Jabez] Fitch preaches the lecture; companys in arms, Govr to view them; much fatigued by the wet [weather].

May 24th Set out for Newbury with Major [Daniel] Davison; visit Mr. [Edward] Payson, and deliver him my wife's present; I hope he is recovering. Dine at sister Northend's [Dorothy Sewall]; brother Northend [Dorothy's husband, Ezekiel] brings us going as far as Capt. [Joseph] Hale's. At sister Gerrishes [Jane Sewall] dismiss Major Davison; visit brother and sister Tappan [Jacob Toppan and his wife, Hannah Sewall], cousin [Samuel] Swett, cousins John, Henry, and Saml Sewall [sons of Sewall's brother John, who died in 1699]. Lodge at sister Gerrishes.

May 25th Saw the sheep shearing, visited cousin [Anne Toppan] Rolf.

May 26th Mr. [Christopher] Tappan preaches. Deacon Cutting Noyes catechises in the afternoon. In the evening visit Mr. Tappan.

May 27th Col. [Thomas] Noyes invites me to his training dinner: Mr. Tappan, [Richard] Brown, [Joseph] Hale and my self are guarded from the green to the tavern, bro[the]r [William] Moodey [Mehitable Sewall's husband] and a part of the troop with a trumpet accompany me to the ferry. Sam. Moody waits on me. Get to brother's [Stephen Sewall] in the night after nine aclock. Mr. [Nicholas] Noyes had left his verses for Mr. Bayley, which I carried with me next morning. Rested at Lewis' [tavern in Lynn] during the rain. Got home well, *Laus Deo* [Praise God].

May 29. Election-day [councillors:], Winthrop 83. Russel, 80. (Cooke 50) Hathorn 68. Elisha Hutchinson, 80. Sewall, 83. Addington 74. [William] Brown 76. [John] Phillips 80. [Jonathan] Corwin 75. [John] Foster 75. Townsend, 78. [John] Higginson, 69. [Andrew] Belcher, 80. Bromfield 55. Legg, 65. S[amuel] Appleton, 47. [Samuel] Partridge, 58. [John] Thacher 79. [Nathaniel] Pain, 79. [Isaac] Winslow, 86. [John]

Cushing, 47. E[liaki]m Hutchinson, 75. ([Joseph] Hammond 62.) [Ichabod] Plaisted, 46. Leverett, 42. Walley, 37. John Appleton, 34.

June 6. In stead of the negatived [defeated councillors Cooke and Hammond] were chosen B[enjamin] Brown, 55. Ephr. Hunt, 42. Mr. James Taylor, Treasurer; James Russel esqr Commissr of the Customs.

This Court Mr. Lillie preferred [brought forth] a petition about his reals not accepted by the Super. Court to go by tale, which was untrue in one material article as to matter of fact, and the justices much reflected on. Mr. Paul Dudley was attorney for Mr. Lillie. I prayed the petition might be dismissed, or those reflections abated; the Govr brake forth into a passionate harangue respecting the Roxbury carters. He might be run through, trampled on, &c no care taken of him. Finally, at another time it was agreed that there should be a hearing, only Mr. Lillie should first come into Council, make some acknowledgement, withdraw that petition, and file another. The Govr was very hot and hard upon me at this time, insomuch that I was provoked to say it was a hardship upon me that the Governour's son was Mr. Lillie's attorney. At which the Govr stormed very much. Some days after Mr. Lillie came into Council. The Govr presently said, Sir, shall I speak for you, or will you speak for your self, and so fell a speaking—at last Mr. Lillie said with a low voice, I have preferred a petition which I understand is not so satisfactory; I did not intend to reflect upon the judges, and desire that petition may be withdrawn, and this [new petition] filed in the room of it. Withdrew, Govr asked it might be so, and that the first petition might be cass [void] and null. Secretary [Addington] whispered the Govr that the petition had been read twice in Council, whereupon the Govr took the pen and obliterated the minute of its having been read on the head of the petition. And then after the hearing before the whole Court, when the deputies were returned, the Govr bundled up the papers and sent them in to the House of Deputies, without asking the Council whether they would first go upon them, with whom the petition was entered. After many days, the deputies returned the papers agen by Mr. [Nathaniel] Blagrove, expressing their desire that the Council would first act upon them, seeing the petition was entered with the Secretary.

Some time after, the Govr sent in the papers again, and then the deputies voted upon them and sent it in, but before any thing was done in Council, the Court was prorogued to the 7th of August, &c., &c. Major Walley sick, staid at home two Sabbaths; came out agen July 27th.

July 28. 1706. Col. Hathorne comes to town, dines and lodges at our house.

July 29. Col. Hathorne, Major Walley, Sewall, ride to Cambridge in the hackney coach. Mr. Sheriff, his son, and the steward of the college met us at Brooklin, drank a glass of good beer at my son's [Sam], and passed on. My case was called in the afternoon and committed to the jury.[5] I would have come home but then Major Walley also would come; which made me stay and send the coach to town empty. Lodged at Mr. [William] Brattles.

July 30. College Hall at Cambridge, the jury brought in for me costs of courts. Charlestown gentlemen and their attorneys said not a word that I could hear. Col. Hathorne with Mr. [John] Valentine, Charlest[own] attorney, examined my bill of cost and so did the clerk, and afterward Col. Hathorne shewed it to Majr Walley and Leverett, and then allowed it, subscribing his name.

Augt 7. Genl Court meets.

Augt 10, 1706. A conference is held in the Council-chamber, at the desire of the deputies. Mr. Speaker [Nehemiah Jewett said], The House is doubtfull whether they have not proceeded too hastily in calling that a misdemeanour, which the law calls treason; and are doubtfull whether this Court can proceed to try the prisoners. Mr. Jewet [said], committee that were appointed to prepare for the trials, were doubtfull and unsatisfied that they had called the crime of the prisoners a misdemeanour. If any wrong steps had been taken, tis fit they should be retrieved. Mr. Blagrove [said], If that which the prisoners are charged with, be made treason by the law of England; this Court must not make laws repugnant to the law of England.

The Governour answered, he had not seen the papers, and could not say that what they had done was treason. After this the deputies sent in the papers. And about Augt 13, Govr put it to vote in the Council, whether the prisoners should be tried by the Genl Court according to the order of last sessions. There were 17 at the board [meeting:] nine Yeas, and eight Nos. Secretary was in the negative as well as I.[6]

---

[5]In 1650, the town of Woburn gave up land in Wilmington in exchange for land in Charlestown. The Charlestown land was then sold to several prominent inhabitants. In 1683, John Hull, Sewall's father-in-law, bought some 1,100 acres of the Charlestown land formerly in the possession of Francis Willoughby. Sewall took possession of the Hull estate upon Hull's death; consequently, when Charlestown claimed rights to the land in question, Sewall was forced to appear before the Cambridge court (September 1705) and the Superior Court (July 1706). Both courts decided in Sewall's favor.

[6]The prisoners in question were Samuel Vetch and his companions, who were charged with selling supplies to the French and their Indian allies. Vetch and the others were fined by the General Court in 1706 for their activities. Governor Dudley's opponents hoped to try Vetch for treason, to implicate Dudley himself in the illegal trading, and to force the governor from office. Sewall, as we shall see, became a central figure in the confrontation between Dudley and his accusers.

Friday Augt. 16. Capt. [Samuel] Vetch was brought to his trial in the afternoon, in the Court chamber.

Note[:] I came home on Wednesday morn, and went not again till the Govr and Council sent for me by Mr. [John] Winchcomb Friday morn. I went though I had a cold; spake that a suit of cloaths might be made here for Mr. Williams.[7] Deputies would have had Mr. John Eliot, and Cousin [Jeremiah] Dummer M.A. to have assisted Mr. Attorney: Govr did not consent; they insisted so long that the forenoon was spent, and I fairly got home.

Augt. 17. I am told Mr. [John] Borland and [George] Lawson [associates of Vetch] are brought to their trial. Mr. Borland pleads that he was a factor [commissioned agent] in the management of this affair.

Note[:] Govr would have had the judges manage the conference, I declined it because was against the procedure. And so declined joining with the judges to prepare for it because I was against it. Col. Hathorne was at Salem with his sick son; so that only Majr Walley, and Mr. Leverett were active in the matter. And Mr. Leverett said at the board that he did not interpret that clause in the charter of imposing fines &c. as if it did empower the Genl Court to try delinquents.

Feria secunda [second day, i.e., Monday], August 19th 1706. Went and visited my son and daughter [Sam and Rebeckah] at Brooklin, and dined there; went to Cambridge; gave Mr. [Andrew] Bordman, Town-Clerk, seven pounds in two bills of credit to help build the new-meetinghouse; fourty shillings of it upon consideration of my ancient tenant, the widow Margaret Gates, and her family, going there to the publick worship of God. Gave him also ten shillings for Mrs. [Barbara] Corlett, widow. Visited [son] Joseph, Mr. [Henry] Flint [Harvard tutor], congratulated Mr. [John] Whiting upon his being chosen a fellow. Went into hall and heard Mr. Willard expound excellently from 1 Cor. 7.15, 16 [But if the unbelieving depart, let him depart . . . For what knowest thou, O wife, whether thou shalt save thy husband? or how knowest thou, O man, whether thou shalt save thy wife?]. It was dark by that time I got to Roxbury, yet I visited Mr. Bayley, and gave him the fourty shillings Mr. John Eliot sent him as a gratuity: He was very thankful for the present, and very glad to see me. I told him, coming in the night, I had brought a small illumination with me. Rid home;

---

[7]John Williams, minister of Deerfield, and his family had been captured by Mohawks on February 29, 1704. John Demos, *The Unredeemed Captive: A Family Story from Early America* (New York: Alfred A. Knopf, 1994), offers a sensitive account of the experiences of the Williams family, and especially of Eunice Williams, who was seven years old in 1704 and remained with her Indian family and community for the rest of her life.

twas past nine by that time I got there. Found all well; *Laus Deo* [Praise God].

Augt. 26. 1706. feria secunda [second day] About 2 P.M. Mr Bromfield and I set out for Martha's Vinyard;[8] got well to Cushing's [in Scituate] about day-light shutting in. *27,* to Morey's. *28,* to Sandwich, *29,* to lecture at Pompesprisset [near Plymouth]; on the way thither, a small stump overset the calash, and Mr. Bromfield was much hurt, which made our journey afterwards uncomfortable. *30.* rested: saw the harbour, burying-place, mill-pond. *31.* Went to Succanesset [Falmouth] but could not get over [to Martha's Vineyard].

Septr 1. Mr. [Samuel] Danforth preached there. Lodged at Mr. [Barnabas] Lothrop's.

Septr 2. embarked for the Vinyard; but by stormy rough wether were forced back again to Woods's Hole. Lodged at B[enjamin] Skiff's, he shewed me the bay, and Mr. Weeks's harbour.

Septr 3. Went to the Vinyard with a fair wind, and from Homes's Hole to Tisbury and I to Chilmark, to Mr. Allen's.

Septr 4. to Gayhead, Mr. Danforth, I, Mr. Tho. Mayhew, Major Basset.

Septr 5. Dined at Mr. Mayhew's: went to Homes's Hole to wait for a passage to Rode-Island, or Bristol. There lay windbound.

Septr 8. Mr. Danforth and I go to Tisbury meeting, Mr. Josia Torrey preached forenoon; Mr. Danforth after noon. Returned to Chases [tavern on Martha's Vineyard] to Mr. Bromfield.

Septr 9. Monday, embarked with a scant wind; put in to Tarpoling Cove: Mr. Bromfield not yielding to go to Cushnet. There spake with Darby who shewed us the prisoners fines; spake with Mr. Weeks.

Septr 10. Gave the squaw that has lost her feet, ten pounds of wool. When the tide served, sailed for Cushnet, had a good passage; lodged at Capt. [Seth] Pope's; he not at home: borrowed six pounds of Mrs. Pope; were entertained there.

Septr 11. Wednesday, five Indians carried Mr. Bromfield in a chair from Spooner's, to Assowamset, and so to Taunton. Twas near midnight by that time we got there, where by Lt. Leonard, whom we accidentally met late at night, we were informed the Bristol court was not held for want of justices; and that Majr Walley and Mr. Leverett adjourned *de die in diem* [from day to day]; jury-men murmured. This

---

[8]The Commissioners for Indian Affairs ordered Sewall, Edward Bromfield, and the Reverend Samuel Danforth of Taunton to go to Martha's Vineyard to inquire into the state of the Indians inhabiting the island.

put me upon new straits; but I resolved to go to Bristol, and so did, next day, *Septr 12. Thorsday,* Capt. Hodges's son waiting on me; got thither about 2. Saved the afternoon. Mr. Blagrove is cast, asks a Chancery in writing; Major Walley and Leverett will by no means suffer it; I earnestly pressed for it.

[September] 13, 14. Court held, and then adjourned *sine die* [indefinitely]. But twas so late, there was no getting out of town.

Septr 15. Lord's Day, Mr. [John] Sparhawk preaches forenoon; Mr. [Nicholas] Sever in the afternoon. Sup at Mr. [Nathaniel] Pain's.

Septr 16. By Mr. [Samuel] Niles's importunity, I set out with him for Narraganset. Dined at Bright's; while dinner was getting ready I read in Ben Johnson, a folio:

> Wake, our Mirth begins to dye:
> Quicken it with Tunes and Wine
> Raise your Notes; you'r out; fie, fie,
> This drowsiness is an ill sign.
> We banish him the Quire of Gods
> That droops agen:
> Then all are men
> For here's not one but nods.

> Fol.13.

SEJANUS

> ————great and high
> The [world] knows only 2, thats Rome and I,
> My Roof receives me not, 'tis Aer I tread
> And at each step I feel my advanced head
> Knock out a Star in Heaven————

> f. 144.

> Howere the Age she lives in doth endure
> The vices that she breeds above their Cure.

> 211.

I went to wait on Govr [Samuel] Cranston [of Rhode Island]; but found him not at home. Ferried over, got to Narraganset shoar a little before sunset. Twas in the night before we got to our lodging about 5 miles off the ferry. Tuesday and Wednesday spent in settling bounds between Niles and [Thomas] Hazard; and the widow Wilson; at last all were agreed. I was fain to forgo some acres of land to bring Niles and Hazard to peace and fix a convenient line between them.

Thorsday 7r [September] 19. Forenoon I got Mr. Mumford, the surveyor, to goe with us, and we found out and renewed the bounds of an

80 acre lot, just by Place's. Place went with us and assisted. After dinner, went to Point Judith, was pleased to see the good grass and wood there is upon the Neck. Just as we came there the Triton's Prise passed by, all her sails abroad, fresh gale, S.S.W., standing for Newport. (News Letter, 7r 30.—8r 4.)[9] Woman of the house sick; house miserably out of repair. Twas night by that time we got home.

Friday, Septr 20. go into the Quakers Meeting-house, about 35 long 30 wide, on Hazard's ground that was mine. Acknowledge a deed to Knowls, of eight acres, reserving one acre at the corner for a Meetinghouse. Bait [ate and rested] at Capt. Eldridges. From thence to the fulling-mill [mill for processing woolen cloth] at the head of Coeset [Coweset] Cove, and there dine; a civil woman, but sorrowfull, dressed our dinner. From thence Niles brings me to Turpins [tavern] at Providence, and there bait: From thence over Blackston's River, and there I send him back, and travail alone to Freeman's [tavern], where I meet with Piriam, the under-Sheriff, and Capt. Watts, whose company was helpfull to me.

Satterday, Septr 21. Baited at [John] Devotion's, who was very glad to see me. Dined at Billinges [inn at Roxbury]; by Piriam and him was informed of Mr. Bromfields being well at home. Baited at Dedham. Was trimed at Roxbury; my barber told me the awfull news of the murder of Mr. Simeon Stoddard [Jr.], in England, which much saddened me. Got home a little before sunset; found all well, *Laus Deo* [Praise God].

Septr 25. Mr. Bromfield and I took the hackney coach to wait on the Govr; met his Excellency on this side the gate; went out of the coach and complimented him, and then went on and visited Mr. Bailey.

Thorsday 8r [October] 17. Son [Sam, Jr.] and daughter Sewall and their little Rebeca, son [Grove] Hirst and his family, dine with us; all here but [son] Joseph. He keeps his thanksgiving at Cambridge.

Friday, 8r 18. I visit Mr. Baily; as I enter, he saith, I am even gon, even gon! said he had a fever; the night before and that day had subdued his nature. In his paroxism said, cutting, cutting, cutting all to pieces: My head, my head; could not bear the boys chopping without door [outside].

Tuesday, 8r 22. I go to Roxbury lecture, Mr. Cotton Mather preached from 1 John 5.13 [that ye may know that ye have eternal life] concerning assurance, with much affecting solidity and fervor. Went to see Mr.

[9]The initial issue of the weekly *Boston News-Letter*, the first regularly published newspaper in the colonies, appeared on April 24, 1704.

Baily, whose mouth and tongue were so furred, he could hardly speak at first; said he had been a long time in a storm at the harbours mouth, hoped he should not be swallowed on quicksands, or split on rocks. God had not yet forsaken him, and he hoped He never would. Said, Here I wait!

Wednesday, 8r 23. Court meets; but the Govr has signified his pleasure that nothing be done till he come from Piscataqua; adjourn till 3 P.M. after lecture tomorrow. After dinner I go and take the acknowledgment of Mr. Nathanl Henchman and Anna his wife to a deed to their brother, the schoolmaster. She was lying on the bed sick of a fever; yet very sensible and set her hand to the receipt.

Thorsday, 8r 24. Mr. Wadsworth appears at lecture in his perriwigg. Mr. Chiever is grieved at it. Court meets, read Mr. Secretary's letter to Mr. Constantine Phips; adjourn to ten in the morn. This day I am told of Mr. [Samuel] Torrey's [minister of Weymouth] kinswoman [stepdaughter], Betty Symmes, being brought to bed of a bastard in his house last Monday night. I visit Mr. Chiever.

Novr 7th 1706. I invited the Govr, Col. [Jonathan] Tyng, Mr. Sol. Stoddard, Simeon [Stoddard], Mr. [Ebenezer] Pemberton, Capt. [Andrew] Belchar, Mr. Bromfield, Capt. [Cyprian] Southack. I supposed Mr. Stoddard had preached the lecture. Mr. Cotton Mather preached. He did not pray for the Super. Court, or judges in his first prayer, that I took notice of: but in his last, mentioned the Genl Court, and any administrations of justice. I invited him to dine by Mr. Cooke; he said he was engaged.

Novr 8. There is a hearing of Roxbury, Spring Street, about another Meeting-house, and of Billericay proprietors and farmers. Deputies treat the Govr at Homes's [tavern].

Feria Sexta [sixth day, i.e., Friday] Novr 8, 1706. I visited Mr. Bayley; find his sister [Sarah] Cheyny with him. He was very low at first; but after awhile revived and spake freely; has been very ill this month; especially last Satterday and Sabbath day night. Desired his service to brother, sister, Mr. [Nicholas] Noyes, with much thanks for his verses which had been a great comfort to him; to Mr. [John] Higginson, Mrs. [Mary] Higginson. I gave him 2 five shilling bills of credit to buy a cord of wood, which he accepted with great thankfulness. I told him it was a time of great expense; he was in prison, and Mrs. Bayley in fetters. Upon my coming in, Mrs. Bayley went to Sol. Phip's wife, who was hurt by a fall out of her calash. I staid with him about 2 hours or more, went from home at 3 and returned past seven.

Lords-Day, Novr 10. Andrew Belchar, Nicholas Bows, Debora Green, and Sarah [blank] are baptised by Mr. Willard. *Tingitur* [there was dipped] *Andreas, Nicolaus, Debora, Sarah.*
This morning Tom Child, the painter, died.

> Tom Child had often painted Death,
> But never to the Life, before:
> Doing it now, he's out of Breath;
> He paints it once, and paints no more.[10]

Novr 11th 1706. Went to Salem with Mr. [Paul] Dudley.
Novr 14th Returned with Mr. Leverett, Mr. Dudley. Had very comfortable journey out and home.
Novr 15th Midnight, Mrs. [Mary Clark] Pemberton is brought to bed of a dead daughter. Her life was almost despaired of, her bleeding was so much, and pains so few.
Novr 27. Mr. John Hubbard comes in and tells me Mr. Bayley is very sick, and much changed as he thinks; is desirous of seeing me.
Novr 28, 1706. Visited Mr. Bayley after dinner; went in the coach. I mentioned heaven being the Christian's home: Mr. Bayley said, I long to be at home; why tarry thy chariot wheels? Told me twas the last time he should see me. Was born, July, 1642.
Decr 3. I went with Col. Townsend, and Mr. Em Hutchinson, and visited Capt. Legg: He is in a low and languishing condition. Then went and talked thoroughly with Mr. Cotton Mather about selling [schoolmaster Richard] Henchman's house; he seemed to be satisfied; tells me Mr. Williams is to preach the lecture. Yesterday Mrs. Walker of the Neck was buried, I followed for one; I saw none else of the Council there. Mrs. Hannah Oliver is to be buried tomorrow.
Decr 4, 1706. I was at the burial of Mrs. Hannah Oliver.
Decr 5th Mr. John Williams preached the lecture.
Decr 6. I went to Mr. Sergeant's and heard Mr. Pemberton preach from Ps. 4.6 [Lord, lift thou up the light of thy countenance upon us].
Decr 7. 1706. The Genl Court is prorogued to Wednesday the 12th of February, at 10 *mane.* I invited the Govr to dine at Holms's. There were the Govr, Col. Townsend, Bromfield, Leverett, Williams, Capt. Wells, [Joseph] Shelden, Hook, Sewall.
Midweek, Decr 11th I visited Mr. Bayley, find Mr. Walter with him; I moved that seeing Mr. [Nehemiah] Walter and I seldom met there together, Mr. Walter might go to prayer; which he did excellently; that

---

[10]Thomas Child was a painter-stainer who, among other things, painted coffins.

Mr. Bayley and we our selves might be prepared to dye. Mr. Bayley is now, the night before last, taken with pleuretick pains, which go beyond those of the stone; new pains; cryes out, My head! my head! what shall I doe? Seems now to long, and pray for a dismission. At parting I gave his sister Cheyny a ten-shilling bill for him, to help to buy some necessaries; I could not help them to watch. Mr. Bayley said he thought he should dye of a consumption of the lungs; by his cough he found they were touched. When he mentioned the pain in his side, I said, twas sad for a man to be circumvented with his enemies. He answered pretty readily, he hoped there were more with him than against him. He desired me to write to his brother Joseph to come and see him.

Decr 13. I gave my letter to J. Bayley to Mr. Simkins, who said he had one to send it by.

Note[:] By reason of the storm yesterday, the Council met not; Govr was not in town, but writt a letter to the Secretary that the Council was adjourned to Friday; I told the Secretary, the Council that met not, could not be adjourned; yet, Govr nominated Mr. [John] Plaisted to be a justice of peace in Yorkshire, and drove it throw, though he be a dweller in Hampshire; and has a brother Ichabod Plaisted, that is of the Council.

This day Mr. [Jacob] Melyen dies. Aetat. [aged] 67. Mrs. Mary Pemberton is very low, dangerously ill.

Decr 14th [son] Joseph comes to see us, brings word that [John] Wyth, the mason, dyed yesterday at Cambridge. Goodman [John] Swan is in a fair way to be received into the [Cambridge] church again; was cast out in Mr. [Urian] Oakes's time [excommunicated in 1684], in a very solemn manner, in my sight and hearing.

Decr 18. 1706. Bastian [John Wait's black servant] lops the elm by my Lord's [Earl of Bellomont] stable; cuts off a cord of good wood. Mr. Sergeant came up Rawson's Lane as we were doing of it.

Decr 19. mane, [John] Maxwell comes in the Governour's name to invite me to dine at Roxbury with his Excellency at one aclock tomorrow. Mr. C. Mather preaches the lecture in Mr. [Thomas] Bridges turn, from Gal. 3. 27——have put on Christ. Preached with allusion to apparel; one head was that apparel was for distinction.

Mr. Walter dines with us, and leaves with me £13.10.9. Roxbury money. Mr. Sergeant marries Mrs. Mehetabel Cooper.

Decr 20, feria sexta [sixth day], very rainy day; Mr. Winthrop, Russel, Elisha Hutchinson, E[liaki]m Hutchinson, Mr. Foster, Sewall, Townsend, Walley, Bromfield, Belchar dine at the Governour's, Mr. Secretary. Go in coaches. After dinner I visit Mr. Bayley; is in great extremity, paroxisms return in about 1/2 hour; seemed to desire death; and yet once I took notice that he breathed after some space and recovery of strength before went hence: leave all to God's unerring providence. He told me he heard Sister Shortt[11] was dangerously sick; heard of by Jonathan Emmery. Came home to the meeting at Mr. Bromfield's, Mr. Williams of Deerfield preached;[12] very rainy day, and dirty under foot. When came home, or a little after, had a letter brought me of the death of sister Shortt the 18th inst[ant] which was very surprising to me. Half [of my brothers and sisters] are now dead.[13] The Lord fit me for my departure.

Decr 21. Not having other mourning, I looked out a pair of mourning gloves. An hour or 2 after, Mr. Sergeant, sent me and my wife gloves; mine are so little I cant wear them. Mr. Cooper's son brought them, I gave him Dr. [Increase] Mather's treatise of tithes [*A Discourse Concerning the Maintenance Due to Those that Preach the Gospel* (Boston, 1706)].

Decr 23. I visit Mr. Sergeant and his bride; had ale and wine. Mr. Cook, Col. Hutchinson, Mr. [Benjamin] Colman, [Eliphalet] Adams, Capt. [James] Hill, Mr. [Henry] Dering were there. After came in Mr. Bromfield, and Cousin [Jeremiah] Dummer.

Decr 24. Feria Tertia [third day, i.e., Tuesday] My wife and I execute a lease to Mr. Seth Dwight, for 21 years, of the House he dwells in. Mr. Eliezer Moodey writt the leases; and he and David Sinclar [Sewall's servant] were witnesses; twas transacted in our bedchamber.

Feria tertia [third day], Decr 24. 1706. I went to Brooklin, and visited my son [Sam] and Daughter Sewall and little Rebekah; paid my son 30s in full, and he is to send me 15 fountains, which are paid for in the mentioned sum. He has been ill, and is not very well now. Mr. Read, with whom he has been, tells him he is melancholy. Dined on salt fish and a spar-rib.

Visited Mr. Bayley as I came home; he has a very sore mouth. He tells me he has left off observing the distance of his fits, is tired and

[11] Sewall's sister, Anne, married Henry Short in 1692. Anne's first husband, William Longfellow of Newbury, died in a shipwreck in Sir William Phips's 1690 expedition to Quebec. It will be recalled that in 1685 Sewall was mortified by Brother Longfellow's appearance at a private fast, "he being so ill conditioned and so outwardly shabby," and that the following year, upon giving Longfellow some money and arranging to have him provided with clothes worth £5, Sewall advised his brother-in-law "to be frugal."

[12] Reverend John Williams's daughter, Eunice, was still in captivity.

[13] Of Sewall's seven brothers and sisters, John died in August and Hannah (Toppan) in November of 1699, Mehitable (Moodey) in August of 1702, and Anne (Longfellow Short) in December of 1706.

done. I gave him a Banbury cake, of which he eat pretty well, complaining of his mouth.

Mid-week. Decr 25. Shops open, carts come to town with wood, fagots, hay, and horses with provisions, as usually. I bought me a great toothed comb at [Seth] Dwight's; 6s.

Feria septima [seventh day, i.e., Saturday], Decr 28, 1706. A large fair rainbow is seen in the morning in the norwest. Madam [Sarah] Walley called her husband [John] into the shop to see it. The Govr being indisposed with the gout, called a Council to meet at Roxbury [nearer his home]; and by that means I gained an opportunity to see my friend Bayley once again. He is now brought very low by his stone, fever, sore tongue and mouth; could hardly speak a word to me. But he said, sit down. His wife asked him if he knew me? He answered, with some quickness, he should be distracted, if he should not know me. He thanked me when I came away. I said Christ would change his vile body, and make it like his glorious body. And when the coach-man called, saying the company staid for me, I took leave, telling him God would abide with him; Those that Christ loves, he loves to the end. He bowed with his head. His wife and sister weep over him. He called for mouth-water once while I was there, and then for his little pot to void it into; I supposed it was to enable him to speak. Though he doth not eat at present; yet I left the banbury cake I carried for him, with his wife: And when came away, called her into next chamber, and gave her two five-shilling bills. She very modestly and kindly accepted them and said I had done too much already. I told her No, if the state of my family would have born it, I ought to have watched with Mr. Bayley, as much as that came to. I left her weeping. Mark the perfect man &c.[14] When returned to the Governour's, I found the other coaches gon; the sun down some time. Major Walley, Col. Townsend, Mr. Bromfield and I came home well together in the hackney coach; though the ways are very deep by reason of the long, strong southerly wind and thaw. Serene day. Wind w[esterly].

Decr 31. 1706. Madam Dudley, and Mrs. Anne Dudley visit my wife just a little before night and inform of our son's [Sam, Jr.] illness, which they were told of at midnight: Will send us word if he grow worse.

Mr. [Aeneas] Salter makes us a little chimney in my chimney, make a fire in it to try it.

---

[14]James Bayley died on January 18, 1707. Since the onset of Bayley's illness, Sewall had visited his friend in Roxbury at least nineteen times. After Bayley's funeral, Sewall consoled friends and family members by noting that Bayley had "gon to rest after a weary race."

4

"This Daughter Was
Much His Delight"

The decade after 1706 began with Sewall mired in public controversy. His embattled kinsman, Joseph Dudley, faced a serious challenge to his administration in the form of a petition to Queen Anne calling for the governor's removal. According to his accusers, Dudley had profited from a treasonous scheme in which his accomplices had traded with enemy troops in Canada while England and France were at war. In answering this charge, Dudley asked for a vote of confidence from the Council on November 1, 1707. He urged that body to "vote an abhorrence" of the petition itself, which the Council did unanimously. Sewall, however, was not comfortable with his vote. As he explained later, the governor presented the matter to the Council "about noon" on Saturday, "a time very hurrying with us" because of preparations for the Sabbath. Yet when Sewall requested a postponement of the vote until Monday, Dudley "would not hear of" it.[1]

Sewall's subsequent inquiries, including a discussion with one of the men implicated in the illegal trade, and his reading of *A Memorial of the Present Deplorable State of New-England,* which supplied supporting affidavits to the charges against Dudley, deepened his "uneasiness." Three weeks after casting an affirmative vote in Council, Sewall was ready to reverse himself. When he heard Dudley declare at a joint conference of councillors and deputies that "every one of the Council remained steady to their vote, and every word of it," Sewall sought "to extricate" himself publicly from the governor's position. At the end of the meeting of the Council on November 25, Sewall notified Dudley of his intention to withdraw his earlier vote and presented the governor with

---

[1]M. Halsey Thomas, ed., *The Diary of Samuel Sewall, 1674–1729,* 2 vols. (New York: Farrar, Straus and Giroux, 1973), 1:574; Sewall to Nathaniel Higginson, March 10, 1708, in *Letter-Book of Samuel Sewall,* Massachusetts Historical Society *Collections,* 6th series, 1–2 (Boston, 1886–88), 1:361.

the reasons for his reversal. In his formal statement, which was later printed as a broadside, Sewall objected to the "very short time" that the Council had been allowed to decide on a matter of such "great concernment" and to the fact that the motion had been drafted by the governor himself when it "ought to have been debated and framed by the members of the Council apart by themselves, in the absence of the Governour." Dudley was not pleased. "The Govr often says that if any body would deal plainly with him, he would kiss them; but I received many a bite," Sewall recorded.[2]

Dudley survived this challenge to his administration and the very public defection of his own "brother-in-law" in part because of his vigorous defense of the Massachusetts frontier during Queen Anne's War (1702–13). Sewall himself admitted in his statement of withdrawal that the governor's orders were "truly excellent" with respect to the "suitableness of the orders themselves and the quickness of their dispatch." Even more important to the survival of Dudley's administration, however, was the protection afforded it by the governor's patrons in London. Dudley's opponents in Massachusetts were ineffectual as long as his friends in England were in power. This situation changed dramatically after the death of Queen Anne in 1714 and the triumph of the Whig party in 1715. Following their electoral victory, the Whigs proceeded to purge the government of Tory leaders and their placemen. New leaders, many of them strangers to Dudley, reserved the spoils of victory for their own clients.[3]

Ironically, the end of Dudley's tenure in 1715 came at a time when some Bostonians who had formerly been among his most vociferous critics were beginning to argue for his retention as governor. After thirteen years of doing battle with Dudley, they were accustomed to his

---

[2]Thomas, ed., *Diary*, 1:576–79; Sewall to Higginson, March 10, 1708, in *Sewall Letter-Book*, 1:361; [Cotton Mather?] *A Memorial of the Present Deplorable State of New-England, With the Many Disadvantages It Lyes Under, by the Male-Administration of their Present Governour, Joseph Dudley, Esq.* (Boston, 1707), reprinted in Massachusetts Historical Society *Collections*, 5th series (1879), 6:33*–64*. Dudley's defense appeared as *A Modest Enquiry into the Grounds and Occasions of a Late Pamphlet, Intitled A Memorial of the Present Deplorable State of New-England* (London, 1707), and the renewed attack on Dudley appeared as *The Deplorable State of New-England, by Reason of a Covetous and Treacherous Governour* (London, 1708); both pamphlets are reprinted in Massachusetts Historical Society *Collections*, 5th series (1879), 6:65*–95*, 97*–131*. *The Deplorable State of New-England*, perhaps also the work of Cotton Mather, included a copy of Sewall's explanation of his reversal (pp. 110*–11*) with the prefatory comment that Sewall was a "-brother-in-law to the Governour" and a "Judge of the Superior Court, but a person of unspotted integrity."

[3]Thomas, ed., *Diary*, 1:579; Richard L. Bushman, *King and People in Provincial Massachusetts* (Chapel Hill: Univ. of North Carolina Press, 1985), 66–67.

antics or at least familiar with his worst characteristics. There was no guarantee that a stranger sent from England would be better than Dudley; indeed, given the prevailing political climate of the mother country, there was good reason to expect that he would be worse. For his part, Dudley was less confrontational in his last years. Perhaps sensing that he could ill afford to alienate any of his newfound support, he did not negate the election of Elisha Cooke to the Council in 1715. In any case, when news arrived from England that Dudley's term as governor was ended, few Bostonians celebrated. Sewall and others called on the outgoing governor and joined in expressions of "sorrow for the change."[4]

The appointment of Colonel Elizeus Burgess to be Dudley's replacement did nothing to ease the regrets of many Bostonians. To those especially who had opposed Sir William Phips two decades earlier because they found the one-time ship's carpenter to be too crude, too poorly educated, and too apt to engage in fisticuffs to serve as their royal governor, the new appointee was even less acceptable. Phips may have proven to be an embarrassment as governor, but at least he was once a local hero. Born into humble surroundings in Kennebec, Maine, he had moved to Boston, married a wealthy widow, become a naval adventurer, taken a Spanish galleon laden with gold to London, and led the Massachusetts troops on a successful assault on the French position at Port Royal during King William's War. Burgess possessed all of the faults and none of the virtues of Phips. He was a military commander with a reputation for profanity and intemperate actions (he threatened to slit the throat of one of his opponents in Boston), and a stranger to Massachusetts. In the end, the colony was spared what promised to be a stormy administration when Burgess accepted payment of a thousand pounds sterling in exchange for resigning his governorship before ever having set foot in Massachusetts. In the wake of Burgess's resignation, "certain news is brought that Samuel Shute is made our Govr, to our great joy," Sewall recorded.[5]

In his private life, the years after 1706 were also filled with joy and sorrow for Sewall. His son Joseph graduated from Harvard in 1707, took a master's degree in 1710, and was ordained as colleague pastor to

[4]Richard R. Johnson, *Adjustment to Empire: The New England Colonies, 1675–1715* (New Brunswick, N.J.: Rutgers Univ. Press, 1981), 349–51; G. B. Warden, *Boston, 1689–1776* (Boston: Little, Brown, 1970), 80; Thomas, ed., *Diary,* 1:804–5.

[5]T. H. Breen, *The Character of the Good Ruler: A Study of Puritan Political Ideas in New England, 1630–1730* (New Haven: Yale Univ. Press, 1970), 184–88; Johnson, *Adjustment to Empire,* 352–53; Thomas, ed., *Diary,* 2:821.

Ebenezer Pemberton of the South Church in 1713. Joseph's marriage to Elizabeth Walley a month after his ordination simply consummated the satisfaction that Sewall found in his son's accomplishments. The only sour note on that occasion, a portent of things still ahead, was Rebeckah Dudley Sewall's refusal to spend the night at the home of her in-laws. In the months and years that followed, we know that Sewall came to harbor serious doubts about the virtues of Rebeckah; over the same period, he nurtured a deep affection for Elizabeth. He helped Joseph and Elizabeth welcome the birth of their first child, "Little Samuel, *de Josepho*," and mourned with them ("Alas! Alas!") when their second child, Joseph, suffered convulsions and died in infancy. As a measure of his esteem, after Hannah died in 1717, Sewall presented Elizabeth with Hannah's wedding ring, "saying I hoped she would wear it with the same nobility as she did who was the first owner of it." Honored by the gesture, Elizabeth treated Sewall to some "excellent sackposset." The sweetened milk and wine drink put Sewall in a genial mood. "I told her the ring I had given her was her mother's wedding ring; and this entertainment savored of a wedding." By the time he took his leave of Joseph and Elizabeth, the day had turned cold and wet; still, Sewall walked home "in the rain" contented.[6]

The marriage of the Sewalls' tenth child, Mary, to Boston bookseller Samuel Gerrish in 1709 was a similarly joyous event. But here the joy was short-lived. On November 9, 1710, fourteen months after the reception at which her father had given each guest a "large piece of cake wrapped in paper," Mary went into labor with her first child. As was his custom, Sewall "sat up late" awaiting word of the birth. Although complications seemed to have attended the difficult delivery, Mary gave birth to a daughter at dawn on the tenth. Three days later, Sewall visited his daughter and new granddaughter, whom the Gerrishes had named Hannah. Samuel Gerrish reported that Mary was "something disordered," but neither he nor Sewall "apprehended . . . [any] danger." The Sewalls sent Mary a portion of their thanksgiving dinner on November 16, which, they were told, "she eat of pleasantly." But when they visited her that night, they knew that their daughter had not regained any of her strength. While Hannah spent hours at Mary's bedside, Sewall prayed with her and then sought solace in the company of Grove Hirst. The Sewalls left the Gerrish residence later that night only to receive an urgent summons to return there an hour or two after midnight. "All the family were alarmed and gathered into our bed-

6Thomas, ed., *Diary,* 2:791, 871, 929.

Figure 8.
Joseph Sewall, pastor of the South Church from 1713 to 1769. Mezzotint of the portrait by John Smibert. Courtesy, American Antiquarian Society.

chamber," Sewall remembered. Returning to the Gerrish home, he was astonished to find Mary so weak that she "could not speak to me." Because Gerrish was apparently unable to get Benjamin Wadsworth to come in time, Sewall sent for Experience Mayhew, who came promptly and "prayed very well." Then, before sunrise on Friday, Mary died. "My dear child expired, being but nineteen years, and twenty days old," Sewall lamented. When he returned home and told Hannah the sad news, "a dolefull cry was lifted up."[7]

The sadness the Sewalls felt over the death of Mary was compounded when Mary's daughter became "very sick" on April 21, 1711. Barely five months after they had buried their daughter, the Sewalls found their granddaughter "little Hannah Gerrish in an agony." Two days later, between two and three in the morning, Sewall was again awakened by a summons to the Gerrish home, but "my little Hannah expired before I got thither." Hannah's death was followed in quick order by the deaths of three other Sewall grandchildren. Sam, Jr., and Rebeckah's fifth child, Mary, died on August 24, 1712, at the age of one. And two of Grove and Betty Hirst's children, both named William, died before their first birthday; the first William died on April 6, 1713, and the second on March 13, 1714. In less than three and a half years, the Sewalls had buried a daughter and four grandchildren, and more sorrow was in store for them.[8]

After she had lost her last two sons in infancy, Betty developed a "grievous cough and a returning fever." Eight pregnancies in a span of twelve years had taxed Betty's constitution, which was never robust. Sewall, who was particularly fond of Betty and her husband, closely monitored his daughter's health problems throughout her years of marriage. For Sewall, visiting "my sick daughter Hirst" or having her lodge "at our house to promote her revival and strengthening" or praying and asking for prayers for Betty, who was "very weak and low," became something of a routine. But in 1716, a change for the worse was clearly evident in Betty's health. Confined mainly to her home by a fever, Betty was beginning to despair. She "was ready to think she was dying." Sewall, busily arranging for prayers in the Hirst's home, was himself fearful that "her stay with us is short." As Benjamin Colman, William Cooper, Ebenezer Pemberton, and Increase Mather joined Joseph Sewall in prayer on separate days in late June and early July, Betty grew progressively weaker. On the evening of July 10, Sewall must have suspected that the end was near. Although Hannah went home a little after nine, Sewall, in Joseph's words, "tarried all night." Betty grew restless as the night wore on. She called for a gown to fight the chill, for linen to be laid on her hands, for something to drink "which she had much adoe to take though given her in a spoon," and for help in turning from her right side because "she was weary of lying on that side." All the

---

[7] Ibid., 2:625; 644–45.
[8] Ibid., 2:658–59, 697, 709, 788.

while, Sewall kept watch, moving from side to side and inquiring after her comfort. The end came swiftly about midnight. Betty uttered, "I am a-going, call Mr. Hirst." She moaned "lower and lower till she dyed."[9]

"Thus have I parted with a very desirable child not full thirty five years old. She lived desired and died lamented," Sewall wept. He did not return home immediately after Betty's death; rather, he lingered at Betty's side until morning. Joseph Sewall understood. "Great & very awfull is the breach . . . made on my Father's family," he wrote, for Betty was the "Flower & Ornament of the family." Joseph sensed the depth of the loss for his father: "This daughter was much his delight."[10]

Diary

1717

January 1. 1717. Very warm sun-shiny pleasant weather. Mr. [John] Danforth, of Dorchester, visits me, gives me his sermons [*Judgment Begun at the House of God* (Boston, 1716)]. John Quinsey here. I visit Madam [Frances] Banister to condole with her; find her sister [Mary Banister] Dyer there, and condole her, all under one.[1] Had no noise this morning; I yesterday used means with Mr. Master to prevent it.

Jany 2. Midweek, dine with the Court and Govr [Samuel Shute]. Commissioners meeting, Mr. [Experience] Mayhew.

Jany 3. Fair day, Mr. [Joseph] Sewall's Text Hab. 2.3. The vision [is

---

[9] Ibid., 2:594, 612, 661, 712, 815, 816, 823–25; Grove Hirst's observations on Betty's illness and confinement are quoted in Benjamin Colman, *A Sermon Preached upon the Death of the Truly Vertuous and Religious Grove Hirst* (Boston, 1717), 93.

[10] Thomas, ed., *Diary,* 2:825; "Diary of Joseph Sewall, 1711–1716," MS, Massachusetts Historical Society, entry for July 10, 1716.

[1] Thomas Banister died in a shipwreck off the coast of England in December 1716. Interestingly enough, Sewall's past encounters with Banister indicate that he disapproved of the latter's personal conduct. In June 1708, Sewall recorded that the Court had fined Banister for lying, cursing, and "breach of the peace for throwing the pots and scale-box at the maid." More recently, in February of 1714, Sewall had accompanied Constable Henry Howell to a South-end tavern after nine at night in an effort to quiet Banister and his drunken compatriots, who were drinking to the "Queen's Health" and many "other Healths." Sewall "threaten'd to send some of them to prison" and specifically admonished Banister, who among the revellers "had been longest an Inhabitant and Freeholder," that he must mend his ways and "set an Example" for the rest. Banister responded by inviting the crowd to his house "and away they went."

yet for an appointed time]—102. Psal: 11–18. G. 2 1/2 staves. 'Twas a good discourse, and large assembly. Dined with the Govr at Major [Thomas] Fitch's. Mrs. Bream was before Mr. [Grove] Hirst and [Elisha] Cooke [Jr.]. I would not speak; because one party's bringing justices upon those that are handling a cause is the way to disturb and confound a judicial process.

Jany 4. Friday, Govr dines at Mr. [Addington] Davenport's. Sets out for Cambridge. I visit the widow [Katherine] Jeffries [whose husband, David, died in the same shipwreck that took Thomas Banister's life].

Jany 9. Mr. Mayhew goes away by water, for Duxbury, having sold his horse.

Jany 6. Great rain last night; but fair, moderate weather. Hannah Sewall [Sewall's daughter, thirty-six years old] taken into the South Church [as a member]. Lord grant it may be in order to her being taken into heaven! Visit Madam [Eunice] Willard [widow of Reverend Samuel Willard].

[January] 7. 2[nd day]. Moderate [weather].

[January] 8. 3[rd day]. Cool N. east wind, but holds up and is Moderat. Great assembly at the New South [Church], which is the first. Dr. Increase Mather began with an excellent prayer, Mr. [Benjamin] Wadsworth preached from Rev. 2.23. I am he which searcheth the reins—Mr. [Benjamin] Colman prayed excellently and blessed the people. Lt. Govr [William Dummer] and Col. [Adam] Winthrop go home with me at noon. [January 8] P.M. Mr. Sewall prayed, Dr. C. Mather preached from John 2.17. The zeal of the house hath eaten thee up. Mr. [Ebenezer] Pemberton prayed, appointed the 2d part of the 84th Psalm to be sung. Mr. [Nathaniel] Williams of the Old Church set the tune D. and read it. Mr. Pemberton blessed the people. In the fore-seat in the morn. Lt Govr Dummer, Sewall, Lynde, Joseph [i.e., Joseph Lynde], [Edward] Bromfield. P.M. was also Major Genl [Wait Still] Winthrop and Col. [Elisha] Hutchinson. Madam Winthrop in the foreseat. 'Tis sad it should be so, but a virulent libel was starched on upon the three doors of the Meeting-house, containing the following words:

TO ALL TRUE-HEARTED CHRISTIANS.

Good people, within this House, this very day,
A Canting Crew will meet to fast, and pray.
Just as the miser fasts with greedy mind, to spare;
So the glutton fasts, to eat a greater share.
But the sower-headed Presbyterians fast to seem more holy,
And their Canting Ministers to punish sinfull foley.

Jany 9. Mr. [Ebenezer] Thayer preaches at his brother's from Gal. 6.9. Be not weary—son J[oseph] and I heard him to very good content. *Jany 10.* Mr. [John] Webb preaches a very good sermon from 1 John 3.3. Every man that hath this hope—after lecture grant Mrs. Mary Norton the administration of her husband's goods. Lord make me ready for my change.

January 11. I shew the answer I had drawn up to Barrington Shute esqr [John Shute, Viscount Barrington]; they appointed Mr. Davenport, Winthrop and others to peruse it against tomorrow. Prayer at Mr. comissary's [Andrew Belcher] on account of his son and daughter. Mr. Wadsworth, Colman prayed; Mr. Pemberton preached from Philip 4.6. Be carefull—Mr. Sewall prayed; part of the 34th Ps. sung, L. Came home with my son and Madam Willard in the coach. Mrs. Mary Wheelwright dies: Mr. Treasurer [Jeremiah] Allen's only daughter; was brought to bed yesterday of a son; would have been 20 years old the 22th of April next.

[January] 13. 1[st day]. The new South [Church] have their first Sabbath assembly. Mr. [William] Cooper preaches A.M. Sanctify my Sabbath—Mr. Colman P.M. [Ps.] 132.9. Let thy priests [be clothed with righteousness; and let thy saints shout for joy].

[January] 15: 3[rd day]. Mrs. Wheelwright buried. Bearers, Lieut Govr [Dummer], Thomas Hutchinson esqr.; Mr. [Henry] Harris, Wm Hutchinson esqr.; Mr. Wm Clark of the Common, Mr. Russel. Visited cousin S. Sewall and his new married wife.[2] As I went to Mr. Hirst's to dinner, I tripped at wood, and fell down all along just over against Mr. Fenno's, with my hand in the canal, but with little or no hurt, Blessed be God.

16. 4. Went to Mr. Pemberton, and carried home his Baxter;[3] he gave occasion to speak of him. I objected against his exposition of 2 Cor. 3d. He seemed to excuse him, and said not a word against it that I observed. Went to the funeral of James Mirick; to the meeting.

---

[2]Stephen Sewall's son, Samuel, married Katharine Howell, the recently widowed stepdaughter of Cotton Mather, on January 1, 1717. Mather, who once described Katharine's first husband, Boston merchant Nathan Howell, as "the worst of Men; a sorry, forward and exceedingly wicked Fellow," welcomed the latter's passing. Indeed, shortly after Howell's death on May 2, 1716, Mather boasted that he had earlier prayed for three days that "this wicked Creature" might be delivered "into the Hands of the holy God." His prayers were answered when "God smote the Wretch, with a languishing Sickness." For six months, physicians tried unsuccessfully to restore Howell's previously "strong, lively, hearty" condition, Mather noted, but "glorious GOD putt a Period unto the grievous Wayes of this wicked Man."

[3]Sewall is probably referring to Richard Baxter's *A Call to the Unconverted . . . The Thirty-first Edition* (Boston, 1717).

17. 6. Dr. C. Mather preaches, Rev. 14.7 Fear God [and give glory to him; for the hour of his judgment is come: and worship him that made heaven, and earth].

19. 7. Capt Cayley's men make a rout in the town at night by pressing [forcing men into service] without order, cut one man's head with a sword.

20. 1. Mr. [Nathaniel] Appleton preaches at the New South, A.[M.] and P.M.

21. 2. Lt Govr calls a Council, writes to Capt. Cayley to demand two men mentioned by name. He sends them ashore.

January 29. 1717. Super[io]r Court at Charlestown held by the 5 justices with their new commissions from Govr Shute, which were read. I read the attorney's oath to them to refresh their memory. The afternoon was taken up with the admiralty cause. Mr. [Robert] Auchmuty and Smith for the libel, Mr. [Paul] Dudley and [John] Vallentine against it. Court unanimous in the prohibition.

Note[:] This day my dear sister Gerrish [Jane Sewall] dies between 1 and 2 P.M.; was born 8r [October] 25, 1659 at Baddesly, in Hampshire [England].

Jany 30. Storm of snow; go to Charlestown with the chief justice [Wait Still Winthrop] as yesterday; finish the Court. When I came home met with the sad news of my sister Gerrishes death. Send my eldest son with Sam Moodey [son of Sewall's sister Mehitable] the messenger; went away before seven, proposing to go to Meadford to shorten their journey to-morrow.

Jany 31. Very cold; yet Sam and his cousin [Samuel Moodey] ride from Meadford to Newbury by 3 P.M. and assist at the funeral.

Jany 31. 1717. My sister Gerrish's bearers were: Mr. Justice [Joseph] Woodbridge, Col. Somersby; Mr. John Kent of the Island, Majr [Thomas] Noyes; Deacon William Noyes, Deacon Nathanl Coffin. The Govr comes from Ipswich to Cambridge; lodges at Col. [Spencer] Phips's.

Feb. 1. Friday, The Govr dines with Col. [William] Dudley, then comes home.

Feb. 2. 7[th day]. I wait on his Excellency with Mr. Bromfield.

Feb. 8. 6. The hearing of Capt. [Christopher] Taylor is put off till Tuesday 19 because the original will [of his father James] was not produced. Mr. Pemberton is very sick; I visit him in his little bed-room next [to] the study.

Feb. 10. Mr. Pemberton prayed for as there being hopes of his being better. Mr. Sam Fisk preaches in the afternoon.

Feb. 11. 2. A number of the [South] Church meet at Mr. [Joseph]

Sewall's and pray for Mr. Pemberton.[4] Mr. Wadsworth, Dr. Cotton Mather, Mr. Colman, Mr. Webb, Mr. Cooper, Mr. Sewall, in the west-room. Psal. 41.1–4 sung Windsor tune.

Feb. 12. 3. I go to Charlestown with Mr. [Francis] Willoughby to wait on their committee. 'Twas very cold, and I grew sick in Capt. [Samuel] Phips's stove-room; vomited; went to the 3 Cranes [tavern in Charlestown], vomited again, fain to lay down on the bed, had 4 evacuations downward. Much ado to get home, Mr. Willoughby going before and preparing a coach for me at landing. Mr. [Thomas] Graves was very courteous and helpfull to me, as a physician. How pleasant was my own chamber to me. *Laus Deo* [Praise God].

Feb. 13. 4th[day] Susan [Susanna Thayer, Sewall's domestic servant] brings word that Mr. Pemberton had a good night, was much better. Yet afternoon am sent for to him as approaching his end. When came was finishing his will. Then I went in to him. He called me to sit down by him, held me by the hand and spake pertinently to me, though had some difficulty to hear him. Mr. [Joseph] Sewall prayed fervently, and quickly after he expired, bolstered [Pemberton] up in his bed, about 3/4 past 3 after noon in the best chamber. The Lord sanctify it to me, and to all. My son writ a letter to Dr. Cotton Mather to preach for him, and before 'twas superscribed, he [Mather] came in, which [we] took as a token for good. I spake to Mr. [Ezekiel] Lewis, and he approved of it.

Feb. 14. Dr. C. Mather preaches and prays excellently, Come my people enter into thy chambers—Isa. 26. P.M. Mrs. Hannah Clark, widow of Saml Clark, was buried in the old burying place, aged 53. Bearers, Wait Winthrop esqr. Sewall; [Thomas] Fitch esqr. Oliver, Daniel; Mr. Saml Phillips, [William] Welsteed.

Febr. 15. 6[th day]. The Revd Mr. William Brattle died last night at mid-night. He was a father to the students of Harvard College, and a physician. My fast friend. I wish it be not portentous that two such great men [Pemberton and Brattle] should fall in one week! *Deus avertat omen* [may God turn away the omen].

Febr. 16. 7. Is a great storm of snow and sleet, so that the burying of Mr. Pemberton is put off to Monday, and notice sent accordingly.

Febr. 17. 1. Serene, Mr. Wadsworth preaches at the South [Church] excellently, from 2 Pet. 1.15 [that ye may be able after my decease to have these things always in remembrance].

---

[4]When Joseph Sewall became Pemberton's colleague pastor at the Old South Church in 1713, Pemberton presided over the ordination ceremony and provided the "chief Entertainment" afterwards.

Febr. 18. 2. Great storm of snow; yet good going under foot. Mr. Pemberton is buried between 4 and 5 in Mr. [Samuel] Willard's tomb. Bearers, Mr. John Leverett, president [of Harvard], Dr. Cotton Mather; Mr. Wadsworth, Colman; Mr. [Joseph] Sewall, Webb; Dr. Increase Mather, Majr Genl Winthrop. Col. [Elisha] Hutchinson not there, by which means it fell to me to wait on his Excellency: Twas good going, a broad path being made. Col. [Joseph] Lynde of Charlestown was there. Mr. [Joseph] Stephen's wife [Sarah Lynde] brought to bed of a daughter this morn. I saw not him there; nor Mr. [Henry] Flint; Col. [Nathaniel] Byfield, and Counsellour Cushing there. Mr. [Peter] Thacher of Milton.

Febr. 19. Serene, cold, snow blows, Council does nothing as to Mr. James Taylor's will, because Col. [John] Appleton came not. Mrs. Story buried.

Febr. 20. The pleas are made and evidences produced: Council confirms what Col. Appleton had done as judge of probat for Essex [pertaining to James Taylor's will]. I propounded to have had an adjournment till after lecture, to consider it. But that was not harkened to. Then I propounded, the not persuing Mr. Taylor's order as to his grandchildren, Pains [the children of Mary Payne, Taylor's deceased daughter, who were not mentioned in Taylor's will]; and the not signing the will in the witnesses presence; Mr. Davenport read the law of Posthumous Children, which seemed to explain it.[5] And the running it over with a pen before the witnesses, seemed to satisfy; especially, because Mr. Taylor used to sign alone; the difficulty of his palsy so inclining him. But if the grand-children, Mr. [William] Pain's children, shall not by law take as their mother [Mary Taylor Payne] would have done if living; I am still in doubt. This did so well come in my mind of a sudden, and I, and I think every body, voted an affirmance of Judge Appleton's decree [to include Mary Payne's children as beneficiaries]. About 1/2 an hour past one my son [Sam, Jr.] and I set out for Mr. Brattle's funeral in Capt. Belchar's slay; got thither in good time. Bearers, President [Leverett], Mr. [Samuel] Anger; Mr. [John] Hancock, Mr. Wadsworth; Mr. [Simon] Bradstreet, Mr. Stephens. Scarvs and rings. Governour [Shute] and [former] Govr Dudley went first; [Lieut.] Govr [John] Usher and Sewall 2d. Were many ministers there, Mr. [John] Rogers and [Jabez] Fitch from Ipswich. Came home from the

---

[5]The "Act providing for Posthumous Children," passed in 1701, ensured that children left out of a parent's will would receive a portion of the family estate equal to what their share would have been had that parent died intestate.

burying place: Cousin Elithrop drove. Got home very seasonably. Another snow coming on. *Laus Deo.*

Febr. 21. 5[th day]. Extraordinary storm of snow; yet many men at lecture to hear Mr. Colman preach the funeral sermon of Mr. Pemberton and Mr. Brattle, from John 9.4 [I must work the works of him that sent me, while it is day: the night cometh, when no man can work]. Compared Mr. Pemberton to Elijah; Mr. Brattle to Moses. After lecture the storm increases much, grows more vehement.

Feb. 22. 6. It was terribly surprising to me to see the extraordinary banks of snow on the side of the way over against us.

Feb. 23. 7. Serene and pleasant. Cousin [Edmund] Quinsey's servants essay to get their cattel home that came hither on Wednesday, leaving their sleds &c. here. I congratulate Madam [Katharine Brattle] Winthrop's return on Wednesday night; was afraid she was imprisoned at Cambridge. Condole with her on the loss of her excellent brother [William Brattle].

Feb. 24. 1. Violent storm of snow, which makes our meeting very thin especially as to women. Mr. [John] Cotton of Newtown here. Hardly any of the ministers at Mr. Brattle's funeral are got home. [As a result,] 'Tis feared many congregations failed [to meet]. There was none at the New-South [church].

Feb. 27. 4. Council held about a divorce. Capt. [Christopher] Taylor's petition for an appeal [of the action taken by the Court on 20 February] referred to a Genl Council.

Feb. 28. Storm. Dr. Cotton Mather preaches excellent from Psal. 147. He sendeth his word and melteth them. Applyed it also to the conversion of the Jews.

March 1. 6. Serene, visited Col. Hutchinson. He has recorded the nominations of many years in a quarto[-sized] parchment-covered book. Visited Col. [Penn] Townsend, who hurt his legg by a fall last Tuesday, which confines him. Mrs. Anne Henchman was buried this week. Cousin Susan Porter dines with us.

March 2. Rain. Capt. [Nathaniel] Oliver comes to me, and declares his unwillingness to make his confession before the congregation [as was customary for wayward members seeking to be restored]; his friends advise him. I said, you did run well, who hindered you?

March 3. 1[st day]. Fair good wether P.M. Robert Calef is baptized; and Mr. Abiel Wally, John James, Mrs. Margaret Wally and Susan Thayer [Sewall's domestic servant] are admitted [to church membership]. Mr. [Edward] Holyoke dined with us, who is still kept here by the snow that makes the ways unpassable.

March 4. I discourse Dr. [Oliver] Noyes about Mrs. Bream's appeal; he will not meddle, leaves it to his father[-in-law Andrew] Belchar.

March 5. The sheriff comes to me, and shews me a copy of Capt. Wyborn's petition to the Govr, wherein he charges the chief justice [Winthrop] with injustice for signing a bill of cost against him. Says the Govr bid him shew it me.

March 6. The Govr sends Zech. Sias to me. This midweek, the old [First] Church have a meeting, and chuse Mr. Thomas Foxcroft [as colleague pastor to Benjamin Wadsworth]. Sore storm in the day, and lightening and thunder at night; yet the messengers go to Cambridge the same day.

[March] 7. 5[th day]. Mr. Wadsworth preaches excellently from [Ps.] 119.50. This is my comfort [in my affliction: for thy word hath quickened me].

[March] 8. 6. Mr. Sewall preaches at Capt. Hab[ijah] Savages.

[March] 10. 1. Lord's Supper at the South. Comfortable weather. Son [Joseph] propounds the turning the lecture into a fast. Sundry of our fathers in the ministry think it proper; which I mention that I may have your concurrence with them in the seasonable solemnity.

[March] 11. 2. Visit Mr. Davenport, who was in his chamber; has had a sore pain in his side this 14 night; takes him when warm in his bed. Visit Mr. [John] Rawlings; give him a crown. Court prorogued to the 10th of April. Mr. [John] White chosen Moderator at the town meeting by papers [written ballots]. Same Selectmen as last year.

[March] 12. 3. The marriage of [John] Battersby [to Sarah Phelps] in Boston by Dr. C. Mather [on 28 February 1711] is declared to be henceforth null and void because he had a wife at Kinsale in Ireland. Order for a fast drawn up by Col. Winthrop, is voted, to be Apr. 4th. I put in [included in the order for a fast] losses by sea of lives and estates; New Jerusalem. Govr [Shute] propounded it might be [for] religious and civil liberties. I said religious was contained under civil; arguing that civil should go first. Capt. [Thomas] Hutchinson spoke that religious might go first. I mentioned adjourning Plimouth court to the Govr by reason of the difficulty of the road, and Mr. Davenport's indisposition. His Excellency seemed to discountenance it.

[March] 13. 4. Visited Capt. Ephr. Savage. Our private meeting is to be this day 14 night by reason of the fast to morrow.

[March] 14. 5. Fast, Mr. Webb begins with prayer, Mr. Colman preaches; text, Feed me with food convenient—Prov: 30. Prays. P.M. Mr. [Joseph] Sewall prays, Mr. Wadsworth preaches: text, 107. ult., whoso is wise—Prays; sung. Great congregation. F[orenoo]n and

aft[ernoo]n Dr. Incr., Cot. Mather, Mr. Cooper not there, by reason of indisposition. Governour was present in the forenoon only. Col. Townsend absent by reason of his lame leg; Mr. Davenport sick.

[March] 15. 6. Eclipse seen.

[March] 16. 7. Visit son [Samuel] Gerrish [husband of Mary Sewall] confined by his lame legg.

[March] 17. 1. pleasant weather.

[March] 18. 2. Warm weather. Give my letter to C[apt]. Belcher for Mr. [Experience] Mayhew; News-Letter of adjournment Super[io]r Court.

5 Fasts. Madam Paul Dudley brings Hannah Sewall of Brooklin, our grand-child [Sam, Jr., and Rebeckah's daughter, aged nine], to our house, in the chariot of her grandf. Dudley.

[March] 19. 3. Rain, Mr. [Joseph] Marsh calls and thanks me for my book. Hear Hannah S[ewall] read the 12. Psalm, which I had been reading in course.

[March] 21. 5. Mr. Sewall preaches: Christ is our hope.

[March] 24. 1. Mr. Thomas Foxcroft preaches at the South [Church] in the morn. Mark the perfect man.

[March] 25. 2. Mr. Bream returns my paper, says he could take up with it.

[March] 26. 3. Pleasant weather; I ride to Cambridge to the fast in company of Mr. Stephens, very bad way. No sled, cart or calash has gone [before us] that I can see. Mr. [Aaron] Porter [minister of Medford and husband of Sewall's niece Susanna] began with prayer, Mr. Bradstreet preached, Mr. Stephens prayed; sung the first part of the 80th Ps. Mr. [Nicholas] Fissenden set York tune very well; Mr. Bradstreet prayed. Began about 11 [A].M. had done by 3 P.M. Visited Col. [Francis] Foxcroft who has been confined a quarter of a year by the gout. Came home with Mr. Bradstreet, Stephens, Fisk. Got home well before twas quite dark. *Laus Deo.* None of the Council there but myself that I saw.

[March] 28. 5. Lightening and thunder in the night. Mr. Webb preaches from Matt. 25. 13. Watch, therefore, for ye know neither the day nor the hour when the Son of man cometh. I visit Mr. Cooper, Davenport. Mr. Tho. Lothrop arrives this day from Virginia, 6 days passage, brings news of the death of the Duke of Marlborough, Pretender, alliance with Great Britain and France.[6] 'Tis now 8 weeks from London.

Wiar arrived also from the bay this day. Am told of the death of Mr. [Samuel] Treat of Eastham. The Lord fit me for my turn.

---

[6]Great Britain, France, and Holland completed a triple alliance in January of 1717.

Took an inventory, gave an administration. I was helped in the night and this morning to pray earnestly for the pardon of my past sins, and for amendment of life. *Exaudi Deus* [may God hear me].

March 31. Now about 'tis propounded to the Church whether Capt Nathanl Oliver's confession should be before the church [members only], or before the [entire] congregation. I opposed the former as not agreeing with the universal practice; 'twas brought on by our late pastor [Pemberton] with the design that it should be before the congregation. Not fit that the penitent should prescribe before what auditory [audience] his confession should be. Some said there was little difference; I said twas the more gravaminous that Capt. Oliver should insist on it. I think it was the congregation's due, all being offended, when a person is [re]admitted, the congregation are acquainted with it. 'Twas carried for Capt. Oliver, and he was restored, but I did not vote in it. When he spake to me, I said, you did run well, who hindered you? He mentioned the advice of some friends. I suppose Col. [Nicholas] Paige. When Mr. [Nathaniel] Williams spake to me, I said let him as a Capt. take courage and make it before the congregation.

April 10. Genl Court sits 11, 12. Mr. Webb prays.

[April] 17th. Commissioners meeting.

[April] 18th I go with [daughter] Judith and [grandson] Sam Hirst [eleven years old] to the funeral of his grandmother [Mary Hirst of Salem]; rained to Lewis's [tavern in Lynn]; Mr. [Edward] Holyoke came in before we went thence. Sister Hirst buried.

[April] 19. Very comfortable day home. Bearers, Col. [John] Higginson, [Benjamin] Lynde; [Daniel] Epes, Col. [Samuel] Brown; Mr. [Josiah] Woolcot, Stephen Sewall. Scarfs and rings. I had a scarf and ring. Coming and going were in danger of oversetting the calash. But did not through the goodness of God. Got home very well. *Laus Deo.*

April 20. I go with Mr. Wadsworth to Capt. [Jeremiah] Dummer's. He prayed with him; I was very glad had motioned it. When Mr. Wadsworth asked him what to pray for, he said, for faith and patience. Asked me whether I was going, having occasion, and gave me his hand at parting. I mentioned to Mr. Wadsworth before we went up, as long as we are tacking, let us be praying, alluding to Mr. Bayly when in Ipswich-Bay.

April 21. Capt. Belchar tells me of the plot of Sweden's making a descent on Scotland.[7] It brought to mind my last night's dream. I dreamed of all being in a military flame, Major [John] Walley on foot led an ex-

---

[7]Charles XII of Sweden might have contemplated an invasion of Scotland, but nothing came of it.

traordinary troop of horse; I heard Col. [Thomas] Noyes at prayer with another company of soldiers.

April 22. By reason of the rain, I set not out for Plimouth till 7 m[ane], with David [Sinclair, Sewall's domestic servant] on horseback, and I in a calash which much defended me from the remaining rain. Baited at Capt. Mills [tavern at Braintree]. Dined at Cushing's [tavern at Scituate]. Baited at Bairsto's [tavern at Scituate]. From thence Mr. [Joseph] Briant went with me. Got to Mr. [Ephraim] Little's about sunset. Major [John] Bradford met me. All the company being gone, I lodged there. In the morning Mr. Allen and Seabry his brother in law came to me. Mr. Sheriff [Joseph] Lothrop of Barnstable, met me there with a number of men. Got to town a little after nine. I excused it to Mr. Isaac Lothrop that I had occasioned him double trouble. But to my surprise found he met not the judges. I bid Mr. Crocker tell him I should not set out till Monday; to prevent his coming too early. But I intended to go thorow; and I suppose had done so had not the rain hindered me in the morn. Mr. Little prays at opening the Court; excuses his dining, because he was going to see a man 6 miles off at the point of death (Zebulun Thorp).

April 24. The Court are informed that the said Thorp was dead of a fall from his horse Monday about sun-set, died a little before sunrise.

Apr. 24th. Mrs. Hedge and her Ethiopian woman were dismissed their attendance. Zeb. Thorp was accused by this negro of ravishing her. All were bound over. Thorp has said, if he were guilty he wish he might never get alive to Plimouth. He was a very debauched man; being presented to Barnstaple court Ap. 16. He went drunk into court; so that he was ordered to goal [jail] where he lay till next day, and then was proceeded with. He was said to be in drink when he fell, riding swiftly; had 19£ odd, Mr. Little found in his pocket; some say, he brought £50. from Yarmouth.

Apr. 25. Mr. [John] Watson the crowner's [coroner's] return is read in court.

April 26th I go early into Plimouth-Meetinghouse, and have much communion with God in prayer. Col. [William] Whiting dines with us, and reads the king's speech of Febr. 20 which he had copied out. Give Mr. Little the funeral sermons on Mr. Pemberton, Brattle, Dr. Mather's treatise of Councils, with an Angel bill of credit.[8] Set out for Cushing's.

[8]Two sermons were printed shortly after the deaths of Pemberton and Brattle: Benjamin Colman, *Industry and Diligence in the Work of Religion. A Sermon Preached in Boston, after the Funerals of . . . the Reverend Mr. William Brattle . . . and the Reverend Mr.*

Got over the worst way, and into Hingham bounds while had some considerable light; then the way was open and lightsome. When came in found the gentlemen at supper, whom I expected to have been gone to town. Supped with them very comfortably.

Apr. 27. Baited at Mills's. My calash defended me well from the cold drisk [drizzly mist]. Got well home about 3 P.M. *Laus Deo.*

Apr. 29. 30. We have the good news of the pirate's [Samuel Bellamy's ship the *Whidaw*] being broken to pieces on the Cape on Fridaynight. 24 guns. On Friday Apr. 26. Zeb. Thorp was brought dead to Plimouth and buried there.

May-day, Govr defers going eastward till next week.

Thorsday May 2d Mr. Sewall in his thanksgiving [sermon] on account of the dissipation of the pirates, mentions Job 34.25. Knewest the works overturned them in the night. Text, Mal. 4.[2] Sun of righteousness [arise with healing in his wings]. P.M. Trustees meet.

Thorsday, May 9. Jeremy Phenix arraigned in the Court-chamber.

[May] 10. Tryed in the Old Meetinghouse. Mr. Auchmooty [Robert Auchmuty] was counsel for the prisoner and had family with him in the fore-seat of the women, though he be bound over for notorious words against the government. About 14 of the Jury were challenged peremptorily. Was brought in guilty a little before night. Tryal held about five hours.[9]

May 11. 7[th day]. I passed sentence upon Phenix [that he be executed], the chief justice being absent. This was done in the Court-chamber.

May 13. 2. Set out for Salem with Col. [Nathaniel] Thomas from Meadford. Went to the funeral of Col. [John] Hathorne. Bearers, Mr. [Jonathan] Corwin, Higginson; Epes, Lynd Ben.; Col. Brown, Woolcot. Ten minut guns [i.e., guns fired at one-minute intervals] were discharged at the fort and battery.

[May] 14. 3. To Newbury, met the funeral of Mr. [Humphrey] Bradstreet [Newbury physician], stood still under Deacon [Nathaniel] Coffin's apletree while it passed by.

[May] 15. 4. From the Green Dragon [tavern in Boston], where we lodged, to Hampton, went in to Mr. [Theophilus] Cotton's. Dined at

---

Ebenezer Pemberton (Boston, 1717); and Joseph Sewall, *Precious Treasure in Earthen Vessels* (Boston, 1717). Increase Mather's treatise appeared under the title: *A Disquisition Concerning Ecclesiastical Councils* (Boston, 1716).

[9]Jeremiah Phenix, a Boston innkeeper, struck rope maker Ralph Moxtershed with a hatchet on August 7, 1716. Moxtershed died of the wound on November 11, 1716.

Wingets' [tavern in Hampton, New Hampshire]; to Newington [NH], Kittery [Maine]. *Laus Deo.*

[May] 16. 5. Mr. [John] Newmarch prayed. Bro[the]r [William] Moodey dined. No cousin [Samuel] Moodey of York [husband of Sewall's niece Hannah], but a letter.

[May] 17. 6. Mr. [Benjamin] Lynde goes over to Newington. Gave Mr. Newmarch the funeral sermons and an Angel in them.[10] Major [William] Vaughan's daughter, [Mary Vaughan] King, was buried May 16.

[May] 18.7. To Newington, Hampton, Newbury: where found Mr. Lynde very sick to our great surprise. By reason of its being six-a-clock, and Mr. Lynde's sickness, went not to Rowly, though brother Northen [Dorothy Sewall's husband, Ezekiel Northend] met us there to desire it.

[May] 19. 1. Mr. Lynde went with us to meeting. Cold day. Heard Mr. [Richard] Brown of Reading. Dined with Col. [Thomas] Noyes.

[May] 20. Mr. Lynde had a very bad night; yet after noon rode in the calash with Col. [Nathaniel] Thomas to Ipswich.

[May] 21. Open the court, Mr. [John] Rogers prays.

[May] 22. Mr. Lynde goes home on Mr. sheriff [William] Gedney's horse, the sheriff accompanys him on his.

[May] 23. 5[th day]. To Salem, Meadford, lodge at Cousin [Aaron] Porter's; see and hear the dulcimer.

May 24, then to Charlestown with Col. Thomas's wife's daughter then well home. *Laus Deo.*

[May] 28. 3. Adjourn the Court. 2 of the justices being absent, Lynde, Davenport; dine at the Dragon [tavern], pay for all that dine with us.

[May] 31. 6. Court sits, and adjourns *sine die* [indefinitely].

June 2. 1. Mr. R[owland] Cotton preaches A.M. Mr. John Williams post m[eridiem]. My son [Joseph] having the ague in his face; yet he is so far recovered as to administer the Lord's Super, and baptise Anna Gerrish.

[June] 3. 2. Mr. [Thomas] Blower preaches from 1 Sam. 16.18 [I have seen a son of Jesse the Bethlehemite . . . a mighty valiant man, and a man of war . . . and the Lord is with him]. Mr. Edward Hutchin-

---

[10]An Angel was an English gold coin bearing the image of the archangel Michael slaying a dragon. It was last coined by Charles I. After it ceased to be coined, a small medal with the same imprint was substituted for it. Sewall gave Newmarch copies of the sermons that Benjamin Colman and Joseph Sewall had preached after the deaths of Ebenezer Pemberton and William Brattle in February 1717.

son is chosen Captain, Capt. N. Oliver [is chosen] Lt, [John] Greenough [is chosen] ensign. Governour gave the staves on the change by reason of the wet weather.

[June] *6. 5.* Mr. Jona[than] Belcher speaks to me on change after lecture that Mr. [John] Boydell might be clerk [of the Superior Court] instead of Mr. [Elisha] Cooke [Jr.] when he laid down. Col. Noyes dines with us.

[June] *7. 6.* Hearing of Dorchester case. In the evening, Mr. Cooke treats the Governour, Lt Govr, and Councillors.

[June] *8. 7.* Capt. Wybourn dyed last night; Lt Col. [Thomas] Savage is taken with a convulsion at 5 m[ane]. Hearing of Nantucket Indians complaining of wrong done them by the English.

[June] *9. 1.* Mr. Sam. Haugh buried; Mr. Edwards, Ellis, Williams retailer, were 3 of the bearers. I had a scarf: Mr. Eliakim Hutchinson and I followed next after the mourners. 42 upon the coffin.

[June] *12. 4.* Hearing between Cambridge and Charlestown which should be the shiretown. Mr. Auchmooty pleaded very well for Charlestown: His first discourse was very well worth hearing. Mr. [Jonathan] Remington alleged and proved for Cambridge very pertinently and fully.

[June] *13. 5.* A very great congregation to hear the last sermon preached to poor Jer. Phenix by Dr. Cotton Mather[11] from Matt. 10. 28 [fear him which is able to destroy both soul and body in hell].

Council declares that Cambridge is the shire-town for Middlesex. I do not remember any dissenting save Majr Genl Winthrop, Elisha Hutchinson esqr, Thomas Hutchinson esqr.

[June] *14. 6.* The deputies concur. Could not tell by lifting up the hands, were fain to divide the House; they for Cambridge went to the north side; they for Charlestown, to the south; Cambridge had 46. Charlestown, 41, as brother Northend one of the monitors informs me. Charlestown had 2 deputies that voted; [Charles] Chambers and [Jonathan] Dows; Cambridge only one, viz: Remington. Cambridge was under great disadvantage because many favoured Capt. Saml Phips, the present register, and were loath he should be forced to move to Cambridge or quit his office.

[June] *14. 6.* I dine with the Majr Genl [Winthrop] and his Lady with Col. [Edmund] Quinsey and Majr [John] Quinsey.

[June] *15. 7.* A day is set apart for nomination [of] officers. Some ob-

---

[11]Cotton Mather, *The Valley of Hinnom. The Terrours of Hell Demonstrated and the Methods of Escaping the Terrible Miseries of the Punishments on the Wicked* (Boston, 1717).

jected that the 25th was Salem court [day], but no alteration was made.

[June] 19. 4. I waited on his Excellency [Gov. Shute] in the morn between 9 and 10; and prayed his favour as to the judge of probate's office, that if he saw convenient, I might have it. He very frankly promised me, which I thanked his Excellency for. Mentioned Mr. Boydel, for register; I said if he could condescend, 'twas a laborious place.

[June] 17. Monday, Col. [Nathaniel] Byfield storms at the answer to Dr. [Edmund] Calamy &c. letter, acknowledging the goodness of the king in sending the Lieut. Govr. Hot words began to pass between him and Capt. Belcher. Takes leave, being sent for home by express by reason of Madam [Deborah Clark] Byfield's great sickness.

[June] 18. Tuesday, The widow [Mary] Norton, Mr. Davenport, Mr. P. Dudley, Col. Quinsey, Col. [Samuel] Thaxter met at my house, to see if an accommodation might be between her and her son [John Norton, Jr.]; but the son came not, nor sent any excuse nor answered my kind letter. Col. Thaxter told me he had my letter, and shewed it him. Col. Thaxter said, if Madam Norton would give her son her land in Boston which she promised, he thought there would be no money wanting.

[June] 19. 4. Bro[the]r [William] Moodey [husband of Sewall's sister, Mehitable] comes to town. Madam [Bridget] Usher, [sister Mehitable] Moodey, cousin [John] Hunt and wife [Ruth Quincy] sup with us. I delivered Madam Usher the long sealed paper Lydia Kay desired me to keep for the said Usher, when she went to Mr. Nathaniel Henchman's.

[June] 20. 5. Mr. [Peter] Thacher of Milton dines with us.

[June] 21. 6. Deputies treat the Govr at the Green Dragon [tavern].

[June] 22. 7. Council vote next Thursday fortnight to be a fast. Govr sends me in with the message [to the Assembly]: Mr. Speaker, next Thursday 14 night, the eleventh of July, is appointed for a day of publick prayer with fasting in complyance with the message sent by this honorable House. Before night it began to rain, and rained plentifully all night. Blessed be God who answers before we call; as Mr. Colman prayed in Council this morn He would. *Laus Deo!*

[June] 23. 1. Capt. Clark tells me that Madam Byfield died yesterday, which will prevent Col. [Nathaniel] Pain's being at the nomination [meeting] on Tuesday.

Midsummer Day [June 24], Mr. Colman's New Steeple is raised. Joseph prays with us in the evening, brother Northend being sick of a fever.

June 25. 3. General Council; voted that all of the Council be inserted in the commissions for the [justices of the] peace. Consented that Mr. Paul Dudley be a justice. Then the Govr nominated Mr. [Thomas]

Palmer, many spake as before, that might have time for consideration. And the Govr adjourned to Friday morning.

June 26. 4. Major Nathan Gold, Dep. Govr of Connecticut, and Col. [John] Otis dined with me. Green pease, cherries. Tells me Major Fitch was imprisoned by the Govr at Hartford till he humbled himself on account of his anti-proclamation. Visited Madam Usher. Morn pleasant. Sweet rain in the morn.

July 2. Mr. Exp. Mayhew and Cous. [Moses] Hale [husband of Sewall's niece Mary Moodey] come to town.

July 3. Last night my wife was taken very sick, this extraordinary pain and fainting was of long continuance, whereby I was obliged to abide at home and not go to the [Harvard] commencement. This is the second year of my absence from that solemnity.

[July 20] Great plenty of rain quickly after the fast which was July 11th. Mr. Mayhew preaches at Roxbury. July, 20. I bring Mr. Mayhew going, and view the brick work of the fortification, Govr rides by towards Roxbury as I was doing it.

Now about I have my ear sirringed to great benefit. A great pellet of wax brought out.

[July] 21. 1. [Capt.] Norris arrives, wherein comes Mr. [Thomas] Prince. I heard he was to preach at the Castle. He was at our meeting P.M. But not thinking of him, and he having a wigg on and russet coat I saw him not at all.

July 25th Mr. Prince puts up a note. Mr. Sewall preaches from John 5.25 [the dead shall hear the voice of the Son of God: and they that hear shall live]. Only Dr. Cotton Mather and Mr. Colman were in the pulpit. Govr, Govr [Gurdon] Saltonstall [of Connecticut], Majr Genl [Winthrop] and Col. Hutchinson in the fore-seat.

July 26. 6. Great rain. Madam Usher removed this week to Mr. Henchman's, after a sore fit of sickness.

July 28. 1. Govr Shute and the Lieut. Govr come to the South-meeting, P.M. Mr. [Robert] Stanton preached. One child baptized.

July 30. 3. Sam. Pegun and Sam. Abraham come to me earnestly to desire that John Neesnumun may be procured for them [as their minister]. They heard him July 28 and yesterday they had a meeting, from whom they are sent to express this their unanimous and earnest desire.[12]

For my voyage to Arrowsick in Kenebeck River, see my octavo

[12]Pegun, Abraham, and Neesnumun were Indians. In 1709–10, Neesnumun, a preacher, worked with Experience Mayhew to revise for separate printing portions of John Eliot's Indian Bible.

paper book. Twas begun Thorsday Augt. 1 and ended Friday night between the 16 and 17th of Augt. at 2 hours after midnight.[13] Mrs. Bant was buried in our absence, in one of the 21 tombs building in Hull-Street.

Augt 20. Went to the funeral of Mrs. Mary Hayman, whose maiden name was Anderson. Her first husband's name was [Thomas] Lynde, by whom she had Mrs. [Mary] Toft; her second, Shepard, the Reverend Mr. Thomas Shepard, by whom she had Mrs. [Hannah] Smith; her third husband was Samuel Hayman esqr., whose widow she was; died in the 67th year of her age. Was buried in her husband Shepard's tomb, which she built for him, as I was told; bearers, John Usher, esqr., Elisha Hutchinson esqr; Saml Sewall, Edw. Bromfield esqr; Mr. Leverett, president, John Clark esqr. Has the reputation of a pious gentlewoman.

Augt 22. Mrs. Mary Winchcomb was buried in the old burying place, in the 67th year of her age, as her relations tell me; though the [head]stone bear 69; died suddenly.

Augt 23. Went to Charlestown lecture. Mr. Stephens gave us a very good discourse from Rev. 14. 13 [Blessed are the dead which die in the Lord]. Mr. Prince was at the lecture. I dined at Mr. Bradstreet's, whither Mr. Prince came.

As I came home, I viewed the tombs building in Hull-street. Gave the workmen 2s dreaners [drain-makers], 6d. Visited Madam Usher, David [Sinclair].

---

[13] In August, Sewall and a half dozen other dignitaries accompanied Governor Samuel Shute to Arrowsick Island to negotiate with the Penobscot Abenaki Indians. Although the Abenaki greeted the expedition cordially enough on August 9, "their answers & Gouv's reply" the next day made it clear that both parties disagreed over one point in particular. The Abenaki were "against a[ny] more houses being builded" on Arrowsick. When they received no satisfactory adjustment of the colony's terms, they "went away something dissatisfied." In this tense atmosphere, the governor's ship "fired 21 guns" and the expedition enlarged its watch with "more sentinels set out." Finally, on August 11, according to Sewall, the Abenaki apologized for their "unsutable manner of going away" the day before, offered Shute "two belts of wampum," and brought the proceedings to a "desirable conclusion." On the morning of August 12, the "Indians come and sign & seal their Agreem[en]t," and the expedition "gave them all to drink. The young men gave volleys; made a dance; and all was managed with great Joy." Upon returning to Boston, Sewall was reflective: the expedition to Arrowsick had managed to avoid any contact with pirates, escaped without injury when Shute's frigate ran aground, experienced fair winds for most of the journey, and negotiated successfully with the Abenaki who were "standing off at first." Furthermore, he personally, although tormented by "musketoes," was "well all the time at sea & shoar whereas many were very sea-sick; others much troubled with fluxes." Sewall was thankful, "Laus Deo." Sewall's journal entries of his journey to Arrowsick are printed in an appendix in M. Halsey Thomas, ed., *The Diary of Samuel Sewall, 1674–1729*, 2 vols. (New York: Farrar, Straus and Giroux, 1973), 2:1123–27.

[August] 24. 7[th day]. Col. Byfield visits me, says Mr. [John] Sparhawk preached last Lord's Day; preaches but seldom. Intends to come hither when the dog-days are out; by which means we are like to want his company in the court-week.

[August] 25. 1. Great storm of rain. Mr. Prince preached P.M. Col. Byfield and Mr. Attorney[-General Paul Dudley] with us.

[August] 27. 3. Visit Dr. Incr. Mather and carry him Cousin Moodey's sermon.[14] Being sent for, I pray with Joshua Cornish, he seemed to bewail his apostasie. Has much adoe to speak; dyes before morning.

[August] 28. 4. Read an excellent sermon at Mr. [Josiah] Franklin's about communion with God; sung the 4th part of the 73d Psalm [For there are no bands in their death: but their strength is firm]. Prayed.

[August] 29. 5. Mr. Colman preaches excellently from [Ps.] 119.32 [I will run the way of thy commandments, when thou shalt enlarge my heart]. Son [Joseph], the minister, dines with us, his wife [Elizabeth] being at Brooklin. Mr. Sheaf and I followed next after the relations of Joshua Cornish to his funeral.

As I came out of the Meetinghouse, Mr. Eliot's youth told me Govr Dudley would speak with me at Mr. Attorney's [Paul Dudley's place]; I said, I think it will be best after dinner; and went accordingly, after a little waiting on some probate business, which I thought not of. Govr Dudley mentioned Christ's pardoning Mary Magdalen; and God hates putting away; but did not insert *sine causa* [without reason] as [David] Pareus [Heidelberg theologian, 1548–1622] notes. I said my son [Sam] had all along insisted that caution should be given, that the infant lately born should not be chargeable to his estate. Govr Dudley no ways came into it; but said 'twas best as 'twas, no body knew whose twas. [illegible] to bring it up. I said I hoped to speak with Mr. P. Dudley in the circuit [court]. As Govr Dudley went along, took little Hannah [Sam, Jr., and Rebeckah's daughter, aged seven] into his chariot, and carried her home without any forewarning.

Augt 30. 6. I went with the Majr Genl [Wait Still Winthrop] to Roxbury in his coach to speak to Hely about making a wheel; by this means I had the pleasure to view the wall of our city [between the bays

---

[14]Samuel Moody, *The Children of the Covenant under the Promise of Divine Teachings* (Boston, 1716). Moody's sermon was occasioned by the death of Sewall's nephew, Thomas Sewall, who had been a sophomore at Harvard.

on Boston Neck], and pass in and out at the gate; the work being closed postern [back gate] and all. The LORD keep the City!

Augt 31. My indispositions hold, from Tuesday or Wednesday; am this day seised with a flux, which makes me refrain from going to Council, forenoon and afternoon. Mr. [Samuel] Fisk visits me; I encourage him to accept the call of the New South [church]. Mr. Wadsworth visits me, says he intends for Salem next week.

Septr 1. Went to the solemn assembly P.M., the rather that I might hear Mr. Josiah Oakes, who preached very well, from Psal. 73.25 [Whom have I in heaven but thee?].

Septr 2. I hoped my sickness had been over, and sat up too long; was taken with shivering for an hour or two, could not get heat though wrapt my feet in flannel, and put flannel on my breast; had a very restless night; was fain to send for Dr. [Thomas] Oakes at an hour past midnight. My son was assaulted by the way near Col. [Adam] Winthrop's, but had no hurt. Found sensible benefit by Dr's. physick.

Septr 5. kept from lecture which Mr. Prince preached in my son's turn.

Septr 8. Detained from the publick solemnities of the Sabbath by my indisposition; and from [riding] the Bristol circuit. Judge Davenport and Mr. Colman set out 7r [September] 6th to Sabbatize there.

Septr 15. Went to the solemn assembly P.M. A fast was agreed on to humble ourselves for the breach made in the South church by the death of Mr. Pemberton; and to seek unto God by prayer for a sutable and seasonable supply.

[September] 17th. I went to Mr. Thomas Clark and paid him one hundred and eighty pounds in five-pound bills of credit; and of this province all save one; for the account of an anonymous and unknown person, who supposed he might have wronged him; and now, out of conscience, made restitution; presumed Mr. Clark might have wronged him considerably. I laid that before Mr. Clark in order to have some of the money returned; but Mr. Clark after some time, and going out of the room declined it, saying the party might have balanced it himself. So I took his receipt for the whole.

[September] 18. 4[th day]. Went to the barber's, visited Madam Hubbard [Anne Leverett, daughter of former governor John Leverett] who is very low.

[September] 19. 5. Went to lecture, heard Mr. Cooper from 1 John 2, 8.—Because the darkness is past, and the true light now shineth.

Shewed that was a powerfull argument to inforce new obedience. The Govr turned to talk with Col. Townsend; so his back was upon the ministers as they went out.[15] Went to Council at 4 P.M.

[September] 20. 6. Went to Charlestown lecture, where Mr. Bradstreet preached from [Ps.] 143.10. Teach me to do thy Will. Dined with Mr. [Thomas] Graves, where was likewise the Revd Mr. Sparhawk seeking to recover his health. The Governour went through Charlestown in the morn, towards Piscataqua, carrying M[ada]m Paul Dudley in his shay. Coming home I visited Dr. Incr. Mather, who had a good night last night, no hiccoughs to day. Visited David [Sinclair], and prayed with him.

7r [September] 22. Went to the Lord's Supper: heard Mr. Prince in the afternoon from the same text he preached on this day 4 weeks [ago].

7r 23. Gave Mr. Wadsworth the receipt of the £180 I paid Mr. Tho. Clark this day sennight; did it in my bed-chamber.[16]

When I first came down to prayer in the family about 7r 13, I was greatly refreshed by reading in course Psal. 66. and by singing in course the 3d pt of the 71 Psalm [Be thou my strong habitation, whereunto I may continually resort]. 7r 15. m[ane]. The Lord help me to pay my vows and walk in new obedience. *Laus Deo.*

7r 24. To day the companies train, as yesterday, when the commissions of the field-officers, Col. [Thomas] Fitch, Lt Col. Edw. Hutchinson, and Major Hab. Savage were read.

7r 23. The eclipse was seen. Mr. Sparhawk visited us.

7r 25. Fast at the South Church: Mr. [John] Webb begun with prayer, Mr. Sewall preached from Jer. 3.15, give you pastors [according to mine heart, which shall feed you with knowledge and understanding]. Mr. Cooper prayed and gave the blessing. P.M. Mr. Colman prayed, Dr. Cotton Mather preached from John 6.11. And Jesus took the loaves

[15]Sewall is indicating that Shute was being disrespectful to Cooper and Colman. Custom dictated that the congregation stand, face the ministers, and wait for them to proceed first out of the meetinghouse.

[16]In other words, the "anonymous and unknown person" alluded to in the entry for September 17 above was Benjamin Wadsworth, pastor of the First Church. Sewall, Clark, and Wadsworth were engaging in a social charade. Upon presenting Clark with the £180, Sewall suggested that Clark might return at least a portion of the money to the "anonymous" person who "might have wrong'd him" as a gesture of good will and because Clark himself was not blameless. For his part, Clark, knowing the identity of the "unknown" supplicant, refused to accommodate Sewall's suggestion and demanded instead a personal apology from Wadsworth by insisting that the latter "might have balanced it himself."

and distributed to the disciples, and the disciples to them that were set down. Mr. Wadsworth prayed. 23d Psalm sung, D. Mr. Sewall blessed. Twas a good day. Mr. Sparhawk was there.

7r 26. Dr. Cotton Mather preached the lecture from Jonah, 4.6. So Jonah was exceeding glad of the gourd. Part of the 39 Psal. sung O., who shall the same up take. Only Majr Genl and Col. Hutchinson in the fore-seat. Govr Dudley and Col. [William] Tailer were at meeting; latter sat in Mr. [Elisha] Cook's pue. He arrived on Satterday in Capt. [John] Gore, I visited him.

7r 27. Write to Mr. [Samuel] Moody of York by neighbour Briggs, sit with Mr. Boydell and take out presidents [precedents?]. Rain.

7r 28. I and my son S[am] and Mr. [Samuel] Gerrish [former husband of Mary, Sewall's deceased daughter] go to Hog-Island, went off about 11; had a good passage, wind and tide. Viewed the reparation of the causey [causeway]; and gave him leave to dig clay in the place he proposes to make bricks; he promises not to use any of the Island wood to burn them; but to bring it from Lin. Charged him not to fetch any more shingle from the point, to mend the causey; bid him dig gravel just by, where he has dug some. Dined with pork and fowls, and excellent good butter. Bastian [servant] was with us, and helped to bring some pumpkins &c. Landed at the Salutation [tavern?] an hour before sun-set. *Laus Deo.* The tenant says I hant been there these 5 years.

7r 29. The church is staid, the calling a church meeting is propounded to confer about getting supply in the work of the ministry. Majr Genl and Mr. [Nathaniel] Williams oppose it! 'Tis voted [approved]. Then the time was debated; Monday morning and Friday were proposed; which was opposed; both voted [on] but neither carried it. At last Tuesday come sennight at 3 P.M. is voted [approved]. Voted twice before could tell whether 'twas a vote [in favor] or no.

Went to the funeral of Mrs. Anne [Leverett] Hubbard widow, just about 65 years old: Bearers, Col. Tailer, Majr Genl Winthrop; Col. Hutchinson, Sewall; Mr. Eliakim Hutchinson, Dr. Clark. She was a gentlewoman of a meek and quiet spirit and great patience.

7r 30. Monday, P.M. I view the training in the Common.

Octobr 1. Visit Mrs. Ruth Cutler; David Sinclar [Sinclair], gave him an Angel [coin], as had done to his wife ten days before. I asked him whether I should put up a note for him; he seemed very desirous of it; and said he counted it the best medicine.

Wednesday, Octobr 2. Fast at the Old North [church]. Dr. Cotton Mather begins with prayer: Mr. Colman preaches from Isa. 6.5, 6, 7, 8

[Woe is me! for I am undone; because I am a man of unclean lips . . . Then flew one of the seraphims unto me, having a live coal in his hand . . . And he laid it upon my mouth, and said, Lo, this hath touched thy lips; and thine iniquity is taken away, and thy sin purged. Also I heard the voice of the Lord saying, Whom shall I send, and who will go for us? Then said I, Here am I; send me]. Mr. [Joseph] Sewall prays and gives the blessing. P.M. Mr. Wadsworth prays; Dr. Cotton Mather preaches, John 10.11. I am the good shepherd. Dr. I. Mather prays: sing two first staves of the 65th Psal. D. set by deacon [Edward] Procter. At noon Dr. Clark entertained me very courteously. In the fore-seat were Sewall, Bromfield, Oakes, Clark, Hutchinson Thomas. *Laus Deo.*

Octobr 3. Mr. Prince, and my son Joseph and his wife [Elizabeth] dine with us.

Octobr 6. Mr. Thomas Walter preaches with us, prayed well, and made a very good discourse from Luke, 2.10, 11 [And the angel said unto them, Fear not: for, behold, I bring you good tidings of great joy, which shall be to all people. For unto you is born this day in the city of David a Saviour, which is Christ the Lord].

Octobr 7. North Church have a meeting warned [announced] yesterday, just before the blessing concluding the solemnity of the Lord's Supper. But nothing is done but to adjourn to the 14th instant. Mrs. Prudence Swan [Rebeckah Dudley Sewall's cousin] was buried last Lord's day night. I and my son S[am] at the funeral.

Octobr 7. Are acquainted that our Cousin Mrs. Anne Holman *alias* Quincy died yesterday. She was born June 1. 1685. Was baptized the 7th, on which day her excellent Unkle Mr. Thomas Shepherd dyed.

Octobr 8. The rain hinders my son going to the funeral.

8r [October] 15. My wife got some relapse by a new cold and grew very bad; sent for Mr. Oakes, and he sat up with me all night.

[October] 16. The distemper increases; yet my wife speaks to me to goe to bed.

[October] 17. Thursday, I asked my wife whether twere best for me to go to lecture; she said, I can't tell; so I staid at home; put up a note. It being my son's [Joseph] lecture, and I absent, twas taken much notice of. Major Genl Winthrop and his Lady visit us. I thank her that she would visit my poor wife.

Friday, 8r 18. My wife grows worse and exceedingly restless. Prayed God to look upon her. Asked not after my going to bed. Had the advice of Mr. Williams and Dr. [John] Cutler.

7th day, 8r 19. Called Dr. C. Mather to pray, which he did excellently in the dining room, having suggested good thoughts to my wife before

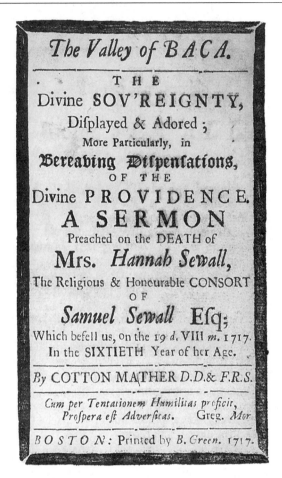

Figure 9.
Title page of Cotton Mather's funeral sermon on Hannah Hull Sewall, 1717.
Courtesy, Massachusetts Historical Society, Boston.

he went down. After, Mr. Wadsworth prayed in the chamber when 'twas supposed my wife took little notice. About a quarter of an hour past four, my dear wife expired in the afternoon, whereby the chamber was filled with a flood of tears. God is teaching me a new lesson; to live a widower's life. Lord help me to learn; and be a sun and shield to me, now so much of my Comfort and Defense are taken away.

8r 20. I goe to the publick worship forenoon and afternoon. My son has much adoe to read the note I put up, being overwhelmed with tears.

8r 21. Monday, My dear wife is embowelled and put in a cere-cloth [burial cloth treated with wax], the weather being more than ordinarily hot.

Midweek, 8r 23. My dear wife is interred. Bearers, Lt Govr Dummer, Majr Genl Winthrop; Col. Elisha Hutchinson, Col. Townsend; Andrew Belcher esqr and Simeon Stoddard esqr. I intended Col. Taylor [William Tailer] for a bearer, but he was from home. Had very comfortable weather. Bro[the]r Gerrish [Reverend Joseph Gerrish, former father-in-law of Sewall's deceased daughter, Mary] prayed with us when returned from the tomb; I went into it. Govr [Shute] had a scarf and ring, and the bearers, Govr Dudley, Brother [Stephen] Sewall, [William] Hirst, [Joseph] Gerrish. Was very destitute for want of the help of son Hirst [Grove Hirst, who had been Betty's husband], and cousin Jane Green. This was the first day of the Genl Court. Gave the deputies books. Allen's Alarm.[17] They sent Mr. Isa. Tay and Capt. Wadsworth to me to thank me.

8r 24. Went to lecture.

8r 25. Went to see Mr. [Grove] Hirst whom I found very sick. He took solemn leave of his father and me. Prayed me to forgive. I said, I doe it heartily; and prayed him to forgive me, defects, excesses; in many things we all offend. Afterward I told him he was in a great degree the Stay and Comfort of my life.

8r 26. He [Grove Hirst] sent to me by Mrs. King as I was in the counting room, to take Sam [Sewall's grandson, Samuel Hirst, twelve years old] home to my house, which I did.

8r 28. Mr. Hirst grows much worse; seemed to pray hard to be spared longer. I sent for Mr. Colman, who after considerable discourse with him, prayed for him in the counting room, at Mr. Hirst's election. Desired me to take Elizabeth Hirst [eleven years old] with me, to his brother the minister's [Joseph Sewall] house, till the controversy should be ended. I did it late at night. Mr. Hirst expired between 3 and 4 past midnight.

8r 30. Midweek, Mr. Hirst interred; bearers, Addington Davenport, Josiah Woolcot esqrs.; Oliver Noyes, Edward Hutchinson esqrs.; Mr. Francis Willoughby, Mr. Nathanl Green, father of the apprentice. I led Mary [Hirst, aged thirteen]; Sam [Hirst, aged twelve], Betty [Hirst, aged eleven]; Hannah [Hirst, aged nine], Jane [Hirst, aged eight]; My

---

[17]Joseph Alleine, *An Alarme to Unconverted Sinners* (London, 1672).

eldest son [Sam] led Madam Price [Grove Hirst's sister, Elizabeth], Joseph [Sewall] his sister Judith [aged fifteen]. Put up a note.

8r 31. Mr. Cooper preached: the wicked driven away in his wickedness; but the righteous hath hope in his death.

Novr 1. 6[th day]. Mr. Saml Phillips drowned, was now buried. Majr Genl Winthrop was at the funeral. Quickly after he was taken sick.

[November] 3d 1[st day]. In the evening I visited him, and sat with him a considerable time as he lay on his bed. I asked him whether he had his old pains; he said he was pained all over; spake of the difficulty of the passage of death; desired prayers.

9r [November] 6. Midweek, Capt [Andrew] Belcher buried. Bearers, Lt Govr Dummer, Col. Hutchinson; Sewall, Eliakim Hutchinson; Addington Davenport, Col. Fitch esqrs. Scarfs, rings, gloves, escutcheons. What three sad Wednesdays have these been!

Novr 7. 5. Last night died the excellent Waitstill Winthrop esqr., for parentage, piety, prudence, philosophy, love to New England ways and people very eminent. His son not come, though sent for. Dr. [John] Cutler, a very usefull physician, dyes now, and my amiable tenant Deacon Thomas Hubbart; Help Lord!

Novr 9. Satterday, poor David Sinclair [Sewall's servant] dyes just about eleven aclock. Court adjourns *sine die* [indefinitely]. Cousin [Samuel] Moodey grows much better. *Laus Deo.*

Monday, Novr 11. Set out for Salem, though it rains hard; worst was going over the ferry; was sheltered in the coach thither, in the calash to Meadford, where I lodged because the rain there would be just in our face. Mr. Porter, father and son, and Mr. Trowbridge came and visited us; which was very refreshing to me.

9r 12. Serene; set out near an hour before the rising of the sun. Got to Salem before noon. All four justices there. In the evening visited cousin [Walter] Price [husband of Grove Hirst's sister Elizabeth].

[November] 13. Sent many funeral sermons about. Mr. [Joseph] Gerrish from Wenham visits and dines with us. Mr. [Nicholas] Noyes opens the court with prayer. Adjourn *sine die* [indefinitely].

Novr 14th Set out homeward quickly after sun-rise: got home before three. John Arcus waited on me. Attend the funeral of Majr Genl Winthrop; the corpse was carried to the Town-House the night before; now buried from the Council chamber. Bearers, His Excel. the Govr [Shute], Govr Dudley; Lt Govr Dummer, Col. Taylor; Col. Elisha Hutchinson, Saml Sewall; scarfs and rings. The regiment attended in arms. Mr. John Winthrop led the widow [his mother]. Twas past five before we went. The streets were crowded with people; was laid in

Govr [John] Winthrop's tomb in Old Burial place. When returned I condoled Mr. [John] Winthrop, Madam [Ann Winthrop] Lechmere, the province, on the loss of so excellent a father. Councillors had scarfs; the Deputies, gloves.

Novr 15. Friday, Mrs. Hannah Melyne buried. Bearers, Sewall, Bromfield; Col. [Samuel] Checkley, [James] Hill; Capt. Timo. Clark, Mr. Daniel Oliver. She was truly a daughter of Sarah, *Priscis moribus, antiqua fide* [venerable in manners, upright in faith]. Scarvs, gloves.

Novr 16. Very great rain which keeps the Salem gentlemen in town.

[November] 17. Lord's Supper. Col. Sommersby dines with us.

[November] 18. Mr. [Robert] Windsor and his wife; and Mr. [Henry] Dering and his wife buried. Such a sight has not before been seen in Boston. Bearers to Mr. Dering, John Usher, esqr, Col. Hutchinson; Sewall, Eliakim Hutchinson; Deacon Hill, [Joseph] Maryon.

Mrs. Dering [Elizabeth Packer, wife of Henry Dering, Jr.], Col. Townsend, Mr. Sim. Stoddard, &c. Mr. [Joseph] Baxter came in and prayed with us to my great refreshment. Gave him a pair of gloves, and books for Arrowsick.

Tuesday, 9r 19. Mr. Prince visits me in the evening and prays in the family to great refreshment.

Midweek, 9r 20. Ordination of Mr. Thomas Foxcroft, pastor of the Old [First] Church. Dr. Cotton Mather began with prayer, Mr. Foxcroft preached from Colos. 1.28, 29. Whom we preach [warning every man, and teaching every man in all wisdom]. Mr. Colman prayed, Mr. Wadsworth [minister of the First Church] ordained [presided] very notably. Dr. Increase Mather, Dr. C. Mather, Mr. Wadsworth, Colman, [Joseph] Sewall laid on hands, Dr. Incr. Mather gave the right hand of fellowship: said he had done it 3 times in the South [Church], and this was the third time of his doing it here. Sung the 4th part of the 118 Psalm, D. Mr. Foxcroft gave the blessing. Exercise lasted about four hours. In the fore-seat were the Governour, Lt Govr, Col. Taylor, Sewall, Joseph Lynde, Mr. President Leverett. I hope we have a token for good that God will still dwell among us. *Laus Deo!* Entertained at Mr. Wadsworth's. Mr. [Peter] Thacher calls; I gave him a ring, because he had helped my wife with visits and advice as a physician; and was an old acquaintance of hers.

Thorsday, 9r 21. I hear of the death of my old schoolfellow Jacob Adams; I met him very well this day sennight [a week ago] as I came from Salem; and hear he was well last Friday. The Lord prepare me for my change, call me into the ark, and shut me in. I hear also of the death of Mr. Eaton, the representative of Reading, as Adams was of Suffield;

of the death of Mr. [William] Tilly, a great loss to the South-church, and to the town; of Doctor Clark's wife, a vertuous gentlewoman. Mrs. [Elizabeth Clark] Monk, an old acquaintance of mine, being Elder Clark's eldest by her mother. She had languished long. The other four died of the fever. O Lord! as I have often prayed, draw not the line of Hingham over Boston![18] But pity and spare thy people. Mr. [Henry] Flint preached the lecture from Philip 3.7. Loss for Christ; made a very good discourse. First six verses of the fourth Psalm sung, York tune. Visited Mr. Belcher, who took it very kindly. Visited the widow Belcher, Cousin [John] Powell; left sermons with all, and for Mrs. [Mehitable] Lillie delivered her, and for her sister [Abigail] Arnold. *Laus Deo.*

Novr 22. Son prays in the Council. The Governour makes a very sharp speech, chiding with the Deputies because they gave him no more money [no salary increase]. Prorogued to the fifth of February. Went to Major [John] Walley's to shew Mr. Brown of Narragansett the deed for the school and the certificate of its being recorded in their town. He thanked me for it, and acknowledged their error in not gratefully accepting it at first. John Eyre grows better. Went to the funeral of my old schoolfellow Jacob Adams, who was representative for Suffield; seized with a violent fever last Satterday, and buried this Friday, in less than a week's time. Lord make me ready for thy coming! Sewall, Davenport, Tho. Hutchinson. Brother Northend was gone home, before I came to dinner. Sent a good scarf to Mrs. Mary Hale by her brother Saml Moodey, and sermons to all my cousins.

Saturday, 9r 23. Mrs. Clark is buried; bearers, Col. Tailer, Davenport; Tho: Hutchinson, Adam Winthrop; Mr. Wm Pain, Edw. Hutchinson. Col. Hutchinson and I followed next after the gentlewomen. Madam [Wait Still] Winthrop's coach was there. Mrs. [Increase] Mather is gone to Hampton again to her sick daughter [Dorothy] Gookin.

Novr 24. Mr. Tilly buried in the evening. Tho. Hutchinson esqr; Tho' Palmer esqr; Daniel Oliver esqr, Wm Welsteed esqr; Mr. Hill the distiller, and Mr. Gray.

Novr 25. Did much business in my probat office, *Deo juvante* [with God's help]. At Mr. Tilly's funeral were told of the death of Mr. George Curwin [minister of the First Church of Salem]. Alass! Alass!

---

[18]Sewall may be alluding to a passage from Isa. 28:17—"Judgment also will I lay to the line, and righteousness to the plummet"—in his prayer that Boston be spared further affliction.

Novr 29. This day Hannah Sewall is carried to Brooklin. Sam Hirst takes physick.

[November] 27. 4. Visit sundry persons, ministers and others.

[November] 28. 5. Very comfortable thanksgiving day as to the moderation of the weather and exercises of worship, forenoon and afternoon.

[November] 29. 6. Col. [Nicholas] Paige is buried from Capt. Oliver's. Bearers, John Usher esqr, Wm Tailer esqr; Sewall, [Nathaniel] Thomas; Col. Byfield, Col. Checkley. Scarvs and rings. Laid in a tomb in the old burying place. Govr and Lt Govr had scarvs and rings. Mr. Experience Mayhew and his daughter Experience come to town, whom I saw after my return from the funeral.

Novr 30. 7. Sam Bridge died last night; was at work [as a carpenter] on Monday last. The good Lord stay his hand! Great rain last night. Granted administration to Mrs. Mary Cutler.

Decr 1. Madam Winthrop comes not to meeting in the afternoon. I enquire of Mr. Winthrop [her son]. He saith she was not well at noon, but was better [now].

Decr 2. Serene and cold. Dr. Cotton Mather dines with us. I visit Madam Winthrop at her own house; tell her of my sending Hannah [Sewall] to Salem tomorrow; ask her advice to selling Mr. [Grove] Hirst's goods: she advises to sell all but plate and linen. I ask her to give and take condolence. She thanks me for my kindness; I tell her she is beforehand with me. When I came away I prayed God to dwell with her, counsel and comfort her. She desired my prayers. Goe to Mr. Hirst's and there meet with Mr. Oliver.

Tuesday, Decr 3. Serene pleasant wether. I goe and hasten Nathanl Green away with Hannah Hirst in the coach about 10 [A.]M. Visit Mr. Secretary [of the Province Josiah] Willard, who came to town last night from Cape-Anne, where he arrived on the Lord's Day, 7 weeks from the Downs.[19] Go to Mrs. [Sarah] Turin's; only her daughter at home, I speak to her earnestly, to warn her mother and aunts, that of necessity they must now take up their mortgage; she promised to do it, and shewed her inclination. P.M. I go to the funeral of Mr. Saml Bridge. Col. Townsend was one of the bearers: Six Councillors followed the relations: Sewall, Em Hutchinson; Bromfield, Cooke; Tho. Hutchinson, Col.

---

[19]Ships destined for New England were sometimes windbound between the mouth of the Thames and the straits of Dover, an area known as the Downs. Sewall is indicating that Willard's ship took seven weeks to cross the Atlantic.

Winthrop. The air was grown very cold, and snowed before we got to the grave. As came back, visited Mr. J. Sewall, Mr. Abiel Walley was with him, with whom he had much pleasant discourse. Then went up to my daughter [Joseph's wife, Elizabeth Walley], and gave her my wife's wedding ring, saying I hoped she would wear it with the same nobility as she did who was the first owner of it. While her husband and I were fitting part of his sermon for the press, she came in and gave us excellent sack-posset [a sweetened milk and wine drink]. I told her, the ring I had given her was her mother's wedding ring; and this entertainment savoured of a wedding; went home in the rain.

Midweek, Decr 4. There is now much snow on the ground, and continues a great storm of it. Flag warns a Council to meet at ten. The Govr sent word, the weather was bad and nothing to be done but reading the Secretary's [Willard] commission, we might proceed without him. But the Council went unanimously to the Governour's house, where the commission under the broad seal was read, the oaths taken, declaration subscribed, and the proper oath belonging to the office taken by the Secretary and certified by the Govr on the back side of the patent dated June 17, 1717. Govr treated us with a cup of warm wine.

Decr 5. Mr. John Winthrop, Mr. Saml Sewall and Katherine his wife dine with us and Jonathan Sewall.[20] Mr. Winthrop sent home Mrs. Sewall in his coach. By the Governour's direction I ordered a commissioners meeting on Friday at 1/2 hour after 3 P.M. But upon the Governour's sending to me Mr. Frost, I sent again to appoint at 10 in the morning Satterday Decr 7. I called on the Govr and put him in mind of filling up the number of the justices of the Super Court; but two in town; said he would do it.

Decr 7. P.M. I visited Col. Hutchinson, sick a-bed. Dr. Cotton Mather came in, discoursed with him and prayed with him. Col. Hutchinson discoursed very Christianly; said Christ was able and ready to save those that came to him. He prayed that he might be enabled to go to Christ and believe in Him and depend on Him alone for salvation. At my coming away desired my prayers. Visited Henry Sewall [Stephen Sewall's son, aged sixteen], taken sick last night. Dr. Davis administers to him. *Laus Deo.*

Lord's Day, Decr 8. Mr. Secretary puts up a note for thanksgiving for his safe arrival. Madam Winthrop for the recovery of her only son [John].

P.M. Mr. Jonathan Belcher comes to the assembly and very patheti-

---

[20]Samuel and Jonathan were the sons of Sewall's brother, Stephen. See footnote 2 on page 194 for a description of Katherine Howell Sewall's relationship to Cotton Mather.

cally acknowledges God's distinguishing mercy towards him. At night the Church is stayed, and Mr. Thomas Prince's two months [at the South Church] being compleat; Friday the 20th current is appointed for the Church to meet to consider what further steps are to be taken [regarding the appointment of a permanent successor to the deceased Pemberton]. Scipio [Sewall's servant] brings Jane Sewall [the oldest among Stephen Sewall's unmarried daughters, aged twenty-two] to her [sick] brother Henry.

Monday, Xr [December] 9th Do a great mornings work in the office of probate. Am much refreshed with Mr. Sol. Stoddard's letter of condolence, which is excellent. I soked it in tears at reading. Sent to enquire of Col. Hutchinson, who grows worse. Hear of Mr. [John] Watt's death at Arowsick, a great loss to that infant plantation. I take Mr. Stoddard's letter to be an answer to my prayer for God's gracious looking upon me. *Laus Deo.* Judith [Sewall's daughter] is better.

Decr 10. Susanna Nash, Susan's [Susanna Thayer, Sewall's domestic servant] mother, goes home. I gave her my wife's old stays which she much wanted, and by Hannah asked for; and gave her my stuff coat, for service as good as new, for her husband. She is very thankfull.

Decr 13. The president [Leverett of Harvard] calls here to desire me to go to Cambridge next Tuesday with the rest of the committee. Cousin Cutting Noyes and Moses Gerrish lodge here.

Decr 14. Mr. Exp. Mayhew goes homeward with young Mr. [William] Homes. Mr. Boydell coming hither to have me sign an administration, I by him presented his excellency the Governour with Dr. [Edmund] Calamy's abridgment of Mr. [Richard] Baxter's Life &c. in two volumes, cost me 30s are very new and handsome. I said to him, The Governour's grandfather [Reverend Joseph Caryl] had a very good character in it. And if he had had a bigger and better [part] he deserved it; as I knew, who was acquainted with his works; by Mr. Plimpton of Meadfield who dines with us, I sent a letter to Mr. Samuel Fiske to come to Col. Hutchinson's funeral next Monday; I desired to speak with him. When I returned from the funeral of Mr. Clap, just at night, I found Jonathan Sewall [Stephen Sewall's son] at our house who said he was come to tell me the bad news of Mr. [Nicholas] Noyes's [minister of the First Church of Salem] death. He was at my brother's till near 9 at night, rather better than formerly, was taken very sick about midnight, and died about 3 P.M. Friday, Decr 13, 1717, wanted 8 or 9 days of 70 years old; a sore loss to Salem and New-England. He was *Malleus Hereticorum* [hammer of heretics]! my most excellent and obliging friend. Salem will be now much less pleasant to me, since I have not my constant friend to meet me there. O Lord who livest for ever, do thou be ever my friend, and from henceforward more than ever!

Decr. 16. Col. Hutchinson is buried, the regiment being in arms. Bearers, His Excellency the Governour, Lt. Govr Dummer; Col. Tailer, Saml Sewall; Col. Townsend, Simeon Stoddard esqr. Was buried in the South burying place, in Mr. Freak's tomb, where his last wife was buried. Now I have been a bearer to three of my wife's bearers in less than two months time. Lord mercifully fit me for my turn. Let me be clothed upon in order to my being unclothed! Mr. President Leverett asked me if I would go to Salem [for Noyes's funeral], he goes. I desired him to speak to Mr. Austin for a slay; which he promised to doe.

Tuesday, Xr. 17. Cloudy day and cold and snow, which hinders my going to Salem. President went. Mr. Noyes's Bearers were: President, Mr. [Jeremiah] Shepard; Mr. [Joseph] Gerrish, Mr. [John] Rogers; Mr. [Christopher] Tappin, Mr. Blowes [Thomas Blowers]. At the private meeting at brother [William] Manly's I was so hoarse with my cold, that I got brother [Josiah] Franklin to set the tune, which he did very well.

Xr. 18. Sung Ps. 119.65–72, and 75.6 verses 6. Text was hear the rod.

Fifth-day, Decr 19. Lecture-fast; serene sharp day. Thin assembly; Mr. Webb prays. Dr. Cotton Mather preaches from Job, 21.17. God distributeth sorrows in his anger. Mr. [Joseph] Sewall prayed.

P.M. Mr. Colman prayed; expressly mentioned the bereavements of Salem in the death of Mr. Curwin and Noyes [both ministers of the First Church of Salem]. Dr. C. Mather preaches, concluding his text; Mr. Wadsworth prays, mentions Salem expressly. Sung the 17, 18, 19, 20, 21, verses of the 107th Psalm. Dr. Mather gave the blessing, as Sewall *mane.* Supped at my son's in company of Mr. [Nathaniel] Appleton of Cambridge, 12 or more met to prepare things for the church meeting tomorrow.

Friday Xr. 20. Church meeting. After debate voted by papers [written ballots], whether would now proceed to the choice of a pastor [for the South Church]; 40 Yeas, 27 Nos. Then voted for a pastor, and Mr. Thomas Prince had 48. Mr. Saml Fiske, 12. Appointed a committee to wait on Mr. Prince and acquaint him with the Church's call, and their desire of his acceptance; Deacons, Gent[leme]n of the Fore-Seat, Justices, Mr. Nathanl Williams [on the committee].

Decr 21. Waited on Mr. [Paul] Dudley, and helped to abridge his character of Mr. Noyes, and then carried it to Mr. [John] Campbell's; and he now sent it to the press to be inserted, which he refused before. Had talk with Madam Dudley about the affairs of Brooklin [Sam and Rebeckah's marital problems].

Lord's Day, Dec. 22. The congregation is acquainted herewith and the committee told them [of the choice of Thomas Prince as minister], and mention is made of some nominated for the congregation, if they approved of them.

Decr 22. 1717. Lord's Day, we had great lightening and three claps of loud thunder, the last very sharp and startling. This was a little before the rising of the sun. Two houses in Boston were stricken with it; Col. [Samuel] Vetches that was stricken before, and Leeches near Peter Oliver's dock.

Decr 23. Committee met at Mr. [Joseph] Sewall's. From thence went to Mr. Prince about 6 P.M. There were of the congregation, Mr. David Jeffries, Col. Thomas Savage, Capt. [John] Gerrish, Mr. Wm Foy, that I remember. We thanked him for his labours with us in the ministry these two months. The Church had sent us to acquaint him of their choice of him last Friday to the pastoral charge, and to desire his acceptance. Disabled himself, twould require time, would not be hurried. Told him his answer was not expected presently, would not precipitate him. He desired our prayers, we his. At parting said, that as his preaching with us had been acceptable, edifying, we desired the continuance of it, and so might have the best opportunity to pray mutually for the direction of God. Had discourse of thunder yesterday.

Decr 24. Visited Mr. and Mrs. [John] Mico.

Decr 24th Agreed with Obadiah Gore, carpenter, to let him the house at Cotton-Hill in which Mr. Hirst lately dwelt, for four and twenty pounds per annum, to pay quarterly, term ten years, beginning the last day of this inst December. To have the accommodations Mr. Hirst had.

Decr 25. Snowy cold weather; shops open as could be for the storm; hay, wood and all sorts of provisions brought to town.

Decr 26. Lectr Day, ways very bad by reason of extraordinary rain; yet Mr. Wadsworth preached and prayed excellently: His text Joshua 1.7 [Only be thou strong and very courageous, that thou mayest observe to do according to all the law]. Many seats and pues quite empty.

Decr 27. Went to Cambridge to see about adding another building to the college. Dined in the library. Mr. Wadsworth went; Lt Govr, Col. Taylor. Dined in the library: Had a comfortable journy out and home. Col. Fitch and I went together in a calash. *Laus Deo.*

Decr 28. A Council is called wherein Castle muster-roll &c are passed, but no mention is made of calling a Council for appointment of judges.

Decr 29. Lord's day. Very snowy and louring [threatening] cold weather. Madam Rebekah Dudley is dangerously sick.

5

"I Am Happy in a Third Wife"

"I could not expect those events in the year 1716 that many others did," Sewall wrote in 1717. Perhaps among the most unexpected of happenings, and certainly the most unwelcomed, was the death of Hannah. "In October my wife was seised with a vehement cold, which began to abate, and as I hoped, was going off," he explained to the Reverend Thomas Cotton, who was then visiting in London, "but upon the 15th of that month, it returned with much greater force." Hannah's health deteriorated, "her pains grew intolerable, and she expired on the 19th, on Saturday a little before sun-set, which filled our house with a flood of tears." "I have lost a most constant lover, a most laborious Nurse for 42 years together," Sewall lamented as he asked Cotton to pray for him in his "desolate condition." What made his situation even more heartbreaking was the death of Grove Hirst on October 28. Hirst developed a "violent fever" on the "very night after my wife died" and never recovered from it. The death of his "worthy and dear son-in-law" coming so soon after the death of Hannah, his "comfort and defense," compounded Sewall's grief. The "causes of our mourning are so multiplied," Sewall wrote, that it felt as if "breakers were passing over me, wave after wave, wave after wave, in a most formidable succession."[1]

Despite his losses, Sewall did not wallow in misery. Puritan doctrine prohibited it, and friends and neighbors would not allow it. By February 1718, four months after Hannah's death, he was the subject of some speculation concerning his marital prospects. When he called on Francis Willoughby to settle a business account, Mrs. Willoughby humored him about his future, hinting that "persons had need be ware how they

[1] Sewall to Thomas Cotton, August 28, 1717, in *Letter-Book of Samuel Sewall,* Massachusetts Historical Society *Collections,* 6th series, 1–2 (Boston, 1886–88), 2: 78–79; Sewall to Gurdon Saltonstall, January 15, 1718, ibid., 81; also Sewall to Cotton Mather, October 29, 1717, ibid., 73–74; Sewall to John Storke, October 30, 1717, ibid., 76–77.

married again." In March, during a long visit with John Marion, which included a "great deal of discourse about his [Marion's] courtship," Sewall learned that members of the Winthrop family wished him to court Katharine, the widow of Wait Still Winthrop. A few days later, Cotton Mather, concerned because the "widows of the flock are numerous," reminded Sewall to do that "which are expected from you." The following month, as he proofed the will of William Denison, a friend of the deceased informed him that the widow Dorothy Denison "was one of the most dutiful wives in the world." Not surprisingly, Sewall soon found himself "wandering in my mind whether to live a single or a married life."[2]

By the end of May 1718, Sewall had decided. On June 9, he "discoursed thorowly" with Dorothy Denison and, despite her protests that "'twould be talked of," informed her that he "intended to visit her at her own house next lecture-day." Sewall thus began a five-month schedule of regular visits to Roxbury to meet with the widow Denison. But it was not to be. On November 1, he "told her 'twas time now to finish our business" and offered her, as part of his proposal of marriage, "two [hundred?] and fifty pounds per annum during her life" if he should precede her in death. Dorothy, apparently, was not interested. According to Sewall, she indicated that her sacrifice would be too great, that "she should pay dear for dwelling at Boston" and that therefore "she had better keep as she was." Because Dorothy made no counterproposal, Sewall suspected that the courtship was ended. However, in late November, at the behest of the Reverend Nehemiah Walter, he again met with Dorothy. The meeting went poorly. Dorothy accused Sewall of being less than forthright in terminating their relationship, and he repeated the words he said she had spoken about "paying dear" if she moved to Boston. At the end, Dorothy "gathered together the little things" Sewall had given her and offered them back to him; he told her they were hers to keep.[3]

Ten months after his last meeting with Dorothy Denison, Sewall began his courtship of Abigail Tilley. This time the affair proceeded more smoothly. Sewall, who had presided over Abigail's first marriage, to James Woodmansey in 1686, and had remade her acquaintance after the death of her second husband, William Tilley, noted that he was en-

---

[2]M. Halsey Thomas, ed., *Diary of Samuel Sewall, 1674–1729,* 2 vols. (New York: Farrar, Straus and Giroux, 1973), 2:882, 885, 889, 890, 892; *Diary of Cotton Mather,* Massachusetts Historical Society *Collections,* 7th series, vols. 7–8 (1911–12); Reprint, *Diary of Cotton Mather* (New York: Frederick Ungar Publishing, [n.d.]), 2:516.

[3]Thomas, ed., *Diary,* 2:895–912 passim.

couraged by friends almost immediately to commence a courtship. From Mrs. Eliezur Armitage he learned that Abigail had been a "great blessing to them, and hoped God would make her so to me and my family." Mary Clark Pemberton, the wife of Joseph Sewall's senior colleague, "applauded" his interest in Abigail. For her part, the fifty-three-year-old Abigail received Sewall warmly. By October, the couple had decided to marry. Thus on October 29, in the best room of the Sewall home, Joseph Sewall married his father and Abigail Tilley.[4]

That Sewall was pleased with his second marriage is evident in his remarks about Abigail. To Jeremiah Dummer he wrote: "She is very kind to me, and to my four children, and six grand-children." With his daughter Hannah "confined to her chamber 14 months by reason of her maimed knee," he found great comfort in Abigail's assistance in "domestic concerns." But Abigail became "oppressed with a rising of flegm that obstructed her breathing" on the night of May 26, 1720, and died so quickly that it was an "astonishment" to Sewall. He put up a note at the South Church announcing the loss of his "dear wife by a very sudden and awfull stroke." Three months later, he was still struck by the unexpectedness of it all. "It pleased God in a sudden and awfull manner to take away my loving wife from me," he wrote to John Storke. The Reverend Timothy Woodbridge reminded Sewall that "to look on any worldly comfort otherwise than withering, is to forget our divine lesson, that all flesh is grass," but it was a reminder wasted on Sewall. "I am again tossed with tempests," he said; "how soon is an earthly Happiness turned into a Condolence!"[5]

Abigail's death, Hannah's confinement, and Judith's marriage and subsequent removal to her new home left Sewall "more lonesome" than he had ever been before. It was under these circumstances that he commenced his courtship of Katharine Winthrop. From its outset in early October of 1720, Sewall's courtship seemed hopeless. Katharine offered little in the way of encouragement; indeed, she "instantly" rejected Sewall's suggestion that she "might be the person assigned" to him as his next wife. Although Sewall called on the widow Winthrop throughout the remainder of October and the first week of November in an effort to persuade her to change her mind, she would not. "She could not leave her house, children, neighbours, business." By early

[4]Ibid., 2:927, 929, 931–33; Sewall to Jeremiah Dummer, February 23, 1720, *Sewall Letter-Book,* 2:109.

[5]Thomas, ed., *Diary,* 2:950–51; Sewall to Jeremiah Dummer, February 23, 1720, *Sewall Letter-Book,* 2:109; Sewall to John Storke, August 30, 1720, ibid., 116; Timothy Woodbridge to Sewall, [August?] 1720, ibid., 117–18.

November, Sewall noticed that Katharine had become distinctly less courteous to him. On two separate occasions, "her dress was not so clean as sometime it had been." Upon receiving a gift of almonds, "she did not eat of them as before; but laid them away." For one of their meetings, she positioned her granddaughter's cradle so that it "was between her arm'd chair and mine." But he remained undeterred until November 7, when Katharine confessed that although she had "great respect" for him, she did not love him. Two days later, when Simeon and Mehitable Stoddard invited Sewall to dinner at their home and asked whether they should also invite Katharine, he answered simply, "No." As an afterword, it is worth mentioning that Sewall harbored no ill will toward Katharine. In June of 1725, when she was seriously ill, he visited her and was solicitous enough to notice that "her hand felt very dry." When she died shortly thereafter, Sewall was one of the six bearers of her coffin.[6]

Sewall's next courtship, of Mary Gibbs, was brief and straightforward. On January 12, 1722, Sewall wrote a remarkable letter to Mary in which he recalled an episode thirty years earlier, when Mary and her first husband, Robert Gibbs, were about to get married. Sewall recollected that at the time "you were minded that I should marry you, by giving you to your desirable bridegroom." The purpose of his current "epistolary visit" was to determine "whether you be willing that I should marry you now, by becoming your husband." Because he was "aged, and feeble, and exhausted," and perhaps wiser for his failed courtship of Katharine Winthrop, he requested a "favourable answer to this enquiry, in a few lines, the candor of it will much oblige." Mary did respond quickly and favorably, and in early February the couple announced their intention to marry. On March 29, 1722, the day after his seventieth birthday, he and Mary were "joined together in marriage by the Rev. Mr. William Cooper," Sewall's son-in-law.[7]

"I am happy in a third wife," Sewall told Jeremiah Dummer eight months after his wedding. By then, we know, Mary had proven to be a "great blessing" to the family. She was indispensable in nursing Hannah, whose "maimed knee" needed to be dressed at least once a day. For Sewall, who was beginning to slow down, Mary's assistance became "necessary." In his last years, he complained more and more frequently about his various infirmities: "a feverish indisposition . . . which made me less able to bear the cold"; "my voice being enfeebled"; "the

---

[6]Thomas, ed., *Diary,* 2:957–67 passim, 1035, 1037.
[7]Ibid., 988–93.

indisposition in my back"; a restless night followed by a "sudden forcible vomit"; "my fever and sore leg"; "my sickness i.e. lameness." Small wonder that Sewall thanked "God in his Goodness" for "my wife."[8]

Even as he began to complain about the frailties of old age, Sewall's public career reached its zenith. In February 1718, around the time that Sewall was deciding whether to court Dorothy Denison, Governor Samuel Shute called on him. The governor "tells me he would make me Chief Judge" of the Superior Court, and that "it was just it should be so." Sewall was undoubtedly pleased by the appointment ("I humbly thanked his Excellency"), but the governor's favor may have accentuated the awkwardness of Sewall's position. Suspicious of the changes instituted in Massachusetts politics after 1691, he had nevertheless welcomed every offer of preferment made by royal governors whose powers of appointment resided in the charter that had undermined the old Puritan magistracy. Moreover, by virtue of his official standing, Sewall was unavoidably drawn into the personal and political confrontations that were reaching new heights of intensity in 1718.[9]

The crisis began when Shute, apparently on the advice of former governor Joseph Dudley's son Paul, at whose home he had resided since his arrival in Boston, vetoed the election of Elisha Cooke, Jr., to the Council. In early 1719, Cooke, Jr., mindful that his father's election to the Council had been negatived for twelve consecutive years by the elder Dudley and still smarting over his own rejection, confronted admiralty judge Robert Auchmuty. Sewall witnessed the exchange of unpleasantries. Cooke, Jr., "looked Mr. Auchmuty in the face and asked him if he were the man that caused him to be put out of the Council?"

Auchmuty said, "No! I could not do it; but I endeavoured it, I endeavoured it!"

Cooke, Jr., replied, "The Govr is not so great a blockhead [as] to hearken to you."

A week later, the two men appeared before Governor Shute and the Council in answer to a complaint. At first, Cooke, Jr., tried to dismiss the whole episode as a case of simple misunderstanding, that his use of the epithet *blockhead* was in reference to "he himself." But confronted with evidence to the contrary in the form of "written affidavits," he

[8]Ibid., 885, 886, 898, 1013, 1014, 1052; Sewall to Jeremiah Dummer, November 20, 1722, *Sewall Letter-Book,* 2:146; Sewall to Jonathan Dickinson, February 22, 1724, ibid., 160; Sewall to Solomon Stoddard, March 14, 1724, ibid., 162.

[9]Thomas, ed., *Diary,* 2:884.

"owned the truth" of the charges. The governor then left the room and the Council condemned Cooke, Jr.'s, words as "rude, injurious, and reflecting on the Governor."[10]

On the strength of the Council's vote, Shute maneuvered next to have Cooke, Jr., dismissed from the only office he held in the provincial government. He "declared that Mr. Cooke was such an enemy to his master the king and to him his lieut[enant], that he expected he should be removed from his clerk's place" on the Superior Court. The five justices of the court must have realized that, coming in the wake of Shute's veto of Cooke, Jr.'s, election to the Council, a vote for removal would identify them as part of the governor's faction in the rapidly escalating political contest. To make matters worse, one of the justices, Addington Davenport, was Cooke, Jr.'s, cousin, and Davenport was opposed to the dismissal of his kinsman; thus a court vote against the clerk would be a personal affront to one of its own members. Caught in a quandary, the justices decided to postpone voting on the issue for two weeks. When Chief Justice Sewall went to inform the governor of the court's postponement, he was immediately reminded of the wages of spoilsmanship. Paul Dudley told him that if Cooke, Jr., was removed from his post, he, Sewall, should "nominate" the new clerk. Afterwards, in private prayers with his son Joseph, Sewall asked for "divine favour to help in this difficult season."[11]

When the justices finally addressed the issue, they decided, with Davenport dissenting, that "all things considered, twas convenient to dismiss Mr. Cooke." The result could hardly have been unanticipated. Although unanimity returned to the Superior Court because Sewall allowed the justices to select Cooke, Jr.'s, replacement after "freely confer[ing] about it," factionalism came to plague the rest of Shute's administration. Shortly after his dismissal in 1719, Cooke, Jr.'s, supporters elected him to the Assembly, and the following year that body chose him as its speaker. Shute promptly rejected the lower house's decision, but the representatives ignored his rejection and refused to elect another speaker. An exasperated Shute dissolved the General Court and fired off a letter to the Board of Trade. "The common people of this Province are so perverse," he wrote, "that when I remove any person from the Council, for not behaving himself with duty towards H[is]

[10]G. B. Warden, *Boston, 1689–1776* (Boston: Little, Brown, 1970), 92; Thomas, ed., *Diary,* 2:833–34, 915, 916.
[11]Ibid., 2:916–17.

M[ajesty] or his orders, or for treating me H.M. Govr. ill, that he becomes their favourite, and is chose a Representative."[12]

When Shute reconvened the General Court two months later, he prevailed to the extent that the new Assembly elected Timothy Lindall as its speaker. But Lindall's victory over Cooke, Jr., came on a divided vote in the third ballot and said little about the latter's continuing influence in the Assembly. Indeed, there is good evidence to suggest that Cooke, Jr., had already begun to marshal his supporters into an effective political organization that was the forerunner of the famous Boston Caucus of the period after 1740. It was soon apparent that the lower house under its new speaker was no friendlier to the governor than the previous one had been. Ten days after it had reconvened, the house voted to reduce the governor's six-month salary from its usual £600 to £500. An angry Shute sent the Assembly a "note expressing his disacceptance" of the reduction, but there was little else he could do that had not already been tried by his predecessor.[13]

From the outset of Joseph Dudley's administration in 1702, royal instructions required Massachusetts governors to demand of the Assembly a fixed salary. Dudley did, but to no avail. The lower house jealously protected its power to vote from year to year on bills appropriating certain amounts of money to the governor. It was the one reliable countermeasure possessed by elected representatives of the people against the elevated powers of the governor under the 1691 charter. The governor could prorogue or dissolve the Assembly, but in so doing he might jeopardize his income. Perceived misbehavior might similarly reap punitive monetary damages. In 1709, amid charges of maladministration if not criminal activity on Dudley's part, the Assembly voted to reduce his salary.[14]

When the Assembly reduced Shute's salary in 1720 and offered him the same reduced salary the next year, it was exercising what by then it considered to be a time-tested check on the governor. Shute responded in 1721 by dissolving the General Court and making what Sew-

---

[12]Ibid., 2:917, 950, 951; Richard L. Bushman, *King and People in Provincial Massachusetts* (Chapel Hill: Univ. of North Carolina Press, 1985), 95. After voting to dismiss Cooke, Jr., the court voted to hire two clerks instead of one. Davenport was given the chance to nominate his own son, eighteen-year-old Addington, Jr., but declined to do so because "his son was under age."

[13]Thomas, ed., *Diary*, 2:953; Warden, *Boston*, 92–95. Sewall recorded that Cooke, Jr., received more votes than any of the other candidates for the speakership, including Lindall, on the first ballot. Some representatives undoubtedly voted for Lindall on subsequent ballots simply to avoid another dissolution of the General Court by the governor.

[14]Bushman, *King and People*, 118–19.

all called "a very sharp speech" in which he rebuked the Assembly for its effrontery and threatened to forward all offending material to authorities in London. The representatives were unmoved by the governor's threat, however, and when Shute later reconvened the General Court, they insisted on challenging him on yet another issue: the power of adjournment. On July 12, in an obvious attempt to claim a greater degree of independence for itself, the Assembly adjourned for six days, until July 18, without "acquainting the governor" of its action. Shute, alive to the challenge, ordered the representatives back "to their House to business," Sewall recorded. "But the speaker, Mr. Cooke, and others so much oppose it that nothing is done." Unwilling to surrender the point, Shute declared the whole court adjourned until Wednesday, July 19, and directed the "deputies [representatives] not to meet on Tuesday," July 18, as they had planned. But the governor's directive fell on deaf ears. The deputies met on Tuesday anyway, and then, as if to accentuate their defiance, declared themselves adjourned until Wednesday. The Assembly thus met on the appointed day, July 19, but by whose appointment remained unclear. The next day, unable "to bring the deputies to acknowledge their error in adjourning for 6 days without his allowance," Governor Shute dissolved the court.[15]

The truculence of the lower house convinced Shute that he needed to present his case in person to the Privy Council, and he abruptly announced his intention to do so at the end of 1722. Several members of the Council, apparently including Sewall, voted to send a delegation "to compliment the Govr" before he left Boston, but the deputies in the Assembly were in a contrary mood. Rather than complimenting their old nemesis, they dispatched Cooke, Jr., to England to justify their recent actions and to accuse Shute of abuse of power. In England, the Privy Council was decidedly sympathetic to Shute. As a result, the crown issued an explanatory charter in 1726 that amended the 1691 charter by explicitly recognizing the governor's right to approve of the speaker and by prohibiting the Assembly from adjourning for more than two days. Shute had prevailed, but he never returned to Massachusetts.[16]

[15]Thomas, ed., 2:978, 981; Bushman, *King and People,* 113.

[16]Thomas, ed., 2:1001–2; Bushman, *King and People,* 67–68, 114, 119–20; Warden, *Boston,* 98–99. Lieutenant Governor William Dummer served as the colony's chief executive officer until the arrival of Governor William Burnet in 1728. Dummer was married to Catherine Dudley, the daughter of former governor Joseph Dudley and the sister of Samuel Sewall, Jr.'s, wife Rebeckah. He was, as Sewall anticipated, by "birth and education" more apt than Shute to make concessions to the Assembly. Burnet, however, adopted a confrontational style; like Shute, he was also determined to secure a permanent salary for himself as governor. For two years, Burnet and the deputies in the lower

Diary

1726

January. Presented his Honr the Lt Governour [William Dummer] a ring weighing 3 p. wt 6 grains with this engraving—Jany 2. 1725/6 *Pace fruamur* [may we use this in peace], which he kindly accepts.

This winter I gave Mr. [John] Boydell a silver spoon in remembrance of his son Edward. E.B. 1724 [Edward Boydell had been baptized on December 12, 1724/25]. Gave my grand daughter Pepperell [Mary, daughter of Sewall's daughter Betty and Grove Hirst, both now deceased] a silver spoon in remembrance of her son Andrew, born Jany 4. 1726.

Thorsday, 1726 February 17th Mr. Thomas Walker was buried; bearers, Sewall, [Penn] Townsend; [Samuel] Checkley, Bennet; [John] Barnard, Capt. Thomas Cushing. Rings and gloves. I went thither in the coach with my wife and son. From the tomb in the Old Burying place I went again to the house of mourning, and carried Mrs. Jones with me in the coach, at the desire of her bro[the]r [Thomas] Walker. When come home, took in Col. Townsend, Checkly, Barnard. Got home very well. *Laus Deo.*

Friday, Feb. 25. His Honr the Lt Govr comes up from the Castle [Fort William] and adjourns the Genl Court, or prorogues it, to the 13th of April next.

Febr. 28. I find the mortgage of Thomas Baker and Thankfull, his wife, to Madam [Bridget] Usher; and send for Mr. George Nowell, boatbuilder, and going with him to the register [court clerk], I cancel the mortgage and take it off the record. There was an omission in that no reference was made on Nowell's bond to this mortgage, as there ought to have been. For Nowell negotiated the whole; took up Baker's bond; gave his own, and has honestly paid both principal and interest, for doing which it seems there was a double security for the same individual sum; Baker's mortgage and Nowell's bond without manifesting their cognation.

Going home called at Mr. [John] Campbell's, found only Mrs. Mary

---

house of the General Court were locked in a standoff. Burnet's unexpected death in late 1729, the result of a fever, left the issue unsettled. His successor, Jonathan Belcher, was a native-born inhabitant of Massachusetts and not disposed to press hard on the issue of a permanent salary, especially in view of the fact that he had been in London presenting the Assembly's case against a fixed salary at the time of Burnet's death. Beginning in 1735, the Privy Council acceded to Belcher's advice and allowed the governor to accept an annual salary granted at the start of the legislative session. As a result, Bushman notes, the "salary issue was peacefully buried."

Pemberton [Campbell's wife] at home; mentioned her sympathy with my daughter Hannah [who had died on August 16, 1724], gave her a 20s bill, invited her to my house.

Called at Mr. [Thomas] Prince's; but Madam Prince was not at home.

Sent the Revd Mr. William Waldron [of the New Brick Church, built in 1722] one of Mr. [Samuel] Willard's folios lettered on the back; sent by Ben [Swett, Sewall's thirteen-year-old attendant], at Mr. Cooper's [William Cooper of the Brattle Street Church, husband of Sewall's daughter Judith] intimation.

3d day, March 15 1726. Mrs. Palsgrave Walker, (whose maiden name was Edwards) is buried. Bearers, Sewall, [Addington] Davenport; Dr. [John] Clark, Col. [Thomas] Fitch; [Jonathan] Belcher esqr., [Thomas] Palmer esqr. Was laid in her husband's tomb in the old burying place. Lt Govr there. Ministers, Mr. [Benjamin] Colman, Mr. [William] Cooper; Mr. [Samuel] Myles, Mr. [Henry] Harris. After the funeral Mr. [Benjamin] Walker told me, their marriage relation had continued 44 years, 2 months 3 days.

March 17. Mr. [Peter] Thacher and his son [Samuel] Niles dined with us after lecture. They tell me Mr. [Joseph] Marsh his bearers were, Edmd Quincey esqr, Mr. Thacher of Milton; Mr. Joseph Mors, Mr. Samuel Niles; Mr. John Webb, Mr. Thomas Paine.

March 15. Sam Hirst [son of Sewall's daughter Betty and Grove Hirst, aged twenty] got up betime in the morning, and took Ben Swett with him and went into the Common to play at wicket. Went before any body was up, left the door open; Sam came not to prayer; at which I was much displeased.

March 17th [Sam Hirst] Did the like again, but took not Ben with him. I told him he could not lodge here practising thus. So he lodged elsewhere. He grievously offended me in persuading his sister Hannah not to have [marry] Mr. Turall [Reverend Ebenezer Turrell of Medford], without enquiring of me about it. And played fast and loose with me in a matter relating to himself, procuring me great vexation.

6th day, March 25th In the morning I made Madam [Mary] Saltonstall guardian to Mad[am] [Hannah] Clarks five children. *post merid.* I went with my wife to Col. [John] Phillips's funeral. Bearers, Sewall, Townsend; [Nathaniel] Byfield, [Jonathan] Dowse; [Charles] Chambers, Cary. Much rain fell, and 'twas very dirty under foot. I went not back to the house 'twas so near night; but went in my calash directly to the ferry, and so over; His Honour the Lt Govr rode with me to the ferry and back.

2d day, March 28. I proved Elder Preston's will, &c. My sons Saml and Joseph, and Mr. [Thomas] Prince dined with me. Yesterday Mr. Prince [of the Old South Church] preached out of Exod. 12. Comparing the Passover with the Lord's Supper; made good work of it. P.M. Mr. Sewall preached from Hab. 2.3.—For the Vision is yet for an appointed time &c. very well.

5th day, March 31. Dr. [Cotton] Mather, Mr. John White of Glocester, and son Cotton and daughter [Reverend John Cotton and his wife, Sewall's stepdaughter, Mary Gibbs] dine with us after lecture.

7th day April 2. Nathanl Pitcher, 15 years old next June, trimmed me for the first time. Mr. Secretary [Josiah Willard] and my Cousins S.S. and J.S. dine with me.

Lord's Day, April 3. My son [Joseph] preached in the fore-noon from Gen. 1.26 [And God said, Let us make man in our image, after our likeness: and let them have dominion]. Read the whole chapter and commented pithily and well upon it; and after that spoke to the 26th verse. I desire with humble thankfullness to bless God, who has favoured me with such an excellent discourse to begin my 75th year, withall delivered by my own son, making him as a parent to his father!

2d day April 4th Mrs. Sarah Clark was interred in one of the tombs in the South-burying place next the Common; bearers, Sewall, [Edward] Bromfield; [Addington] Davenport, [Daniel] Oliver; [John] Marion, [Daniel] Powning. Gloves and rings. Aets 69. Mr. T[homas] Foxcroft [of the First Church] prayed after returning from the grave. I inquiring of Mr. Jonas Clark, and understanding it was to be so, I stayed and all the bearers, and enjoyed the benefit of that excellent prayer. It seems Capt. Clark lived with his beloved wife almost 48 years.

3d day April 5th. I gave Madam Hannah Clark her oath to her account.

5th day April 7th Mr. J. Sewall marries the hon[ora]ble Josiah Willard esqr and Mrs. Hannah Clark widow.

7th day April 9th. Mrs. Sarah Middlecott dyes Aetats [aged] 88.

Apr. 14. was interred after the dissolution of the Genl Court, in her husband Middlecott's tomb in the North Burying place; bearers, His Honr Lt Govr Dummer, Sewall; Byfield, Bromfield; Dr. John Clark, Thomas Hutchinson esqr. Gloves, rings, escutcheons.

My Cousin Moses Gerrish [Sewall's nephew, the son of his deceased sister Jane Sewall Gerrish] his wife, Col. Noyes's daughter [Mary], dyed the same day Apr. 9th after long languishing.

Mrs. Mary Atwater, a person of great prudence and piety, and good education; first Mr. John Clark married her, by whom she had her eldest daughter Mary; [daughter Mary was] first [married to Ebenezer] Pemberton and now [to John] Campbell. When she [Mary Atwater Clark] was a widow, Mr. John Coney married her, being a widower, by whom he had four daughters. Mr. Coney died more than three years ago; and now his widow Mrs. Mary [Atwater Clark] Coney died somwhat suddenly on Tuesday morning April 12 and was interred in one of the new tombs of the South-burying place; bearers, Sam Sewall, John Clark esqr; Sam Brown esqr, Thomas Fitch esqr; Sam Checkley esqr. Capt. John Ballantine. Was buried from her daughter Bromfield's [Mary's daughter, Abigail Coney, was the wife of Edward Bromfield, Jr.]. His Honor the Lieut Govr followed his Aunt [William Dummer was the son of Ann Atwater Dummer, Mary's sister] as a mourner and his Lady. Thus death, by its regardless stroke, mows down all before it, making no distinction between our most prudent and charming friends, and others; may we learn more entirely to delight and trust in God who is altogether lovely and lives for ever. Three Sams being bearers together on the right side, occasioned my binding all bearers up together in this band,

> Three Sams, two Johns, and one good Tom
> Bore Prudent Mary to her Tomb.

Fifth-day, April 21. The swallows unanimously and cheerfully proclaim the spring. They have been discouraged and made much to abscond for about a week, by reason of the constantly N.E. wind and rain. Dr. Mather preached P.M. The Court of Admiralty sits to try James Simons, late master of the sloop Wren, for murder. Commission of K. George is read. His Honr the Lt Govr sworn, then he gives the oath to the members of the Court. Mr. [Samuel] Tylye is appointed Register [clerk], Mr. [John] Read [appointed] Advocate [Attorney General], *pro hac vice* [for this compensation] ('Twas offered to Mr. [Robert] Achmuty by the Court; but he declined it). Mr. Advocate's complaint is read, the prisoner holding up his hand at the bar; was sent for to the prison by a written order; by his attorney, Mr. [John] Overing, he prays time and copy of the complaint, alleging he has witnesses at Beverly— granted and the Court adjourned to Satterday, at ten in the morning.

Satterday, Apr. 23. Court voted the prisoner not guilty; to be discharged paying [court] costs.

Monday, April 25. Judge Davenport, Mr. [William] Cooper and I set out for Plimouth [court] in Blake's coach, Ben Swett [Sewall's attendant] waiting on us; got thither a little after sun-set. Lodge at Mr. Cushman's [tavern].

3d day, Ap. 26. Court opened, Mr. [Nathaniel] Lennard prays.

Satterday, Apr. 30. 11 [A.]M. Mr. [Paul] Dudley returns home [to Boston]. 3 P.M. Mr. Justice Quincey ditto. Sewall, [Benjamin] Lynde, Davenport continue to hold the court [in Plymouth] till about 6 P.M. and then adjourn *sine die* [indefinitely].

Lords-Day, May 1. The Revd Mr. Wm Cooper preached forenoon and afternoon, from Heb. 4.9 [There remaineth therefore a rest to the people of God]. Justices dined together at Cushman's.

2d day, May 2. gave Mr. Lennard a 20s bill. Mr. Cooper prayed on Satterday morn. Baited [rested] at Bairstow's; dined at Hingham; had a noble treat set before us at Col. Quincey's. Got well home a little before nine. The honoured ancient Elder France,[1] and Deacon [David] Jacobs of Situat kindly visited me. *Laus Deo.* The good news of M. Usher's chest, plate, box of books being delivered, birth of cous. Joseph Moodey's son Samuel, Ap. 18, and a *Good old Age* [Cotton Mather, *A Good Old Age. A Brief Essay on the Glory of Aged Piety* (Boston, 1726)], met me at my coming home.

May 16. 1726. Set out for Ipswich with Benj. [Swett] by Winnisimmet. Baited at More's [tavern]. From thence Mr. Read accompanied us, having his wife with him in a calash. By the pilotage of the Lt. Governour's servant bound home. Went the way by Mr. [Benjamin] Prescott's Meetinghouse. Dined at Phillips's [tavern in Wenham]. Got seasonably to Mr. [John] Rogers's.

May 17. Super[io]r Court at Ipswich. Full Court. Mr. Rogers prays at the opening of it and *sic deinceps* [so in turn].

Friday, May 20. Court adjourns *sine die*. Visit Col. [John] Appleton with Judge Dudley.

Satterday, May 21. Took leave of Mr. Rogers; gave him Mr. Willard's Body of Divinity; to his son, who is called by the church of Ipswich, Dr. [John] Owen's volume printed by subscription. Visited Col. Appleton with J.D. Went to sister [Dorothy Sewall] Northend [in Rowley].

Midweek, May 25. Went to Salem, 'twas late before I got to Salem.

Thorsday, May 26. I took my widowed sister Sewall [Margaret, Stephen's widow], and brought her with me in the calash, called at Madam [Bethia] Kitchen's, saluted us very courteously as we sat in the calash and gave us spirits; no body brought us going. Dined at Moor's [tavern]. Got seasonably to Winnisimmet. Boat just ready, got over in good time; but were fain to sit there a considerable time before Ben

---

[1]In 1741, Thomas Faunce of Plymouth, ninety-five years old, identified a rock that supposedly served as the platform that received the first Pilgrims—Plymouth Rock.

[Swett] could get a calash. Mrs. Young first, and then he himself entertained us with agreeable discourse; set down sister [Margaret Sewall] safely at her son's in the Common by good day-light. Mr. Mercier [Andrew Le Mercier, minister of Boston's French Huguenot Church] and Benj. Sewall [brother Stephen's son] came to the gate. *Laus Deo.*

Thorsday, June 9. Mr. [Experience] Mayhew returns home.

July 8, Friday, Madam [Elizabeth] Cotton dyes.

July 9. Satterday, is interred in the South-burying place in a tomb. Bearers, Dr. Cotton Mather, Mr. [Benjamin] Wadsworth; Mr. [Benjamin] Colman, [Nathaniel] Williams; Mr. [Joseph] Sewall, [Thomas] Prince. His Honr the Lt Govr followed next after the relations.

July 6. Went to the commencment this year in the coach with my sons Sewall and Cooper; coach sheltered us well from the rain. Went first to Sir [Simeon] Stoddard's chamber,[2] who had invited me, where were nobly entertained; to Sir [Henry] Gibbs—into the Meetinghouse. President began with prayer, then the oration—gave the degrees in the Meetinghouse to 3 or 4 at a time. *Admitto vos* [I admit you]. After dinner it rained so hard that the solimnity was finished in the Hall, oration. Mr. S. Mather well defended his awfull question.[3]— Went to Mr. [Henry] Flint's chamber, and from thence home; I and my son, Mr. Prince and his wife comfortably, notwithstanding the rain. *Laus Deo.* Mr. Cooper lodged at Cambridge. His Honr the Lieut. Govr did so.

July 14. His Honr the Lt Govr sets sail for Casco [Maine], to meet the Indians.[4]

July 23. 7th day, Elizabeth Hirst and Jane Hirst [Sewall's granddaughters, nineteen and seventeen years old] set sail for Newbury in Mr. Josiah Titcomb's. 'Twas near noon July 24 before they arrived.

[July] 27. Went to Mr. [John] Toft's lecture [in Newbury].

Tuesday, July 26. Rode in Mr. Sheriff's calash to Cambridge. Mr. Appleton prays. Entring upon the charge to the grand-jury, I said, Since men's departure from God, there was such an aversion in them to return, that every kind of authority was necessary to reclaim them.

---

[2]Simeon Stoddard was the son of Judge Anthony Stoddard. "Sir" was a title accorded to resident graduates of the college; hence, its usage in referring to graduating seniors was ceremonial and indicative of their newly achieved status. Sewall, mindful of tradition, was careful in following this accepted practice.

[3]Samuel Mather, Cotton Mather's son, as part of the commencement exercise had the affirmative in the following proposition: whether original sin is inherited equally by all.

[4]The meeting formally ended the three years of hostility sometimes referred to as Governor Dummer's War.

Notwithstanding the, singular advantage Cambridge had enjoyed in their excellent pastors and presidents of the college—yet it must be said, *Venimus ipsam Cantabrigiam ad stabiliendos, et corrigendos mores* [we came to Cambridge to stabilize and correct behavior]—Dined at Mr. Stedman's [inn]. Mr. President [Wadsworth of Harvard], [Nathaniel] Appleton, Mr. Professor [Edward Wigglesworth] dined with us. Mr. John Davenport, Mr. Stephen Sewall at several times dined with us. Col. [Francis] Foxcroft. Mr. Appleton invited me, and I lodged at his house, Ben [Swett] with me.

July 27. Adjourned *sine die.* Visited the President and his Lady, Mr. Professor and his. Gave 2s to the workman to drive a nail for me in the president's house. Mr. Sheriff brought me to the ferry in his calash. After landing came home a-foot. Well. *Laus Deo.*

Augt 4. 5[th day]. My wife goes to Newtown to stay one night.

Augt 6. 7. Saml Marion dies; was born Xr. [December] 1654.

Augt 7. 1. Mrs. Elizabeth Cooper dies (She was sister to Mr. Sam. Mather by father and mother [Cotton and Elizabeth Mather]), was buried at the North in the court time, which hindred my going to the funeral. My wife was there. Bearers, [Joseph] Sewall, [Thomas] Prince; [John] Webb, [William] Cooper; [Thomas] Foxcroft, [Joshua] Gee.[5]

Augt. 9. Super. Court at Boston. Mr. Goffe attends as under-sheriff in the room of his father Winslow. Mr. Sewall prays. Minded the grand-jurors of their oaths p. 113. 165.—and with all good fidelity, as well to the Court, as to your clients—Now about Mrs. Hannah Moodey comes to town which was a great refreshment to me [Hannah was Sewall's niece, the daughter of his deceased brother John]; put me in mind of the Reverend Mr. Thomas Thacher's expression—The Lord who comforteth all that are cast down, comforted us by the coming of Titus. It rained the next day, so I hired a coach, and rode with her to the Court, and then sent the coachman with her to the ferry; and gave her wherewith to hire a calash to Peny Ferry, because of the rain and dirt, and her bundles, for she was hastening over to her distressed daughter.

[August] 13. 7[th day]. Adjourn to 15. Then to 16. Made a rule of Court about taxing bills cost; which I was very glad of; though some opposed it. Gave the judges, attornies &c., each of them, one of Dr. Mather's sermons of the glory of aged piety [Cotton Mather, *A Good Old Age*].

---

[5]All of Elizabeth Cooper's bearers were Boston ministers: Sewall and Prince of the Old South Church; Webb of the New North Church; William Cooper of the Brattle Street Church; Foxcroft of the First Church; and Gee of the Old North Church.

[August] 21. 1. Now about reading the 139 Psalm in course, those words, v. 16. Thine eyes did see my substance yet being imperfect—were a great cordial to me. What though men may not vouchsafe to look upon me in a way of common courtesy, God looked upon my substance in that circumstance, and I hope will not now forbear to humble Himself to see me.

The hon[ora]ble John Usher esqr. died 7r [September] 1. 1726. at his country-seat near Meadford. Was brought in the Castle [Fort William] pinnace to Boston, and buried from his own house. 7r 5. Bearers, His Honr the Lt Govr, Col. [William] Tailer; Sewall, [Nathaniel] Byfield; [Addington] Davenport, [Francis] Foxcroft esqr. Old Burying place. Aets 79.

Septr 22. Mr. Eliph[alet] Adams gave an excellent discourse from Psal. 112. 7.—He shall not be afraid of evil tidings—which was a great comfort to me.

2d day, 7r [September] 26. Mr. Payson [Reverend Edward Payson of Rowley] marrys Madam Elizabeth Appleton at Ipswich, and carrys her to Rowly.

3d day 7r 27. Cousin Mr. Moses Gerrish [Sewall's nephew] marries Mrs. [Elizabeth] Perce *virginem* [virgin], at Newbury.[6]

---

[6]The death of Mary Noyes, Moses Gerrish's first wife, on April 9 is noted above under the entry for April 14.

Epilogue

At the time of his death in 1730, Samuel Sewall had been a member of the South Church for over half a century. It was fitting, therefore, that the colleague pastors of the Old South were his principal eulogizers. Thomas Prince, the junior colleague who had assumed his position eleven years earlier after some cajoling orchestrated by Sewall and who had been a source of "great Refreshment" to a grief-stricken Sewall after the death of Hannah, spoke first. His was a sermon about public duty and sacrifice and the promise of personal improvement. "Universal mourning," yes, but what about the lessons to be gleaned from the "death and life of that honourable and aged person, who has sat so long among us"? Prince's Sewall was the "Scripture Samuel." He heard the pleas of the people, received appeals, restrained the vicious, settled controversies, and issued "righteous decisions." For the sake of the "publick justice," he learned to accommodate the "inclemencies of the weather" and to adjust to the "inconvenience of inns or roads" in going "year to year in circuit." The provincial Samuel had earned the love of his mourners because he "had spent his life to serve them." Here, then, was a "pattern of integrity" worthy of emulation: from the "days of his youth," Samuel had served the cause of "piety, justice, goodness, and every public virtue that could make a people easy and happy."[1]

Prince's eulogy was focused on Sewall's "office, life and character"; it directed the audience's attention to Sewall's public persona. *A Sermon upon the Death of the Honourable Samuel Sewall, Esq.* was at once a reverential tribute to the deceased and a reminder to the "great assembly" of listeners of the beauties of a life well spent in pursuit of one's calling. Because he was concerned with the dissemination of public virtues among the faithful, Prince emphasized certain qualities in

---

[1] M. Halsey Thomas, ed., *The Diary of Samuel Sewall, 1674–1729,* 2 vols. (New York: Farrar, Straus and Giroux, 1973), 2:868; Thomas Prince, *A Sermon at the Publick Lecture in Boston . . . upon the Death of the Honourable Samuel Sewall, Esq.* (Boston, 1730), 1, 18, 19, 29.

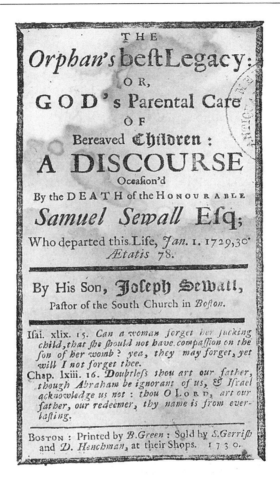

Figure 10.
Title page of Joseph Sewall's funeral sermon on Samuel Sewall, 1730. Courtesy, American Antiquarian Society.

the Sewall he knew: "faithful discharge" of duty, "pains he took for the Publick Good," "strict integrity," and "stedfast perseverance." In sum, he was describing, Prince acknowledged, the qualities of a "Public Father."[2]

The next sermon, by the senior pastor of the South Church, offered

[2]Prince, *Sermon upon the Death of Sewall,* 2, 11, 19, 29.

a different though complementary portrait of Sewall: his life as a family patriarch. No one was better qualified to do this than the second speaker, Joseph Sewall. What was *The Orphan's Best Legacy?* At one level, Joseph's message was the stuff of Thursday lectures and Sunday sermons: The only permanent security and comfort in this life was to be found in God. "The fathers of our flesh are Mortal, and must in a little time forsake us, if we are not taken from them first, but God the Everlasting Father lives for ever." Children, trust in God. The very "course of Nature" dictates that parents will die before their offspring.

And yet, Joseph could not help but reflect on his own situation. He was forty-one years old; Sam, Jr., was fifty-one, and Judith, twenty-eight. Some parents live a long life; they "continue till their children are grown up." The children of such parents are the beneficiaries of the "favour of God." Joseph himself had grown to adulthood under the "presence, counsels and prayers" of a long-lived father. But precisely because of this, he would have his audience believe, he felt the loss more acutely than those whose parents had not lived "to a good old age." His was a bereavement that "ought to be lamented." Consider what he had become accustomed to and now lost: "exemplary conversation," "counsel," "instructions," "advice," "parental care and love," "almost invincible affection," and "tender love and care." He had lost a "protector," an "ever loving" companion, his "choicest friend" and "helper." What was left to be said? "I acknowledge my self unworthy of the honour & privilege I enjoyed in such a Parent."[3]

In January 1730, Thomas Prince and Joseph Sewall summarized for the South Church congregation, and perhaps for the larger New England community as well, the public and private ideals exemplified in the life of Samuel Sewall.

---

[3]Joseph Sewall, *The Orphan's Best Legacy: A Discourse Occasion'd by the Death of the Honourable Samuel Sewall* (Boston, 1730), 2, 3, 7–9, 11, 14, 15, 18, 22, 23.

A Sewall Chronology
(1629–1730)

1629

Massachusetts Bay Company receives its charter from Charles I; the great migration to Massachusetts begins in 1630 and continues until 1642.

1634

Henry Sewall, Jr., the father of Samuel Sewall, arrives in Massachusetts.

1646

March 25: Henry Sewall, Jr., marries Jane Dummer; both return to England with Jane's parents in the winter of 1646.

1652

March 28: Samuel Sewall is born at Bishop Stoke, Hampshire, England; he is the second of eight children that Henry and Jane Dummer Sewall had together.

1659

Henry Sewall, Jr., returns to Newbury, Massachusetts.

1660

Navigation Act is passed by the Restoration Parliament of Charles II. It stipulates that goods imported into or exported out of any English colony must be carried in English-built or English-owned ships that are manned by crews that are at least 75 percent English; and that certain enumerated products, including tobacco and sugar, must be shipped only to England or her colonies. Subsequent navigation laws enacted in 1662, 1663, and 1673 were intended to close loopholes used by colonial merchants to evade the terms of the 1660 law.

Figure 11.
Samuel Sewall's tomb in Granary Burying Ground, Boston. Photograph by Mel Yazawa.

1661

July 6: Jane Dummer Sewall and the rest of the Sewall family, Samuel and his two brothers and two sisters, arrive in Boston and are escorted to Newbury by Henry, Jr.

1667

August: Sewall is admitted to Harvard College. He receives his B.A. in 1671 and his M.A. in 1674.

1675–76

King Philip's War between the New England colonists and a coalition of Native Americans led by the chief of the Wampanoags, King Philip. Although the peace was not concluded until 1678, King Philip was killed in August of 1676, and the major part of the fighting was over by the end of that year.

1676

February 28: Sewall marries Hannah Hull, daughter of John and Judith Quincy Hull. Hannah was born in Boston on February 14, 1658.

1677

March 12: Sewall attends his first town meeting in Boston.

March 30: Sewall is admitted to membership in the South Church.

April 2: John, the Sewalls' first child, is born; he dies on September 11, 1678.

1678

May: Sewall is made a freeman of the colony by the General Court.

June 11: Son Samuel, Jr., is born.

1680

February 3: Daughter Hannah is born.

1681

December 29: Daughter Elizabeth (Betty) is born.

1683

October 1: John Hull, Sewall's father-in-law, dies.

November 7: Sewall is elected to the General Court as a deputy from Westfield.

1684

May 7: Sewall is elected to the Court of Assistants.

July 8: Son Hull is born; he dies on June 18, 1686.

October 23: Massachusetts Bay Company Charter of 1629 is revoked by the Court of Chancery.

1684–86

Plans for unifying all of New England are being considered by Charles II and his successor James II; meanwhile, a provisional government under Joseph Dudley governed Massachusetts for seven months in 1686.

1685

December 7: Son Henry is born; he dies on December 22, 1685.

1686

December: Sir Edmund Andros arrives in Boston as governor and captain-general of the Dominion of New England.

1687

January 30: Son Stephen is born; he dies on July 26, 1687.

1688

August 15: Son Joseph is born.

November 5: William of Orange lands in England with a Dutch army. James II, deserted by all but a few of his people, flees England.

November 22: Sewall sails for England to protect his land claims in Massachusetts; lands at Dover on January 13, 1689. He leaves England on October 10, 1689.

1689

April 11: Joint coronation of William and Mary in England; Glorious Revolution accomplished without bloodshed. In Boston, opponents of Andros arrest the governor and his chief assistants and bring an end to the rule of the Dominion.

1689–97

King William's War or the War of the League of Augsburg. In 1690, Sir William Phips leads a Massachusetts expedition against the French position at Port Royal and captures the whole of the Acadian peninsula. The war ends with the Treaty of Ryswick, September 30, 1697.

1690

August 13: Daughter Judith is born; she dies on September 21, 1690.

1691

October: New charter for Massachusetts makes the colony a royal province.

October 7: Sewall is appointed as a member of the Council under the new charter.

October 28: Daughter Mary is born.

1692–94

Sir William Phips arrives in Boston in May of 1692 as the first royal governor of Massachusetts under the charter of 1691. Phips leaves for England in late 1694 to answer charges of gubernatorial misconduct; he dies there in February 1695, about a month after his return. Lieutenant governor William Stoughton acted as the province's governor from 1694 to 1698.

1692

May 25: Sewall is appointed to the special Court of Oyer and Terminer to rule on cases relating to witchcraft at Salem.

December 6: Sewall is appointed to the Superior Court of Judicature. Under the new charter, the Superior Court replaced the Court of Assistants.

1693

August 7: Daughter Jane is born; she dies on September 13, 1693.

1694

November 21: Daughter Sarah is born; she dies on December 23, 1696.

1696

Navigation Act is passed during the reign of William III, which strengthens the implementation of navigation laws dating back to 1660. It bolsters the powers of the customs officers, tightens obligations on colonial governors to enforce the navigation acts, and prepares the way for a system of vice-admiralty courts (which have no juries) to facilitate the conviction of violators of the trade laws.

May 21: Stillborn son.

1697

November: Sewall's first book is published; *Phaenomena Quaedam Apocalyptica ad Aspectum Novi Orbis Configurata.*

1698–1701

Richard Coote, Earl of Bellomont, serves as governor.

1699

October 14: Sewall is appointed as commissioner of the Company for the Propagation of the Gospel in New England and Parts Adjacent, better known as the New England Company; he served until April of 1724.

1700

June 24: Sewall's *The Selling of Joseph, A Memorial* is published.

1702

January 2: Daughter Judith is born.

June: Joseph Dudley returns to Massachusetts as royal governor, thirteen years after the collapse of the Dominion of New England and Dudley's arrest for his role in the Andros regime.

1702–13

Queen Anne's War or the War of Spanish Succession. In 1706–7, Governor Joseph Dudley was implicated in a scheme involving trading with the French under the guise of prisoner exchanges. The war ended with the Treaty of Utrecht, April 11, 1713.

1710

November 17: Daughter Mary, aged nineteen, dies after giving birth to her first child.

1713

September 13: Joseph Sewall is ordained as pastor of the South Church.

1715

January: Elizeus Burgess is appointed governor of Massachusetts, but remains in London. After much partisan maneuvering on all sides, Joseph Dudley surrenders control of the province to lieutenant governor William Tailer in November.

December 9: Sewall is appointed as judge of probate for Suffolk County.

1716

April: Samuel Shute is appointed governor in the wake of Burgess's resignation; arrives in Boston in October.

July 10: Daughter Betty dies; aged thirty-four.

1717

October 19: Hannah, Sewall's wife of forty-one years, dies.
October 29: Grove Hirst, Betty's husband, dies.

1718

April 16: Sewall is elevated to chief justice of the Superior Court of Judicature.

1719

October 29: Sewall marries Abigail Woodmansey Tilley.

1720

May 26: Abigail Tilley Sewall dies.

1722

March 29: Sewall marries Mary Gibbs.

1723

January: Governor Samuel Shute, after numerous confrontations with the lower house of the General Court, leaves for England to present his case in person to the Privy Council. Shute never returned to Massachusetts. Lieutenant governor William Dummer served as acting governor until 1727.

1724

August 16: Daughter Hannah dies; aged forty-four.

1725

June 4: Sewall declines reelection to the Council after thirty-three consecutive terms; he cites as his reasons: "my enfeebled state of health; the other publick employments lying upon me, and very weighty business of a more personal concern."

1726

Explanatory charter amends the charter of 1691 by clarifying the power of the royal governor to approve of the election of the speaker of the lower house.

1728

June: William Burnet's commission as governor of Massachusetts arrives; the crown's instructions required him to confront the lower house on the issue of a permanent salary for the office. Burnet died unexpectedly on September 7, 1729. Lieutenant governor William Dummer served as interim chief executive until Jonathan Belcher's appointment as governor in 1730.

July 29: Sewall resigns as chief justice of the Superior Court of Judicature and as judge of probate for Suffolk County.

1730

January 1: Sewall dies in Boston at the age of seventy-seven.

Questions for Consideration

1. How trustworthy is Sewall's diary as a source of information for his actions and those of his neighbors? Does he create a favorable image for himself? Is he being honest?

2. In what ways is a diary different from an autobiography as a source of information for a researcher? Is one preferable to the other? If so, under what circumstances?

3. What are the components of the popular stereotype of the New England "Puritan"? In what ways does Samuel Sewall's life confirm the stereotype? In what ways does his life contradict the stereotype?

4. Was Samuel Sewall a "good" father? Explain.

5. How did Samuel Sewall cope with the deaths of his children?

6. The portions of the diary reproduced in this edition cover a period of over forty years. What evidence is there in the diary entries that Sewall's life was changing over the course of those years? If the diary entries were not identified by years, would one be able still to place them in their correct chronological sequence? What sort of clues might one look for?

7. How did Sewall respond to the development of political factionalism in the period after 1691? On which side was he in the division between the supporters and opponents of the new charter?

8. Sewall was a domestic patriarch and a public officer with multiple responsibilities. Is there any evidence of tension in his life as a result of combining these two demanding roles?

9. If Sewall is indeed best remembered for one or more of the four episodes described at the outset of Part 1—witchcraft judge, antislavery writer, fortunate son-in-law, and overaged suitor—what might account for such selective memories? Are all historical reconstructions selective? Does it matter?

Selected Bibliography

NEW ENGLAND

Bailyn, Bernard. *The New England Merchants in the Seventeenth Century.* Cambridge, Mass.: Harvard University Press, 1955; New York: Harper and Row, 1964.

———. *The Origins of American Politics.* New York: Alfred A. Knopf, 1968.

Boyer, Paul, and Stephen Nissenbaum. *Salem Possessed: The Social Origins of Witchcraft.* Cambridge, Mass.: Harvard University Press, 1974.

Bushman, Richard L. *King and People in Provincial Massachusetts.* Chapel Hill: University of North Carolina Press, 1985.

Conroy, David W. *In Public Houses: Drink and the Revolution of Authority in Colonial Massachusetts.* Chapel Hill: University of North Carolina Press, 1995.

Cook, Edward M., Jr. *The Fathers of the Towns: Leadership and Community Structure in Eighteenth-Century New England.* Baltimore: Johns Hopkins University Press, 1976.

Craven, Wesley Frank. *The Colonies in Transition, 1660–1713.* New York: Harper and Row, 1968.

Godbeer, Richard. *The Devil's Dominion: Magic and Religion in Early New England.* Cambridge: Cambridge University Press, 1992.

Greene, Lorenzo J. *The Negro in Colonial New England, 1620–1776.* New York: Columbia University Press, 1942.

Greven, Philip J., Jr. *Four Generations: Population, Land, and Family in Colonial Andover, Massachusetts.* Ithaca, N.Y.: Cornell University Press, 1970.

———. *The Protestant Temperament: Patterns of Child-Rearing, Religious Experience, and the Self in Early America.* New York: Alfred A. Knopf, 1977.

Hall, Michael G. *Edward Randolph and the American Colonies, 1676–1703.* Chapel Hill: University of North Carolina Press, 1960.

Hoffer, Peter Charles, and N. E. H. Hull. *Murdering Mothers: Infanticide in England and New England, 1558–1803.* New York: New York University Press, 1981.

Hull, N. E. H. *Female Felons: Women and Serious Crime in Colonial Massachusetts.* Urbana: University of Illinois Press, 1987.

Johnson, Richard R. *Adjustment to Empire: The New England Colonies 1675–1715.* New Brunswick, N.J.: Rutgers University Press, 1981.

Kawashima, Yasuhide. *Puritan Justice and the Indian: White Man's Law in Massachusetts, 1630–1763.* Middletown, Conn.: Wesleyan University Press, 1986.

Labaree, Benjamin W. *Colonial Massachusetts: A History.* Millwood, N.Y.: KTO Press, 1979.

Lockridge, Kenneth A. *A New England Town, the First Hundred Years: Dedham, Massachusetts, 1636–1736.* New York: W. W. Norton and Company, 1970.

Lovejoy, David S. *The Glorious Revolution in America.* New York: Harper and Row, 1972.

Ulrich, Laurel Thatcher. *Good Wives: Image and Reality in the Lives of Women in Northern New England, 1650–1750.* New York: Alfred A. Knopf, 1982.

Zuckerman, Michael. *Peaceable Kingdoms: New England Towns in the Eighteenth Century.* New York: Alfred A. Knopf, 1970.

PURITANISM

Breen, T. H. *The Character of the Good Ruler: A Study of Puritan Political Ideas in New England, 1630–1730.* New Haven: Yale University Press, 1970.

Cohen, Charles Lloyd. *God's Caress: The Psychology of Puritan Religious Experience.* New York: Oxford University Press, 1986.

Davidson, James West. *The Logic of Millennial Thought: Eighteenth-Century New England.* New Haven: Yale University Press, 1977.

Dunn, Richard S. *Puritans and Yankees: The Winthrop Dynasty of New England, 1630–1717.* Princeton: Princeton University Press, 1962.

Foster, Stephen. *The Long Argument: English Puritanism and the Shaping of New England Culture, 1570–1700.* Chapel Hill: University of North Carolina Press, 1991.

———. *Their Solitary Way: The Puritan Social Ethic in the First Century of Settlement in New England.* New Haven: Yale University Press, 1971.

Hall, David D. *Worlds of Wonder, Days of Judgment: Popular Religious Belief in Early New England.* New York: Alfred A. Knopf, 1989.

Hambrick-Stowe, Charles E. *The Practice of Piety: Puritan Devotional Disciplines in Seventeenth-Century New England.* Chapel Hill: University of North Carolina Press, 1982.

Middlekauff, Robert. *The Mathers: Three Generations of Puritan Intellectuals, 1596–1728.* New York: Oxford University Press, 1971.

Miller, Perry. *The New England Mind: From Colony to Province.* Cambridge, Mass.: Harvard University Press, 1953.

———. *The New England Mind: The Seventeenth Century.* New York: Macmillan, 1939.

Morgan, Edmund S. *The Puritan Dilemma: The Story of John Winthrop.* Boston: Little, Brown and Company, 1958.

———. *The Puritan Family: Religion and Domestic Relations in Seventeenth-Century New England.* Rev. ed. New York: Harper and Row, 1966.

———. *Visible Saints: The History of a Puritan Idea.* New York: New York University Press, 1963.

Oberholzer, Emil. *Delinquent Saints: Disciplinary Action in the Early Congregational Churches of Massachusetts.* New York: Columbia University Press, 1956.

Pettit, Norman. *The Heart Prepared: Grace and Conversion in Puritan Spiritual Life.* New Haven: Yale University Press, 1966.

Rutman, Darrett B. *American Puritanism: Faith and Practice.* Philadelphia: Lippincott, 1970.

Silverman, Kenneth. *The Life and Times of Cotton Mather.* New York: Harper and Row, 1984.

Stannard, David E. *The Puritan Way of Death: A Study in Religion, Culture, and Social Change.* New York: Oxford University Press, 1977.

Stout, Harry S. *The New England Soul: Preaching and Religious Culture in Colonial New England.* New York: Oxford University Press, 1986.

Winslow, Ola Elizabeth. *Meetinghouse Hill, 1630–1783.* New York: Macmillan Company, 1952.

BOSTON

Bridenbaugh, Carl. *Cities in the Wilderness: The First Century of Urban Life in America, 1625–1742.* New York: Ronald, 1938; New York: Capricorn Books, 1964.

Henretta, James A. "Economic Development and Social Structure in Colonial Boston." *William and Mary Quarterly,* 3rd series, 22 (1965): 75–92.

Nash, Gary B. *The Urban Crucible: Social Change, Political Consciousness, and the Origins of the American Revolution.* Cambridge, Mass.: Harvard University Press, 1979.

Rutman, Darrett B. *Winthrop's Boston: Portrait of a Puritan Town, 1630–1649.* Chapel Hill: University of North Carolina Press, 1965.

Warden, G. B. *Boston, 1689–1776.* Boston: Little, Brown, 1970.

———. "Inequality and Instability in Eighteenth-Century Boston: A Reappraisal." *Journal of Interdisciplinary History* 6 (1976): 585–620.

Whitehill, Walter Muir. *Boston: A Topographical History.* Rev. ed. Cambridge, Mass.: Harvard University Press, 1968.

SAMUEL SEWALL

Brown, Richard D. "Information and Authority in Samuel Sewall's Boston, 1676–1729." In *Knowledge Is Power: The Diffusion of Information in Early America, 1700–1865.* New York: Oxford University Press, 1989.

Chamberlain, N. H. *Samuel Sewall and the World He Lived In.* New York: Russell and Russell, 1897.

Hall, David D. "The Mental World of Samuel Sewall." In *Saints and Revolutionaries: Essays on Early American History,* ed. David D. Hall, John M. Murrin, and Thad W. Tate. New York: W. W. Norton, 1984.

Strandness, T. B. *Samuel Sewall: A Puritan Portrait.* East Lansing: Michigan State University Press, 1967.

Winslow, Ola Elizabeth. *Samuel Sewall of Boston.* New York: Macmillan, 1964.

DIARY AND LETTERS

Diary of Samuel Sewall, 1674–1729. Massachusetts Historical Society *Collections,* 5th series, vols. 5–7 (1878–82). Reprint. 3 vols. New York: Arno Press, 1972.

Letter-Book of Samuel Sewall. Massachusetts Historical Society *Collections.* 6th series, vols. 1–2 (1886–88).

Thomas, M. Halsey, ed. *The Diary of Samuel Sewall, 1674–1729.* 2 vols. New York: Farrar, Straus and Giroux, 1973.

Van Doren, Mark, ed. *Samuel Sewall's Diary.* New York: Russell and Russell, 1963.

Wish, Harvey, ed. *The Diary of Samuel Sewall.* New York: G. P. Putnam's Sons, 1967.

Index